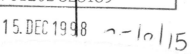

WINTON LIBRARY
WIMBORNE ROAD
BOURNEMOUTH BH9 2EN
TEL: 01202 528139

15. DEC 1998   ⁀-|₀||5

CW00677674

BOURNEMOUTH LIBRARIES

2009779720

THROUGH A
GLASS DARKLY

In memory of my mother

MARIE BEAUCHAMP REVANS
(1913–1991)

who died as this book was completed.

When I was a child, I spake as a child, I
understood as a child, I thought as a child:
but when I became a man I put away childish things.
For now we see through a glass, darkly;
but then face to face ... And now abideth faith,
hope, charity, these three; but the greatest of
these is charity.

St Paul's Epistle to the Corinthians
Chapter 13, Verses 11 and 13

The glass is falling hour by hour, the glass will fall forever,
But if you break the bloody glass you won't hold up the
weather.

LOUIS MACNEICE 'Bagpipe Music'

LIBRARY

THROUGH A GLASS DARKLY

The Life of Patrick Hamilton

Nigel Jones

Scribners

DORSET COUNTY

1992

LIBRARY AS

A Scribners Book

First published in Great Britain in 1991
by Scribners, a Division of Macdonald & Co (Publishers) Ltd
London & Sydney

Copyright © Nigel Jones 1991

The right of Nigel Jones to be identified as author
of this work has been asserted by him in accordance with the
Copyright, Designs and Patents Act 1988.

All rights reserved.
No part of this publication may be reproduced, stored in a
retrieval system, or transmitted, in any form or by any means,
without the prior permission in writing of the publisher, nor be
otherwise circulated in any form of binding or cover other than
that in which it is published and without a similar condition
including this condition being imposed on the subsequent
purchaser.

British Library Cataloguing in Publication Data
Jones, Nigel
    Through a glass darkly: the life of Patrick Hamilton.
1. Fiction in English. Hamilton, Patrick, 1904–1962
    I. Title
    823.912

    ISBN 0-356-19701-8

Typeset by Leaper & Gard Ltd, Bristol
Printed and bound in Great Britain by Mackays of Chatham PLC,
Chatham, Kent

Scribners
A Division of
Macdonald & Co (Publishers) Ltd
165 Great Dover Street
London SE1 4YA
A member of Maxwell Macmillan Publishing Corporation

2009779720

WINTON LIBRARY
WIMBORNE ROAD
WINTON BH9 2EN
Tel: 528139

3554

Contents

Contents

Acknowledgements

The writing of any kind of book inevitably leaves an author in debt to innumerable people. With no genre is this more true than biography. It is only possible to piece together the fragments of another person's life with the aid of other people's views, recollections and opinions.

I would like to thank the following for their invaluable assistance: Jack Beeching, Richard Beswick, Simon Blow, Timothy Boulton, the late Dallas Bower, Arthur Calder-Marshall and his wife Ara, Patricia Cockburn, Andy Croft, Roger Davenport, Polly Devlin, Tomas D'Ornellas, Gwen Ffrangcon-Davies, Geraldine Fitzgerald, Cy Fox, Dr Henry Geldard, Ben Glazebrook, Angus Hall, Aileen Hamilton, Michael Holroyd, Douglas Hyde, Hermione Lee, Doris Lessing, Majorie Lewel, Maruja Mackehenie, Brian Mackenna, James Marsh, George Matthews, Lady Audrey Morris, Sean O'Brien, Mary Orr Denham, Peter Parker, Don Paterson, Chris Petit, Stephen Plaice, Allan Prior, Arnold Rattenbury, Sir Kenneth Robinson, Eva Salzman, John Russell Taylor, Lynne Truss, Jenny Uglow, Stephen Ward, and Lord Ted Willis.

To the staffs of Westminster School, the National Portrait Gallery, the London Library, Brighton, Hove, Chiswick and Hammersmith public libraries, the Theatre Museum, the British Library Newspaper Library, the Inner Temple, the Home Office,

Kensington Police Station, and the Savile – my thanks for helping me unearth information relating to Patrick.

Lastly, I thank my wife Claudia Richardson. This book is as much hers as mine.

Introduction

WHEN PATRICK HAMILTON DIED IN 1962, his reputation as a writer had sadly declined. He had not published a book for seven years, and the quality of his last novels – the uncompleted series chronicling the criminal career of a con-man and murderer, Ernest Ralph Gorse – did not match the high standards of his best, wartime work: the marvellous *Hangover Square* and *The Slaves of Solitude*. The successful stage thrillers *Rope* and *Gaslight*, although they had been hits around the world and, together with their Hollywood screen versions, assured him a healthy income, were works from his distant youth.

Little wonder, then, that in 1968, Doris Lessing lamented:

Patrick Hamilton was a marvellous novelist who's grossly neglected. And I can't think of any reason for it unless he's not a member of one of the cliques, one of the invisible brotherhoods that exist in England and especially in English literary life. I'm continually amazed that there's a kind of roll call of OK names from the 1930s, sort of Auden, Isherwood, etc. But Hamilton is never on them and he's a much better writer than any of them ... [he] was very much outside the tradition of an upper-class or middle-class writer of that time. He wrote novels about ordinary people. He wrote more sense about England and what was going on in England in the 1930s than anybody else I can think of, and his novels are true now. You can go into any pub and see it going on.[1]

1

But there *was* a reason for this neglect and a clue is found in Lessing's words, 'You can go into any pub and see it going on'. Patrick Hamilton, as his friend and patron J.B. Priestley wrote, 'spent too many of his later years in an alcoholic haze, no longer a social drinker but an unhappy man who needed whisky as a car needs petrol'.[2] Patrick's loving brother Bruce, who told the story of his decline in his tender memoir, *The Light Went Out* (1972), recognised the reality of his brother's alcoholism, but failed to explore the roots of the condition; almost certainly because he himself was a product of the same abnormally close-knit family that nurtured unhappiness like a precious, hot-house plant. Patrick's father, Bernard Hamilton, was a widowed, womanising alcoholic and a bullying, absentee patriarch. His mother, Nellie, was a divorced, possessive, unhappy snob and a suicide. His sister Lalla was a divorced, promiscuous failed actress and an alcoholic. Patrick himself was a divorced, sexually tortured alcoholic who sought solace for his psychological wounds in the pursuit of prostitutes and unattainable dream women – Hollywood film stars and actresses. None of the three Hamilton siblings produced children of their own. There is a pattern behind these brutal facts and teasing it out has been one of the main tasks of this biography.

The neglect that followed Patrick's death has been reversed in recent years and there are now unmistakable signs of a growing revival of his reputation, both as a novelist and as a playwright. To the admiration of his contemporaries and peers – Graham Greene, Anthony Powell, John Betjeman, J.B. Priestley and Osbert Sitwell – has been added the recognition of later generations of critics and writers such as Doris Lessing, Michael Holroyd, Allan Prior, John Russell Taylor and Keith Waterhouse among others.

Coupled with this critical acclaim there have been signs of a popular revival: publication of several of his novels in paperback, well-received performances of his play *Gaslight* in London theatres in 1989 and 1990 and a feminist adaptation of his best novel, *Hangover Square*, also on a London stage. On television, his novel *Mr Stimpson and Mr Gorse* was adapted by Allan Prior as the series 'The Charmer', and the BBC's 'The Late Show' devoted an entire edition to a film about him. (Prior also adapted another novel, *The West Pier*, for the stage, appropriately in its Brighton setting.) This revival has not, as Doris Lessing complained, as yet been matched by any real signs that Hamilton is to join the ranks of writers deemed 'great' by those mysterious judges who decide such things. Why Hamilton should suffer such omission remains something of a mystery: is it because of his lack of an Oxbridge education (he was never a highbrow, or part of a contemporary literary clique)? Is it because he spread himself too thin and committed the unforgivable sin of writing popular theatrical chillers? Is it because – although a professed Marxist – he is difficult to label ideologically? Or is it only because, as his brother, and friends like Claud Cockburn believed, the devastating effects of the road accident he suffered in the 1930s and his later alcoholism hampered his productivity as a writer and clouded his later life?

Whatever the reason, Hamilton has still not achieved the literary stature or indeed widespread popularity he surely deserves. Though Priestley asserted that Hamilton's social vision was narrow, the themes and questions raised by his work – the buried lives of ordinary people; the linguistic and behavioural stratagems by which the quotidian is managed and unpleasant realities kept at bay; the mysterious roots of human evil – are with us today, unresolved and ever-present. In Priestley's words:

> I feel sure that a great many younger readers will be caught and held by Patrick Hamilton's intensely personal vision of life, his enduring sense of homelessness, of the loneliness and solitude so many young men have known, his feeling for the innocence always menaced by stupidity and wickedness, the compassion behind his apparently sardonic detachment. The world that he secretly regarded with horror, in the dark outside the lighted saloon bars, is not better than it was when he was writing . . . it is, if anything, worse . . . I find his stature has increased.[3]

While Hamilton is, as Priestley recognised, 'uniquely individual' his work can be seen as part of a recognisable tradition in the English novel: a tradition exemplified by his beloved

Dickens, continued into the twentieth century by George Gissing, taken up by Hamilton, and renewed in our own time by writers like Colin MacInnes, Harold Pinter and Martin Amis. Hamilton is, as his *Times* obituary remarked, a poet of urban – particularly London – life. His world is that of the streets, pubs, bars and boarding houses of the inter-war years. His attuned ears capture the sleaze and slang of an era with the actuality of a human tape recorder. The results are frequently hilarious, but often deeply sad. His range arguably is a limited one. Neither in Hamilton's life nor in his work did he often venture outside the confines of London and south-east England ('Horrible place, abroad', he would say), but within those boundaries he knew his chosen territory and mapped it on the printed page with the assurance of an expert cartographer. For all his Marxism, Hamilton may be seen as an old-fashioned insular Little Englander and inside this self-defined area he was a king.

My own involvement with Hamilton began early. I played one of his prime stage parts, the madman Gribaud, in a school production of his little-known, but excellent, play *The Duke in Darkness*, became curious about his strange life, and read Bruce's memoir. But his brother's book, which told a tragic tale superbly and with aching honesty, came from a man too emotionally involved with his subject to be fully objective.

It was clear that another fuller account of Patrick Hamilton's life and work remained to be written; but I hardly thought that I would be the person to write it until a chance coincidence brought Patrick's life and mine into collision. I moved to Patrick's native town, Brighton, in the late 1980s and stumbled on the fact that Patrick's last surviving relative, Aileen Hamilton, Bruce's widow, lived around the corner from me. She proved to be a formidable but friendly lady with a blunt and forthright view of her dead brother-in-law: she hated him. She was also the guardian of a suitcase full of Patrick's letters and papers. They had been left untouched since Bruce's death; unread by Aileen because of her disdain for Patrick. This cache was a goldmine for the literary biographer, containing nearly all Patrick's letters to his brother, written at regular intervals from the late 1920s until shortly before his death. In addition, the case contained several unpublished works, including an early play fragment, a dialogue about pubs, his hand-written dictionary of rhyming slang and an attempt at a psychological autobiography, frankly entitled, *Memoirs of a Heavy Drinking Man*. The papers also included the opening six chapters of his unfinished last novel, *The Happy Hunting Grounds*, written by hand in a stiff-backed notebook with corrections added in the Pitman's shorthand he learned at a commercial college in his youth. From that youth there also survives the only known example of a Hamilton short story, a little gem called 'The Quiet Room' which is a merciless account of his own father's drunken bullying and was written before he was twenty-one.

There are other letters too: from Lily Connolly, the semi-literate prostitute he loved in the 1920s and who inspired his magnificent London trilogy, *Twenty Thousand Streets Under the Sky*; from and to his mother, guilelessly revealing an almost incestuous closeness that makes Proust's relationship with his own adored mother look positively healthy. From later in his life there are letters from literary, political and drinking cronies like Michael Sadleir (his publisher, and the author of *Fanny by Gaslight*); from Claud Cockburn, perhaps the greatest intellectual influence on Patrick, who turned his theoretical interest in Marxism into a rigid espousal of the Communist cause; and from John Davenport, boxer, poet, critic and drinker, the great friend of Patrick's declining years.

A glance at this treasure trove told me that here was the raw material of a full biography, and I decided then and there to write it. Closer inspection of the documents, together with early drafts of Bruce's book – which contained at least twice as much material as eventually appeared in his published text – confirmed my resolve. It soon became apparent that Bruce had acted, consciously and unconsciously, as his own censor. Whole chunks of Patrick's letters – revealing and important prime sources – were omitted, presumably because they shed a light on the Hamiltons which Bruce found too painfully revealing. I do not for a moment want to suggest that Bruce dishonestly suppressed the facts, for, compared with many keepers of family flames, he was as honest and open as anyone could realistically expect. But, first and foremost, he was a Hamilton, honourably concerned to guard his brother's reputation from being exposed to vulgar posterity.

For all its revelations Aileen Hamilton's archive provided only the skeleton of a biography. To flesh it out I had to locate surviving friends of Patrick and interview them at length. One of them, Jack Beeching, warned me from his place of exile in France that my quest would be a difficult, if not impossible, task, something akin to Symons' semi-intuitive reconstruction of the life of Frederick Rolfe, *The Quest for Corvo*. Patrick, Beeching wrote, was a secretive, reclusive man; one who took care to cover his tracks and lived much of his life in those places of transience, pubs. To recreate a life from such sketchy traces would clearly be no small undertaking. In the event, this warning proved pessimistic. Friends and acquaintances from Patrick's public and private lives survive in large numbers, and almost without exception proved more than helpful in giving up their time to tell me of him. With the help of these witnesses I was able to fill out my portrait of Patrick and measure Bruce's evidence against the assessment of other, objective outsiders.

At times, it seemed as though Patrick's ghost was at my elbow, gently guiding me through the byways of his hidden life (although, as a militant atheist, he would have laughed this romantic fancy to scorn). I found myself following his footsteps through many of the twenty thousand London streets that he had made, uniquely, his parish. (Occasionally, nursing my sore feet, it felt as though I had tramped them all.) Odd coincidences helped to keep me close to my quarry's shade: I found myself working in an office block in Hammersmith virtually next door to Patrick's old preparatory school, Colet Court. An office outing took me to Henley, where Patrick spent the wartime years and where he wrote *Hangover Square* and *The Slaves of Solitude*. A summer holiday in Norfolk brought me to the remote village of Overy Staithe where Patrick enjoyed some of his rare happy days – and to the house in Sheringham where he died; there I was lucky enough to catch and interview his last neighbour, Majorie Lewel, a week before she moved out. And always I returned to my base at Brighton, the town where Patrick grew up and to which, in his life and his fiction, he was constantly drawn.

Before I reached the end of the long and sinuous trail I had solved some of the mysteries of Patrick's life, without which it is impossible fully to understand his work. These are chiefly to do with a troubled and tortured sexuality which informed his art to a degree which has never been properly appreciated. By identifying and tracing the real-life models of the heroines of his first novel, *Monday Morning*, and his masterpiece, *Hangover Square*, I felt able to forge a link between the life and the art that had long been suspected by his admirers, but never documented. Discussing Patrick's alcoholism, Priestley noted:

> I feel strongly that an increasing desire to blur reality arose from the depths of a profoundly disturbed unconscious. We have to accept this, I believe, fully to understand the man and his work, both the wonderful best of it and the forgivable worst of it.[4]

Exposing the origins and the reality of that disturbance – the trauma that made Patrick at once an alcoholic and a superb writer – and bringing, I hope, a wider audience for his work, are the main aims of this biography.

PART I
1904–1920

1

Forebears and Family

PATRICK HAMILTON, CHRONICLER OF THE LOST and the lonely, the restless and the rootless, came from a long line firmly established in the settled upper reaches of the British ruling class.

His father, Walter Bernard Hamilton, never one to hide his social pretensions, claimed to belong to a cadet branch of the Scottish ducal family of Hamilton and Brandon, which traced its noble lineage back to Robert the Bruce himself. Bernard – he never used 'Walter' – wore a signet ring embossed with the Hamilton family crest, a horse's head, which Patrick inherited and wore in his turn.[1] The ring was engraved with the family motto, 'Ride Through', words spoken to King Charles I by the first Duke of Hamilton in a desperate moment during the first battle of the Civil War, Edgehill. Sadly, the advice failed to save the head of either man.

A later ancestor on Patrick's paternal side also has his niche in history: Colonel Thomas Wildman, a contemporary of Byron at Harrow and the man who in 1817 bought the poet's ancestral home, Newstead Abbey, near Nottingham, for the then huge sum of £94,500. Patrick christened the central character of his second novel, *Craven House*, with the family name of Wildman.

9

Wildman subsequently spent a further fortune of £100,000 on making the crumbling Gothic pile habitable. Once installed, he began to entertain a string of literary and society friends, including Tom Moore, Washington Irving, Bulwer Lytton and Byron's daughter Ada. Wildman fought at Waterloo along with two of his brothers, John and Colonel Edward Wildman, Patrick's great-grandfather. Edward Wildman was evidently a fire-eater, having had his skull sheared by a French sabre in the Peninsular War and having three horses killed under him at Waterloo. He survived to marry the daughter of Sir Hildebrand Oakes, Governor of Malta, the product of Sir Hildebrand's illicit liaison with a Spanish gypsy dancer. The daughter of this union, Patrick's grandmother, became the second wife of the rector of Waldershare in east Kent, the Reverend Walter Hamilton. Patrick's father was the only child of this marriage.

Bernard Hamilton was born in 1863. His mother died when he was seven, but his father's saturnine good looks – 'My dear, that man must have been a menace!' commented a relative when shown the rector's portrait – soon attracted a third wife. Absorbed in each other and in their pastoral duties, the couple had little time or love left for Bernard, an exuberant, adventurous child who was largely left to his own devices, wandering the woods and fields of the surrounding countryside. When the weather was bad, or energy flagged, the boy devoured the books in his father's library, developing an addiction for the novels of Walter Scott that was to last a lifetime.

The Waldershare rectory's tableau vivant could almost have been created by Dickens (a writer to whom Patrick, who owned a complete set of his works, bears strong affinities). The cast of characters in this Victorian stereotype included a distant and neglectful father, a cruel and jealous stepmother and even a sweet and saintly half-sister, who, true to tragic form, was carried away by disease at an early age leaving the surviving child alone to bear the brunt of parental *froideur*. Young Bernard's education completed the picture: dame school at Ewell in Surrey, preparatory school in Windsor and public school at Repton, where, in the best traditions of sensitive sons from the English upper class, he was miserably unhappy.

Bernard's life bloomed when he was sent up to Trinity College, Cambridge, to read History. His devotion to his studies, never strenuous, relaxed into complete neglect when at the age of twenty-one he came into his share of the family fortune. This amounted to the enormous sum of £100,000, which he nevertheless managed to exhaust in a lifetime of self-indulgence.

Celebrating his inheritance in suitable style on the night of his twenty-first birthday, Bernard was at the Empire Theatre in London when he met the woman who became his first wife, and whom he was to attempt to rescue from her life of prostitution. The marriage of the rich boy and the street girl was predictably disastrous and culminated in the woman's suicide under a train at Wimbledon station following her husband's desertion. She left a letter exonerating Bernard from all blame, but this waywardness set a pattern he was to repeat in his second, more respectable, marriage.

Bernard was to maintain a life of selfish indolence for the rest of his days. Leaving Cambridge with an MA degree he was called to the Bar at the Middle Temple in June 1893, but although he habitually referred to himself as 'the author and barrister' and had himself photographed in wig and gown, complete with the monocle he wore for effect, he never put his costume to practical use. Instead he preferred to spend his time as a London clubman (he was a member of the Junior Athenaeum and the Savage), wining and dining in the best restaurants, in restless travel – he roamed every European country and journeyed as far afield as Egypt – and in reading, writing and above all talking. Bernard was a booming and inveterate talker on a wide range of topics – religion, history, politics, morality and military matters – but his favourite subject was undoubtedly himself. He was, in short, a crashing bore; and he soon inflicted his overpowering personality on a second wife.

Ellen Adèle Hockley, known to family and friends as Nell or Nellie, was the youngest of three sisters, the daughters of a London dentist who was reputed to be the illegitimate son of the Irish baronet Sir Anthony Weldon.[2] Both parents died when their daughters were young and the girls were brought up by their elder brother George, also a dentist, at Old Shoreham in

Sussex. The eldest, Bessy, married the local squire; Mary, the middle sister, married a doctor and emigrated to South Africa, while Nellie fell in love with, and married, a Mr Day. Their union was a brief one, for Day proved to be a charming but incorrigible womaniser. He vanished from Nellie's life as rapidly as he had entered it and a divorce concluded the childless marriage. A divorced woman past her first youth was not exactly eligible in late-Victorian society, so when Bernard Hamilton began to pay her court perhaps Nellie can be forgiven for not looking too closely in the gift-horse's expansive mouth. They married in 1895 and although three children were born it was obvious from the start that the relationship was a mismatch.

Of the sexual side of the marriage we know little beyond a suggestion by Bruce Hamilton that his mother was afflicted by 'frigidity'. This may have been a quite reasonable distaste for the attentions of her husband and it is certain that she was endowed with an immense capacity for a cloying sort of love that was lavished, not on Bernard, but on her children and in particular her youngest son, Patrick. It seems that there was little passion between the couple from the outset and Nellie may well have regarded marriage to the wealthy Bernard as a sensible business arrangement. She was two years older than her husband who, although he had evidently sown some wild oats in his youth, she might reasonably have expected to settle down. If she had such expectations, they were to be grievously disappointed.

They made a handsome enough pair. Bernard was tall and imposing and although he was already running to fat, his ponderous figure and rather flabby features were offset by an upright bearing and a low, deep voice. He probably appeared 'distinguished'; he certainly thought he was.

Nellie was a bundle of bubbling energy, her busy body enhanced by a pretty round face, a plump figure, snub nose and dark hair. But despite an ostensible compatability Bruce Hamilton was explicit in stating, 'As a human relationship the marriage was a failure.' He instanced two anecdotes told him by his mother from the early years of her marriage which seem to have been watersheds in turning her mild affection for Bernard into first distrust and, then, bitter dislike.

On the first occasion the couple were dining out with friends when Bernard became embroiled in an argument with his host. Eventually he rose from the table, commanded his wife to follow and left, contemptuously throwing down a sovereign (five shillings, according to Patrick) to cover the cost of the dinner. Shortly afterwards the Hamiltons were staying with friends in the country. The daughter of the house told Nellie in strictest confidence that she had exchanged vows of love with an ineligible young man, a lowly curate who was her tutor. Trusting to her husband's discretion, Nellie passed on this titbit to Bernard, who promptly informed the parents. A family row ensued, after which the girl, giving Nellie a burning gaze of reproof, severed all relations with her false friend. 'That was when I first realised I hated B.,' Nellie recalled years later.

These incidents may nowadays seem comparatively trivial, but it should be remembered that Victorian couples frequently knew little of each other's personalities until after they were married and Bernard's behaviour must have provided most unwelcome evidence to Nellie of his real temperament.

Nevertheless, the marriage endured. Both partners buried their bitter private differences for the sake of putting on a brave face to the outside world, particularly that of the upper-middle-class county society of Surrey and Sussex. To the members of their caste it was vital to keep up appearances. Bernard had the advantage of being a wealthy man in his own right, which buttressed his frequently outrageous behaviour and arrogant outbursts and, under the hypocritical codes and rules by which the Hamiltons lived, conduct that would have meant social death for the less favoured was forgiven and even applauded; however Nellie's position was far more precarious. To the stigma of being a divorcee she had the added disadvantage of possessing no money of her own. Her fear of descending into an abyss of genteel poverty not only forced her to put up with Bernard's neglect, cruelty and extravagance, but made her even more of a snob than her husband. In the days before the social reforms of the welfare state the prospect of poverty was an ever-present nightmare to the middle classes and terror of falling back into the inchoate world of the working class is a leitmotiv shading the background of Patrick Hamilton's books, as well as the work of contemporaries from similar social backgrounds, such as George Orwell.

The Hamiltons set up their first married home at a house in Hindhead, named, with a nod to Bernard's Scottish ancestry and the Victorian craze for all things tartan, 'Hindhead Brae'.[3] Among their neighbours in the locality was Arthur Conan Doyle, then at the height of his fame as author of the Sherlock Holmes stories. Bernard Hamilton struck up a friendship with Doyle who subsequently agreed to be Bruce Hamilton's godfather (Bruce's first name was Arthur, in Doyle's honour). However the friendship soon foundered on the rocks of Bernard's incurable egotism and pomposity. Years later in his memoirs, serialised in the *Strand* magazine, Doyle recounted how Bernard had been the victim of a put-down by Sir Henry Irving at one of their Hindhead evenings. Bernard was mid-way through an interminable monologue when Irving turned to him and remarked, '*What a low comedian you would have made!*' It is not recorded whether Bernard made one of his grand exits at this point, but at any rate his vanity was hard hit when he read about it in the *Strand*, to which Nellie, as an occasional contributor of stories, subscribed. The author and barrister eventually took his revenge by writing a book, *One World at a Time*, mocking Doyle's devotion to spiritualism.

Both Bernard and Nellie were published writers. Bernard's first book was *The Light?* which appeared in 1898, shortly after his marriage to Nellie, who was its dedicatee. *The Light?* is a monstrous five-hundred-page bag of a book into which Bernard stuffs all his favourite religious and historical obsessions, saddling them with a thin and wildly improbable plot which draws on his travels in the near East to drag in ancient Egypt, reincarnation, and scenes from contemporary Victorian life, including the Franco-Prussian War and the East End, where Bernard had briefly worked at Toynbee Hall social centre during his university days. It is the sort of book that only a Victorian gentleman, with endless leisure on his hands, could write for an audience of similarly placed social peers. For those with less time, Bernard helpfully included asterisks in the text to show his readers where particularly turgid passages could be safely skipped, without interfering with the dramatic sequence of the tale. The preface is full of similarly eccentric mannerisms and statements of intent:

> The following pages, while endeavouring to voice the silent spirit of the times, deal with mythology, but uphold every essential element of the Christian religion ... As a reviewer, to reviewers, I venture, with diffidence, to call attention to one or two points ... This book is a humble attempt to give utterance to the unspoken thoughts of this great dumb majority.

Beneath the clotted prose *The Light?* is a blast against the Anglo-Catholic Oxford Movement, then a fashionable force within the Anglican Church, and a plea for tolerance and respect for other religions. It proved too shocking for two of Bernard's aged aunts living in Canterbury who, on reading the book, diverted to the Church a further fortune of £100,000 in Wildman money which had been destined for their nephew.

Bernard's next book, published in 1899 with a dedication to Doyle, was *A Kiss for a Kingdom*, a Ruritanian romance about an American millionaire who tries to become monarch of San Marino. Then came *Coronation*, a mediaeval yarn with an appalling alliterative opening:

> Boom! went the bell of St Botolph's, bidding her boys from book and board. Clang! came the curfew of Carfax, calling the citizens from counter and cloth-yard.

Not to be outdone by Bernard's burgeoning career as a writer, Nellie, too, settled down to her *éscritoire*. She wrote two novels under the pseudonym Olivia Roy the titles of which give some indication of their author's abiding concerns: *The Husband Hunter* and *The Awakening of Mrs Carstairs*. They are light social romances which do much to justify Bruce Hamilton's suspicion that his mother was not a natural writer, but took it up as a hobby under her husband's influence. Novel-writing was a fairly common pursuit of the leisured upper-middle classes, a skill analogous in their minds to piano-playing or singing. Nevertheless the fact that the Hamilton children were born into and brought up in a household where both parents fancied themselves gifted practitioners of the art makes it unsurprising that all three found vocations in the same field. Bernard took his own literary pretensions extremely seriously, seeing himself as a disciple of his beloved Scott and a peer of his near-contemporaries Carlyle, Anatole France and Victor Hugo.[4] Patrick was later to remark that the quartet had a disastrous influence on Bernard's own literary style.

The coming of children ended Nellie's brief writing career and from then on she devoted her time and talents exclusively to their welfare. Bernard, for his part, was often absent from home. After a short break he had resumed his amorous activities, acquiring that essential accessory of the Edwardian Englishman, a mistress in Paris, named Marthe. He spent a considerable period of time with her and also made frequent visits to the famous spa of Karlsbad, taking the cure for gout and his increasing obesity. Even when he was in England he would stay for weeks at his bachelor barrister flat in the Temple, 1 Pump Court, where he could safely carry on what amounted to a second life as a gallant lover and clubbable man-about-town, far from the vexatious demands of his growing family.

The first child of the marriage was born in July 1898 and christened Helen Dorothea Elisa, but was known in the family as Lalla. Two years later came a boy, baptised Arthur Douglas Bruce (Douglas was the Hamilton ducal family name). When Bruce was two, the Hamiltons moved from Hindhead to Dale House at Hassocks in the Sussex Weald. Dale House was a mid-Victorian, rambling, gabled affair, overlooked by the South Downs and containing in its grounds a wood, a stream, a lake with islands, as well as lawns, stables, summer-house and kitchen garden. The building was demolished in the 1930s to make way for those Hamiltonian symbols – a cinema, a garage and a housing estate; here, on 17 March 1904, Patrick Hamilton was born.

2

When I was a Child

THE NEW BABY, WHOSE BIRTH had been easy for his mother, was christened at the nearby parish church of Keymer and baptised Anthony Walter Patrick. His first name was possibly given in honour of his supposed maternal great-grandfather, Sir Anthony Weldon, his second was after his father and paternal grandfather, but it was his third – given because he shared his birthday with Ireland's patron saint – by which he was always known. A sleepy and silent child he was from the first the pampered apple of his mother's eye. Significantly, Bruce's earliest memory of his younger brother concerned a quarrel during which he bit the newcomer's arm. Patrick's cries summoned his ever-watchful mother to the scene and Bruce was banished to his bedroom while a special trip to Brighton, the first of many in his life, was laid on to soothe and divert the injured party.

Sibling rivalry played a major part in Bruce's earliest memories of his brother and it can be deduced that Patrick suffered his share of the normal jealousy and resentment reserved for an unwanted younger rival by his elder brother and sister. One typical row between the brothers resulted in the dismissal of their German governess, known to the children as 'Frorline'. The argument arose during a cricket match when Patrick called Bruce a 'demon', the vilest epithet in his infant vocabulary. 'Frorline' overheard the insult and, mistaking the offender, fetched Bruce a

17

light box on the ear. This incident was witnessed from afar by
Nellie who was preparing for a social outing. Dressed all in
white, her jewellery jingling, she bore across the lawn like an
avenging angel. 'How dare you!' she said to the hapless
'Frorline', 'How *dare* you!'. The governess was instantly
dismissed and sent to pack her box.

Patrick was quick to spot and exploit the weaknesses in his
brother's armour. The shy and gentle Bruce was easy to tease
and Patrick could be relied upon to play upon his naivety and
kindle sparks of resentment into a raging fight. While Bruce
expended his energy in spitting anger, Patrick remained calm,
solemn and watchful. When naughtiness in the nursery brought
adult investigation and the threat of retribution, Patrick was
more skilful than his elder brother in evading the consequences
of his crimes. On one occasion Bruce was moved to protest. 'Of
course you believe him', he told their mother, 'he's got such
insinuating manners.'

Patrick was precocious in displaying traits that were later to
characterise him as a writer; particularly the quality, noticed by
many who knew him, of quietly observing the conversation and
behaviour of others. From his earliest years he was intellectually
curious, storing up impressions of people and objects and unin-
hibited in asking frank questions about things which puzzled
him. He was also able to establish greater intimacy with adults
than the tongue-tied Bruce.

A series of stays in London presaged the family's departure
from their idyllic life at Dale House. They lived for almost a year
in Gloucester Terrace, from where the children could see the
green trains entering and leaving Paddington station, and
another year was spent in Norland Square, off Holland Park
Road, from where the children were taken to play in the
Kensington Gardens which had been recently immortalised as
Never-never land by J.M. Barrie in *Peter Pan*. Early impressions
of London life which imprinted themselves on Patrick's mind
included a fire engine, pulled by white horses, which seemed
themselves to breathe smoke as they thundered down the road.
On a more terrifying occasion the children saw a convict,
complete with broad-arrowed prison uniform, being dragged in

manacles along a pavement by two grim policemen.

In 1908 Dale House was let and the family moved to Hove on the Sussex coast. Initially the Hamiltons lived in a series of flats while Bernard sought a permanent residence for his brood. It was at about this time that the children began to notice the increasing frequency, not only of Bernard's absences, but of their mother's too, as she engaged in her social round. Very often the young Hamiltons were left alone in the charge of nurses and governesses. However, by Christmas of that year, the family unit was reassembled in a rented house in Hove's Palmeira Avenue, where Bernard condescended to read passages from *The Pilgrim's Progress* and *The Arabian Nights* to his two elder children. The following January a house was bought at 12 First Avenue, which was to be the family home for the next six and a half years. A tall, five-storey structure standing in a terrace of similar properties within yards of Hove's seafront, it is today divided into flatlets and bedsits and, despite the recent addition of a plaque commemorating Patrick,[1] it exudes decay and desolation.

It was of First Avenue that Patrick had his earliest coherent childhood memories; towards the end of his life, hospitalised for alcoholic depression, he was quizzed by two medical students seeking the origins of his drinking:

They questioned me pleasantly and eagerly. Was it hereditary? Did I think it was something caused automatically by the constitution of the body, or was it the result of nervous strain – of some underlying frustration or major disorder in my life? Could it be traced to unhappiness in childhood or boyhood? And many other rather naive and delightful questions of the same sort – all equally impossible for a conscientious witness to answer with a straight yes or no.

I can remember answering, though, that I had been offered, on the whole, about as happy a childhood as one could reasonably hope for, and I think that this was true. At the age of four I was the youngest member of a well-to-do middle-class household of about nine people (mother, father, sister, brother, three or four servants and myself) established at First Avenue, Hove. I have often thought that First Avenue, Hove, could be adequately described by only one living writer – Osbert Sitwell – and I can, actually, remember this writer's eyes lighting up, with a sort of novelist's relish, when I told him that this had been my early background.

I myself can only say that it is quite unlike anything else I have ever seen on earth. The grey, drab, tall, treeless houses leading down to the King's Gardens and the sea convey absolutely no social or historical message to me. They are not even funny, or ostentatious, or bizarre, or characteristic, so far as I know, of any recognised form of taste. There are grounds for believing, though, that in 1908 the residents, so far from showing any sort of amazement or bewilderment at what they saw from their front windows, were complacent and even vain about their houses – regarding the Adelaide Crescent and Brunswick Square areas which lay eastwards as being inferior not only from the point of view of convenience and beauty, but socially.

In Bernard's absence the household was presided over by the tiny, increasingly rotund, figure of Nellie, brimming with vitality and volubility, but with her sensitivity barely concealed by her powdered skin. At nearly fifty (the age she attained in 1911) she was still full of energy but her high spirits were sometimes interspersed with outbursts of temper that the children later ascribed to her marital unhappiness. Like many Edwardian parents she attempted to inculcate high ideals into her offspring, drumming in her personal motto, 'It's worth trying for.' In the evenings she would entertain the family by playing the piano, accompanying her own rendition of songs like 'Who is Sylvia?' or 'Dinah Doh'. The walls of the house were decorated with her own paintings – copies in oils she had executed after the English masters Turner, Gainsborough, Reynolds and Romney. The children would often receive written injunctions and reminders, scribbled in her ungrammatical hand: 'Besure [sic] to put on your thick vest and pants if the weather turns any colder'.

She fussed frequently over her children's health, imprisoning them in the schoolroom if the weather was bad and piling on layers of clothes – galoshes, gloves, gaiters, coats and umbrellas – if it was merely vaguely inclement. Patent medicines were poured down their young throats with abandon in a bid to ward off maladies real and imagined. In line with the thinking of most turn-of-the-century middle-class mothers Nellie took a keen personal interest in the movements of her children's bowels. Her particular enemy was constipation and she kept a 'constipation calendar', which was a diary of the children's bowel movements. A typical week in the calendar reads: 'Mon: Good. Tue: Fair. Wed: Fair. Thu: Poor. Fri: Bad. Medicine. Sat: Excellent. Sun: V. good', and nurses were instructed to inspect the contents of the lavatory before flushing if the children were thought to be less than honest about their internal condition.[2] Such rigid toilet training is not easily shaken off.

Although writing with the disillusioned hindsight of late middle-age, Patrick's incomplete and fragmentary attempt at an autobiography *Memoirs of a Heavy Drinking Man* is adamant in ascribing many of the mental worries that plagued him in later life to the experiences of his early childhood in Hove:

> Here I was well fed, well cared for and well clothed: and I suffered no physical violence of any sort. But this does not mean that there was any absence of anxieties and neuroses of all sorts, which were made more expressive, rather than disentangled, by various women with whom I spent most of my time – at this period and in that class called nurses (not 'nannies').

Patrick proceeds to compile a charge sheet against his nurses:

> They said that if the wind changed while a person was making a face then the face would remain permanently distorted and hideous and the mind wandered . . . between belief and disbelief. To believe was to accept the existence of a constant personal danger: to disbelieve was to accept that one's powerful . . . informant was a liar, and therefore hateful, or idiotic, or both.
>
> They shouted that the toes were pigs – that one went to market, that one stayed at home, that one had roast beef, that one had none and that one went 'Wee-wee-wee-wee!' all the way home. But what was 'market'? Why did one pig have roast beef and the other none? Where did justice lie? Which pig gained? Could toes, in fact, be pigs?

The future poet also claimed to be disturbed by the 'complete and ugly abandonment of scansion' in the last line of the rhyme and by the knowledge that the word 'home' did not rhyme with the word 'none' and that the final use of the word 'home' was a repetition and not a rhyme.

Patrick's acute reaction to the common currency of an Edwardian nursery – his refusal to swallow rhymes, tales and saws that other children would have bolted with a smile – suggests that the finely tuned antennae which were to be his great strength as a writer were already up and operating in his infancy. But there is something both disturbed and disturbing in his wounded hyper-sensitivity; here are the first stirrings of the complexes and terrors that were to beset him sorely as an adult. There is, for example, his open misogyny:

> Children are absolutely humourless, and least of all smiled [sic] to the ponderous drolleries of these humourless women put in charge of them.
>
> In their stern, formal logic, though, children can easily discern the differences between inconsequent untruthfulness and avowed fiction, and will take the utmost delight in well-constructed fiction presented honestly as such. Hence their delight in fairy stories, which analysis shows are for the most part witch-stories, and their constant demand for them from their nurses. My own nurses here were hatefully disobliging, and instead of cordially declining resorted to their usual unpleasant mental trickery.
>
> I can remember two particularly below-the-belt ruses they used when I asked to be told a story. In one case, pretending to consent, they would say 'Very well . . .', and I was waiting eagerly for what was to follow. Then, slowly and pointedly recited, came the following rhyme:
> 			'I'll tell you a story of Jack O'My Nory,
> 			And now my story's begun.
> 			I'll tell you another of Jack and his brother,
> 			And now my story's done.'
> In the other case they would again feign consent and begin, with a heavy dramatic air which filled me with pleasure and hope: 'It was a cold and frosty night . . . and the King of the castle said to his servant: "Tell me a story." And this is how he began: "It was a cold and frosty night . . . and the King of the castle said

to his servant: "Tell me a story." And this is how he began: "It was a cold . . .' and so on, again, and again and again until my patience tired. And no amount of entreaties brought forth anything but the same cruel, deliberate formula.

The crushing impact of this drawn-out and tortuous teasing on Patrick's forming mind is the obvious origin of some of his most characteristically obsessive traits: his frequent repetitions, his delight in suspense and his interest in the macabre and the frankly sadistic. We can trace the torments of the victim's parents in *Rope* to these agonising minutes in the Hove nursery, as they await the arrival of their son who is, all the time, dead in the chest on which they are dining. It is here where we may find the frustrations of Bob in *The Midnight Bell* as he continuously tries to make a telephone connection with his beloved but uncaring Jenny, or the dull pain of the stubborn, plodding Bone in *Hangover Square* as Netta heaps humiliating coals of derision on his bowed and patient head. Here is the female as bitch; as the omnipotent writer Patrick wreaked his revenge on women, in part compensating himself for his powerlessness as a child: as Bob is neglected by Jenny in *The Midnight Bell* so in his turn Bob neglects Ella who so patiently loves him. In *The Slaves of Solitude* before turning the tables on her tormentors, poor, sad Miss Roach is victimised in turn by the sadistic Mr Thwaites, the opportunist American officer and the sinister Vicki Kugelmann. It is a world in which all the protagonists are at once victims and torturers, prisoners and executioners, locked in a hell from which there is no release.

Patrick laid the blame for his adult alcoholism squarely on the horrors of Hove. 'All this sort of thing, almost certainly, helps to nourish in a child's mind those plants of doubt, distress and anxiety which are ultimately the main causes of heavy or excessive drinking.' But despite the hatred he cherished in his heart for his nurses, Patrick was ultimately too honest and too self-aware to hold them solely to blame for his mature problems and obsessions: 'These ignorant women – "ignorant", it may be noted, was a word in which they delighted – could not be held responsible for many of the neuroses which in due course appeared seemingly for no reason.'

Obsessive-compulsive behaviour has long been known to psychology. It is a sure sign of profound insecurity and is usually found only in adults. When exhibited in young children it is a mark of an unusually disturbed child. It is not, perhaps, too fanciful to suggest that at least part of the cause of this disturbance, not overtly recognised by Patrick in his account, was the absence of his parents. It is quite likely that this led to fears of abandonment and a terror of the outside world into which his parents so frequently and, to a young child, inexplicably, vanished. Any rage against his mother for forsaking him was swiftly and deeply repressed.

The painful sensitivity – albeit recalled with an adult's perspective – with which Patrick described the details of his early childhood burnt itself into his consciousness. A more robust child would have forgotten or ignored these incidents. To Patrick, they were an ever-present torment that haunted him for the rest of his days. They were his undoing as an emotionally mature man, but they were the making of him as an acutely sensitive writer. And there were other horrors yet to be endured:

> This way of thinking and behaving was very much more painful and harmful when it was combined with a fear of the dark, of isolation in the dark. Thus, when I was put to my bed by my nurse with the assurance that if I needed anything I had only to summon her from the kitchen far below, I was soon, strenuously as I tried not to be so, restless, agitated and really afraid ... I do not know how many times each night this nurse had to climb, at the end of her day, from the basement, and up through the equivalent of two capacious flats, to soothe me. I should say half a dozen at least. But she knew as well as I did that this was not caprice, self-indulgence, impertinence or foolishness on my part: it was panic.

To placate the sheer fear gripping Patrick's infant imagination,

> A night-light was given me. But this made matters worse. For the night-light, in its saucer on the mantelpiece – dim, wavering, and sinking – was even more suggestive and anticipative of evil than darkness itself.

'Master Pat' was four or five years old at the time of these incidents. It may be suspected that the adult Patrick, recalling his childhood terrors, if not in tranquillity, at least from a safe distance, was exaggerating them for dramatic effect. But it cannot be coincidental that in his writing the ephemeral warmth and safety of the light is frequently contrasted with the unknown and unnamed dangers lurking in the dark. The flickering shadows of the malevolently manipulated mantle in *Gaslight* and the darkness in which the murderers conceal their deed in *Rope* are pale reflections of the magnified terror of the tiny, uncertain flame of the night-light in the child's bedroom.

During Patrick's childhood the financial position of the Hamiltons steadily declined. At Hove, the domestic servants' payroll was cut to half of what it had been in the Dale House days when Bernard had employed a staff of ten, including gardeners, governesses, maids and a groom to look after his horse. The groom had been dismissed, along with his horse and carriage and Nellie had to send a servant to the top of the avenue to call up a horse-drawn 'fly' from the rank if she was moved to make a social call.

Nellie's domestic tyranny extended outside the home to the local tradesmen who attempted to cater to her needs. At least six butchers were tried out and dismissed before one was found to give satisfaction. Inside the walls of her domain justice was still as rough and swift as in the days of 'Frorline': Patrick's favourite nurse, the sympathetic Alice Swain, was sacked on the spot for returning late from a dance. Nellie, conforming to the codes of her caste, divided the world into 'Gentlepeople' (one of us); 'Common' (not quite one of us); or, the 'Lower orders' (beneath notice). Bruce's first fumbling attempt to make a friendship outside his family was foiled when his mother discovered that the boy's parents owned a chain of bakers' shops and were therefore deemed 'in trade'.

Both Bernard and Nellie worshipped titles and did their best to play up to their aristocratic pretensions. Bernard installed panes of coloured glass carrying the heraldic devices of the Hamilton and Wildman families that cast a gloomy light over their successive homes; Nellie was pleased to include a

'Baroness' and a 'Lady' in her address book and her husband
went into ecstasy when he learned that Lalla had got to know the
daughter of the Duc de Clermont Tonnerre.

The snobbishness of the Hamiltons was a common attribute of
their type in a rigidly class-bound era, but there was always
something artificial about Bernard's efforts to emulate his alleged
ancestors and claim kinship with the highest in the land. (He
even told Patrick he was the rightful heir to the Scottish throne.)
Bernard had a canteen of cutlery engraved with the Hamilton
ducal crest which passed to Bruce on his death and was inherited
in turn by Bruce's widow Aileen. She assumed the set was solid
silver and took it to a jeweller to have it valued. After a cursory
examination the man exclaimed that it was certainly not silver
and moreover that it was the first time in his experience that he
had known anyone go to the trouble of engraving plate.[3] The incident typifies Bernard's bogusness, notwithstanding which his
obsession with family and ancestry was dinned into his children
from an early age: pictures of the two Colonel Wildmans,
bristling in their uniforms, and of the old ancestral home,
Newstead Abbey, had pride of place alongside Nellie's paintings
on the walls of the various Hamilton houses.

Probably Patrick rumbled his father early on; significantly in
his novel *The West Pier* he equips his criminal creation Ernest
Gorse with an ancestral signet ring *à la* Bernard. At any rate he
was to display a clear-eyed interest in and insight into the minds
of con-men in his work. Both Patrick and Bruce came later to
despise and ridicule the sort of snobbery practised by their
parents, but for long formative years they were tightly bound by
social conventions which they were slow to throw off and never
entirely succeeded in escaping.

The town where the Hamilton children were growing up was
changing with the country. As the new century dawned Victoria
was succeeded by her son, the rakish Edward VII, a frequent
visitor to Brighton and Hove. Brighton had enjoyed its first
heyday under George IV, who was in many ways a similar sort
of character to the new King; virtually boycotted by Victoria
because of its raffish atmosphere, it now looked forward to a new
lease of life. The easygoing resort was a place where, in summer,

according to local journalist George Sala:

> [It] means bathing, it means donkey-riding ... the building of
> sham fortifications with pebbles on the beach; it means the
> collection of seaweed and shells by the small folk; it means much
> reading by young ladies of cheap novels, or knitting, or in some
> way whiling away the time in shady places or on the pier.[4]

It was a town patronised by high society in spring and autumn
for the sea air and by the London working classes in summer,
down on cheap-day rail excursions to escape from the 'Smoke' in
search of sun and fun.

The Hamilton children got to know Brighton through household servants, like their cook, Mrs Collins – known to them as
'Collie Dog' – who delighted the young Hamiltons by letting
them participate in the creation of home-made toffee and soda
cakes. She was the wife of Captain Collins, skipper of a well-known
local institution, the pleasure craft *Skylark*, and at whose feet a
wide-eyed Patrick heard embroidered yarns of nautical derring-do.

Both Bruce and Patrick felt the first faint stirrings of sexual
awakening inspired by one of their nurses, Nellie Gates, a beauty
known to the boys from her crisp uniform as the 'Blue Nurse'.
She had a mass of red-gold hair and an English rose complexion
with a curvaceous figure held promisingly in check by her
starched uniform. She entertained the brothers with her gift for
rapidly executed watercolours, her silvery voice and her knack of
enthralling storytelling. These tales, recounted on daily walks
along the Hove seafront, consisted of excitingly detailed accounts
of memorable whippings she had received at the hands of her
father and boasts about her first sexual conquests, among whom
she claimed to have numbered two Sussex sporting stars: the
county's cricket captain and later Hollywood actor, C.L. Aubrey
Smith; and Brighton and Hove Albion's legendary outside-right,
the auspiciously named Ernest Longstaff. But the lucky suitor
who finally won the heart and hand of the erotically compelling
Blue Nurse was a man of more humble name and occupation,
one Albert Sugden, a driver on the Volks Electric Railway which
plied (and indeed still plies) the Brighton seafront.

Albert had wooed and won the not-unwilling Nurse Nellie when, family visits having been exchanged and a date fixed for their wedding, he succumbed to double pneumonia. It was the younger Hamiltons' first experience of death and Bruce recalled the morning when the Blue Nurse heard the news, sitting at the schoolroom table, her magnificent head buried in her arms, sobbing as if she would never cease. Embarrassed, Bruce made a strategic withdrawal to the dining room, but Patrick stayed on, lying stomach down on the schoolroom floor, his head propped on his hands, taking in the tragic scene and storing it for future retrieval.

The boys' most constant companion during the early years at Hove was their teenage cousin, Frank Bridger, son of their mother's sister Bessy and heir to broad acres at nearby Shoreham. He infected the brothers with his own enthusiasm for steam railways, condescended to play hide-and-seek with them and escorted them on visits to the West Pier and the King's Gardens, scene of memorable encounters with the King himself. The monarch was often in Hove, staying with his friends the Sassoons at their house in Grand Avenue. On sunny days he would take the sea air in the King's Gardens, preceded by a flurry of equerries who would escort the King to his favourite seat in a sunny shelter. A cordon of gardeners and flunkies shooed *hoi polloi* away to a safe distance while the King relaxed and dozed. With bated breath the Hamilton boys would watch their sleeping sovereign and after an hour or so the King would rise and ponderously return to his base. It was at this point that the brothers would swoop and race each other to the Royal bench in order to secure the honour of sitting on it while still warm from the heat of the Hanoverian hindquarters.

All too soon, school, the inevitable spoiler of childhood idylls, beckoned. Lalla was sent to a local girls' academy, St Michael's Hall, while Bruce attended the kindergarten of the same establishment. Patrick's first experience of learning outside his domestic environment was an infant school, Norlandholme, run by a Miss Cadwallader from her home in the Drive, off Hove's Wilbury Road. The curriculum consisted mainly of handicrafts and here Patrick acquired his first friend, a boy named Nigel

Elmsleigh. Nigel, evidently a fun-loving lad, initiated Patrick in the traditional boyhood sports of ringing doorbells and running away, or stopping a grown-up to ask directions to some fictitious destination. At home, after the jealousies and quarrels of Dale House, Patrick and Bruce had established a brotherly *modus vivendi*: Bruce taught Patrick how to ride a bike, how to dodge their enemy, 'the Panther', the soft-shoed local park-keeper, and gave Patrick early lessons in the art of storytelling. Bruce, by his own admission, 'a ready, though implausible, liar', regaled Patrick in their bedroom after lights out with a series of fables and fantasies. Together they invented a family, the Thankyou-bells, who lived in nearby Norton Road and wove a sort of serial around their adventures, telling each other alternate episodes each night in what became a long-running Hove soap opera.

But there were clouds on the horizon. Bruce became aware that he was jealous of his younger brother, noticing that Patrick possessed an engaging quality that he himself lacked – adults appeared more attracted to the bright but taciturn younger boy – and Nellie had an annoying habit of holding up Patrick's behaviour as an example to be emulated. Once, Bruce broke his two front teeth when Patrick cannoned into him during a bout of horseplay. He was taken to the dentist where the teeth were mended, but cried during the ordeal. A little while later Patrick was sent for some dental work and endured the experience with Spartan equanimity. The dentist compared his stoicism favourably with Bruce's squeamishness and Nellie wasted no time in passing this on to her elder son.

A further humiliation for Bruce lay in store when the children spent the summer of 1910 at Orchard Farm, a rural guest house between Hassocks and Burgess Hill. The Hamiltons teamed up with a fellow guest, Marjorie Read, who consented to be crowned Bruce's consort as 'Queen' of a tiny island in a local lake. The coronation was carried out in deadly earnest, complete with paper crowns, curtains converted into robes, and nurses acting as attendants. However no sooner was the reign inaugurated than Marjorie jilted Bruce for Patrick and within a week a similar ceremony was held to celebrate their 'marriage'. King Bruce was not amused.

Orchard Farm was a paradise for the children; it was the place where Patrick, at the age of seven, finally learned to read under his brother's tuition. Less studious pursuits were also available in abundance: a German waiter, Karl, and a cowman, Bennett, were there to teach the tricks of their respective trades. There was a calf to be petted, a boat to row on the lake, a tree hanging over the tennis court to be climbed and the inevitable presence of 'Mummie' – as the brothers referred to her throughout their lives – to accompany them on walks to a nearby water-mill and thrill them with ghost stories from Newstead Abbey. The holiday was repeated the following year, the brilliant summer of 1911; and then the time came for Patrick to follow Bruce and take his place in his first proper school.

3

Mummie's Boy

HOLLAND HOUSE WAS A PREPARATORY SCHOOL for boys that occupied two houses in Hove's Cromwell Road, conveniently adjacent to the Sussex county cricket ground. George Orwell, an almost exact contemporary of Patrick, left a vividly horrific account of life at a Sussex prep school in the early years of the century in his essay 'Such, Such were the Joys'.[1] In Orwell's account, St Cyprian's, the school he attended at Eastbourne, becomes a mini-version of Oceania in *1984*, a state run by fear and policed by the Headmaster, Sambo, and his terrifying wife, Flip.

Patrick's schooldays were altogether happier. The main difference between his life and the ordeal Orwell was simultaneously undergoing a few miles down the coast was that Patrick was a day boy, while Orwell was a boarder. If life got too tough at Holland House, home and the comforting presence of Mummie were only a few yards away. Nellie had laboured hard to create a bolthole, which her children were ready to exploit. Patrick has left us a portrait of Holland House in *The West Pier*[2] and here he maps out the social hierarchy of the school in characteristic fashion:

What may be roughly called an aristocracy of five or six boys came from the squares and avenues – Brunswick Square, Grand Avenue, First Avenue and the like. What may be roughly called a bourgeoisie (the sons of merchants, dentists, estate agents, doctors, clergymen, retired officers and well-to-do local tradesmen) came from the roads – Wilbury Road, Holland Road, Tisbury Road, Norton Road: while the rest came from the villas – Hove Villas, Ventnor Villas, Denmark Villas – or from obscure crescents and streets at the back of Hove or of Brighton, or from humble western regions verging upon Portslade. A few of this third class approximated to the *sans culottes*: at any rate their clothes were laughed at, and they were known to be 'common'.

Patrick is careful, here, to number his own residence among the élite, while the last disparaging line, ostensibly mocking schoolboy snobbery, carries a disturbing hint of Nellie's own prejudices.

The teaching of the forty boys at Holland House was in the hands of its Headmaster, W.B.C. 'Bill' Cawood, and three fulltime assistant masters. Discipline at the school was relaxed compared to similar establishments, but Cawood occasionally felt it necessary to check his charges' transgressions with the cane. School games were played on the sacred turf of the county cricket ground, which Patrick and Bruce came to refer to as their own Elysian Fields.

The eight-year-old Patrick quickly found his feet at the school and made his mark as a leader of a gang known as the Sporting Club. His chief sidekicks were a friend named Claude Chepmell and Herman Treutler, the son of a German doctor and the gang's minor mischief-making consisted of trespassing in half-built houses and scaring each other with ghost and spy stories and tales of thieves and murderers. Soon Patrick established a military hierarchy in the club, with himself as undisputed General and Officer-in-Command, while a boy named Stocker acted as his Regimental Sergeant-Major, complete with three stripes chalked on his sleeve.

Bruce continued to suffer small humiliations at the hands of his favoured younger brother: on one occasion Patrick was asked to share a promised treat with Bruce – an outing to see a film with the Hamiltonian title *Temptations of a Great City* – but the younger boy steadfastly refused and Bruce had to content himself with a trip to another cinema showing a different film.

Patrick was keen to emphasise his greater daring and independence and he began to indulge in some minor pilfering. After stealing a box of coloured chalks from a local department store he came home and boasted of the deed: an outraged Nellie marched him back to the shop the next day and made him hand over his ill-gotten gains.

However in contrast to the selfishness of these two occasions, Bruce noticed a more sympathetic quality growing in his brother at this time: the germs of a tormented compassion for the weak, suffering and oppressed masses of humanity that was to become the hallmark of the mature Patrick Hamilton. One vivid incident illustrated the boy's growing awareness of the rigid barriers shutting off class from class and the hard lot endured by those beneath Nellie's lofty contempt. Patrick was travelling home with his mother from Brighton station in a horse-drawn fly, laden with luggage, and all the way to Hove – a distance of at least two miles – they were pursued by a 'runner', a sort of Edwardian coolie who hoped to make a few pitiful pence by chasing cabs in order to do some portering at the journey's end. Patrick, sitting with his back to the driver, watched the perspiring man with fascinated horror. On reaching home Nellie dismissed him peremptorily, without giving him a halfpenny. Patrick was appalled and never forgot the runner's pallid face and the sound of his heaving lungs.[3]

Both brothers became ardent aficionados of the cinema, then in its infancy as a popular mass medium. They attended Brighton's plushest picture house, the Queens, although Nellie placed other cinemas in the town out of bounds for being 'common' and probable sources of nameless infections. Their other main entertainment outside home was the theatre, in particular the Brighton Hippodrome. Here the brothers would pay sixpence for a front-row balcony seat to see the great names of the Edwardian stage including George Formby Snr and even Sarah Bernhardt herself. Magicians and illusionists were also favourites, such as David Devant, Carl Hertz and Chung Ling Soo. Each year at Christmas the boys went to see pantomimes at the Theatre Royal or the Grand; and sometimes they trekked to the end of the West Pier to see shows such as Conan Doyle's *The*

Speckled Band. (Patrick was later to see a performance of his own play *Rope* at the same theatre.)

Christmas and church-going were recurring features of Patrick's young life. The elder Hamiltons made an effort to paper over the gaps in their marriage during the festive season and put on a traditional display for the children's sake, complete with stockings at the foot of their beds and generous presents laid out on the schoolroom table after breakfast.

Patrick recalled:

I should not like to say I enjoyed Christmas Day as a whole. I can remember that the stocking, opened and enjoyed in tranquillity, gave ecstasy: but after that the emotions were confused and not altogether happy. Many of the presents given after breakfast were unintelligible: and the over-fervent explanations, given by parents and nurses, of their delightful uses and charms, only increased that decidedly ungracious stare with which a child so often looks upon gifts. And little pleasure could be taken in presents if the recipient was reminded that he was soon to be hurried off to church.

The midday (Christmas) meal was certainly exciting – almost certainly more from an aesthetic and dramatic point of view than an eating one. On the aesthetic side there were the fanciful crackers, the glorious boxes of dates (the boxes, with their pictures of camels in sunsets, gave even more happiness than the shining dates), the dried figs, the almonds and raisins, the walnuts and the glittering silver walnut-crackers. On the dramatic side came the Christmas pudding being brought in on fire, the threepenny bits discovered in the pudding and, long-awaited, the climax of the explosion of the crackers. But, alas, the crackers did not always explode, and there was a good deal of ugly wrenching and tearing and cheating and even quarrelling. Their contents, too, were for the most part quite seriously disappointing. The child quickly detected that there was little humour in the paper hats, and that the trinkets and small toys were almost fraudulently valueless. The mottoes which went with them were often cheaply printed, with unintelligible words ...[4]

This palpable disappointment, the discovery that beneath the superficially attractive surface glitter lay dust and ashes was to

remain with Patrick all his life. The sense that once the gaudy
wrappings were ripped off, life itself was a let-down, a cheat,
was to seep into him and gradually shaped his wary cynicism.

Sunday afternoons were a regular gloomy purgatory of church
attendance at nearby St John's. The Hamilton children, starched
into their Sunday best, fidgeted and giggled their way through
the interminable services. In later life, perhaps preferring to
forget that he was, as a young adolescent, a fervent believer and
went so far as to undergo confirmation in the Church of England,
Patrick set down some scathing memories of the *ennui* of the
English sabbath:

> With children, anxiety, along with a heavy feeling of the over-
> bearing illogicality of the universe, which is always with them, is
> almost always at its acutest on Sundays – and in a lesser degree
> this is true of adults.
>
> A day of rest is undoubtedly necessary (in the absence of
> staggered holidays during the week): but it is unnatural, and to
> that extent curiously bare for the soul. To anyone sensitive – child
> or adult, townsman or countryman, worker or idler, there is, on
> Sundays, a seriously depressing and ... disturbing qualitative
> change in ... all phenomena – the sky, the sun, the trees, the
> birds, the flowers, the houses, the roads, the walls, the pave-
> ments and the chimney-pots – a change which would still be felt
> even if it were not emphasised by the ... disappearance of all
> normal traffic, the strange dress of the children, and the distant
> smell and noise of Sunday joints being cooked everywhere.[5]

The Marxist in the mature Patrick then gets an outing:

> Many people – workers, peasants and intellectuals – bravely
> attempt to escape the discoloration of the spiritual atmosphere –
> seldom with success. The worker may lie on in his bed forgetting
> himself by reading the *News of the World* practically in its entirety,
> but as soon as he is out in the street on the way to the public
> house, he is smitten by what, quietly and greyly, goes on outside:
> and in the burbling, bubbling public houses all is much too noisy
> for their attempts to rid themselves of it [sic]. The peasant may
> engross himself in his own patch of soil instead of another's, but
> his obligation, ultimately and uneasily, to wear a different suit

and shirt in public with his wife, hangs over him. And the intellectual, going out perhaps, to buy the *Sunday Times* or the *Observer* is more sensitive than others to the uncanny group movements, and is distressed by the later opening and earlier shutting of his week-day drinking haunt.[6]

The sabbath's horrors were capped by a 'formal, frightening, and hideously heavy – heavy on the soul and stomach – Sunday lunch' – a meal made worse for the children by the knowledge that their father, back from London, was home and had to be faced.

Patrick's intellectual curiosity was deepening. Having been taught to read comparatively late by his brother, he rapidly made up for lost time and overtook his teacher. He was well into *The Pickwick Papers* – Dickens was a first, and abiding, love – while Bruce was still immersed in comics like *Chums*. Patrick was soon recommending such treats as *The Scarlet Pimpernel* to his elder brother and, though he wrote nothing down at this stage, further glimmerings of creativity showed in his invention of a detective named Seymour Grey, whose adventures were narrated to Bruce in bed at night.

Beyond the backwater of Hove, the Edwardian age which had encompassed Patrick's childhood was passing away. The outbreak of war in 1914 is one of those rare watersheds when gradual social changes are accelerated by a dramatic external event. The decade before the Great War has since been suffused with a shimmery golden glow; the summers were warmer, life more leisurely, behaviour more gracious. Technological progress was rapid, but designed towards peaceful ends. Humanity appeared launched on a steady curve of painless progression towards broad sunlit uplands. War, and rumours of war, appeared something from a darker age. It was a mirage, but not a complete one. In J.B. Priestley's words:

> Edwardian England is a time and a land seen across the vast dark chasm of war. Over there the afternoons seem to linger in the mellow sunlight, the nights are immediately romantic. There is illusion here, of course, but it is not all a cheat: something did go, something was lost.[7]

Patrick was perched uncomfortably on the cusp between one age and another. His childhood had been spent in the cosy glow of a secure and stable era; his adolescence was to be experienced during a time of unprecedented and brutal change, both domestically and in the outside world. Britain's unquestioned dominance of an Empire upon which the sun never set, was bled away into the Flanders mud. The middle class's assumption of its God-given superiority gave way to a strange new age during the war years where servants became insolent, expensive and hard to find. Families like the Hamiltons found themselves uprooted from large, comfortable homes and pitched into boarding-houses. For a boy of ten it was a puzzling and unsettling transformation. It would be strange if these changes were not reflected in Patrick Hamilton's mature work and it is easy to see certain themes and attitudes that stem directly from the abrupt break between his secure pre-war position as a child of an upper-middle-class family and the unfamiliar, transient life of rented rooms, boarding-houses and sudden switches of school that he was about to join. Indeed the most striking note that was later to resound from his novels is a sense of mistrust, an awareness that nothing is ever as it seems to be. Even when characters establish a temporary home or resting place, we are aware that their position is permanently menaced by dangerous external forces that will shortly dislodge them from their fleeting enjoyment of some sort of happiness.

For Bruce and Patrick, however, the summer of 1914 seemed even more flawless than usual. Brighton filled with day-trippers; Britain's imperial power appeared to be at its invincible acme, impressively demonstrated to the Hamiltons when the Home Fleet anchored off the town and the boys were among the crowds who flocked to the pleasure boats to enjoy a sightseeing cruise around the grim warships. The sun shone ceaselessly; Holland House won fourteen of its cricket fixtures and drew the other two, and then a shadow fell: an Austrian archduke was assassinated in an obscure Balkan town and within weeks, unbelievably, Britain was drawn into a European war for the first time in nearly a century.

This reality was brought home sharply to Patrick when one

afternoon in late August he was sitting in the county ground watching Sussex play Yorkshire. His home county were doing well: the previous day Joe Vine and Vallance Jupp had enjoyed an unbroken second-wicket partnership of 250 runs. Just after three o'clock the spectators heard the blaring sound of martial music. The noise got louder and then a file of khaki-clad soldiers appeared, preceded by a brass band. Ignoring the match, the parade strode across the ground and marched on to the pitch itself, where they proceeded to wheel and turn in formation, under the commands of a bellowing RSM. The cricketers stood gaping, 'flannelled fools at the wicket', unable to comprehend that the gentle sporting activities of an England at peace were giving way to an older and sterner tradition, that of the 'muddied oafs' of the military. At last the umpires drew stumps and the players straggled off the pitch.

When Patrick uses this striking scene in *The West Pier* he is in no doubt of its significance:

> This entirely unnecessary, gratuitous and largely bestial assault upon the players (curiously akin in atmosphere to the smashing up of a small store by the henchmen of a gangster) beyond doubt ended in the victory of the aggressor – though at the time of its happening very few people present were able vividly or exactly to understand what was taking place.

He places his protagonist, the young Ernest Ralph Gorse, in the crowd following the military thugs:

> He inhaled unconsciously the distant aroma of universal evil and was made happy ... Astute and precocious as he was, he was unable to tell himself in so many words that his day had come.

Something that remains unmentioned in the Hamilton brothers' copious correspondence is that Patrick appears to have borrowed this scene directly from Bruce's novel *Pro*, published five years prior to *The West Pier* in 1946. It seems typically characteristic of both Patrick's artistic high-handedness and his brother's humility that there is no record of any acknowledgement of this near plagiarism. Here, at any rate, there was an element of cross-fertilisation, for the hero of *Pro* commits suicide in almost exactly the same circumstances as George Harvey Bone in Patrick's earlier *Hangover Square*. Bruce always emphasised his debt to his brother – a compliment which was not, however, usually returned.

The outbreak of the war signalled a crack in the family life of the Hamiltons; Bruce departed to public school at Westminster, while Patrick stayed on for another term at Holland House. His Headmaster, Bill Cawood, a captain in the Territorial Army, left for garrison duty in India, where he died within months of heat stroke, ironically enough after nothing more bellicose than a cricket match. Patrick reported this and other news in regular letters to Bruce, the beginning of a lifelong correspondence between the often-separated brothers. In a style described by Bruce as 'direct, serviceable and quite arresting', Patrick related his lachrymose farewell with Bill and his deputy 'Barty' Barton as they left for the war. 'But nobody else wept,' he concluded. Bill's regime was replaced by that of a harsher successor, an elderly, yellow-faced man, with the Dickensian name of Girdlestone, who swiftly abandoned all pretence of inculcating learning into the boys in favour of military drill.

Although the outbreak of war was something of a shock, Britain's private schools had long been preparing themselves for combat and were ready to answer the call. Almost all schools – and Holland House was no exception – had their own Officers' Training Corps where boys received frequent military training, augmented by summer camps alongside regular army units. The spirit of patriotism, self-sacrifice and a willingness to fight, and if necessary die, for the old school and the Old Country had been dinned in to several generations. The war was a God-given opportunity to put this into practice.

In common with almost every other private school in the country, a mania of martial ardour gripped Holland House. With fathers, older brothers and younger masters joining the colours, the elderly teachers left behind saw it as their sole duty to impart patriotism and military values to their charges. Patrick describes the daily drilling in *The West Pier*:

In the afternoon they were dressed in the boots, puttees, tunics
and caps of private soldiers and, carrying wooden imitations of
rifles, were marched down to the county ground and drilled –
made, with their coarse puttees tickling their immature legs, to
shoulder arms, present arms, port arms, form fours, right dress,
stand at ease, etc., never, never satisfactorily, and again and again
and again until they were stupefied. In the latter condition they
wore a bewildered, staring, idiotic Bedlam, Bridewell look – many
of them, during class, biting their nails, blinking their eyes, or
showing other nervous, twitching gestures. This habit of staring,
brought on by bewilderment and boredom, was almost certainly
the original cause of the myopia which would make so many of
them in later life wear spectacles.

Patrick, like Bruce and Bernard, began to wear glasses – or
'windows' as the brothers called them – at this time, although
hereditary astigmatism seems a likelier cause of his shortsighted-
ness than an excess of mindless drill.

As it became clear that the war would not be over by
Christmas as the optimists had predicted, its malign presence
began to impinge more and more on ordinary life. Food short-
ages began as housewives hoarded scarce supplies; even Nellie
was reduced to the indignity of buying flour in bulk and baking
her own, lead-heavy bread. More seriously, fear of bombardment
from the sea caused Bernard to sell the Hove house and uproot to
London, where a new home – a substantial six-bedroom
property, built in solid red and yellow brick – was rented at 2
Burlington Gardens, in the Turnham Green area of Chiswick. In
the chaos of the move, both Patrick and Bruce missed a term at
school and renewed their old intimacy in the new environment
of London's western suburbs.

If the boys' peripatetic education was cause for parental
concern, however, it was nothing compared to the problematic
Lalla who, nearly sixteen, was increasingly preoccupied with
boyfriends. Her early good looks had developed, by her teens,
into real beauty. As a guest at a Holland House Christmas party
Lalla was voted 'Loveliest Lady' and her attractions soon led to a
succession of suitors hovering moth-like around the Hamilton
home. Lazy and sensual by disposition, Lalla did little to

discourage her admirers, and Bernard and Nellie, disturbed by her precocious sexuality and lack of academic progress, withdrew her from her school in Hove and sent her to a college for young ladies in Lausanne. After a year she returned with a fund of experience – though not of the type intended by her parents – and having failed to learn any foreign languages. She was sent next to Brighton High School for Girls, in the hope that in its colder climate, her intellectual abilities would at last flourish. Alas, beyond a fondness for singing and the stage, the Hamiltons' only daughter continued to be largely concerned with the opposite sex. (Lalla was to inherit her share of the Hamilton artistic gifts – she was later to write a play with Bruce – and as a teenager wrote and performed plays and stories with her family and friends as audience.) However, it was not so much her lack of formal academic skills but her highly developed interest in men that really worried her parents – her first affair took place when she was just thirteen. Nellie was near to despair for she nurtured high ambitions for her daughter; but if she could not awaken her mind she was determined to exact a high price for her body. The succession of lumpen youths who presented themselves as candidates for Lalla's hand simply would not do (she even fell in love with the bus driver who drove her to school) and Nellie was about to send her daughter for an extended stay at the Beacon Hotel in Crowborough, in the hope of matching Lalla with one of its high-born and wealthy visitors, when the war put a stop to such social ambitions.

As for the rascally Bernard, the children had grown up regarding him as an occasional and erratic visitor to their home rather than as an active and caring parent. During his visits, his casual geniality and heavy-handed humour were often displaced by a didactic and overbearing manner that terrified his family. He meted out corporal punishment to all the children, including Lalla, and all three came to regard him with fear and outright loathing. One of his obsessions was his children's regular reading matter. He had never outgrown his youthful love of Scott and considered the author the only suitable writer for his own children. His first question on appearing at the house would be, 'What have you been readin'?' and it was an interrogation they dreaded, for the real answer was comics like the *Magnet* and the *Gem*. Copies of these had to be hidden from Bernard's monocled eye, but on one occasion he discovered Bruce's secreted *Boy's Realm* and tore it to pieces in front of the miscreant. Bernard, however, was more violent in speech and manner than in action. His bark, although it was heard frequently, was much worse than his bite and it was another aspect of his behaviour that the children found more disturbing – his drinking.

The great debate continues among researchers into alcoholism as to whether the condition is primarily caused by hereditary or environmental factors. Recognition of alcoholism as a disease has a relatively modern provenance; the Edinburgh doctor Thomas Trotter first defined alcoholism as an illness in 1804: 'The habit of drunkenness is a disease of the mind.' The idea that a tendency to alcoholism is hereditary, however, is an ancient one: Aristotle declared that drunken women, 'Bring forth children like themselves', and it was Plutarch's view that, 'One drunkard begets another'. For many years the folk wisdom of alcohol abuse passing from generation to generation went unquestioned; it was only with the rise of psychoanalysis in the 1920s that investigators began to switch their attention to social and environmental factors. But while psychologists and sociologists succeeded in establishing that alcoholics were often neurotics, they failed to demonstrate that the neuroses preceded the alcoholism. In the 1960s, therefore, research turned back to a search for biological/hereditary causes. A Swedish study has shown that sons of alcoholic fathers have a higher incidence of alcoholism than other men of the same age.[8] However, the evidence suggested that the sons drank after the example of their elders, rather than through a genetically-inherited weakness.

More recently strong evidence that alcoholics are genetically predisposed to the disease has come in a detailed study which has found that the sons of alcoholics, with no contact with their biological parents, have a fourfold greater incidence of alcoholism than the children of non-alcoholics. Researchers seem agreed that a tendency to alcoholism is familial, although it is not yet clear whether this is genetic or by example. A seeker after the

main root of Patrick Hamilton's alcoholism need look no further
than Bernard, his father. It is significant that as many as two of
Bernard's three children – Patrick and Lalla – became alcoholic,
though Bruce remained a moderate drinker. Patrick shared with
his sister the marital, sexual and emotional problems associated
with the alcoholic – while the placid Bruce enjoyed a comparatively stable marriage and lifestyle. In Bruce's case, the environmental causes needed to trigger latent alcoholism into activity
were lacking. In Patrick, disastrously, they were not.

Patrick himself cleared Bernard of any blame for passing on
his drink problem to him, but then spoilt his case by telling
numerous anecdotes about his father's boozing, which might
suggest that even if his addiction was not handed down genetically, Bernard's bad example was probably enough.

> This [Patrick's] ultra-anxiety, then, exhibited so early, may be
> evidence that there was some constitutional defect which might
> lead finally to alcoholism. It might also be said that a fondness for
> drink was in my case inherited from my father. I do not person-
> ally believe either of these things. I think that this early longing
> for re-insurances of insurances are experienced by most children
> – and although my father, during his lifetime, was very often
> drunk, he had not the smallest tendency to alcoholism. Alco-
> holism means bottles in the bedroom and elsewhere. There was
> never anything of this sort. This does not mean, though, that my
> father was not a cause of grave external anxiety, as often during
> his sobriety as when he had been drinking.[9]

Patrick's own evidence is stark confirmation of the fear his father
inspired:

> Unbearable pathos ... is the last thing a child can recognise and
> at First Avenue the feeling in the schoolroom ... was one of
> complete dread and consequent absolute hatred. He was, happily
> for us, in London during the greater part of the week, spending
> only the Friday, or sometimes, only the Saturday to Monday at
> Hove. On his return he was, I think, nearly always 'On' [Nellie's
> euphemism for drunk] ... and anxious to express aggressive
> views about London and everything to my mother ... [In] the
> school-bright electric light of the schoolroom there was, in the
> winter, an atmosphere of pallid oppressiveness fully an hour

before he arrived – which would be between half-past six and seven. It seemed, indeed, that the whole house shuddered feebly, as it were, in anticipation, before, at last it shuddered truly and forcibly under the impact of his ferocious and often cruel slamming of the front door. This slam resembled, and was probably meant to resemble, the tapping of a conductor with his baton before conducting an orchestra: he was now conducting the house. What happened then, overheard with dreadful intentness from the schoolroom, varied considerably. Sometimes there would be a long and inexplicable silence: sometimes the sound of his footsteps: an intermittent, slow sound, very deliberate, giving no clue to his actual movements or intentions. Sometimes, whatever on earth he might be doing was accompanied by the sound of hostile murmuring, like the growlings of the double-bass. Sometimes he went to the top of the basement and shouted for a servant, who would quickly answer, and at whom he would shout. But all these curious variations were certain to end with his slamming open the dining-room door (he had the gift of slamming doors open) and greeting my mother.

What then happened in the dining room, over his dinner with my mother, could not be ascertained from the schoolroom. Only an occasional mumbling sound could be heard from the other side of the thick wall – mumbling, mumbling, mumbling, going on and on and on and on and on. To listen to this was somehow even more terrifying than the earlier anticipation of his entrance, and the eavesdropping on its variations.

There is something of Dickens in all these childhood memories, something of the quaking felt by David Copperfield as he awaited the wrath – slow, deliberate but inexorable – of the dreaded Mr Murdstone. But there is something else that is peculiar to Patrick, the contrast between the 'school-bright electric light' and the 'pallid oppressiveness', for example. And his writing comes full circle in that, in this final memoir, penned just before his death, he attributes human qualities to inanimate things (the shuddering of the house awaiting Bernard), just as in his first story, 'The Quiet Room,' written forty years before, he had described an empty room as being 'in a state of billowy, undignified laughter'.

Apart from his drinking, Bernard continued to stray in his love life. He set up his French mistress in a flat in the West End, from where she walked out without warning and escaped to Canada with another lover. Heartbroken, Bernard made a transatlantic crossing in a futile bid to win her back and when he was forced to return empty-handed he began to look around for other prey. While Nellie was absent for months with Lalla at her Swiss school, the incorrigible Bernard arrived at First Avenue with a young actress in tow, along with her mother as chaperone. Ostensibly, the object of the visit was to discuss a possible part in Bernard's only staged play, *The Combat*, a one-act Roman drama put on for a week at a Bournemouth Music Hall. Despite the presence of the mother, the Hamiltons' housekeeper, Mrs Hancock – loyal, like the rest of the household, to Nellie rather than Bernard – discovered conclusive evidence that he had given the young woman the casting-couch treatment and summoned Nellie home. She was long used to Bernard's infidelities, but now she was outraged that the adultery had taken place under her own roof, in her children's home. She seriously contemplated divorce, but eventually economic considerations and her fears for her children's welfare caused her to content herself with extracting a further chunk of Wildman money from a chastened Bernard.[11]

With the beginning of the war Bernard's waywardness found a new outlet: he enrolled as a Special Constable before fulfilling, at the age of fifty-one, a lifetime's ambition for martial glory. He received a commission in the Territorial Division of the Royal Horse Artillery and prepared to depart to Leamington for training. Patrick and Bruce were left largely alone in Chiswick with Nellie. The boys were bored, distracting themselves with games of ping-pong, cricket, fives or target practice with Patrick's new air-gun and the first surviving scrap of Patrick's writing dates from these days: it is a sort of treaty, patching up a brotherly quarrel:

I promise on my honour that I will not quarrel with Bruce if we go into rooms, while in the bedroom, at meals, or any other time. I've fixed it up with him, and I really don't think we will if we try.
 Patrick.
P.S. When I say on my honour I mean I've taken a solemn oath.

The adolescent Bruce was now increasingly assailed by the hormonal upsets of puberty and became a prey to exciting new lusts and obsessions. Sharing a bedroom with his brother, he poured out all his fantasies and guilty secrets in a one-night dialogue lasting some six hours. As a safety-valve for his sexual energies Bruce plunged into a phase of feverish artistic creation: modelling a Plasticine head of the Kaiser to which, much to his patriotic parents' annoyance, he became inordinately attached; drawing comic postcards and landscapes; writing short stories and compiling his own magazine, the *Meteor*.

Patrick appeared to regard his brother's activities with an ironic detachment that smacked of precocity: he decided, instead, that he wanted to become a Boy Scout. Bernard heartily approved of this decision to join the ranks of Baden-Powell's army and drafted a letter of application to the movement's journal, *The Scout*: 'Dear Sir, I wish to become a Boy Scout. My father, the author and barrister, wishes me to do this. Will you kindly tell me the address of the local branch in the Chiswick area?' Boldly, Patrick suggested a minor amendment: would it not be better, he tentatively suggested, to say 'An author and barrister' rather than 'The author'? Bernard poo-pooed this: 'They'll know me, my boy,' he replied airily, 'They'll know me.' Patrick duly enrolled in the Chiswick troop, went on a few route marches and picked up a badge or two before apathy got the better of him and his scouting career lapsed.

It was time for Patrick to pick up his schooling again after the dislocations of 1914. In the summer term of 1915 he enrolled as a day boy at Colet Court, a prep school in Hammersmith, while Bruce briefly returned to Westminster, where a dangerous bout of lung congestion soon interrupted his unhappy school life. Doctors prescribed sea air and the Hamiltons temporarily uprooted themselves once more and returned to Hove, taking digs in Lansdowne Place. Bruce went back as a pupil-teacher to Holland House – his first taste of his later career – where the manpower demands of the war had produced a critical shortage of staff. He and Patrick continued to share a room and sometimes had noisy quarrels, only terminated by the voice of their landlady's son calling querulously, 'I say, can't you two keep quiet? A chap must get some sleep.'

These fraternal rows were mainly provoked by Bruce's increasing sexual travails, with Patrick playing the part of moral guardian. Bruce had been driven by his bottled lusts to revolt against Nellie's dire warnings about self-abuse and to indulge in frequent and stealthy masturbation. His feelings of shame led to no great satisfaction; nor did his furtive excursions to Brighton beach to eye up the glimpses of female flesh afforded by girls paddling or sunbathing. Bruce haunted the windows of ladies' haberdashery shops, greedily taking in the sight of women's underwear and prowled around kiosks selling mildly porno- graphic postcards, one of which he even ventured to purchase: the censorious Patrick found the card where Bruce had hidden it, and prevailed on his elder brother to tear it up. In September 1915, Patrick returned to London and Colet Court, for the first time in his life as a boarder, and Bruce was left alone to suffer his libidinous thoughts in peace.

Patrick's first experience of life away from his mother and home was traumatic, but two surviving letters from him to Nellie give little indication of the horrors of an English single-sex boarding school early this century and are comically clichéd in their expression of the eternal concerns of repressed English middle-class youth:

> On Friday we had a football match. It was the boarders against the day boys. We drew them 3–3. It was an awfully exciting match. I kept goal. You know that set of cigarette cards called 'Gems of Belgian Architecture'? I have nearly got the set now. I will have it before I come home I expect. I am sorry I can't say any more but I am in a hurry. And I want to write a note to Lalla. Will you give it to her.
> Very much love.
> Pat.

> Dear Mummie.
> I am writing this in the morning so Lalla has not come yet. I am looking forward to her coming very much. I am working very hard, with good results, because I am top in arithmetic, which is rather good because there are chaps in my form, who are

supposed to [be] miles better than me. I am second in Latin, and I
hope to be top in French. It shows what you can do when you try.
I am keeping very well in every way.... The time is simply flying
with me. If it keeps up like this it won't be long before the end of
term. I am very sorry but I have not got anything more to say this
time so I must say good-bye.
Very much love.
Pat.

The impression given by these letters is that of a priggish boy,
anxious above all to please a fussy, protective mother, and telling
her very little of the realities of school life. Back with Bruce, who
was staying with their former nurse, Alice Swain and her
husband at Hassocks during the Christmas holidays of 1915–16,
Patrick was more forthcoming. He explained what he had
learned of the facts of life to his ignorant, though keenly interested, elder brother. When a man and woman wished to
procreate, said Patrick, they came together genitally under
medical supervision and 'spunk' was drawn from the male, out
of which fluid a doctor, in some mysterious way, fashioned a
baby. The clinical nature of this procedure, as explained by
Patrick, did not square with Bruce's fevered visions of erotic bliss
which he associated with joy, desire and naked ladies. The
younger brother went on to confess what really went on in the
dormitories of Colet Court once the lights went out. Mass
masturbation, individual and reciprocal, was the order of the
day, or night. The ringleaders were the older boys who invited
the younger ones to join them in bed behind curtains made from
rigged-up sheets. Any resistance was met with intimidation and
bullying, alleged Patrick, who spoke of his experiences in terms
of shock and moral reprobation, tempered with healthy curiosity.

Bruce, for his part, made his own confession: that he himself
was now a regular masturbator, though still afflicted with guilt
about the 'bad habit', which the brothers christened with the
code 'B.H.' or 'Billy Hamilton'. Patrick begged his brother to free
himself from the dreaded vice without delay and Bruce promised
to do his best. He continued, however, to give way to the
pleasures of Billy Hamilton and moreover was quite unable to
hide the fact. 'What are you looking so fishy about?' Patrick

would demand when he saw the tell-tale guilt on his brother's face, following up with blackmailing threats to tell Mummie unless Bruce desisted. This cat's cradle of sexual shame, with Patrick threatening to tell Nellie about Bruce's masturbation, and Bruce contemplating whether to confide to her the goings-on in Patrick's dorm, resulted in explosive rows between the brothers and culminated in Patrick making a clean breast of things to Nurse Swain just days before he was due to return to school. The loyal Alice wrote and told Nellie, who was staying near Bernard's camp at Leamington. A telegram came by return: 'Patrick Not To Return To School' and the dark temptations of the dorm at Colet Court were banished.

Soon after, the Hamilton brothers left Hassocks and the family – minus Bernard – reunited once again in Hove, this time in rented rooms in Brunswick Road. Under Nellie's close super-vision once more, Patrick returned to Holland House, again as a day boy. Their cousin Frank Bridger re-entered their lives, treating both boys to the cherries from the sweet Martinis he drank at the Metropole Hotel, and Patrick's first personal acquaintance with alcohol dates from this time, when, he later claimed, he would slip into his father's old Hove club and, on the strength of being Bernard's son, would cajole the barman into giving him schooners of sherry. Frank also straightened the boys out on the facts of life and visions of doctors making babies from spunk in spoons vanished forever.

Bernard was about to be drafted to active service in France, where the war, in the summer of 1916, was reaching a critical stage. The gigantic Allied bombardment preceding the slaughter on the Somme could clearly be heard on the Hove seafront, rumbling across the Channel and bringing the war threateningly close. In reduced circumstances, Nellie was forced to dismiss her last two servants and move into a genteel boarding-house at 60 York Road: this was Patrick's first experience of a territory he was to make very much his own in his writing, the world of the rootless, friendless denizens of the English private hotel. From 1916 until he was able to afford a comfortable flat of his own in the late 1920s after his first success as a writer, Patrick spent a considerable portion of his life as a guest in a series of boarding-

houses, rented rooms and small private hotels in London, Hove
and Brighton. It was the experience of these drifting years and
his encounters with the cast of sad characters met in such
surroundings that indelibly stamped him as a writer. Even in
later life, when both fame and fortune could have taken him
away from the seedy shadowlands of the lodging-house, he was
to return to these places, almost as if he needed to refresh those
early memories and remain close to them as touchstones of
authenticity. In the mid-1930s, when he was earning enough to
maintain himself in a Norfolk country cottage, Patrick would
choose to stay in the small Wells Hotel in Hampstead; and as
late as the 1940s he went into hiding in a nondescript guest-
house in Reading to work on his novel *Mr Stimpson and Mr Gorse.*
Here, he was, according to one acquaintance, in his element and
almost ecstatically happy. This predilection must be considered
highly unusual in a writer of Patrick's class and generation. Most
of his male literary contemporaries – people like Greene, Waugh,
Lowry, Auden and Isherwood – went from the security of
wealthy homes, public schools and Oxbridge straight into jobs as
teachers or tutors and thence to literary and financial success.
Orwell's experience with down-and-outs was more a conscious
act of investigative journalism whereas Patrick, even in the days
of his prosperity, actually preferred the twilight, transient world
of the hotel. It was his chosen ground, and no one surveyed and
charted such territory with more loving exactitude.

While they had been staying at Hassocks Bruce had whiled
away the time between lascivious thoughts in entering a competition launched by one of his favourite comics, the *Magnet*, to
write a story about one of the paper's staple characters, Harry
Wharton, a contemporary of Billy Bunter at Greyfriars. Bruce's
pastiche of Wharton's creator, Charles Hamilton (no
relation), entitled 'The Bounder's Relapse', was duly written and
entered. Some weeks later Patrick set out for the nearest news-
agent to buy the number of the *Magnet* containing the competition winners, while Bruce remained at home, sick with anxiety.
Bruce waited at the garden gate for his brother's return and
when Patrick appeared, wearing a long face and shaking his head
sadly, Bruce was stunned with disappointment. He assumed the

cheerful grin and stiff upper lip of the gallant loser until Patrick dropped his pretence and exclaimed, 'It's all right – you've won, not the big prize, but one of the others.' Bruce duly received his consolation prize, an edition of Tennyson bound in red leather, which he kept until his death together with a letter from the *Magnet*'s editor telling him that his story was to be published in the paper, 'with some touching up'. This confirmed what Bruce had long suspected – that the Greyfriars stories were *not* the sole work of their credited author, Charles Hamilton.[12]

Bruce and Lalla now left the increasingly cramped family nest to strike out on their own. Bruce, having tried a clerk's correspondence course, followed by engineering studies at Brighton Technical College, persuaded Bernard that he intended to join the army as soon as he was old enough. He was sent to a London crammer to study for the army entrance exam and took up residence in a boarding-house in Earls Court where he began to flirt with female fellow guests and at last – or so he claimed – shook off 'Billy Hamilton'. Lalla studied singing in London, before it became clear that her future lay in another branch of show-business – the theatre. Bernard finally got his wish and was sent to Bapaume where, astonishingly enough, he became Area Commandant and later Town Major of Péronne (a sort of honorific position; he was never actually promoted above the rank of Lieutenant), responsible posts close to the front line.

Now a boarder back at Holland House Patrick had become the dominant personality in the little world he found there. Coming back to the old school after his time in London gave him a certain cachet with his contemporaries and he rapidly fell into his old leadership role with his former cronies of the Sporting Club, Claud Chepmell and Herman Treutler. Treutler had wisely changed his name to Holmes in the face of widespread Germanophobia, and Patrick used his considerable influence in the savage world of schoolboy in-fighting to protect his friend from the worst excesses of bullying. Freed from the all-enveloping physical proximity of 'Mummie' (he was never to overcome her emotional domination), Patrick was developing a more independent, less petulant, personality. He was also about to plunge into the first of his life's ruling passions.

4

Patrick the Poet

FOR A SHORT TIME PATRICK CONTINUED the moralistic pose he had adopted with Bruce, going so far as to report to the new Headmaster of Holland House, Mr C.R. de Lyons Pike, a 'smutty' comment by one of his classmates, to the effect that he would like to kiss a friend's sister 'under her belt'. After some consideration the Head sensibly replied that such ideas often came into the minds of growing boys and that not too much notice should be taken of it. Much more important, he stressed, was the necessity of stopping the boys from 'messing about with themselves'.

It cannot be denied that such 'sneaking' – the ultimate schoolboy sin – shows an unattractive trait in Patrick's character, but it should be remembered he was still young and he himself had yet to grapple with the torments of puberty. He was also always the most orthodox of Bernard's children in matters of faith. Now Patrick found his youthful attachment to the tenets of the Anglican Church reinforced by the influence of his teachers, particularly a Mr Smith, a simple youth who was fond of proclaiming his literal belief in the existence of angels, and the Headmaster, who tended to the ritualistic Anglo-Catholic wing of the Church. Under the latter's tutelage, Patrick acted for a short time as a server at St Michael's, highest of Hove's High Anglican churches. But there were counter-balancing influences at work. The third master at the school, Mr Hodgson, was of a more liberal persuasion and after debating the matter with him Patrick decided that he could not accept one of the central articles of the Christian faith: the concept of eternal punishment. He and Treutler pithily expressed this new rejection at a Christmas service, when they sang in unison:

No hell! No hell! No hell! No hell!
Born is the King of Israel!

There was also the mockery of his contemporaries, traditionally directed at the over-pious. Patrick held on to Christianity for the time being, although his own form of secular faith – Marxism – was later to fill the void left by the eventual loss of religious belief. It was Bruce's view that Patrick's became one of those natures tortured by an aching horror at the absurdity of life in a godless, random universe. One of the main wellsprings of his personality, according to his brother, was a deep need for an absolute and unchallengeable truth. Certainly his writing demonstrates a hunger for fixed meanings. In the sharp mockery of his portrayal of the meaninglessness of his characters' lives, and the inanities of their stilted, clichéd conversations, there is an echo of the stern moralist of his youth, pickled by experience into disillusioned bitterness. To the end of his days he remained a disappointed idealist, his sensitive nature wounded by what he considered the horror of reality. Cocooned in his mother's protection, it was a reality he was long unable to confront.

It was at about this time that Patrick began to show the first real signs of a literary inclination. His reading had continued to widen, reflecting a maturity beyond his years, but he was still in thrall to the great English giants of the nineteenth century, Dickens, and his father's old favourite, Scott, whose *Quentin Durward* he read under the sheets in his dormitory after lights out. Here too, the influence of Mr Hodgson was decisive. There is a tradition among writers and creative artists of crediting a particular teacher with the honour of spotting the first flickers of talent among the dull dross of the classroom, and kindling it into flame. In Patrick's case it was the humble Hodgson who lit the fire that, in Bruce's words, led to 'explosive material that shook up and radically altered the boy's whole view of life'.

The complexities of grammar; the mysteries of alliteration,

onomatopoeia and metonymy – which baffled and bored his schoolfellows – were meat and drink to Patrick. Even more to his early taste were the disciplines of poetic shape. He took eager notes on the differences between the Petrarchian and Shakespearian sonnet and the rhyme scheme of the Spenserian stanza. He loved poetry for its form as much as its content, displaying an early interest in the techniques of literary construction that was to stand him in good stead later.

In the summer holidays of 1917, Bruce returned from his Earls Court boarding house to join his mother and brother in Hove. It was six months since he had seen Patrick – the longest separation the two boys had yet endured – and he found him much altered. The changes were primarily physical: Patrick had grown an extraordinary eight inches and was close to attaining his mature height of five-foot-eleven. The open-pored skin of his face was distressingly studded with acne and his habitually serious and mournful expression added to the impression of a troubled youth deep in the difficult toils of puberty. Bruce's pride in his own fledgling literary achievements was dampened when Nellie proudly told him that Patrick had become a poet. Bruce's competitive spirit was immediately fired, and he rapidly composed a poem, 'Ode to Helen', addressed to his sister Lalla, in which the antique darling of Troy was unfavourably compared with the siren of the Sussex shore. Patrick, whose interest in verse had been fired by his conversations with Mr Hodgson and his study of Palgrave's *Golden Treasury*, replied with two poems of his own, both nature pieces couched in sub-Keatsian blank verse. The first, describing the coming and passing of a storm, has disappeared, apart from the lines:

> A flash; a moment's pause; and then as if
> Wrathful because it had been checked so long,
> The rumbling thunder rolls across the sky
> And loses itself in the far distance.

The second poem, inspired by a passage in *The Pickwick Papers* describing a summer cornfield, is a sonnet entitled 'August' which opens:

Then August comes, clothed in her golden robe,
When one remembers nothing but clear skies,
Green fields, and the sweetly perfumed flowers.

and concludes:

A mellow softness covers all the earth.
'Tis now that Nature shows her beauty best.

Beneath, the tyro poet has written: 'Excuse bad handwriting and abominable expression.'

Bruce gave up the fraternal struggle. The older Hamilton was becoming accustomed to playing second fiddle in all things to his talented younger brother. As he ruefully wrote: 'When I returned to Earls Court in September it was with the realisation that in large areas of knowledge and thought I would in future be taking my time from my brother. But I had ceased to resent this.'

Poetic preoccupations continued to absorb Patrick during the Christmas holidays, when the peripatetic Hamiltons uprooted themselves once more and returned to Chiswick, not yet back to Burlington Gardens, but to another boarding-house in nearby Barrowgate Road, run by an academic family named Gwinnell. Mealtimes were dominated by the family patriarch, Professor Gwinnell, a pedant who was apt to bring table talk to a halt with such pronouncements boomed into his beard as, 'Yes, I think on the whole Homer was the greatest poet that ever lived'. The only opposition was offered by another guest, a young man known to the Hamiltons as 'the Nancy' who timorously objected to the professor's enthusiasm for Wagner by squeaking that he personally couldn't stand *Tristan*. The artistic ambience was intensified upon the arrival of the ineffable Bernard, hot-foot from France, who had been composing war verses of a sort somewhat different from the trench poems being written at the same time by Owen and Sassoon. Their flavour can be conveyed by a surviving line, in which Bernard compared the struggles of the BEF with earlier British campaigns in France: 'Agincourt archers march away'. Although he was still reading poetry avidly, Patrick's awe of his father inhibited him from offering his own contributions. The short-lived family reunion broke up in the New Year of 1918, when Patrick returned to Hove with Nellie, while Bruce prepared to sit his army entrance examination in March. Patrick did not, however, go back to Holland House, having apparently persuaded an indulgent Nellie that he needed a fallow period before the rigours of public school at Westminster.

The spring of 1918 brought the supreme crisis of the war for the Allies: the Germans were desperate to finish the struggle before the Americans landed in force in Europe and, bolstered by troops newly arrived from the Eastern Front, Ludendorff launched a series of great offensives in the west that almost cracked the British and French defences. Bruce was infected by the prevailing patriotism and volunteered for active service in the Inns of Court Regiment, even going so far as to cheat at his medical exam by memorising the sight-testing cards in order to disguise his myopia. Patrick, meanwhile, was more engaged by another new enthusiasm. He had been introduced to chess by Claude Chepmell and, in his customary earnest way, he gave over his whole attention to learning and mastering the game. Within two months he was proficient enough to enter and win the junior class of the local boys' championship held at Brighton's Royal Pavilion. As he had outstripped Bruce in litera-ture, so he soon overhauled his chess mentor Chepmell, meeting and beating his friend during the course of the tournament, a feat which reduced Chepmell to tears.

Patrick, though, was now giving the majority of his attention and aptitude to poetry, memorising great chunks of Palgrave, and absorbing Shakespeare (the three parts of *Henry VI* and *Hamlet* being his particular favourites). When the Old Vic under Lilian Baylis staged a production of *Hamlet*, Patrick eagerly wrote off for tickets to a Saturday matinée, but he was bitterly disap-pointed when Baylis herself wrote back to tell him that all seats were booked. Nellie tried to console him with the thought that there would be plenty of chance for him to see the play later, but he was desolate: 'But I want to see it *now*. I won't want to see it later, I *know*!'

As always, Nellie was Patrick's greatest and most dependable fan. No lover of poetry herself, she made an exception in her son's case and gave him the emotional response he needed to the declamations of verse and passages from Shakespeare which he gave after dinner in his mother's room. Patrick would stand, or stride up and down, never consulting the book he held, with his eyes half-closed, spouting verse in the half-cracked voice of adolescence. He would vary the readings with bouts of straight acting, contorting every limb and muscle as he strove to give his all to Hamlet's great soliloquies. Another of his staple performances was the King's nightmare on the eve of the Battle of Bosworth from *Richard III*. For this dramatic rendition the furniture was moved aside and Patrick would commence, building up to a climax which saw him writhing on the sofa, gangling legs askew, as he gasped out, 'Give me another horse, bind up my wounds . . .' concluding with a terrifying scream of, 'Have mercy, Jesu!' which brought frightened fellow-lodgers to the doors of their rooms. Patrick's passion for these recitals was derived directly from his father, although in his maturity this had the adverse result of permanently marring his appreciation for Shakespeare. He later recalled Bernard snatching up a green table cloth as a toga as he acted out Mark Antony's speech after the death of Caesar, leaping on a dining-room chair for added effect and putting on a horrible leer as he reiterated the line, 'Brutus is an honourable man'.[1]

Patrick continued to experiment with his own compositions. At the age of fifteen, the influence of Keats had given way to Shelley, and then to the contemporary romantic hero, Rupert Brooke, newly and unglamorously slain by a mosquito bite while in the Aegean. It was with a piece very reminiscent of Brooke that Patrick first burst into print, when his poem 'Heaven', almost a lift from Brooke's poem of the same title, was published in the prestigious *Poetry Review* in the summer of 1918:

They say, my dear, that far from here,
We two shall meet again.
There is no death, 'tis a loss of breath,
An end to bitter pain.
And there shall be, wise men agree,

A better place than this,
O far above, where only love
Shall enter to our bliss.
But shall we find what we used to mind:
The slumbering English hills,
The sound of bees, the willow trees,
And the laughing daffodils?
And shall we greet what we used to meet:
The talk of men who are witty,
The stinging rain – won't these remain?
And will you be as pretty?

That Brooke's shadow loomed large over Patrick's poem is clear when comparing lines from the original 'Heaven':

Fish say, they have their Stream and Pond;
But is there anything Beyond?
This cannot be All, they swear,
For how unpleasant, if it were!
One may not doubt that somewhere, Good
Shall come of Water, and of Mud;
And sure, the reverent eye must see
A purpose in Liquidity.[2]

Though Patrick's version is not, as Brooke's, a cynical satire on religious belief, it does display doubts about traditional Christian teaching, and marks the end of his short period as an orthodox believer. Despite the unfashionable, sub-Georgian tweeness of the language and pastoral images, this mood of doubt chimed well with the prevailing *zeitgeist* at the end of the war, when millions had seen their naive faith in religious truth destroyed on the battlefields of the Western Front. Perhaps it is not too much to claim that in his groping, juvenile way, Patrick was already showing the first glimmers of the uncanny gift he possessed to seize and express the spirit of the age.

It may seem incomprehensible now that Patrick could display such enthusiasm for the works of Rupert Brooke, a poet so out of fashion that it is almost impossible to look at his work objectively. But we are looking back from the perspective of almost a

century. The savagery and suffering of two world wars, a revolution in poetic technique and themes, and the romantic legend
built up around Brooke for propaganda purposes after his death,
all conspire to obfuscate the real man. In truth Brooke was a far
more complex and interesting figure than the legend of the
boyish 'most handsome young man in England' would suggest:
tortured by sexual ambiguity, neurotic, unable to live up to his
reputation, the death of this poetic Peter Pan may have come as a
welcome release for him. His popularity is easy to explain in
terms of the wartime need for a dead young hero whose
uncharacteristically slushy sonnets of 1914 sold in thousands and
Patrick was only one among millions who swallowed a manu-
factured myth.[3] As Patrick wrote of his autobiographical hero of
his first novel *Monday Morning*: 'Anthony himself was a small
soldier in the great army of young Rupert Brookes – Rupert
Brooke having made as many Rupert Brookes as Byron ever
made Byrons.' Bespectacled, acned Patrick, so far from being a
handsome and romantic figure himself, clearly identified with
the Brooke legend, for the poet was a convenient ready-made
hero to adulate. It says something for Patrick's perception that he
did not take long to shake off this idolatry.

In the late summer of 1918, the Hamiltons set up home again
in their old house, 2 Burlington Gardens, Chiswick. They had
previously been tenants there, but now Bernard bought the
leasehold and it became a firm family base, ending the shifting
uncertain years of wartime boarding- and lodging-houses. But
although they now had a place to call their own, the family were
still scattered: Bernard was only home occasionally on leave;
Lalla was at singing and drama schools; Bruce was now involved
in military training at Berkhamsted and Patrick was about to go
to Westminster. Only Nellie remained permanently in situ at
Chiswick, sheet-anchor to her far-flung clan.

Patrick entered Grant's, one of three residential boarding
houses at Westminster, where his housemaster was a Mr Tanner,
known to his boys as the 'Buck' or 'Turkey Tanner' because of
his strangled, gobbling mode of speech. Tanner was a tall,
gloomy-looking figure whose ash-coloured hair and downward-
swooping moustaches gave him an air of misery, belied by his

pleasant personality. One reason for his universal popularity was his less than strict enforcement of house and school rules, particularly after dark. As at Colet Court, there were 'goings on' in the dorms after lights out, but this time unaccompanied by violence or threats. Perhaps for this reason, or perhaps because 'Billy Hamilton' had by now got a grip on him too, Patrick was not in a position to maintain his unswervingly moralistic stance. We have Bruce's word that Patrick did not have physical homosexual affairs, although he admitted to his brother in later life that this was less from a lack of desire than from a failure of nerve and enterprise.[4] Nevertheless Patrick was not immune to the charms of his own adolescent sex, falling heavily in love with a pretty boy younger than himself. As we know from such contemporary accounts of public-school life as Alec Waugh's *The Loom of Youth* – a book Patrick read at this time – or Robert Graves' autobiography *Goodbye to All That*, such sexless affairs between older and younger boys were the norm at the time and remained so for decades, evolving into elaborate rituals of courtly love, with the older boy playing the protector to the younger and shielding his protégé from the baiting and bullying that was another persistent feature of life at England's grander centres of education. As it turned out Patrick need not have been so diffident in his advances to his beloved. Just like Graves' adored 'Dick' at Charterhouse, the object of Patrick's affection was available: commonly known as 'Grant's whore', he habitually obliged anyone who offered the price of a chocolate bar from the Westminster tuck shop.

The heavily homo-erotic atmosphere at Westminster can only have been reinforced by the slaughter on the Western Front, which took an especially heavy toll of old boys from the school.[5] The Westminster Roll of Honour bears the names of six pairs of brothers killed, alongside three sons of the Bishop of Exeter. As early as 1915, the school magazine the *Elizabethan* reported that a total of 930 old boys were serving their country of which a large proportion had already been killed:

> It is a record of which we may be justly proud, for it should be
> remembered that Westminster, which has contributed more than

three times its own size, is the smallest of the great public schools, and that not more than about eighty Old Westminsters were in the Regular Army when war was declared.

The example of old boys who had died in the trenches was held up for the boys to emulate. Of Captain G.O. Roos, an old Westminster who died with 20,000 others on the disastrous first day of the Battle of the Somme, 1 July 1916, the *Elizabethan* wrote, 'Chaucer might have had him for his "verray parfit gentil knight".' The death of another Old Boy drew forth the encomium:

> Since the days of the Crusades, when Sir Jasper Croft was created a Knight of the Holy Sepulchre by Godfrey de Boulogne at the taking of Jerusalem, AD 1100, the Crofts have continually served their King and Country as soldiers. Members of the family have fought in most of the English wars, notably at the Battle of Agincourt.

A Westminster mother, Mrs Veitch, presented the school with a cricket challenge cup for the highest batting average each season in memory of her sporting son, killed on the Somme.

Patrick's unconsummated homosexual affair curiously foreshadowed his later heterosexual pursuit of the London prostitute Lily Connolly, fictionalised in his novel *The Midnight Bell*. There was the same idealisation of a figure who in sexual matters was hardly a model of conventional morality, and the same reluctance about getting down to the actual business of a physical relationship. There was also an identical repining and anguish when he realised, too late, that both of these objects of desire could have been enjoyed on their own terms if he had had the nerve to broach the matter.

Patrick played the normal school games, which were compulsory, keeping goal for his house football team and though as at Holland House he tended to be a conformist rather than a rebel, even he did not escape occasional corporal correction. These physical punishments were often administered by the school prefects rather than the masters, and in one instance, Patrick's acting talents and his devotion to the cinema got him off the worst rigours of a caning; his impersonation of Charlie Chaplin's famous splay-footed walk as he marched to the whipping point convulsed the cane-wielder with laughter, causing him to land his six of the best with less than the usual severity.

Patrick formed good relationships with his masters, by dint of treating them as human beings rather than the hereditary enemy in a caste war; in return, they respected his obvious intelligence. Even in his weakest subject, French, he established an *entente cordiale* with the teacher, Monsieur Just, whom he pronounced a fair man – 'Just by name and Just by nature'. His art teacher, Mr Neame, was famous for the unpredictability of his random punishments, which chiefly consisted of 'Drill' – marching in single file around Little Dean's yard – or 'Up school' – detention in the assembly hall. The deceptively mild-mannered Neame would make the rounds of the art room, delivering critical comments in a precious voice: 'Yes. Much better. You are beginning to grasp the principles of perspective.' (Pause) 'Up school'; or: 'Quite good. The tip of the nose in line with the forehead. Excellent.' (Pause) 'Two drills.' Patrick confessed that he could never fathom the rationale behind Neame's seemingly casual award of mixed praise and punishment, and ascribed it to simple sadism. To him the art master was the very antithesis of Monsieur Just; Neame was 'Mr Unjust'.

Patrick's own artistic and literary interests continued to flourish under the guidance of his form master, Basil King. As well as his favourites, Patrick was beginning to single out the writers who were not to his taste and he was unabashed about stating his judgements in public. One day King read a Kipling poem to his class and asked for their comments. Patrick put up his hand and piped, 'Please sir, I don't like Kipling very much.' There was a shocked hush in the classroom. This was *lèse majesté* with a vengeance; the bard of Empire was then at the very pinnacle of a public acclaim that fell little short of the idolatry extended to King George himself. The great Rudyard was, to boot, a Sussex man by adoption, and Patrick, a Sussex boy born and bred, was being doubly disloyal. His shocked schoolfellows waited for the roof to fall in, but Mr King, after a pause to take in the import of Patrick's statement, merely inquired, 'Why not?' 'Please sir, I think he's too boisterous, sir,' came the answer. There was another silence, then King mildly remarked, 'I'm inclined to agree with you.' Identifying Patrick as a boy with a mind of his own, Turkey Tanner sought him out for private literary talks. Recommending Hardy with some reservations, Tanner gobbled, 'Don't like *Tess*, don't like *Tess* at all. Try *Under the Greenwood Tree. Under the Greenwood Tree.* Charming book. Charming book.'

But Patrick's principal preoccupation continued, as before, to be poetry, not prose. Westminster, by the narrow hearty standards of most of the major public schools, enjoyed a liberal atmosphere and behaviour such as the writing and enjoyment of poetry, which in less enlightened institutions would have been the occasion for teasing at the very least, was regarded as no more than an amiably eccentric foible. The announcement of the Armistice in November 1918 inspired Patrick to emulate another of those beloved Brooke sonnets that had celebrated the coming of war more than four years before. Patrick's verse began:

Now that the best and worst and last is over

and concluded:

We have found fulfilment, more than words can tell
    Made a wide road for splendour, comforted;
        Flung the great Justice to the hooded night,
And stored up Honour in a Jealous cell.
    Greatly the Live have known for what they bled,
        And the most living Dead have found their right.

Patrick, to his credit, when reminded of his juvenile effusions in later years, would raise his eyes and hands to the heavens and pretend to tear his hair. In mitigation of the lush sentimentality of his poem, we should remember the huge gap between the reality of the trenches and the propaganda-fed home front; Patrick's only direct contact with the war was through his father and Bernard was not the man to dwell long on the details of modern combat, even though he himself returned clinically shell-shocked from its horrors. Others, even more insulated from the war's reality, gave vent to such romantic hyperbole – even the hard-bitten Orwell, whose first published piece was a wartime poem with the deathless title: 'Awake! Young Men of England!'[6] Such ridiculously unrealistic sentiments were the common currency of middle-class, wartime England, and Patrick did not differ from his contemporaries in subscribing to them.

After two terms Patrick was beginning to enjoy himself at Westminster. He collected the school prize for the best paper on a text from English literature (his chosen work was *The Merchant of Venice*) and he was adjusting well to his new social life. Then, in the wake of war, the violent epidemic of Spanish 'flu that was sweeping the country once more aroused Nellie's protectiveness. She decided that Patrick was being put at grave risk of infection by living in the close confines of Westminster and that he must leave the school immediately. This departure signalled the end of his academic career.

In the spring the newly liberated Patrick was sent with Bruce to spend another holiday with Nurse Swain at Hassocks. It was an idyllic few weeks of superb weather, during which the brothers were almost exclusively concerned with poetry. Patrick was still deeply enmeshed with the Romantic movement and the poems he wrote during this period owe much to Wordsworth, Coleridge and Keats.

His devotion to verse alternated uneasily between over-whelming emotion – once, while reading to Bruce, he put down his book with a choked 'I can't go on' – and an acute sense of the absurd. While reading Keats' sonnet which contains the line 'Musing on Milton's fate – on Sidney's bier' he broke into hysterical laughter, having associated 'bier' with liquid refreshment. But despite this lapse, Keats was beginning to replace Brooke as his new hero. Of the other Romantics, he rated the poetry of Wordsworth and Coleridge more highly than their political attitudes, despising the conservatism of their later years. Despite his own ancestral ties – a swordstick reputedly left by the poet had been one of the talismans of his childhood – he initially had little time for Byron, thinking him, 'a great poet who never understood poetry', although he later came to value Byron's lyrics and letters very highly. However, his idolatry of Keats knew no bounds. He read everything by and about the poet that he could lay his hands on and he and Bruce even came to identify themselves with Keats and his family, Patrick naturally taking the part of John, while Bruce deferentially played the role of his brother and confidant George. This passion took a practical turn when Patrick became the first person to subscribe to a fund set up to buy the poet's Hampstead home, Wentworth Place, for the nation, backing his gift with a letter to the *Daily Mail* supporting the project.

Though Patrick was, in 1919, determined to be a poet, and if possible a great one, the realisation soon dawned, as it does to many with this ambition, that poetry does not pay. As he put it in *Monday Morning*, 'I would really rather be a great poet, but novels sell and verse doesn't, so I am reduced to being a great novelist, to make money, to make a name, until I can be a great poet.'His first experiment in prose, a novel with the fashionable title *Disillusionment*, did not get beyond the first couple of chapters and he abandoned it after a reading to Bruce failed to elicit the desired response. Temporarily defeated, he returned to poetry, and compromised by undertaking a long essay in verse which he originally entitled 'Georgianism' but subsequently, in obedience to current trends, re-baptised 'Modernism'. The title was a misnomer, for the poem consisted of a sustained assault on the prevailing fashions in poetry, which were in his view leading away from simplicity and sincerity. Patrick used a scatter-gun approach; among the targets of his attack on the decadence of modern English verse, which he saw as reaching its zenith in the Romantic age, were such hallowed figures as Tennyson and Kipling, who were branded as traitors for allowing plain and even vulgar speech to taint their poetry, after what he considered the purity of the Romantic masters. With the exception of Brooke, he included the Georgians in his indictment, while the realistic war poems of Owen and Sassoon were quite beyond his comprehension.

Kipling was his special *bête noir*. The quality that made his poetry popular, his facility for striking a memorable phrase, was what Patrick had complained of at Westminster – the poet's 'boisterousness'; his exaltation of force, vindication of violence and his hearty, matey use of common speech. It does not need too close an analysis to discover that the qualities Patrick hated in Kipling were similar to those represented by his father. It must have seemed to him that Kipling was merely Bernard in a pith helmet. A couplet from 'Modernism' roasting Kipling displays his distaste:

Guns, ships and wars, and a boisterous English nation,
All go to fill his void of inspiration

although he grudgingly admitted in the next line:

Kipling is merely vile; there are much worse.

Patrick used every trick he knew in 'Modernism', writing in ottava rima, quatrains, heroic couplets and blank verse. The central core of the poem was a celebration and defence of Keats that included an attack on the critics whose wounding reviews in the *Quarterly* and *Blackwood's* magazines had been blamed by Byron for hastening the poet's demise, and it concluded with a plea to the Keats' shade to return and restore English poetry to its rightful concerns. Patrick sent the completed work to Jonathan Cape and Cape himself replied with a kindly letter, declining to publish the sixteen-year-old poet, but praising the poem and expressing an interest in seeing his future work. Patrick was not too devastated. He put the poem, so obviously out of tune with the time, in his bottom drawer. From henceforward poetry was firmly abandoned for prose.

5

The Fractured Family

DISCUSSING PATRICK HAMILTON'S DECLINE INTO ALCOHOLISM ten years after his death, Priestley speculated that the roots of his drinking were to be found early in his life, long before he actually began to hit the bottle:

> There may have been some inherited tendency here, but I feel strongly that an increasing desire to blur reality arose from the depths of a profoundly disturbed unconscious. We have to accept this, I believe, fully to understand the man and his work, both the wonderful best of it and the forgivable worst of it.[1]

Priestley felt that this disturbance came during Patrick's youth and was responsible for both the strengths and weaknesses in his work, in that he never reached the full maturity of an adult artist and continued to see the world through the eyes of adolescence; this brought freshness and immediacy to his early work, but disillusionment and cynicism later on. Patrick, as we have seen, also blamed the stunting of his spiritual growth on his suffering as an over-sensitive child.

In writing about Patrick Hamilton one is driven back to his family time and again. Throughout his life he was shackled by his background and upbringing, returning constantly to the physical places and the mental themes of his childhood. For a long time – far too long – he remained physically tied to his family and he never succeeded – he did not seriously try – in shaking off their bonds. Of these primal links, by far the strongest and most suffocating, was his relationship with his mother. For her part she did her best to strengthen her hold on Patrick as he moved towards adult independence. Bruce Hamilton maintained a fairly rosy view of the relationship, as one might expect from a son who himself only partially escaped the maternal clutches, mainly by virtue of putting an ocean between himself and his mother: 'Mummie remained, as she always had been, at the heart of her sons' lives, always to be relied upon for sympathy and practical help. Constant proximity made it difficult to realise that she was ageing and that her health was deteriorating.' As Nellie grew physically more frail, so her anxiety increased that she was about to be abandoned by her children, who were all approaching adulthood. Psychologically, she had her own reasons to fear desertion: her parents had abandoned her by dying and leaving her an orphan; her sisters had married; and both her husbands had gone off with other women. Her children were her only surviving assets.

Previous writers on Patrick Hamilton, basing their views on Bruce's *The Light Went Out*, have given pride of place to Bernard as the central figure in his childhood and youth. For example, Michael Holroyd has written unequivocally, 'The controlling figure in his life was his father,' and went on to see the course of Patrick's career as a lifelong effort to emulate Bernard: 'From his father he could win no support for his wish to be a writer, although this wish reflected Patrick's need to feel closer to him.'[2] Although it is indisputable that Bernard was an important – if often absent – presence in his children's lives and equally clear that the pattern of Patrick's later years, consciously, unconsciously or by coincidence, held uncanny similarities to his father's, it is also certain that Nellie played an equally vital role. It is time to redress the balance and give her her due – for good or ill – in moulding Patrick's life. The fact that she was at home and her husband, more often than not, was away made the mother–son relationship deeper, more lasting and more deadly to Patrick's psychological health. While he drew his propensity to alcoholism from his father, the neuroses spawned by and causing this drinking were chiefly the responsibility of his mother. Patrick, unable consciously to revolt against Nellie's tyranny in her lifetime, took posthumous revenge in his later life and work. His two wives and the prostitutes he frequented were in their different ways his victims; the women who suffered at the hands of men in his novels and plays were surrogate victims too.

After the war Nellie's mental burden was compounded by health and economic problems. Her dependence on her children reached a pitch of desperation. Patrick, as the youngest and most cherished child, suffered the most from her all-embracing needs, particularly as he was still living under the same roof in Burlington Gardens. For the first time in Nellie's life, economic developments forced her to abandon hired hands. The servant problem was widely shared in middle-class families who, before 1914, would have found it unthinkable to run their substantial homes without such help. The war had changed all that. Girls and women had been recruited on a substantial scale into factory work to replace men who had joined the armed forces. They found that such employment commanded wages four or five times greater than those they had earned as domestic servants and once the war was over, many of them stayed on in their jobs, never to return to the drudgery of domestic duty. Nellie's own financial situation, too, had changed for the worse, for Bernard's fortune was rapidly losing value in the slump of the early 1920s. There were to be no more flamboyant displays to impress the neighbours: for a short time a single resident general servant-woman was kept on, but eventually she was replaced by the occasional visits of a char.

Nellie began to buckle under the pressure. She had to do her own shopping and other household tasks for the first time in her life and aged rapidly under the strain. The pain of worsening rheumatism in her limbs led to insomnia and her temper, always quick, became increasingly ragged. She started to talk about the desirability of 'ending it all', and frequently reminded her children that she lived only for them and once their dependence on her had ended she would simply commit suicide. The burden of guilt thus laid on the younger Hamiltons was enormous and,

not surprisingly, they responded with fervent displays of grati-
tude for all she had done and sacrificed for them and with
demonstrations of affection that went far beyond the usual
tenderness displayed by adult children towards their parents.
Significantly, they saw their very existence as posing a 'problem'
for her. Bruce wrote later:

> She remained indispensable to her children ... but, following the
> laws of their own being and the standards of a different age, they
> took too much for granted and inevitably caused her hours of
> distress.'

It is a familiar cyclical trap: the possessive mother, wishing to
increase and cement her hold over her offspring, sets impossible
standards for them and when they fail to attain her goals,
expresses disappointment and grief in the tones of a wounded
and long-suffering martyr. The children redouble their assurances of affection and attempts to please, while repressing their
natural instincts to rebel and break free of a prison sentence that
has long been spent; such repression can often turn poisonous.
    The first of the children to disappoint her mother's expec-
tations was the eldest, Lalla. Nellie had set her heart on two
conventional attainments for her only daughter: success in the
relatively respectable art of singing and a good marriage. On the
basis of virtuoso performances on the family's upright piano,
Nellie had convinced herself that a successful musical career for
Lalla was a real possibility. She was duly sent off for voice
training but her teacher never succeeded in turning a tin ear into
gold. Too often she would hit a high note flat by a semitone and a
career in the concert hall was clearly a non-starter. Nellie was
distraught. 'But she's *flat* my dear,' she told Patrick, after she had
invested a considerable sum in Lalla's singing lessons, 'She's *still*
flat!' On the strength of her looks rather than her voice, Lalla
managed to get a job as a show-girl in the chorus line of the C.B.
Cochran revue *Oh Joy!*. Stage-struck, she decided to switch from
singing to the theatre and embarked on an acting career under
the stage name Diana Hamilton.
    Lalla was still no better able to please her parents in her love

life. An engagement to one young swain ended when he departed for Siam and another semi-engagement was aborted when the suitor left for the war. Her third serious affair was with a Cambridge student, George Warden, reading for his Mathematical Tripos and tutoring Bruce in the meantime. Although of Austrian descent, Warden, too, went off to the war, and the affair petered out. By then, Lalla's capricious attention had been captured by another man, Vane Sutton Vane, who had been a distant neighbour and acquaintance of the Hamiltons in Hove. The son of a writer of melodramas, he had the theatre in his blood and had begun his thespian career as a puppeteer. A slim volume of verse followed and then a play, *The Blow*, heralded a new departure as an actor and playwright. By the time he renewed his acquaintance with Lalla in 1920, he was established in the theatre and unhappily married. Friendship between the pair soon ripened into a full-scale affair and they set up home together in Paddington. Mummie was mortified; living in sin with a precariously placed married man of the theatre who had a dubious past and an uncertain future, definitely did not fit with her plans for Lalla. Though indirect contact was maintained with the guilty pair through Patrick and Bruce, Lalla became *persona non grata* at Burlington Gardens.

The spotlight of parental attention now switched to the hapless Bruce. Demobilised from the army without having seen action, his anxious parents tried to find him a suitable job. An attempt to get him a post in a Leicester shoe factory having come to nothing, he was given a position as a clerk in a shipping firm in the City of London. Bruce found the work tedious, so Bernard pulled strings to get him a junior job in the City headquarters of his own bank, the London County and Westminster. After a few miserable months, Bruce rebelled and, on his own initiative, found his true *métier* as a teacher. He applied to the traditional standby of young men marking time, the private schoolteachers' recruiting agency Gabbitas and Thring and got a job at a Sussex prep school, Fonthill, near East Grinstead. Bruce spent the next three years, 1920–22, teaching at a succession of small schools, while simultaneously studying for and passing his London Matriculation examinations; these qualified him for a more

prestigious post at a private school in New York State, and in
September 1922 his father accompanied him to the Liverpool
pierhead to put him on a boat bound for the United States.

Bernard himself, back from the war, was a more frequent
presence at his home in Chiswick. He too was ageing rapidly.
His health had been severely shaken by his war experience in
France, but he remained as pompous as ever and his speech was
now larded with military terminology which he used to dress
down his sons as though they were other ranks in his own
private platoon. Patrick and Bruce no longer referred to Bernard
as 'Daddy'. From now on he was, to them, the 'Old Devil' or
'O.D.' The boys regarded their father as a great comic character,
but one whose temper they had to watch. Once installed at
Chiswick he tried to take up the threads of his literary career and
enlisted Nellie's collaboration in attempting to write a best-
selling novel with the title, *Daphne Dale, Typist*, under the
pseudonym A. Myrtle Brown. He also tried his hand at a film
scenario, *The Devil on Two Sticks*, for the infant movie industry
and when this evaporated he turned to another doomed project:
a private printing press to publish the works of the Hamilton
family – his own, his wife's and the not-yet-written bestsellers of
'my budding authors', Patrick and Bruce. In his own clumsy way,
Bernard was proud and pleased that his sons were showing signs
of inheriting his literary interests. But only so long as they did
not challenge his own overweening self-esteem.

Temporarily thwarted in his literary endeavours, Bernard
turned to politics. He joined the Fabian Society, but resigned
after attending only one meeting, having discovered that the
'damned socialists' appeared to be after his money. He
rebounded to the opposite end of the political spectrum and
became a member of a group known first as the Middle Classes
Union and then as the National Citizens' Union,[3] one of a
plethora of right-wing pressure groups which mushroomed at
the end of the war and whose avowed aim was to protect the
middle classes and their property from the menace of socialism.
Bernard took a leading part in a successful campaign to have a
representative of the Citizens' Union elected to Chiswick
Council, but his supporting speech at the Town Hall, which

diversified into his idiosyncratic view of English history, made his audience audibly restive.

Relations between the Hamilton boys and their father were no easier than before the war. Bernard's touchy *amour propre* was easily hurt – as on the occasion when the brothers presented their father with a copy of *Thaïs*, a book by one of his favourite authors, Anatole France. When Patrick wrote a verse inscription to go with the gift beginning, 'O gracious man! O generous heart!' Bernard positively preened, but as the poem went on it became embarrassingly clear that the person thus praised was in fact France and the Old Devil's disconsolation was painful to behold. More and more frequently the brothers found their covert mockery of their father turning to dislike and fear, as his authoritarianism hardened with his arteries. Increasingly often, mostly when in his cups, he would roar out orders to the boys in a parade-ground staccato. Nellie was not exempt from these regimental rows and once, having hit her with a bread roll (according to Bruce; a teacup and saucer according to Patrick),[4] Bernard excused himself by saying, 'I am an artilleryman, and I took a low trajectory.'

The Old Devil continued to frequent his haunts in the West End, dressing up to the nines to go 'up town', but he had been obliged to change his club from the Savage to the Reform after being requested to resign over an incident in which he had broken a glass over the head of a fellow member who had been baiting him. Resentment for his family came out most viciously when the O.D. had been drinking spirits, and they learned to watch for the danger signals and keep out of his way when he returned from one of his jags. Bernard brooded over his diminishing authority and his family's increasingly evident mistrust and dislike of him. It was all monstrously unjust – had he not given them good homes, and kept them free from material want? Was he not flexing every influence to try and secure them a place in the world? He was unable to grasp that his children's rejection of the lives he had mapped out for them in business and commerce stemmed partly from antipathy towards his violent outbursts and partly from artistic aptitudes that ironically they had inherited from him.

As they grew older, Bruce and Patrick began to stand up to their father's assaults with increasing frequency and confidence. Meeting Bernard at Victoria Station, they found him roaring drunk; he immediately pitched into Patrick, calling him to attention and subjecting him to an inspection there and then on the platform. Bruce flew into an uncharacteristic fury and denounced his father as a 'damned bully' who was 'making a beast of himself like a filthy sergeant-major'. Bernard collapsed.

Another spectacular row with Bruce led to the writing of Patrick's first mature piece of prose (though it remained unpublished until long after his death, apparently because he was dissatisfied with it). The story relates an incident that occurred in the late summer of 1922, shortly before Bruce's departure to America. He had been spending the day with Lalla and Vane who, having regularised their relationship in marriage, were spending their honeymoon at Shepperton. On his way home to Chiswick, Bruce was standing on the platform of the Embankment tube station, awaiting a train to Chiswick Park. He spied a slightly swaying O.D. some distance away. Feeling too tired to cope with his father, Bruce quietly slipped down to the far end of the platform, and boarded another carriage. Upon reaching Chiswick, he hopped out and skeltered home. By the time Bernard's stumbling footsteps heralded his first latchkey assault on the front door, Bruce was in bed with his light out. Fearing a late-night confrontation he cautiously climbed out of bed and locked his room. Alas, this manoeuvre was heard by Bernard, who promptly stormed the stairs and rattled Bruce's door. This was defiance! The O.D. started to shout, in his best parade-ground bawl, 'Open the door! *O-pen the door!*' Nervously, Bruce replied, 'I'm not going to let you in, so you might just as well go to bed.' This was more than defiance – it was sheer, open mutiny. Bernard lumbered down the stairs, but was back a minute later to renew the assault. 'Open the door! *O-pen the door!*' he yelled, coupled with the threat, 'If you don't I'll break it down with my cavalry sword!' Bruce next heard the unmistakable sound of his father probing the door panels with his treasured regimental sabre. Weakly, Bruce said, 'If I let you in, will you promise not to stay?'

Sweetly, the O.D. replied, 'I merely want to see to the clasp. You are not on company orders.' Bruce gave in and unlocked the door. Sword in hand, a dishevelled Bernard entered. Laying the weapon on the bed he ordered, 'Come here!' Mistrustfully, Bruce advanced a step. Bernard drew his son to his bosom and planted a smacking kiss, followed by two stinging slaps, to each cheek. Bruce instantly dissolved in tears. Bernard was at once contrite and with oafish gentleness did his awkward best to mollify his son. Then, muttering, 'Don't say anything to your mother. She's a dear, good soul – but she doesn't understand men,' he left. Bruce, who was alone with his father in the house at the time of the incident, related the story to Patrick a week later when they were sharing a holiday lodging in Over Street, near Brighton station. Some time after that, Patrick used it as the basis for 'The Quiet Room'[5] (originally titled 'Violets on the Table'), an extremely mature piece of work for a boy of eighteen. It is a study of the effects of drink on a father's relationship with his daughter. In the story, Bruce's clash with his father is used almost verbatim, except that Bruce becomes the daughter Mary, while Bernard would have been mortified to read of his transformation into the working-class thug Mr Grote, with his sword transposed into a humble poker. Quite apart from its lyrical close, 'Violets – marvellously fresh, showing their sweet wet faces to the moon,' the story is an accomplished demonstration of psychological insight and characterization.

For all his violence Bernard could display another side of his character to his sons that was as absurd as his authoritarian aggression, though far less threatening. He was a self-dramatist *par excellence*, given to grand theatrical gestures in speech and behaviour that were enough to convulse his clubland cronies and his sons in fits of laughter. One characteristic affectation was his habit of identifying with the place he had visited most recently on his extensive travels: from the Scilly Isles he appeared in the guise of a deep-sea fisherman and smuggler, with a rolling seaman's gait. France suggested the part of the dashing and gallant lover; while Italy turned him into a Roman patrician or its cut-price latter-day equivalent, a fascist worshipper of Mussolini, whose bombastic poses perfectly suited Bernard's historical and theatrical pretensions and political prejudices. From Spain he returned as a sherry-pickled grandee, while his ancestral ties with Scotland were enough to turn him into a tartan-tinted clansman. When decanting him from a train at Euston after a visit to his native heather, Patrick was startled to hear Bernard declaim, 'My boy, if it ever comes to war between England and Scotland, you and I go over the border!' Patrick commented:

> He had a 'Hamilton' mania. As such, he once explained to me, in complete sobriety, that the Hamiltons were the hereditary foes of the Douglases, and that it was really my business, if ever I met a Douglas, 'to run him through with my sword'.
>
> He took, then, keen pleasure in being a soldier, which he was: but he took even keener pleasure in being a Frenchman, which he certainly was not. His performances as a Frenchman took place mostly when he was 'On': but they were not at all uncommon in everyday life – particularly when he desired to be either sardonic, sentimental or filthy. There was one fatal flaw in these impersonations: for my father (who actually could speak French quite adequately) constantly wandered into the impression that he was speaking French when in fact he was speaking broken English – that is to say, in the accent of a Frenchman attempting to speak English. 'And after ze soup', he would say to baffled French waiters, 'I haf ze omelette' ... When he was being or talking French in this way, in addition to leering, he nearly always used gestures with his hands – as if he was an orchestra conductor conducting his own performance. I have inherited this love of conducting, and will often stand in front of a window and conduct a symphony. My father, however, would take this enthusiasm so far as to conduct thunderstorms. When a heavy thunderstorm occurred, my mother, the servants and the children were all made to lie on beds and the curtains were closely drawn. He alone would remain on his feet, peeping continuously through an aperture of the curtains to observe the lightning. Immediately after a flash of lightning he would count – that is to say conduct, with his right hand – the amount of seconds intervening between the flash and the ensuing roll of thunder. In this way, I understand, he was able to gauge almost exactly the distance between ourselves and the storm. But an illusion was given that he in fact

controlled the elements, for directly the roll of thunder came he would make a sweep of satisfaction with his hand, as if he had been obeyed exactly.[6]

The overwhelming impression his father made on Patrick as a child was to permeate his writing: Bernard is the prototype of many of the absurd bullies who people his son's books. His bizarre pidgin-French, for instance, is the obvious model for the convoluted 'Oirish' spoken by Mrs Plumleigh-Bruce in *Mr Stimpson and Mr Gorse* when she wishes to patronise her Irish maid, Mary. And Bernard's pompous mode of speech is also clearly the ancestor of what Priestley called Patrick's 'Komic Kapitals' – a stylistic device he sometimes used to excess in his novels.

Patrick witnessed yet another of Bernard's foreign incarnations when his father returned from his abortive trip to Canada after failing to win back the affections of his mistress Marthe: 'He became a Canadian, smoked small cigars, said "Yep", and, without actually giving forth saliva, spat cleverly in the direction of an imaginary spittoon.'[7] But despite all this evidence to the contrary, Patrick is clear that his father was neither bad nor mad:

> The odd thing about all this is that he was not in the smallest way insane. Indeed, when he was not making a fool of himself, he was reasonable, kind-hearted, generous and even wise in the ways of the world.
>
> And although, when making a fool of himself, he caused a great deal of distress and pain to his family, it was impossible, for any of them, at this date, to feel any resentment at what he did. Moreover, his constant absurd inflation and abandonment of reality naturally brought with them their opposites – periods of fearful deflation in the presence of, or the suspicion of, reality. And at such times he had, as he sat thinking, a childish, simple, staring look – unforgettably, almost unbearably childish, simple and unhappy.[8]

Though his sedentary life of cinema going and cricket watching was enjoyable enough it could not have been called productive and the need for Patrick to choose a career was

becoming pressing. Bernard, having seen, somewhat unsatis-
factorily, Lalla and Bruce started off, began to exert his heavy-
handed influence. Patrick was firmer in his opposition to his
father than his brother had been, and made it quite clear from
the outset that his intention was to become a writer. Bernard
accepted this, in theory, as a long-term goal (what else could an
author and barrister do?), but he was equally adamant that, as he
repeated *ad nauseam*, 'Literature can be a walking-stick but not a
crutch.' In other words, he approved authorship as a long-term
ambition, but was concerned about the 'barrister' aspect.
Patrick, Bernard insisted, must carve out a career to supply the
financial cushion necessary for his writing schemes. Bernard
made it clear that he had no intention of keeping his youngest
son in indefinite idleness against the distant day when he might
perhaps achieve wealth and fame as a writer.

Patrick, always a diplomat, managed to induce the O.D. to
accept a compromise: he would start a course to learn shorthand
and typing, which would equip him well for a life either in
commerce or in literature. He settled down to learn the Pitman's
method from the standard textbook and soon became absorbed
in the world of outlines and grammalogues which he found a
powerful vehicle for his fantasies; reading phonographic
symbols in everything he saw – furniture, clouds, even faces. He
evolved shorthand shapes for unusual phrases, turning the
sentence 'If Shelley and Keats were to fish lower down the river'
into two huge billowing curves representing the angling poets.
Having sufficiently mastered the skill to turn out a rapid and
proficient hand that he maintained for the rest of his life, Patrick
then turned his attention to learning touch typing, buying a
Corona portable machine which was to serve him throughout his
career.

Bernard became suspicious of this self-tuition. Patrick
appeared to be spending too much time mooching around the
streets by himself, his head full of unborn literary projects, and
the O.D. insisted that his son enrol in a proper commercial secretarial school in Red Lion Square, Holborn. Patrick agreed,
providing that he be allowed to leave home for lodgings near the
school, but before Bernard would permit this, he drew up a code

to govern his son's conduct while away from parental authority. The document amounts to a vintage collection of the O.D.'s eccentric ravings:

> On Sabbath mornings you will sit, regularly, under the Minister of the Scots Presbyterian Kirk near St Pancras. This is a *parade.*
> You will then proceed to Chiswick, reporting here for dinner at one-thirty, military time – i.e. five minutes *early.* Your costume will be such as befits a gentleman, not a socialist agitator, or a denizen of the Wild West. You will bring with you a weekly report on conduct and progress from your tutors, endorsed by the principal. If any difficulty should arise you are to say that I, your father, require this. You will make inquiries as to membership of the City Volunteer and Cadet companies; I believe such bodies still exist. Understand this is an *order*; excuses will have no more avail with me than the preachments of Mormon missionaries. For exercise, I recommend rowing. Ascertain the conditions of membership of the London or Thames Boat Clubs; you cannot hope for Leander.[9]

The reference to Wild West dress was Bernard's bid to curb Patrick's increasingly flamboyant taste in clothes. A typical ensemble at this stage in his life consisted of a bright green sports coat with well-worn grey flannels and a scarlet knitted tie, surmounted by a greasy old felt hat.

Patrick's interlude at the commercial college was a short one, for it soon became apparent that his general education, abbreviated at Westminster, still left something to be desired. He found himself at Bruce's old crammer, studying for the London Matriculation exam, while living in his brother's former boarding-house, the White House Hotel in Earls Court Square.[10]

Educationally, Patrick achieved as little at the crammer as he had at the commercial school. Lessons were a dreamy interval between the hours of leisure time devoted to his own literary and social interests, but away from the classroom it was a different story: for the first time he began to blossom in mixed company outside the closed circle of his family. At last he was beginning to crack the constricting shell of his upbringing; now he was to tumble out into a fresh new world of friends, girls – and love.

PART II
1920–1927

6

The Pursuit of Unhappiness

THE SENSE OF FREEDOM THAT PATRICK enjoyed in his new environment is vividly evoked in the exhilarating opening pages of his first novel *Monday Morning*, in which the hero, Anthony, is virtually a self-portrait of the young author newly liberated from the smothering possessiveness of his mother and the tyranny of his father. Along with the feelings of liberation Patrick experienced on being freed from the four walls of home, came an eagerness to sample the good things of life, especially the anticipated joys of falling in love. It is almost as though he set himself this as a goal, although it seemed it was not the love-object that was important, but merely the state of being in love. Significantly, he called the second chapter of *Monday Morning* 'The Necessity of Love':

'I am going to fall in love,' he [Anthony] thought, 'I can go no longer without realising in some way that swooning ecstasy which I have so well imagined. I am in favour of an exceedingly unhappy love affair, which I throw from me at last, and take to the open road with the friendship of the hills – the sort of love Rupert Brooke so frequently indicated. Yes, I want a very unhappy affair, ending in disaster and desertion on my part. Her sweet face, nevertheless, will be over me as I die. And I shall possibly encounter her, dear as of old, in the Great Dawn.'

81

His wishes are soon realised in the novel when he is smitten by Diane, the sister of a fellow guest at his hotel. Patrick's experience mirrored that of Anthony. The girl who took his fancy bore the exotic name of Maruja Mackehenie y de la Fuente. 'Maruja is pronounced as Marooha (sounds Japanese!) which is a pet name for Maria.'[1]

The Mackehenies were Peruvians of Spanish–Scottish ancestry, perfectly bilingual in English and Spanish and the father of the family held a consular post at the Peruvian embassy in London. Patrick described him as bearing an uncanny resemblance to Charlie Chaplin. His son Carlos – known to Patrick as Charles – befriended him at the White House Hotel and described his sister in glowing terms; she was currently absent at a Catholic girls' boarding school in Stony Stratford. Before he had even met her, Patrick, his head stuffed full of images of the beautiful but unattainable women in Romantic poetry, was half in love with Maruja:

> Diane's premise was, basically, that being in love was all rot. Anthony thought so too, really. At the same time there were some really Big Loves, and love could absolutely make or mar a man's life. Diane was to look at Keats and Fanny Brawne. There was a difference between being in love and Loving. 'I'm going to wait now,' he said, 'till I can find real love.' 'Yes, there must be such a thing,' said Diane. Here they found each other's eyes.

Living in Lima aged ninety, Maruja remembered Patrick, though charming, as having been painfully shy, unsure of himself and unhappy, though Patrick's unhappiness was also the sort of pose he considered to be appropriate to a young Romantic in love. When Maruja returned to her school, Patrick bombarded her with presents, chiefly anthologies of Romantic poetry. He told her that she was the only person to give meaning and purpose to his existence and that she boosted his confidence in himself as a would-be writer. Despite a tendency to tease and to alternate between surrenders and withdrawals in their games of love, Maruja was essentially kind and affectionate by nature. She was both flattered and bewildered by Patrick's solemn ardour, especially his repeated declarations that he was not *in love* with her; he just *loved* her. She recalled, 'He believed not "in love" but in real loving.'[2]

Maruja certainly looked the part of the love-object that Patrick created in the character of Diane:

> She had bobbed hair. It was thick and profuse ... Her body was slender, alertly, almost primly upright. Her hands, her feet, her shoulders were exact in perfection. Sweet was the word for her face. Neither pretty nor beautiful, though you might have said that it was, like a Shelley lyric, so intensely sweet as to be beautiful. Her eyes were light brown, of an almond shape, and all tolerance. Her skin was lovely as it could only be at her age, which was 17. Her nose was small and her mouth too big, and maddeningly passive. A natural pout and droop at each corner, and so a softly melancholy demeanour when her eyes did nothing. On this night she wore a red silken dress, thin, short, and simply arranged. Anthony said, 'By God, she is rather beautiful.'

Bruce once glimpsed Maruja from the window of Patrick's hotel room:

> The fact that she was exquisitely pretty did not help a peaceful relation. Beautifully made, with fine dark hair bobbed (according to the fashion which Patrick had a thing about) a true peach-like complexion and a generous mouth, she was ripe for lovers if not herself quite ripe for love. I thought to myself, 'God, I don't blame him,' and I could see that her mere appearance made him almost faint with longing. But it was not, at least consciously, a carnal longing; rather an aching to be made one with perfection.

Maruja herself certainly felt an attachment to Patrick – an *'amitié amoureuse'* as she called it – and both she and Carlos believed in Patrick's future as a writer.

Patrick's romantic agony was not assisted by the fact that his beloved was so sexually desirable; although he tried to delude himself into thinking Maruja's beauty was uniquely perceptible to himself. The pangs of jealousy of course added to the sweet pain of his predicament:

He thought of Diane only. She was standing in one corner of the room, looking funnily in front of her while a side-whiskered, dark South American sort of young man sheathed in a blue suit spoke to her. Once she laughed, looking up to him, and looked in front of her again. A disturbing sight for Anthony . . .

The couple's feints and passes in the tourney of love were played out at weekly dances in the hotel's large ballroom. Carlos Mackehenie taught Patrick his first dancing steps, in the Latin manner:

The band started. He asked her to dance. They set off. The room was a wonderful, bright kaleidoscope again. Diane was strange to Anthony's touch. Her hand, poised out with his, was cold, and slid from his hand. She was looking brightly and nonchalantly at the other dancers. Her smooth face was very beautiful and young. There would really be no joy in kissing that face of hers. Perhaps a tender, fatherly joy.

Patrick was eaten up by his obsession to the exclusion of all else. He even forgot his previously punctilious attention to family duties; once, for the only time in his life, neglecting to keep an appointment to meet Bruce. But, as his novel related, the affair came to naught. There was no dramatic break in the relationship, merely a gradually dawning realisation on both sides, over the period of a year or two, that there was no future in it, at least in terms of marriage.

Patrick acquiesced in his defeat with good grace, even masochistically urging a rival suitor to marry Maruja. He remained on good, if distant, terms with her, through her two marriages and the birth of her children: 'We kept in touch and he sent me all his novels as they came out. Our beloved Patrick' and he became a close and lifelong friend of her brother Charles (St John in the novel).

Though only a year or two Patrick's senior, Charles was far wiser in the ways of the world and its wickedness. He had about him a dash of cynicism and Latin machismo, but also a profound and sensitive appreciation of history and literature. At the time Patrick got to know him, Charles was working in the City as a preparation for following his father into the Peruvian diplomatic service, in which he eventually rose to become his country's ambassador to the United Nations. Patrick delighted in his company, not least, perhaps, because Charles believed in his genius and, thrown together by their shared interest in literature and Maruja, the two young men become bosom friends and close drinking companions. Beer was their main tipple – it was only subsequently that the consumption of spirits became a major and essential feature of Patrick's life – and their drinking sprees in the West End were undertaken as light-hearted binges; they were occasions for short bouts of release from the drudgery of their everyday lives, more than the serious boozing that Patrick was later to undertake in seeking an opiate or way of escape from mental and physical suffering. Bruce joined them for one of these escapades after meeting his brother by chance in the street and kept a count of their libations as they sat together with Frank Bridger in the saloon bar of the Courtfield Hotel in Earls Court. He noted that they each downed eleven half-pints of bitter – a personal record for the elder Hamilton – and got 'quite tight'. Without undue concern or censure, he also noticed that Patrick appeared more used to alcohol, and more in need of it, than he.

During his time at the commercial college and the crammer, Patrick twice felt the need to escape from his London milieu to the seaside. The first holiday was taken at Margate in the summer of 1919, which he spent principally in reading poetry in his boarding-house room and attending rather poor open-air concert parties at a venue called the 'Oval'. In the late autumn of 1920 he and Bruce took another holiday with Alice Swain and her husband, Mr Pye, who had moved from Hassocks to St Leonards-on-Sea, near Hastings. The brothers were given the family's cosy front sitting room in the Pyes' flat, which was located over a butcher's shop in the resort's Norman Road and here they again achieved something of the old uninterrupted intimacy of their boyhood. Here too, Patrick initiated Bruce into a new-found interest that was to become a lifelong recreation: golf. Patrick had been introduced to the game by his father, who had enrolled him as a junior member of his club, the mid-Surrey, at Richmond. He was given professional coaching and became quite addicted, assiduously attending match-play tournaments and gradually turning into a fair player in practice and a brilliant one in theory. At St Leonards Patrick discovered an abandoned nine-hole course near the town's railway and spent many happy hours on his own, slicing shots in the direction of passing trains. Bruce was persuaded to join in the fun, which was brought to a premature end when a farmer appeared, claiming that his herd of cows was endangered by high-velocity golf balls.

An idea of the almost sensual joy Patrick found in golf – diffi- cult for the unconverted to comprehend – is acutely conveyed in his novel *Hangover Square*, written two decades later. In the book's only uncompromisingly uplifting scene, the pathetic and inadequate protagonist, George Harvey Bone, experiences the one sense of achievement in his life by completing a round in sixty-eight:

> He pulled his next drive, but it lay well, and he hit a screaming number four up to the back of the green. He was playing golf! He knew he was playing golf! You either had that feeling or you didn't! He had got it. He was going to hit the blasted ball all the way round.
>
> He got his bogey four, and at the next hole – a five – got his four with a glorious chip (like a pocket-knife closing) and a putt. Nothing could stop him now. He was out for their blood. He had gone 'mad' and he was going to keep mad.
>
> He was out in thirty-four. He chuckled aloud as he sunk his putt and he breathed deeply and braced himself for the battle home ... He walked along the Downs, this sad, ungainly man with beer-shot eyes who loved a girl in Earls Court – carrying an old bag of borrowed clubs and thinking of nothing but his game of golf. His face shone, his eyes gleamed, and he felt, deep in his being, that he was not a bad man, as he had thought he was a few hours ago, but a good one. And because he was a good man he was a happy man, and if he could only break seventy he would never be unhappy again.

Patrick himself was at this time a deeply unhappy man. He brooded in self-indulgent misery over his hopeless love for Maruja and he suffered from a world-weary aesthetic sense of the absurdities of life, common to over-sensitive young men. Bruce described it as a 'dead' period in Patrick's inner life, anticipating the word used in *Hangover Square* to depict Bone's schizophrenic blackouts, when the reality of the outer world becomes muffled and mysterious and a wall slams down to isolate him in misery. Bruce ascribed Patrick's condition at St Leonards to a reaction against a too absolute surrender of his self to emotion: aesthetically, through an over-indulgence in romantic poetry and sexually, through his obsessive love for Maruja.

His insensibility to anything but his obsession was demonstrated to Bruce when the brothers made a trip to Fairlight Glen, well known as a local beauty spot, although to Patrick it was anything but picturesque. Bruce made a banal remark about the loveliness of the scene, but Patrick, almost in tears, replied brokenly, 'But I can't feel it. I can't *feel* it.' Somehow he had exhausted his capacity for spontaneous aesthetic emotion. It was never to be fully restored.

Once during this holiday, the brothers got into real physical danger; returning from another disappointing outing to Fairlight Glen by way of the seashore, they found themselves cut off by the rapidly incoming tide. Patrick panicked, but Bruce, for once taking command, started to scale the sheer cliff face, commanding his reluctant brother to follow. With the agility of a mountain-goat – albeit myopic – Bruce assaulted the cliff face, yelling words of encouragement at Patrick and physically hauling him upwards when his courage failed. More by luck than judgement they succeeded at last in scrambling to the cliff-top where they collapsed on the grass with the feelings of mingled relief and excitement that a successful brush with danger usually brings. They celebrated by smoking cigarettes, a habit then unfamiliar to Patrick, although Bruce was already a confirmed nicotine addict.

But seaside diversions were not solving Patrick's career problems; to his father's marked and growing irritation, his neglect of his studies at the Earls Court crammer had made it clear that he would probably never be in a position to take the London Matriculation examination with any hope of success. Father and son were in the midst of a battle that would last for years over the question of Patrick's employment, with Bernard continuing to press his younger son to take up a business or commercial post and Patrick baulking at such an unpleasant prospect. Once again, a temporary compromise was reached: Patrick would leave the crammer – and the White House Hotel with all its bitter-sweet memories of Maruja – and get a job. Not in the field of commerce, but in the far more congenial world of the theatre.

7

Stage-struck

IT WAS LALLA WHO TRANSFORMED PATRICK'S life with his first paid employment. She had formed a professional partnership with Sutton Vane, who had embarked on a serious attempt to make his name as a playwright, and they enjoyed a tacit understanding that Lalla would have the pick of the plum parts in any show that Vane should write.[1] By the autumn of 1921, he had found a backer and assembled a cast for a play called *A Case of Diamonds*, a melodramatic comedy-thriller, and Lalla approached Patrick with the offer of a job as actor/assistant stage manager with the company. Patrick leapt at the chance.

The lead roles in the play were taken by Lalla and Vane himself, who played his own creation, a comic detective called Sir Charles Dorley, cast in the Hercule Poirot/Lord Peter Wimsey mould. To avoid the further appearance of nepotism in his company, Vane supplied the stage-name Patrick Henderson for his brother-in-law to go on the posters and programmes for the show (this was the origin of the nickname 'Hen' by which Patrick was known to his close friends and with which he often signed his personal letters), and *A Case of Diamonds* went on tour in provincial theatres in the hope that it would catch the eye of a promoter who would back a West End production.

Patrick's first, and somewhat starry-eyed, encounter with the stage is recalled in his novel *Twopence Coloured* in the character of the book's heroine, Jackie Mortimer, who contains elements of Lalla and of Patrick himself:

89

Jackie never forgot the dressing-room, where she found herself with seven or eight others; she never forgot the blazing electric bulbs, lighting the red-ochre walls, and reflected by blazing little mirrors on the wooden shelf all around; she never forgot the mad disorder of everything; the swarm and smell of greasepaint – Number 9, Number 5, Number 2 – carmine, blue pencil – the clouds of powder and the scent of flesh. She never forgot the torrents of strident and lewd imprecation pouring forth around her with the monotony of a solemn, set incantation. She never forgot the call-boy's raps upon the door, his buoyant 'Arfnar Peas!' at the half-hour – his sinister 'Quartnar Peas!' at the quarter . . . She never forgot how the curtain softly and suddenly arose amid the noise – how its rising gave the same breathless, irrevocable and utterly elusive sensation as a diver might feel in mid-air . . .

However Patrick's career in the theatre actually turned out to be rather more prosaic. It almost began in disaster when Vane unwisely entrusted him with the sole script of his play which Patrick, in a fit of abstraction, promptly left in a taxi. General consternation in the company ensued when he confessed his crime, but, by a miracle, frenzied efforts at recovery paid off when the cab driver retrieved and returned the script. Compounding his original error, Vane again handed the play over to Patrick for safe-keeping. Again, the novice ASM succeeded in abandoning it, this time in a Lyons tea-shop. But the fates were kind once more and Patrick was able to secure the precious document.

Patrick's inexperience nearly scuppered the play a third time when it was finally staged. One of his tasks was to hand over an envelope to an actor whose role was to pass it to one of the principals, named Clarke-Smith, who was supposed to read on stage the letters 'G.I.Q.S.' – standing for his nickname 'Get-it-quick-Sam'. As a joke, Patrick substituted the letters 'R.S.V.P.', which Clarke-Smith only narrowly avoided saying. The actor was furious, and angrily lectured Patrick in the Green Room after the show, though despite this inauspicious beginning, the two became firm friends and Patrick was later instrumental in securing for Clarke-Smith the lead role in his first radio play, *Money with Menaces* in 1937.

One of the venues visited by the company was the Palace Pier Theatre in Brighton and this gave an opportunity for a Hamilton family reunion when Patrick, Lalla, Vane and Bruce – who was teaching at a nearby school, having lost his post in America – met up in the Old Ship Hotel for dinner. Bruce was most struck by his brother's dapper personal appearance, an early foretaste of the fastidious elegance that had replaced the flamboyance of his early youth, and was also impressed by what he considered Patrick's new sense of maturity and self-possession, vividly illustrated when, in the course of acting out an anecdote, his brother's grand gesture succeeded in sweeping a cup off the table, smashing it to fragments. Patrick ignored the incident and finished his story with lordly insouciance.

A couple of nights later, the two brothers met for a more private talk in one of Brighton's most luxurious hotels, the Metropole. (It is in the cocktail bar of the Metropole that Patrick's villainous creation, Ernest Ralph Gorse, succeeds in persuading the hapless Esther Downes into parting with her pathetic fortune in *The West Pier*.) Patrick presented Bruce with a copy of Dostoevsky's *The Brothers Karamazov*, a novel which he had begun with great eagerness but because of his distaste for the saintly figure of Father Zosima he had never succeeded in finishing – an indication of Patrick's increasingly rigid rejection of any form of religion.

Despite his initial ignorance of theatrical matters – asked to compile a 'listerprops' by the stage manager he naively asked what 'listerprops' were and when a 'list of props' was spelled out, admitted that he had no more idea what 'props' were – Patrick gamely struggled on, acquiring a wealth of experience that he would fully exploit in the future. By keeping his eyes and ears open, he learned the rudiments of stagecraft and came to know what would and would not work in the theatre. At the end of his life he told a young novelist and admirer, Angus Hall, who visited him in his last home in Norfolk:

Writing a money-making play is very simple, really. Just give the actors something good to say. I used to be one, myself, once, and

I know that's all they're interested in – good, long, self-indulgent speeches.[2]

Here Patrick was clearly indulging in that well-known ploy of the successful – making it look all too easy. In truth, the skill which he later demonstrated in his stage hits *Rope* and *Gaslight* was learned in the hard school of provincial repertory.

Patrick's acting gifts were, however, distinctly limited. *A Case of Diamonds* called for him to appear in a non-speaking role but later in the tour, when another actor was temporarily indisposed, Patrick took over his part and played the juvenile lead. His own verdict on his performance was that he had not disgraced himself, but it was clear to everyone that he was not destined for a thespian career.

A Case of Diamonds made the round of the provinces twice, but when, after the end of the second tour, it became obvious that the big impresarios were failing to bite, the play closed, the company dispersed and Patrick was unemployed. Once more Vane came to his rescue. He had landed a part in an American melodrama, *The Squaw Man*, known in its British incarnation as *The White Man*, and managed to secure a job for Patrick as ASM, understudy and actor of bit parts. Patrick's role as a comic parson in a Western saloon was hardly a starring one. His only lines came when he was required to lift up his hands in protest at the swearing of the cowboy clientele and say, 'Language!', and then at a card table when he uttered the immortal words: 'Dearly beloved brethren, I will go three.' Bruce caught up with the play at an East End theatre, and recalled that Patrick's delivery of these lines failed to win any laughs from the audience.

The actor-manager staging *The White Man* was a member of the family who ran London's Lyceum Theatre, Andrew Melville, whose chief characteristic was extreme parsimony. Although Patrick's salary was small, he often had to go cap in hand to Melville to request it. On one occasion, the manager intimidated his creditor by melodramatically shouting, '*What* is this face looking at me from the morgue?' Reginald Carters in *Twopence Coloured* was based on Melville:

Mr Reginald Carters was an untidy, thickly built, sunburnt list-
less little man of 45, with a small moustache and very blue and
innocent eyes. He had been actively concerned in this business
for 40 years, and was indeed something of a landmark and a rock
in his profession. His theatre, the Old Strand, which he had
inherited from his father and now shared with his sister, had
reached a legendary status – and from this legend he had made
no attempt to break away. The titles of the plays and revivals
with which he had, for the last 20 years, had almost exclusive
connection, were revealing of this tendency. Such titles as *Just a
Girl*, *Married for Money*, *A Girl's Best Friend*, *A Soul for Sale*, *Three
Lasses from Blackpool*, *Tried and True*, *Merely the Drudge*, *Only a
Working Girl*, or *Waifs from the Workhouse* were representative and
immediately identifiable ... The plots of these melodramas
accorded with these titles and were similarly identifiable –
dealing, as they did, exclusively and traditionally with infamously
monocled scoundrels, pathetically credulous young women, oily-
mannered (but black-hearted) solicitors, young men vaguely on
His Majesty's Service (but with plenty of time for white flannels,
father-defying and yachting caps) ... Mr Carters was, in fact,
more of an artistic excavator of the past than a modern producer.

This litany of Hamiltonian figures tells us more about Patrick
than Melville – a monocled scoundrel and a credulous young
woman being the chief characters of *The West Pier* – and shows
how his theatrical experience was to influence his novels as well
as his plays.

Offsetting his financial meanness, however, Melville was an
emotionally generous man who offered a home in his company
to a whole range of waifs and strays, some of them frankly
unemployable. He was one of the last exponents of old-
fashioned Victorian melodrama and it is clear that Patrick picked
up from him many of the techniques he was later to employ with
such success in *Gaslight*.

At first the company was more or less permanently on the
road, with weekly stays at a variety of venues around the
country, packing up and moving on Sundays. This lifestyle was
quite congenial to Patrick, who had not himself had a settled
home for several years. Finally, however, the players came to
roost on familiar ground and the Grand Theatre in Brighton

became their home for many months. Here their standard reper-
tory consisted of late nineteenth-century classics like Charles
Reade's *It's Never too Late to Mend* and Dumas's *The Count of
Monte Cristo*. Patrick took digs at a house in Brighton's Over
Street, then one of the town's slummiest areas, near the railway
station. It was a far cry from the luxury of First Avenue, Hove
and he was to give the humble address both to Esther Downes in
The West Pier and to Jackie Mortimer in *Twopence Coloured*.[3]

Bruce came to Brighton to see Patrick play in a piece entitled
OHMS in which he had three parts: Ned Farley, an unshaven
seaman with a rich West Country burr; the policeman who
arrests the villain and his moll at the end of the play saying to the
villain, '*You* are under arrest on a charge of murder,' and to the
moll, 'As for *you*, I have a warrant for *your* arrest on a more
serious charge'; and a scarlet-coated guardsman in a bearskin. In
this impersonation Patrick performed the role of feed to the
play's principal comedian and Bruce was surprised to see the
professional way in which his brother tackled the part. Patrick
had a mobile, plastic face which he could twist into all manner of
contortions to comic or grotesque effect. A later photograph of
him grinning in a ghastly, death's head way, in which he bears
an uncanny resemblance to the comedian Arthur Askey, gives
some idea of this ability. In fact he was abnormally self-
conscious about his facial appearance. According to the testimony of friends and judging by early photos, the young Patrick
was not bad looking, in a sombre and serious sort of way, but the
injuries he was to receive in a road accident in 1932 – and in
particular the plastic surgery carried out on his nose, which
changed it into a clown-like blob – transformed his sensitivity
into an obsession, with the most damaging effects.

Patrick's initial self-consciousness was the result of a very
unpleasant incident: another member of the cast, who was viru-
lently homophobic, heard him speak in warm terms of a fellow
actor who happened to be homosexual. He instantly concluded
that Patrick was also homosexual and, in the dressing-room
after the last night of the play's run, without warning delivered
a smashing blow with his fist to Patrick's face. A colleague intervened in Patrick's defence and peace was eventually restored,

but the accusation and the attack rankled, and Patrick wrote to his assailant demanding a retraction and an apology. Only a letter from the man's wife, pleading that her husband was mentally unhinged, persuaded him to drop the matter. On this painful note, Patrick's stage career ended. The competition of the cinema spelt doom for the sort of shows that Melville was putting on and he dissolved the company: this time neither Vane nor Lalla was able to find Patrick another job in showbusiness.

Once more the vexed question of his future employment loomed large. The O.D. was in a more than usually awkward mood after Bruce's crestfallen return from the United States, and it seemed politic for Patrick to placate him by accepting a commercial job in the City of London, without in any way renouncing his by now fixed ambition to become a writer: the job, his sole experience outside the theatre of regular salaried employment, was to be of brief duration. He secured a position as a shorthand typist at the City headquarters of a company called Wales Estates (Demerara), part of the sugar firm Sandbach Parker. Patrick suffered the usual boredom and frustration of many creative people tied to the drudgery of daily office routine, finding, though, some mild relief in ironic observation of his fellow employees, which he turned to good account in his second novel, *Craven House*:

The first person Master Wildman encountered at the office this morning was Mr Casing, who welcomed him, showed him a few things, and said that Mr Creevy would show him the rest. Shortly after, Mr Creevy arrived, said, 'Oh – good morning,' in a scared but friendly way, and quickly retired into an inner room with Mr Casing. Hence, after three minutes' mumbling over the new typist, he emerged breezily, blew his nose, looked at the weather to see what was to be said about it, and said it was beautiful weather.

Mr Creevy then began to 'show' Master Wildman a few things. He was shown the filing cabinet, and the Books, and where the stamps were kept, and where the ready cash was kept, and where the stationery was kept, and where (incidentally) the Tea, and the Sugar, and the Biscuits were kept; and he was shown the press-copying apparatus, and told how to use it, and how not to get the rags too wet, for 'Our Worthy Boss', said Mr Creevy, 'is very particular about our copying.' Lastly he was shown the typewriter and given a shorthand notebook. He sat down looking and feeling uncommonly like [a] little boy ...

'Our Worthy Boss' in real life was one of the partners in the firm, Mr Parker, described as 'a breezy sudden type blowing in and out of the office, with a loud public-school voice which eliminated many of his consonants so that he was often almost incomprehensible'. Patrick portrayed him in the novel as Mr Shillitoe. Number Two in the office was a Mr Prest,[4] an enigmatic figure who alternated weeks of silent gloom with sudden, sunny outbursts of warmth and good humour; an instability which his colleagues and underlings attributed to liver problems. He is Mr Casing in *Craven House*. Patrick's immediate superior was the principal clerk, Mr Bossom, a prim but friendly slave to convention, the Mr Creevy of the novel:

Mr Creevy had a clean-shaven, small face like a healthy red apple's face, pince-nez over small grey eyes, and a diminutive inquisitiveness of nose. And just as Mr Creevy's features were on a rather miniature scale, so were Mr Creevy's general gestures in life accordingly thin and exact – Mr Creevy being a great expert in all the more Lilliputian and dapper activities of life – an experienced and exquisite pencil-sharpener, a highly finished umbrella-roller, a brilliant apple-peeler, a scintillating fountain-pen-filler, a pince-nez polisher of the first order. Any blunders made by other persons in these or similar functions caused Mr Creevy the sharpest spiritual agonies pending actual interference. An orderly and fearfully exact citizen was Mr Creevy, too. A man who pulled all doors he was told to Pull, and Pushed all doors he was told to Push, who went in by the Way In, and came out by the Way Out; who naturally went the longest way round, if it was the shortest way home; who Bewared of the Trains, or the Bull; who Did not Smoke, who Shopped Early, who Knocked and Rang; and DID let you have a line from Ventnor on his holiday ...

This gallery of dull dogs is drawn with gusto, and exhibits

Patrick's skill in pouncing on the minutest traits of speech or behaviour and spotlighting them to demonstrate wider social or psychological implications. In whatever situation he found himself, whether the colourful world of the theatre, or the greyer hues of a City office, his writer's eyes and ears were always hard at work: observing, recording, setting down the usually un-remarked small change of life and reminting it in his own indi-vidual coinage.

While Patrick was working in the City, he and Bruce took shared digs in Delancey Street, off Regent's Park. The rooms were cramped and claustrophobic and sometimes the reality of living in one another's pockets led to violent rows and arguments. They went their separate ways during the working week; Patrick to his offices in Leadenhall Street near the Monument, Bruce to University College in Gower Street, where, financed by an annual £200 allowance from Bernard, he was reading for a history degree. But during the evenings and at weekends, the brothers resumed their long walks, longer talks and twice-weekly visits to a cinema in Kentish Town. Saturday mornings were devoted to the weekly ritual of hot ablutions at public baths in Endell Street (their digs were without a bathroom), followed by a visit to Mudie's lending library in New Oxford Street to change their books. On Saturday afternoons Bruce would frequently make his way to White Hart Lane to see Tottenham Hotspur play while Patrick, who did not share this enthusiasm for soccer, remained in their rooms, reading.

Vane and Lalla had meanwhile holed up in a flat in Castle-town Road, West Kensington, where Vane was hard at work on a new play. When he finished it, Bruce was given the typescript to read. A drama entitled *Outward Bound* (though ostensibly about passengers on a sea voyage, during the course of the action the actors and audience come to realise that they are dead and in limbo), the play was accepted for production at the Everyman Theatre, Hampstead, with Lalla cast in one of the leading roles.

Patrick and Bruce were present on the first night. They feared the worst when they overheard the *Observer* theatre critic St John Ervine announce loudly, 'Well, I certainly hope crossing the Styx isn't going to be such a dull business as this', but the play was warmly received by the audience and the reviews, apart from the *Observer*'s, were positive. The play was an evident hit and in a short time transferred to the Garrick, where it enjoyed a run of nearly six months. A triumphant American production followed and later came films, revivals and foreign and amateur stagings. This success enabled Vane and Lalla to leave their humble quarters and move to a smarter apartment in South Kensington; they also rented a country villa at Cookham, on the Thames in Berkshire, where they entertained Patrick and Bruce to a succession of weekends, tennis and river-parties, concerts and musical evenings. Vane and Lalla were open-handed with their new wealth, especially with Patrick who received gifts, clothes, meals and free theatre passes, and even a week with Lalla in Paris – his first visit to a city and country he was to come to cordially detest.

Patrick was undoubtedly dazzled by the cornucopia of riches so suddenly showered on his sister and brother-in-law. It was his first real experience of the high life and provided a vivid demonstration of the material advantages a theatrical hit could bring. It hardened his own determination to become a writer and prove that whatever Vane could do, he could surely do better. But there was a dark downside to the success story: Lalla confided to her brothers that her husband had begun to drink heavily. At first it was merely a case of him arriving home late at night, tight, explaining lamely that he had bumped into an old friend or comrade from the war. Then, one day Lalla found half a dozen brandy bottles in Vane's wardrobe. Further investigation revealed a huge number of empties, stowed in ingenious hiding places all round their flat.

Soon Vane's drinking began to affect Lalla directly: whether to keep up with her husband's copious consumption of spirits or because the strain of playing the role in *Outward Bound* was beginning to tell, her own normally modest social drinking accelerated dramatically. One night Patrick and Bruce visited her dressing-room a few minutes before she was due to go on stage and noted with concern that she downed two enormous gins, although apparently without adversely affecting her performance. At any rate, whether the drink was a symptom or a cause of the problems brought by their joint success, a rift began to open in the previously happy marriage which was to lead eventually to a break-up with disastrous results for both partners.

Undeterred by this direct evidence of the problems of artistic success, Patrick settled down at the end of 1923 to the serious business of becoming a writer. From now on, nothing was to stand between him and his chosen goal.

8

Monday Morning

THE OPENING OF THE YEAR 1924 saw another diaspora of the Hamilton family: Bernard let the house in Burlington Gardens, Chiswick and took himself off for an extended sojourn in his beloved France; staying first at Grenoble and later in Paris. Away from the disapproving eyes of his family, the O.D. felt free to give his fantasies their full flight. He wrote from Grenoble asking that letters should be addressed to 'Colonel Hamilton', since that was the rank by which he was known to his fellow guests at the pension where he had taken lodgings. (In England he had already promoted himself from his wartime rank of Lieutenant and painted his trunk with the words, 'Captain Hamilton'.)

Patrick clearly had his father's military pretensions in mind when he opened his novel *Mr Stimpson and Mr Gorse* with a prolonged meditation on colonels:

There are, clearly, in England and all over the world, countless Colonels with hard-working, valiant and enchanting characters. Why, then, is the thought or mention of a 'Colonel', purely in the abstract, faintly laughable, or even faintly displeasing, in some people's minds? Why, for instance, did the eminent cartoonist, Low, make Colonel Blimp a Colonel, rather than a Captain, say, or an officer holding a different rank?

Colonel Blimp, of course, though laughable, was to a very

large extent lovable. Many people, however, do not think of
Colonels as being in any way lovable. Such people, on the
contrary, can only picture Colonels either as moustached bullies
bawling at men on parade grounds, or as uttering idiotic,
outmoded and reactionary sentiments from the armchairs of
Clubs.... Retired colonels have, perhaps, brought about the faint
ignominy attached to their retirement upon themselves. So many
of them, for instance, have become seedy, inactive men
committing the grave social error of permitting or encouraging
themselves to be addressed as 'Colonel' long after they have left
the Service in which they were never regular soldiers. Others –
the rather self-consciously 'peppery', 'fiery' or 'choleric' type –
attempt to use these attributes against servants or old ladies in
the boarding-house in which they usually end their days.

Patrick's opinion of Bernard's fantasies can also be deduced from
the fact that he had the book's anti-hero, Ernest Ralph Gorse, use
a fictitious rank and claim a wartime career.

Once installed at the Pension Boos, Bernard began work on a
book about Georges Danton, called *The Giant*, and Nellie, no
doubt heaving a sigh of relief at getting shot of him, began
another phase of her life in rented rooms, alternating between
Hove and Kensington.

As soon as his father was safely across the Channel, Patrick
lost no time in giving up his job in the City and settled down to
write a novel. He buckled down to the task with relish, taking a
room in Talgarth Road, West Kensington. He was supported
financially by his mother, who paid his rent; by Lalla, who gave
gifts of cash; and by Bruce, who was living in digs in nearby
Comeragh Road and who paid for their beer and sandwiches on
regular evening pub crawls, during which he heard accounts of
the novel's progress. Bruce also forked out for their outings to
the cinema and even paid for the odd shirt, tie or pair of socks for
his impecunious younger brother.

Patrick also found time to read, as well as write, and began to
absorb the influence of some powerful personalities who were to
affect his view of the world. He had discovered Freud, whose
Psychopathology of Everyday Life he found oddly naive; Arnold
Bennett, whom the O.D. once cornered in the Reform Club,

accusing him of encouraging Patrick's literary aspirations by example; and the socialist writings of Wells, Shaw and Sinclair Lewis. Neither Patrick nor Bruce yet professed themselves socialists, but they were increasingly aware of social injustice, and haunted Collet's newly opened left-wing bookshop in the Charing Cross Road in search of ammunition to bolster their awakening convictions. The times were ripe for the growth of radical social thought among newly impoverished upper-middle class young men. The trauma of the Great War had been followed by severe inflation and a rise in mass unemployment, largely caused by the demobilisation of millions of servicemen. Lloyd George's promise to create 'a land fit for heroes' began to look increasingly hollow and after Ramsey MacDonald formed a minority Labour government of impeccable respectability, there was a strong sense of betrayal in the socialist movement.

It was not an example to inspire young hearts and minds, and certainly played a part in forming Patrick's lifelong derision for the Labour Party. The residue of a bourgeois contempt for the proletariat was also, no doubt, another factor. It is noteworthy that none of the central characters and few of those on the periphery in his books are genuine proletarians; most are middle class, and those that are not are generally, in a Marxist sense, 'lumpen' – prostitutes, barmen, barmaids and domestic servants.

Bruce was a constant witness to the creative process that was laboriously giving birth to Patrick's first book. The novel was given a variety of working titles including, 'Immaturity', 'Adolescence' and 'Ferment' – which give a good idea of its theme: the tribulations of an adolescent youth as he struggles to come to terms with his education, the outside world, girls and his overpowering desire to become a writer. It is almost entirely autobiographical.

One evening in his room at Talgarth Road, Patrick dictated to Bruce a long chapter of the book describing a tedious Sunday train trip undertaken by a troupe of actors as they journey to a theatre in Sheffield. Bruce commented:

It was quite clear that he was not improvising, but had carefully worked out the scene in the course of a walk earlier in the day, and was dictating from memory. I made one or two suggestions for small alterations, which he willingly accepted. At that time I had neither read nor had read to me any part of the book, and the quality of what I was given that evening was an eye-opener.

By the end of 1924, Patrick's novel was finished to his satisfaction. Once again Lalla and Vane's contacts proved invaluable. They introduced him to their theatrical agent, Dorothea Fassett, who in turn provided an introduction to Audrey Heath, doyenne of the literary agency A.M. Heath & Co., and the manuscript started to make the rounds of publishers as its youthful author waited anxiously. After being rejected by Cape, Chatto and Heinemann, Audrey Heath wrote to Patrick with the news that it had been accepted by Constable. An ecstatic Patrick made the journey to Constable's office in Orange Street to meet the firm's senior editor, Michael Sadleir. It was the beginning of a happy association between author, publisher and editor that was to last through all but the last years of Patrick's creative life.

Sadleir was a man after Patrick's own heart. A novelist himself (his best known book remains his exposé of Victorian prostitution, *Fanny by Gaslight*), he was an immensely learned bibliographer with an unrivalled knowledge of Victorian life and literature and whose two-volume *Nineteenth Century Fiction: a Bibliographical Record* is still a standard authority. He was also the country's leading expert on Trollope. As is shown in *Fanny*, Sadleir himself had a taste for London low-life that matched Patrick's own. The two hit it off instantly at their first meeting, with Sadleir heaping praise on what he considered an enchanting novel. He suggested the title be changed to *Monday Morning* and also tactfully proposed some cuts and alterations to the text which Patrick gladly accepted.[1] A contract was drawn up, giving the nineteen-year-old author an advance of fifty pounds, and the novel proceeded swiftly towards publication.

Monday Morning is above all else a young man's book, with all the advantages and faults that this implies. Fresh as new paint, vivid and charmingly naive, it dashes through a series of snapshot scenes to a misleadingly happy conclusion. Almost all Patrick's own experiences, interests and early obsessions are set down in its pages; his literary enthusiasms, ranging from Keats and Rupert Brooke through to Freud, Wells and Shaw loom large, his hobbies are there too – chess and golf – as well as scenes from his early life.

The plot, such as it is, is slight. The framework around which the book is hung is Patrick's love for Maruja. Beginning with their meeting at the White House Hotel (renamed the Fauconberg in the novel), the story unflinchingly regales the reader with all the awkward joys and agonies of adolescent love – the fumbled first kiss, the mingled hopes and fears over who is to partner whom on the dance floor – with everything observed as if through a kaleidoscope:

> Diane was in black satin evening dress, with a thick woolly coat over it. The coat was a green sort of dark-blue colour . . . Anthony knelt and put out the noisy gas fire. The hollow shouting abruptly stopped, and the red asbestos faded to chilly grey . . . It was a yellow, drizzling day . . . the colours were really beautiful . . . all about was adorable pink and heavenly light blue. There was a satin mauve dress. One girl danced in pure white. The men were in gay, black evening dress. Some old women with elaborate grey hair and heavily beaded frocks sat in the room and watched.

Drink is not a major theme in the book, but it appears in enough scenes to suggest that alcohol was already playing a part in Patrick's life. There is, for example, an early introduction to what became his standard tipple, whisky:

> 'I'll go and have a drink,' he said. He went into the saloon of the nearest public house. It was ill-lit by daylight. There was the soft murmur of men's voices, and the noise of levers jerking, the ring and the clatter of the till. He ordered a double whisky, and took it without the offered water. The first sip was very bitter – then fine warmth inside him. The rest of the sips were bitter and nasty.

Patrick was clearly aware of the dangers of alcoholic abuse:

> One night Anthony was taken out by the Swede and given some whisky, and this intoxicated the young man – not seriously, but

his eyes became a trifle steadier than they should have been. Diane saw him in this condition. Next morning Diane said to him, timidly, 'You mustn't do that again.'

'No, I know I mustn't. And if you say so I won't.'

'I do say so.'

'Well, I'll never go near whisky again.'

Alas for good intentions. Whether, had he married the stern-willed Maruja, Patrick would have been steered clear of the bottle, must remain an open question.

In the novel Diane departs for her boarding school and a disconsolate Anthony is left to find a remedy for his sorrows in work. He gets down to writing a novel, but no sooner is it begun than he is beguiled into the fascinating world of the theatre: a fellow guest, Brayne (a portrait of Vane) befriends him and Anthony accepts an offer to join Brayne's company touring with *The Coil*. The play's peregrinations around England – Sheffield, Manchester, Liverpool, Torquay, Cheltenham, Brighton – mirror the actual tours of *A Case of Diamonds* and there are strikingly drawn scenes of life in the theatre, on the road and in the squalid rooms of actors' digs. The realism of these episodes contrasts with passages of fantasy in which Anthony imagines Diane seeing his fanciful theatrical triumphs. Patrick did not, however, spare himself in telling of his early humiliations and discomfiture as he found his feet among his fellow actors.

The tour ended, Anthony returns to London and buys an expensive pendant for Diane, whose letters from school have become increasingly cool. She returns to the Fauconberg Hotel, is presented with the pendant, but informs Anthony that she is about to depart to France for a holiday with her mother and refuses his desperate proposal of marriage. Devastated, Anthony burns her letters and photograph and flees to Brighton to compose an elegy for his doomed love affair. He wraps the poem round a stone and casts it into the sea from a beach beneath the West Pier, but the sea, mockingly, throws it back:

The sea, however, rejected the timid offer, and with an air of quick finality, snatched the poem away from the stone, and sent it flying up to a far bank of the beach ... Anthony ... began to walk homeward. 'And now I'm never going to think about her again,' he said.

But sure enough, this pathetic act is false in every respect: Anthony has kept a copy of the poem and when he returns from a second theatrical tour Diane is back at the Fauconberg.

The book builds up to its contrived happy ending: in what is perhaps an approximation of what really happened between Patrick and Maruja, Diane tells Anthony that she is going to get married to someone else and Anthony, lying through his teeth, ripostes, 'Diane, this is weird. So am I.' But fiction takes over when it is revealed that both engagements are a fantasy and Patrick has the reunited lovers walking off together into the sunset:

> They went on aimlessly through the clear, resounding Squares, and Diane's cold, funny hand was in Anthony's greatcoat pocket.

Monday Morning describes two scenes that bode ill for Patrick's future behaviour, and which are presumably drawn from his personal experience. In the first, disillusioned with Diane, Anthony picks up a prostitute in Piccadilly:

> They stopped a passing taxi. 'Where ARE we going? asked Anthony. She gave an address to the taxi man.
>
> They crossed Piccadilly with many stoppages. Anthony looked out of the window.
>
> Suddenly he turned his face to her and looked very shocked indeed. 'Good lord!' he said. 'I've just remembered a terribly urgent appointment. I say. I must go. Look here, will you pay this man? I'll get out here. I really must go ...' Anthony stumbled out into the street.

Although Anthony makes his excuses and leaves, it can safely be assumed that his creator's own experience of London's night life was by now more intimate. We do not know when or in what circumstances Patrick lost his virginity, but this passage would suggest that his tormented affair with the prostitute Lily

Connolly in the late 1920s was not his first brush with street-walkers. Given the Victorian/Edwardian divisions between 'nice' girls to whom young men paid court and eventually married, and 'naughty' ladies whom they slept with and then jettisoned, divisions that were still operative in the 1920s, we can speculate that Patrick, like thousands of other young men of his class, lost his virginity to one of the professional women who thronged the streets of the West End until the 1957 Wolfenden Report drove London prostitution underground. Respectable girls like Maruja were the object of an almost courtly love ethic, while those unfortunates like Lily Connolly who had to live off the streets were the physical reality, receptacles for male lust. Patrick made the mistake, when pursuing Lily, of confusing the two.

The second scene occurs in the final paragraphs of the novel when the perils of drink are again displayed:

> Once they passed two drunk men. 'Let us weigh the matter out,' said one drunk man to the other. 'You're a good fellow, but let us weigh the matter out.'
>
> Diane and Anthony slipped around a corner. 'You wait till we're married, Diane, I'll come back miles worse than that . . .'

Monday Morning was published in the autumn of 1925, with a dedication to Bruce. The reviews were almost universally kind, for, as Bruce remarked, however slight and flawed, the book is hard to dislike, and skates along with such verve that its defects are not immediately apparent. The first edition sold out and was reprinted, more than paying for the advance. There was also an American edition, published by Houghton Mifflin. All told, Patrick could feel well pleased with his achievement. He had, at the age of nineteen, written and published a novel which had been widely and favourably reviewed and was selling well. He had met a sympathetic editor who was busily introducing him to the great and good of literary London. Above all, perhaps, he had finally proved to his father that his desire to be a writer was no mere chimera. There is no disguising the firm determination of a letter, written to the O.D. on 28 August 1924, in which Patrick rejected a final bid by Bernard to get him a 'proper job' and steer him away from his chosen destiny:

My dear Father,

Many thanks for your letters which I have read carefully over many times. I very much appreciate your kindness and care for me, but I must ask you, on no account to attempt to get a job for me, as I would not take it, however good it might prove. I have no doubt this sounds headstrong and absurd, but you will remember that last August I sent you a letter explaining definitely that, from then onwards, I must follow my own career in my own way, without hindrance or help, standing or falling by myself. That letter is still perfectly valid. I've a carbon copy of it by me, and will forward it if necessary.

You can know at least that I am a very, very hard worker now, and that in itself is a justification to me for my present course, even if I had any doubts of the ultimate wisdom of it, which I have not. Again thanking you for all your kindness and consideration,

I'm your most affectionate son,
Patrick.

Exhausted by his sustained bout of writing and the excitement of publication, and somewhat undernourished through poverty and irregular meals, Patrick fell victim to a bout of dysentery. At once Nellie seized the opportunity to swoop and reclaim him into her own tender care. She took rooms for herself and Patrick as paying guests in a house in Kew and soon they were joined by Bruce, nearing the end of his degree course at University College. Bernard remained in France where he had transferred himself to Paris in order to have access to source books necessary for the completion of *The Giant* (and also, no doubt, to be close to more traditional aspects of *la vie Parisienne*).

As soon as Patrick had recovered from his illness, he began work on another novel. Having run through most of his meagre autobiographical material in *Monday Morning* he cast about for a fresh theme, and found it, in his new domestic surroundings.

9

Craven House

THE RAW MATERIAL FOR WHAT WAS to be Patrick's second novel, *Craven House*, was found among fellow lodgers at the Kew guest-house. No doubt it was something of a regression in Patrick's social and emotional – and probably sexual – life to be living again under Mummie's protective wing, but he saw it as a period of rest and recuperation after the emotional trauma of his unconsummated affair with Maruja and the strain of writing *Monday Morning*.

The Hamilton's hosts at Kew were a Mr and Mrs Doughty. Mr Doughty was a partner in a firm of City wine importers and his wife managed the guest-house. The other inhabitants included an elderly man, who was the 'senior boarder' and with whom Patrick developed an instant relationship of mutual detestation. The man was tyrannically disposed, sneering, snobbish and bullying and he almost certainly earned immortality as the detestable Mr Thwaites in Patrick's later novel, *The Slaves of Solitude*. Their crotchety relationship was summed up by an exchange during a card game when the senior boarder, making a punning dig at Patrick's youth remarked, 'Let me see; we are seven, aren't we?' to which Patrick replied smoothly, 'And we are seventy.'

There was also a pair of American ladies from Wilkes-Barre, Pennsylvania,[1] one of whom took a shine to Patrick. Flattered, he went some way to responding to her advances and this encouraged

the woman to more open and embarrassing displays of affection, such as passing little notes to him on which she had
scribbled such nauseatingly cryptic Cupid's messages as 'Isle of
View' (= 'I Love You'). There ensued some fairly mild kissing
and petting between the pair, but a full-blown affair did not
develop, partly because of Patrick's shy reluctance, and partly
because they could not shake off the woman's companion, who
invariably accompanied them on their outings to Kew Gardens
or the funfair near Kew Bridge. Further possible developments
were halted by the women's departure to continue their Grand
Tour of Europe.

The Hamilton contingent in the household was now congeni-
ally increased by the arrival of Nellie's elder sister, Bessy Bridger.
Patrick and Bruce also profited by the regular hours and the good
food provided by their hostess and her two servants and Mr
Doughty installed a badminton set and a billiard table for their
further entertainment. In these comfortable conditions, Patrick
was doing little actual writing, but was instead lying fallow,
soaking up impressions which he would later put to use. This
peaceful idyll was disturbed by a telegram from Paris at Easter: it
reported that Bernard had suffered a stroke and ended ominously, 'Doctor advises relatives near'.

Bruce and Lalla crossed the Channel at once, their emotions
somewhat jumbled. On the one hand, sentimental affections
welled to the surface; on the other, there was the prospect of
imminent relief from a burden that had blighted and crushed
their lives. However when they reached Bernard's bedside at a
pension in the Rue Clement Marot they found his condition was
not so serious as they had feared, or hoped. Their first sight of
the O.D. was of him sitting up with a necklace of repulsive-
looking black, blood-bloated leeches fixed to his throat and
shoulders. He was able to talk to them – which he did, as usual,
at great length – and the French doctor who was treating him
opined that if he stopped drinking there was no reason why he
should not live out his full span. After a few days, Lalla left, but
Bruce stayed on for a further fortnight, during which the O.D.'s
condition continued to improve. Bruce was befriended by a
fellow guest at the pension, an English journalist named

Lambert, who confided that a bout of heavy boozing had indeed brought on the stroke. When the two weeks were up, Patrick replaced Bruce as nurse. He too took up with Lambert, who accompanied him on some memorable Parisian binges. Eventually Bernard was well enough for Patrick to escort him back to England. The O.D. took up residence at a private hotel in Bayswater where his children continued to pay him periodic visits.

Another crisis marked the close of the year: on Christmas Eve a policeman came to the house at Kew to tell the family the tragic news that Tom Hockley, nephew of Nellie and Bessy, had shot himself under Brighton's West Pier and was in hospital with no hope of recovery. The news came as a total shock, for though the Hamiltons had only occasionally met Tom, he had seemed a pleasant, untroubled man. To Patrick fell the grim task of representing the family at the funeral in Hove. He told Bruce on his return that what had affected him most painfully was the unexpectedly dark depths of the grave into which the coffin was lowered.[2] This incident irrevocably prejudiced Patrick in favour of cremation rather than burial after his own death, though late in life he told an interviewer, 'Once I've gone they can take my body and give it to the dustmen for all I care.'[3]

Nellie and Bessy were severely affected by the tragedy; they seemed to take a positive delight in repeatedly raking over its details, or in recalling some touching anecdote from the dead man's childhood which would dissolve them into simultaneous deluges of tears. This public mourning continued for weeks and the atmosphere in the house became bleakly depressing. To escape it, the brothers, and their cousin Frank Bridger, who had joined his mother at Kew, took to the bottle in the form of frequent outings to the Greyhound pub in Richmond, where they would consume huge tenpenny glasses of port. The trio found the contrast between the mournful atmosphere hanging over the guest-house and their riotous evenings at the pub almost too comic to contemplate.

Another frequent drinking companion was the newsman Lambert, who had returned from Paris and continued to see Patrick. A night at their favourite watering hole having ended in the usual way, Patrick and Lambert staggered out into the dark in maudlin mood. They passed an office of an organisation named the Girls' Friendly Society and when their importunate rings were angrily answered, insisted on seeing some girls because, as they so logically justified their request, 'We want to be friendly'. The door having been slammed in their faces, they moved on to a laundry where Patrick demanded to be washed.

By the middle of 1926, the time was approaching for another domestic upheaval in the nomadic family life of the Hamiltons. The tenants who had taken their home in Burlington Gardens, Chiswick, moved out and the family – minus Bernard and Lalla – reoccupied it. Bernard remained happily ensconced in Bayswater, and seemed disinclined to uproot himself to join his family. However he refused to hand over the house keys without a typically theatrical row with Patrick, who, in a finely calculated outburst of temper, bamboozled the O.D. into thinking that he was doing him a great favour by kindly consenting to live there.

Once installed, Patrick set to work, uninterrupted by those fellow guest-house lodgers who, however, had given him the material for the book he now began to write. Bruce, too, was hard at work, preparing for his finals, but as usual Patrick was the centre of his mother's and brother's attention. Bruce and Nellie would wait impatiently before lunch for Patrick to descend from his room and read them the passage he had been working on that morning. His readings were heard in rapt silence, only interrupted by Nellie's exclamations of 'Beautiful!', 'Exquisite!' or 'Perfect!' and her over-emotional outbursts of laughter and tears.

By the end of the summer, Patrick had contemplated the manuscript of *Craven House*. The novel marked a significant stride forward in his own powers as a writer; if *Monday Morning* had been too obviously autobiographical, by his second book Patrick had more subtly assimilated his material and assumed a more detached and ironic standpoint. In one important sense it is a less conventional novel than *Monday Morning*; there is, in the first half, no continuous narrative movement. Somewhat in the manner of Katherine Mansfield's volume of stories, *In a German Pension*, the book presents a series of portraits of the denizens of Craven House, a guest boarding-house in the western suburbs of London. We learn of their personal foibles, their eccentricities, their tawdry secrets, their petty quarrels and reconciliations. The characters are a distillation of Patrick's early experience of guest-house life in Hove and London and for the first time we get a glimpse of the attitudes and tone that were to stamp all his mature fiction. It is not surprising, therefore, that *Craven House* is often thought to be his first novel, with *Monday Morning* either forgotten entirely, or dismissed as a mere sketch of what was to come.

There is a Dickensian warmth and pathos in the book, as well as a pervasive sense of cosiness. Craven House appears at the novel's outset to be a sort of sheltered accommodation, whose inhabitants are safely insulated against the buffets of the outside world. It is an island, hardly changed since the complacent certainties of the Victorian era. The characters, too, show signs of Dickensian caricature. The pompous Mr Spicer, who leaves the fastness of the guest-house each morning to travel to his tea-importing business in the City is a creation similar to Mr Skimpole in *Bleak House*. It is also a world of 'upstairs, down-stairs', with the domestic servants even more crudely caricatured, from their very names ('Audrey Custard') to their Cockneyfied, stereotyped modes of speech. This last – as it does in Dickens' case – reflects the author's own middle-class origins, and his inability to get inside and accurately reflect real working-class life. Another, and possibly less forgivable, Dickensian trait in the book is its lush sentimentality. Patrick himself was well aware of this fault and endeavoured to correct some grosser examples when he revised the novel for its reissue in 1943, in the very different circumstances of an England caught in the toils of another and greater war. Without re-writing the whole book, however, he could do little about the contrived happy ending in which, as in *Monday Morning*, he has two lovers optimistically walking off into the sunset. This cuts against the whole grain of the book and we must assume that here Patrick bowed to more traditional norms and conventions, and tacked on a conclusion that went against his own better judgement. Thankfully, though, these flaws do not invalidate the novel as a whole.

Craven House opens in 1911, three years before the Great War, with the arrival of its central protagonist, the eight-year-old Master Wildman, and his father, the Major, at the eponymous guest-house. We are introduced to the curious gallery of characters who are its residents and who play out their petty lives within its brooding walls. There is the proprietress, Miss Hatt, forced by exigency to take in lodgers – 'Sort of paying *guests,* you know.' There are her senior boarders, Mr and Mrs Spicer, with whom she is on ostensibly friendly terms and with whom she takes her holidays. There is the villainous and tyrannical Mrs Nixon, with a dubious past, who stunts the life of her daughter, Elsie, a child of the same age as Master Wildman. Downstairs, their presence felt through the muffled banging of oven doors and the 'smashing' of the gong summoning guests to meals, are the two servants Audrey ('Ord') and the cook, Edith ('Eed').

For two years nothing much happens to disrupt the ordered calm of the house. We learn all there is to know about its inhabitants and their ways; the middle-class rules and rituals that govern their ossified lives, the unchanging rhythms of little, middle-England.

We follow Master Wildman through passages that are clearly chapters of Patrick's own upbringing – his arrival at his new school, where he is first bullied, then finally accepted; his enthusiasm for cricket, and less orthodox games of derring-do; his regaling of Elsie with improbable bedtime stories; his endurance of the endless tedium of the English Sunday. Time passes slowly and only gradually do the characters' hidden aspects come to light. For example, we discover that Mr Spicer is not all he seems. The outwardly respectable tea importer is addicted to long 'tramps', which are in fact a mixture of pub-crawls and ogling of the prostitutes frequenting Hyde Park:

Mr Spicer soon began to peer to the extent of downright Nosiness: that his peering was directed towards the numerous young ladies seated, with crossed legs, upon the chairs lining these avenues: that the difficulties arising from an attempt to combine (1) the intense function of peering sideways, with (2) the perfectly nonchalant function of strolling forwards, reduced Mr Spicer's stride to something uncommonly resembling the crab's.

The narrative of the novel marks time for the first hundred pages, content to establish its setting and characters, until Book II 'The Great War falls on Craven House' when, with the outbreak of war, all is set for change. Master Wildman and Elsie are growing up and away from their distracted elders. The boy's emancipation is assisted by his father's demise:

> The very last words that passed between Master Wildman and his father were spoken one evening in the entrance ... into Southam Green Station, as Master Wildman left for his new school.
>
> It was a swift and thunderous moment ... The bare boards cracked, thundered under the boots of the other itinerants; from the booking-office there came the deadened and spasmodic jerking of the ticket machine, and the slap and clink of change; from the High Road, the bawling of the news-sellers; and from below, the disconcerting rumble of a possibly negotiable train. The Major said: 'Well, my boy, I'll be getting along then.' 'Right you are then, daddy,' said Master Wildman. 'Good-bye.' And the next moment his father had gone away. The next time Master Wildman saw his father, his father was a stiff, vividly conscious and regular-breathing entity in a bed, braced and tense for a death which seemed to have taken the precaution of binding him all over first. Miss Hatt said he had had a stroke ...

Master Wildman is given the traditional English panacea to soothe away all fears:

> Soon afterwards a candle-lit Miss Hatt entered, looking rather ridiculous (he thought) in her dressing-gown, and she placed a candle-lit, steaming cup of tea on his table. She said, 'Drink this, dear boy.'

This is perhaps the best passage in the whole book. The young Patrick succeeds in conveying in a few lines the traditional failure of the English middle classes to obey Forster's command, 'only connect'. With economy and verve he communicates to the reader the fatal flaw at the heart of so many relationships: a need for love, but an inability to express it. There is also a sense of the absurdity, the banality of the everyday when set against the final fact of death – the uncaring, hurrying crowd of travellers coming between father and son; the bustling nurse going about her deathwatch; above all the arrival of the cup of tea – the pathetically English attempt to outface the grim reaper. But for all Dickens' influence on the book, Patrick avoids any hint of pathos: the death has all the more impact for being understated and the Major is thankfully no Little Nell.

For a while after the war, life at Craven House resumes the even tenor of its pre-war ways. The action parallels Patrick's own life in the immediate post-war period: under Mr Spicer's encouragement Master Wildman learns shorthand and has a brief experience of life as a clerk in a City office. He falls in love with a more worldly friend of Elsie, Miss Cotterell, who bobs her hair and has a lover in distant Allahabad. He decides to become a writer, and duly begins work on a play. But beneath the tranquil surface, events are stirring below stairs: Audrey Custard is about to Answer Back.

> 'And if I have any more of your laziness and impertinent airs, Audrey,' Miss Hatt is crying, 'you'll be finding yourself in Queer Street! You'll kindly come straight back TO me when I give you a call in future.'
>
> And then it is that Audrey Answers Back.
>
> 'All right,' says Audrey. 'All right. I can't be in two places at once, you know.' And there is an interval of sickening silence.
>
> 'What did you say, Audrey?' asks Miss Hatt.
>
> But no reply is given from below.
>
> 'WHAT did you say, Audrey?' repeats Miss Hatt, raising her voice. 'Will you kindly tell me what you said?'
>
> 'All right,' says Audrey. 'Keep your hair on. Keep your hair on.'
>
> 'WHAT did you say?' shrieks Miss Hatt.
>
> 'I said keep your hair on, ma'am,' returns Audrey, and without another word she shuts the kitchen door.
>
> For one moment it seems that Miss Hatt will not recover. But she gets the better of herself, stays erect for a moment, and then swings into the drawing room with the white, tense face of a lady likely to drop any moment; and there is Mrs Hoare, already standing, under the crisis, with her knitting in her hands.
>
> 'Did you hear that?' asks Miss Hatt.
>
> 'Yes,' whispers Mrs Hoare. 'I heard it.'
>
> 'She Answered Back,' says Miss Hatt.

Audrey's insubordination is the signal for the subversion of the whole social order on which the world of Craven House, seemingly so secure, is grounded. From now on events unravel rapidly towards the final débâcle. Encouraged by Master Wildman, Elsie, previously subservient to the whims of her appalling mother, Mrs Nixon, finally revolts and defies her mother's attempts to beat her.

Master Wildman, too, has his triumph; his play is accepted by a West End theatrical impresario for a production in the provinces. But while youth is victorious, for age, only disaster beckons; Mrs Spicer discovers a letter in her husband's pocket from a prostitute which leaves the true nature of her husband's London 'tramps' in little doubt. Exposure and humiliation for the lecherous Mr Spicer gratifyingly follow. The threads which have bound Craven House together finally come apart at a dinner in the presence of a Russian guest, in a scene which blends high tragedy with low farce. Another visitor to the table is Mrs Nixon's thuggish Scots son, Jock, brought down to teach his half-sister Elsie a lesson, and here, for the first time in his fiction, Patrick makes an explicitly political connection between public fascism and private bad behaviour. Jock, egged on by Mr Spicer, retails in lovingly sadistic detail how he and his friends beat up, and then force fed with castor oil, a local socialist in his native land.

Craven House displays in embryo the concerns that were to become the focus of Patrick's art and attention. In his contemptuous depiction of the reactionary, rentier class of post-war English capitalism he is already identifying his chosen enemy and although Hamilton was not yet a declared socialist, let alone a Marxist, *Craven House* has strong anti-fascist elements; interestingly the reviewers and his growing public did not pick up on these.

Brother Bruce led the chorus of critical praise: Patrick, he wrote, now fully conscious of his powers, poured out the riches of his mind with profusion. 'In none of his later and greater novels is the sheer joy of creation so evident.' The professional critics, when the book appeared in 1926, were equally approving.

10

Twopence Coloured

WITH THE PUBLICATION OF *CRAVEN HOUSE* (complete with a dedication 'To My Dear Mother') Patrick began to become something of a name in literary London. The novel had attracted more reviews than *Monday Morning* and correspondingly higher sales and Michael Sadleir, sure now that he had a commercial writer on his hands, was anxious to show off his young protégé. The older man introduced Patrick into London literary society, where he met Arnold Bennett and W.W. Jacobs, author of the classic horror story 'The Monkey's Paw'. Sadleir proposed Patrick for membership of his first club – the Omar Khayyám Dining Society, whose annual banquets he continued to attend for years. Patrick's publisher also offered to put him up for membership of the Garrick; but Patrick preferred to plump for the similar ambience of the Savile Club in New Bond Street.

Sadleir obviously had good business reasons for promoting his discovery, but he also had more personal grounds for seeking out Patrick's company. The two men got on famously together, with their taste for London low-life and a similar fondness for drinking. Their favourite London watering-hole was Gordon's Wine Bar, outside the Embankment tube station, equally convenient for Sadleir's office at Constable, and for pouring Patrick into a home-bound District Line train. After suffering the adverse effects of port too often, Patrick had now transferred his affections to sherry, and many glasses were quaffed in the dim basement bar at regular evening binges in his publisher's congenial company.

Patrick was not the only member of the Hamilton family to be enjoying a season of success: Bruce had graduated from University College with a good second in history, an event celebrated with Patrick and Charles Mackehenie by a memorable pub crawl through the West End, and now even the Old Devil came into his own again, with an Indian summer of literary activity: *The Giant* was accepted by Hutchinson. Characteristically convinced that he had penned a masterpiece, he wrote to the publisher's publicity department: 'As a puff preliminary you may say that this is the greatest novel ever published – which indeed it is.' Sadly, when the book appeared, reviews were few and unfavourable. Nothing daunted, the irrepressible O.D. produced two further historical novels: *The Master of Mirth* (about Rabelais) and *His Queen* (a romance about Columbus and Queen Isabella). To give his books an additional boost, Bernard was in the habit of sending complimentary copies to eminent figures. Patrick recalled:

... he wrote a book about Danton called *The Giant* and sent a copy, with a remarkably laudatory letter, to Mussolini, who did not reply. He wrote another book about Columbus called *His Queen*, and sent a copy to the King of Spain, who also did not reply, but one of whose employees sent a letter saying that it was 'beneath the dignity' of his master to accept presents from strangers. Always, when writing letters of some moment there appeared, after his signature, the inscription: 'M.A. Trin.Coll.Cam. Barrister-at-Law, R.H.A. (T) retd. Author of *The Light?*, *Coronation*, *A Kiss for a Kingdom*, *The Giant*, *His Queen*, *The Master of Mirth*, etc.[1]

Bernard's last book, *One World at a Time*, was a counter-blast against his old friend Conan Doyle's spiritualist enthusiasms. Bruce commented:

Bernard had always laid claim to spiritual experiences of a rather special nature. If he had held the book to his account of these, his anti-spiritualist arguments, and his fragments of auto-biography, it might, to those able to take his staccato parade-ground style, have been interesting reading. But unhappily, his besetting tendency to give the law on anything and everything proved too strong for him. Almost every known thinker or author or man of action of the time was awarded either good marks or bad – mostly bad. Doyle of course principally got it in the neck; so did Shaw, Wells and most of his sons' favourite writers. The only living person whom he seemed to admire without reservation, indeed becoming almost lyrical about him, was Mussolini, whom he had seen in Rome orating from the Palazzo Venezia.

Patrick's distaste for the attitudes represented by his father hardened. He was hugely embarrassed when Bernard dedicated *One World at a Time* with its panegyric of Mussolini's fascism, to himself and Bruce, but the O.D. was, as was to be expected, quite oblivious to this. Pleased to be back in print he embarked on his travels once more, reaching New Zealand, where he was invited to make a broadcast in which he disparagingly surveyed the state of English fiction, with the exception, of course, of his own works.

The Chiswick household was now increased by the addition of Lalla, whose drink-sodden marriage had collapsed amidst considerable bitterness. She came home to find a contented Patrick and Bruce ticking over in their usual routine of cinema trips and, particularly, pub-crawls. Patrick had rather laughably attempted to regulate his drinking by the invention of a device he christened the Hamilton Drop. Starting off with a double scotch, he would drink about a third of the measure before topping up the glass with water or soda, repeating the process progressively until the whisky had been diluted to almost nothing. By this method a drink could be stretched to last an hour or more, and a mere five or six would be consumed in the course of a long evening. When Bruce was invited to try out the Hamilton Drop he discovered that in practice, the dilutions and toppings-up with real whisky followed each other in such close succession that almost as much scotch was drunk as before. Patrick was also neglecting himself when it came to eating; subsisting chiefly on the stale sandwiches and sausage rolls found under glass on pub bars at the end of an evening. A real meal would, he felt, have interfered with the serious business of drinking and getting drunk.

Early in 1927, Bruce landed a job as a history teacher at a college in Barbados on a three-year contract. On his final night in London before sailing to the West Indies, he met Patrick for a forlorn farewell drink at The Coal Hole in the Strand. A melancholy Patrick presented his brother with a copy of Stevenson's *Prince Otto* together with a tender inscription and a drawing of a pierced heart dripping blood. Then the two brothers hailed a taxi to carry them to the docks, where Bruce boarded a liner taking him to his new life. They were not to meet again for three years.

Patrick was at first, as he had promised his brother, a frequent and regular correspondent. His aim was to keep up Bruce's morale in a strange new environment by giving as upbeat an account of his life as he could and initially there was much to be upbeat about. These letters to Bruce, the majority of which have been lovingly preserved, give us a week-by-week, sometimes almost a day-by-day, account of Patrick's activities. As the year 1927 went by, however, he became embroiled in the affair with Lily Connolly that was to inspire his trilogy *Twenty Thousand Streets Under the Sky* – but of this there is barely a hint in his correspondence. His extramural pursuits caused him to write infrequently, however, and letters were often replaced by brief telegrams assuring his brother that he was still alive and well and living in London, albeit harassed.

In the first letters, written at the end of January, he was still flushed with the success of *Craven House* and working steadily on the book that was to become *Twopence Coloured*:

> I've put off my work till this afternoon, and the time is twenty to one by my alarm clock. This morning is quite easily the coldest we've had yet this winter, and when I woke up there was a thick frost, such as I have seldom seen, covering the trees and the slates. This is now melting under a bright yellow sun in an immaculately cloudless sky. As I passed Turnham Green the grass was glisteningly wet, and the drops were like diamonds – but rather shoddy yellow diamonds against a sickly green – depressing.

It was jolly good of Michael to ask me to this Trollope dinner like that wasn't it? I don't see how he could give me a higher token of his friendship.

Mummie's just come up – rather repentant after the rows with Lalla – and I am to have fried eggs and bacon for lunch, which makes life a little brighter.

... What was *Prince Otto* like? Life is going on just as usual here. We come down every morning to the usual breakfast, and meet again at every lunch, and make jokes and slyly look up to see how Annie's [the maid] taking them – that pastily spectacled and non-committal creature in brown giving nothing away as usual. And Mummie's listening in the dark when you come back from your movie, and Lalla looks as bleared as ever in her old silk kimono, and irons unceasingly. There's not much hope in life.

In his next letter a week later Patrick proudly expanded on the honour of attending a dinner to mark the publication of Michael Sadleir's new biography of Trollope:

You would appreciate it more if you knew the big noise they're making here over Trollope. There was the front-page article in the *Times Lit. Supp.* on the day of publication and a vast notice in the *Outlook* on the same day, and in the *Observer* on the Sunday directly after there was a colossal article, by Garvin, if you please, where I always thought the leader was put. As much row, in fact, as has ever been made over Wells and Shaw – if not more, and that's a fact. And so you can imagine I felt rather proud at being at the dinner, and having *my* work read after it.'

On 3 February, Patrick wrote in verse:

My dearest Bruce – the time is eight o'clock.
I'm sitting up in bed and drinking Bock.
At least, not Bock, but ordinary beer,
Which is the only stuff they give you here.
At least, not beer, but Hammerton's brown Stout –
Useful for milder kinds of drinking bout.

Despite this alcoholic opening, Patrick claimed to be off the booze generally and behaving 'like a self-controlled gentleman from beginning to end', with only one fall from grace:

> an evening with Carlitos [Mackehenie] which began at Earls Court and progressed via a pub crawl through the streets of London, eventually ending at the Rising Sun, Chelsea ... disgraceful episode, as usual. However that is my only one fall, and I haven't touched a thing before or since.

Life *chez* Mummie continued in an atmosphere of tragi-comic crisis:

> Lalla came back from Paris last night and this morning the ceiling fell in her room. The combination of these circumstances was trying. I expect Mummie's told you about it.

Patrick proudly reported on his continuing lionisation in literary London. His letters of this time also contain long philosophical excursions which betray the effect of his current reading, Nietzsche's *Thus Spake Zarathustra*, a book which was to have a great influence on Patrick over the next few years, particularly in the writing of *Rope*, his first stage play.

Patrick was undoubtedly attracted by a simplified conception of the philosopher's idea of the 'Superman'; the gifted exception to the common run of humanity, destined, by force of will, to stamp his mark upon the world. Nietzsche foresaw a future evolutionary stage for man when he would, by trial and error, have learned to master his own destiny. But eager and susceptible young men like Patrick chose to regard the command, 'I sing the Superman; man is something to be surpassed,' as an injunction to individuals to defy given law and custom and create their own values, separate from and superior to the herd morality that governed the common man. Since Nietzsche had declared that the new morality would be 'Beyond good and evil' this could encompass acts, for example, a motiveless murder, inexplicable to those unenlightened ones still ruled by the old order. Patrick was fond of quoting Nietzsche's aphorism, 'Beware lest thou spittest against the wind of the Superman.' His brother thought that in some shamefaced corner of his mind Patrick cherished a dream of having a shot at being a superman himself, and recorded that he more than once maintained the argument that a man of genius could practically choose whether to become a Shakespeare, a Newton, a Napoleon or a Jesus. Certainly the belief in a potential never fully realised was to be one of the shadows haunting Patrick's later life.

In his first 'Nietzschean' letter to Bruce, Patrick exhorted his brother:

> *Now* must I take advantage of a flying start. *This* is the moment. I must *not* rest on my laurels, and consider myself justified in having a rest for a little, so as to recuperate for another attack in the near future. *Now Now Now*!

Patrick's hectoring of Bruce could take on a pompous and didactic tone:

> All life (for men of God like you and I) has got to be labour, so let this set the tone, and inculcate the habit. Also with the classes – use them to sharpen your personality with. Experiment with them, so that you may be fitter for the psychological handling of your fellow men afterwards. And fear nothing – not even making an ass of yourself and being scorned and hated.

Patrick was keen to emphasise that he was practising what he preached:

> It may be some consolation to you to know that I'm working very hard now – just like the old *Craven House* days. You know – rise half past six – bed half past nine with no reading but a little gazing at a gas fire. Also no smoking except while working, and no drinking except with Charles, when the limit is three. In fact I'm getting down to it, because I know that the difference between the failure or half-failure and the successes in this life is the difference between mild self-control and something partially fanatical.

Patrick's lecturing of his brother makes it appear that he, not

Bruce, is the schoolmaster: hypocritically he instructed him not to drink, 'but I know that is not one of your natural vices, as it is with me', to gather material for a novel: 'God! What an epic of schoolmastering you'll turn out one day!' and not to have nostalgic regrets for the joys of Chiswick: 'If you knew how we longed for sunlight and a relief from cold and rain you wouldn't envy us ... and the cars taking revolting females to Twickenham – all, all go on with their dreadful immutability, like obsessions in a sick madman's brain.'

Patrick sent his brother 'A parody of the work of the cele-brated mad philosopher – Neitsche [sic]'(whose name he, inci-dentally, never learned to spell). This pastiche of Nietzsche's Biblical style is entitled 'Upon the Practising of Virtue' and is full of exhortations to 'Mock the voice of the herd!' and to shun those who:

> Practise base preachments ... for Verily, I tell you I love him who preacheth beyond-man and doth not practise his belief, more than I love him who preacheth animal and behaveth like unto one! For the one aspires, and is unhappy, while the other remains base, and is contented in his baseness. The one is scourged by the rod of his own weakness, and endeavoureth to escape; but the other kisseth the rod and crawleth like a slave.

Though Nietzsche's philosophy of ascetic renunciation appealed to Patrick as an ideal for which to strive, it was one he was to remain pathetically unable to fulfil.

Another aspect of the philosopher's teaching that may well have influenced Patrick was his notorious misogyny ('Thou goest to women – do not forget the whip.'). Patrick's contempt for the opposite sex shines through in his letters at this time ('revolting females') and even extended to his own family circle – witness his remark about a 'bleared' Lalla in her old silk kimono 'un-ceasingly ironing'. It seems very likely that this was rooted in his unresolved conflict with Nellie. No doubt he continued to resent her ever-watchful concern for his welfare, but it was a resent-ment that he could or would not express openly, unlike his hatred and contempt for his father: 'Today's Thought – Any

nation in which the sons do not, on reaching a given age of
discretion, kick their fathers with the utmost ceremony down-
stairs, is a nation without a destiny.'

For a while Patrick toyed with the idea of writing a pseudo-
philosophical work, and he was disarmingly open, with all the
arrogance of a young man just turned twenty-three, about the
scope of his literary and artistic ambitions:

> I am rather excited these days about, and am beginning to make
> quite extensive notes for, my Apology for Art. Have you realised,
> if I can carry the thing off (and I feel daily more confident of being
> able to do so) how ominously original the thing would be ... All
> the great reputations of the artist philosophers have been
> founded on some such iconoclasm ... Darwin, Huxley, and their
> more or less important followers destroyed religion, Neitsche
> [sic] and his more or less important followers destroyed morals,
> Bernard Shaw, with apparently no followers whatsoever,
> destroyed Science. It remains for Schleswig to destroy Art. If a
> man can destroy good and evil, as Neitzche [sic] did, there
> shouldn't be much difficulty in tackling art. And the field is open
> to me. I tell you, that book is going to be my making.

To bolster his own expanding self-esteem Patrick quoted reviews
of the American edition of *Craven House* which had appeared in
the *New York Times* and the *Los Angeles Times*, comparing him
with Samuel Butler and Sinclair Lewis. But he soon abandoned
work on the abolition of art for another novel, provisionally titled
The Player's Scourge: 'though about twenty pages behind
schedule [it] has been going *excellently* ... I think it should be
good.'

In April he took a trip to France, accompanied by Michael
Sadleir and his secretary, Martha Smith: 'We lived like Kings ...
ate and drank gloriously all the time.' With a guilty air Patrick
also confessed that he had been enjoying some of the first fruits
of literary success:

> I have got a new suit coming in a day or two's time. This has been
> made by Messrs Curtis of Maddox Street (Carlitos's tailors) and is
> costing ten guineas, and should be the devil of a suit. There's no

doubt that it's economy to get better clothes. First of all you get perfect cut and irreproachableness, which gives one enormous confidence anywhere, and also you get *wear*. I believe that this applies to every kind of garment, ties, socks, everything.

Patrick's slightly shamefaced justification of his expensive taste in clothes betrayed an ambivalence in his life that was to become increasingly evident. On the one hand there was Patrick the clubbable literary man about town, with expensive West End apartments and flawless, even dandified dress; on the other there was the political Patrick, the man who in his work was to become increasingly scathing in his indictment of the rottenness of capitalism, and in his thought was to approach ever nearer to a rigid Marxist condemnation of a society whose 'decadent' pleasures he was the first to enjoy. This same letter to Bruce contains a significant passage about prostitutes, servants and the nature of the female condition in which this duality becomes explicit. He condemns the society which forces women into prostitution, while making use of the services they offer:

Lately I've been making most extraordinary expeditions (with Charles) into Soho – mixing a great deal with the courtesans therein and also the low life. I think I've got an idea for an extraordinary and really valuable novel. I daresay you know it's always been one of my leading ambitions to write about the life of servants – particularly female ones – and their oppressed hideous condition. And it's also been my ambition to write about harlots. I have two first-rate novels with either of these subjects. Now my latest adventures have led me into remarkable sociological obser-vations and enlightenments, and it's suddenly occurred to me that to write a novel which is both about servants and harlots (possibly the slow transformation of the one into the other) would not only be ferociously good as a novel, but really sound work. A kind of *Mrs Warren's Profession* brought up to date.

I can't go into all this now, because I can't tell you in my letter my latest conclusions about women. The cardinal fact is that women *cannot earn a decent living* (as people vaguely think they may). Their position, in fact, if one takes the trouble to examine it, and think hard about it, is *hideous*. I'm going into wages and facts. They are utterly dependent on their sexual attractions for their

salvation. There was never such a need for a huge feminist movement as there is now. I can't explain, but this is so, and I think I
have good work ahead. Contemplate a chambermaid, in a small
hotel, cleaning up your overnight messes.

Here is the first germ of the project that was to become *Twenty
Thousand Streets Under the Sky*, which indeed tells the story of the
making of a 'harlot' and the degradations suffered by a servant.
There is also, to set against his occasional outbreaks of misogyny, Patrick's compassionate espousal of the cause of
oppressed women that was to find expression in a gallery of
exploited female characters in his works; from the prostitute
Jenny and the barmaid Ella in *Twenty Thousand Streets*, through
Mrs Manningham in *Gaslight* to Miss Roach in *The Slaves of Solitude* and Esther Downes in *The West Pier*.

Besides reporting the plans and progress of his own writing,
Patrick's letters also gave enthusiastic, even passionate accounts
of his current reading; his tastes and favours ranged from *Pride
and Prejudice* through the poetry of Matthew Arnold and the
satires of Samuel Butler, to Theodore Dreiser, in whose novels he
took 'an almost sensual, certainly abandoned', delight, boasting
that Constable were making him a present of a full set of the
author's works. There are also charming glimpses of Patrick at
leisure, smoking, drinking beer or just sitting in the garden
trying to catch some 'fugitive sun', and looking 'a fool in a pair of
green sun-specs bought at Woolworths'. Once he is trapped in
his bedroom by a rare home visit from his father: 'I can hear him
from here, elephantly having conversations with Mummie.'

Patrick was still making rapid progress with *The Player's
Scourge* which was threatening to expand out of control:

I'm writing now about 1,500 words daily, and though I daren't
look back, think it is going to turn out well. It's going to be a devil
of a long book though – something like 150,000 I should think.

By June, the book was complete:

I have finished the typing of the book now. During this period . . .

I have been getting up at six and not leaving off until sometimes
as late as half past nine. I'm in a fearful sweat and hurry now
rushing through correcting and getting the ms ready for Michael,
to whom I deliver it on Tuesday ... I have read the book to both
Lalla and Mummie separately. I think it is good. Better than *CH*.
More amorphous and powerful. And more propagandist. But just
as funny.

Patrick's feeling that *Twopence Coloured* (the title substituted at
the last minute by Michael Sadleir) was a better book than
Craven House has not been borne out by the judgement of critics
or public. Like *Monday Morning*, the novel is now almost
forgotten, although an altered reprint was issued along with the
new edition of *Craven House* during the Second World War. The
novel shows some signs of the haste with which it was
composed and is also, as Patrick himself admitted, 'devilishly
long'; too long to sustain its rather thin plot. There is over-use of
several of Patrick's favoured devices, especially his 'Komic
Kapitals', which were employed to emphasise the use of clichés
in everyday speech.

The novel is set in the backstage of the theatre, drawing on
Patrick's memories of his own brief thespian career and on
Lalla's more extensive experience; its heroine Jackie is a wide-
eyed innocent, determined to become an actress, and its message
can be summed up in the Noël Coward song, 'Don't Put Your
Daughter on the Stage, Mrs Worthington'. As in his first two
novels, many of the major characters are drawn from people in
Patrick's life: Jackie herself has some of Lalla's characteristics
(though the author's sister was less sexually innocent than his
fictional creation); Jackie's theatrical mentor and lover, the actor-
writer Richard Gissing, owes much to Sutton Vane; while
Richard's land-owning brother Charles, the squire of 'South-
shore' in Sussex, is a portrait of Frank Bridger.

One of the weaknesses of the book is its narrow vision; while
Craven House with its generational conflicts can be seen as an
effective microcosm of the condition of post-First World War
England, *Twopence Coloured* concentrates exclusively on one
particular profession and makes no larger judgement on the state

of society. Its satire is directed entirely at the trivia of the stage, and in nearly four hundred pages there is just one political reference, a throw-away mention of the growth of fascist organisations in Sussex. Nevertheless, the satire, given its limited range, was accurate and bruising enough to draw yelps of protest from actors, and there are one or two interesting moments of lyricism, such as when the hero and heroine take a walk on the Downs outside Brighton and become lovers. Significantly, this is, with all its reserve, the nearest Patrick comes to depicting physical love-making throughout his writing:

> And then it began to rain ... They arrived together hand in hand: and they looked each other gravely in the eyes, and found themselves in each other's arms, and paused, and kissed each other.
>
> It was the rain's doing. It patted down on the roof of leaves, and stormed slantingly in the open. It was ruthlessly responsible.
>
> The rush of noise was amazing. They were the most quiet of all things on the Downs. After a while she left his face, and put her head on his shoulder.
>
> Then she was lying back, speechless, on the wet turf, and he was leaning over her. And 'Oh, Jackie – dear – dear!' he was saying. And she was taking his head in her hands and kissing it – shamelessly, deliberately and with profound proficiency. She had never done such a thing in her life before, but she was, from some mysterious and beautiful source, an adept. Each contact of her lips was the deliberate signing and sealing of her surrender. She was his for ever, and that was the end of the matter.

After the achievement of *Craven House*, *Twopence Coloured* seems like a step back, although the reviews were generally kind. After three successful books in as many years, it was time for Patrick to close the chapter of his juvenilia and return from literature to life.

PART III
1928–1932

11

Lily

THAT PATRICK WAS READY FOR A momentous sexual adventure can be seen from a letter written to Bruce on 11 July 1927, in which he first gave notice of his new obsession: a prostitute. Typically, he idealised her as 'Esther Ralston', the silent-film star on whom the brothers had enjoyed teenage crushes:

Dearest Ecurb,

I said in my letter last week that Esther Ralston was an empire-smasher after all. I had then met her once. I've seen her six times by now, and I can assure you she's something more than an empire-smasher. She is Perfect. She is the summit of the human race. Her parents ought to be given a gold cup. She's without blemish. She is, really.

Of course I'm hopelessly and madly in love, much more so than ever with Maruja. And honestly I think that a beautiful woman like that enriches life. The fact that she can make Mankind susceptible to the vast and terrific and transcendent emotions which I myself experience in the sixpenny seats – emotions at the pure physical beauty and the aura shining there-from – is enough in itself. She truly ennobles one, for one under-stands, watching her, the terrible power and seductiveness of nature in creating a racial ideal. One is awed, and arises infinitely more Neitzchean [sic] than ever. One knows how great and holy sex is. Also one realises that there can be no compromising, no fooling, with that divine force.

It is probably not for you or I (our lust is the lust for thought and power) and if we can't get it we will not steal furtive little bits of it and torment ourselves, and it can be put aside, if it is put aside with one noble gesture, completely.

How are you in this respect? I can definitely say that with me, I am saved. I have committed no malpractices for months, and for months after that, and (by keeping my head at the right moment) I have no anguish. I have created the habit of celibacy, as Samuel Butler and G.B.S. and any amount of priests and people have also succeeded in doing, [and] don't think it couldn't be roused this moment if I cared.

You and I realised this was the dividing line between the degenerate and the genius, and I've pulled through. The seeing of Esther Ralston has communicated in emotions what I understood in reason.

There was a most enlightening article by H.G. W[ells] in the *Sunday Express* the other day. He said that sex was pure habit and that any man could make himself a rake or a celibate, at will, and without any apparent inconvenience to himself. This confirms all I have said, (and proved) and I was awfully glad.

It is painfully clear that here Patrick protests too much, and that his self-congratulatory celibacy had been more a condition of the enormous expenditure of energy he had put into finishing his novel than any self-willed renunciation. In truth, as his adulation of the image of Esther Ralston makes clear, his repressed sexuality was steaming under the surface, awaiting an outlet. Moreover that Patrick was not being wholly honest in his protestations of celibacy is evident from a letter he had written a few months before to Charles Mackehenie after one of their Soho jaunts:

Touching courtesans, it has just occurred to me that they themselves would be the last to subscribe to our theory of abstinence. 'That is all very well,' I imagine they would say, 'but what about us? Just because you get squeamish about our eyes, we've got to lose decent custom.' Directly you de-sentimentalise the position, and allow they are amply justified in pursuing that course, there is no earthly difference between a courtesan and her less adventurous and courageous sisters. From which it follows that if you reject a courtesan's commodity, you might as well reject a poached egg from a waitress in a sweat restaurant. They are both equally victims, and you are assisting in their victimisation. The waitress deserves rather more consideration, though, for she's having a much worse time. But she would soon lose her job if her patrons were unable to face her eyes. Now as you and I are obviously unable to exist without the waitress, it follows that, as men of honour, we cannot continue to live. But this we will succeed in doing, as will be demonstrated by the fact that when I phone you on Saturday morning you will be at the other end of the line.

This Jesuitical justification for philandering would seem to suggest that during their Soho slumming excursions, Patrick and Charles made full use of the service the courtesans offered. In addition to the seamy side of London's sexuality, Patrick and Charles were trying to get to know how the other half lived. Patrick mentioned one such episode to Bruce in August:

My other bit of news is that last night I slept in a *doss house!* This is literally the truth. And not a Rowton House either, but a real genuine low-down slum *doss house* in Drury Lane.

Patrick explained that he had been at the Admiral Duncan pub with Charles Mackehenie and had fallen into conversation with a down-at-heel artist reduced to selling smutty postcards. In a spirit of drunken bravado, Patrick accompanied this man to a doss-house where he stayed till five-thirty in the morning, leaving early so as to arrive home without Mummie noticing his absence. Patrick added that his doss-house night, plus the ambience of the Admiral Duncan would make 'the most marvellous copy for this book I'm thinking of.'

There is no mistaking the thrilled tones of the sheltered young man doing something daring, albeit furtive – definitely something of which Mummie would not approve – with which Patrick related this adventure. But perhaps he did not give Nellie the credit she deserved for a tolerance she exhibited when such expeditions became a regular feature of his life. This duly happened in the latter half of 1927, as he stepped up his pursuit of Lily, remaining out for most of the night; either meeting her, or prowling around London in pursuit of his tantalisingly elusive quarry.

We do not know exactly in what circumstances Patrick first met Lily, but given his inveterate habit of transcribing his real life experiences in his fiction, it can be deduced that the encounter resembled the meeting in *Twenty Thousand Streets Under the Sky* of the barman Bob and the street-walker Jenny in the pub, The Midnight Bell:

> While the noise was at its height the door creaked open again and two figures entered – a young woman and a young girl – passing straight through the bar and sitting down at a table in the lounge.
>
> It was almost as though someone had suddenly shouted too loudly, or as though a bottle had been smashed. Nearly all eyes were turned upon the couple; many people ceased speaking; and the loudest speakers tempered their tones ... It was not a question simply of good looks – though the heavy dark handsomeness of the elder and the blonde prettiness of the younger might well have excited scrutiny on their own account. It was not because these good looks had, in themselves, an air of being assumed, of being painted on, of being made self-conscious, and over distinct, and too explicit by the lavish use of cosmetics. It was not even the phenomenon of their bold unescortedness, or rather of their own quaint chaperonage. It was not the discrepancy between the comparative costliness of their finery and what must surely have been their original station in society. It was not the strange blending of their isolation with a certain hard and unrelenting self-sufficiency. But it was a mixture of all these things which, stirring the imagination of the crowd in The Midnight Bell revealed them for what they were – revealed the fact that these two were beyond the reach of society because they evaded its burdens: that these two were born to toil but did not toil: that these two were for that reason bold, lazy, ruthless and insensitive: that they were women of the street ... The brief hush and hiatus, then, which marked their entrance into good society as represented by The Midnight Bell ... only lasted for a few

seconds; and directly they were seated the place was as noisy as before – noisier than before. Bob took his tray, and went over to serve them.[1]

This is a key scene, reflecting as it does many of Patrick's own attitudes and prejudices towards prostitutes and their profession. He describes and apparently deplores society's traditional rejection of the 'harlot', but cannot completely disguise the fact that he himself, as a product of that society, is heavily imbued with the same outlook – regarding 'women of the street' as outcasts and pariahs and even criminals (he goes on to compare the prostitutes with pickpockets). At the same time, mixed with the disgust he feels, there is a surging sense of fascinated curiosity – an explosive combination and one which impelled Patrick to further explore the world of the street-walker.

Besides this attraction to forbidden fruit, there were other motives – conscious and possibly unconscious – which caused Patrick to lock into Lily and her life. He told Bruce that she resembled Esther Ralston and it seems that he was attempting to act out in his own life his adoration for the unattainable goddess of the silver screen. Then again there was Lily's undeniable sexual attraction and availability. Patrick endowed her with all the romantic fantasies he nurtured about Esther, but she was no flickering, silent image, but a woman of all too real flesh and blood, sitting with him at a bar, offering her charms at a price he could afford. Finally there was his own family history – his father's disastrous marriage to a prostitute was not forgotten. If the pattern of Patrick's life can be seen, in some senses, as a repetition of Bernard's, then his affair with Lily was perhaps an imitation and expiation of his father's own marital mistake.

Fascinated by Lily, Patrick plunged into her pursuit with passionate abandon. He attempted, though, to make his own rules for the chase: his romantic idealisation of women meant that he could not accept the realities of his beloved's profession, and, like the besotted barman Bob, he did not attempt to possess her on her own terms. (Bruce tells us that he did finally have sex with Lily, not very successfully, when the full force of his passion for her was spent. Whether he paid for the privilege is not recorded.) Although his father's example, and his own common sense, must have told him that he had no real hope of reclaiming her from a life of vice, he wooed her with all the gallantry and attention of a conventional lover. The pursuit consumed so much of his time and emotional energy that it could not be hidden from Mummie and soon Patrick found himself pouring out the whole story to her. He found a more sympathetic hearing than he could have expected and Nellie swiftly became his ally and confidante as the doomed affair ran its inevitable course.

Nellie preserved, and Patrick inherited and kept, a sheaf of notes which he wrote to her on his return in the small hours from his meetings with Lily:

> My own darling, Will you let me sleep on tomorrow. Sleep well, my exquisite. Your infatuated son. Patrick ... My darling. Will you let me sleep on as long as I like tomorrow? Goodnight, my blessed. Patrick ... My dearest, Will you call me at a quarter to eight, my darling, Your doting, doting, doting Patrick ... My own darling, Will you call me with the *gong* tomorrow, and I'll come down and have a cup of tea. I'm feeling ever so fit. Goodnight my angel. Patrick. [This is surrounded by 60 X-kisses.]

Finally:

> My more than darling Mother. I hope (even more than you do) that by the time you read this you will have had a glorious night's sleep. Don't call me *at all* darling, tomorrow. Not even for break-fast. Let me sleep on, and I'll have a cup of tea and a digestive when I wake. But make as much noise as you like, because when I'm sleeping I hear nothing. Your doting, Patrick.

The intimate, almost incestuous, tone of these *billets-doux* leaves little doubt as to the true object of Patrick's affections, despite the storm of his mania for Lily. His passion for the prostitute had drawn him even closer (if that were possible) to his mother, refastening an emotional umbilical cord between them that was to be broken only by her death – and perhaps not even then.

We have little written evidence from Patrick about the course of his affair. He was so bound up by his obsession that his letters to Bruce dried to a trickle and he did no creative writing until the hurricane had passed. But three letters from Lily herself survive, remarkable for their artless charm, in the manner of an Eliza Doolittle writing to her Henry Higgins. The first was penned early in their relationship from her room at 7 Bentinck Terrace, St John's Wood:

> Dearest Patrick,
>
> You can see by the above address that I have changed my address again. And I am with my old landlady again. Well Patrick I was very pleased to read that you are enjoying yourself and also that you are well. I am very sorry that I have not written before but I did not receive your letter until today Thursday as I did not go to my landladys address for my letters until then so you must excuse me dear. Well I I [sic] pleased to tell you that we have a Phone here Primrose Hill 0521 so will you ring me up when you arrive back in town please Well Bye Bye dear
>
> Yours truly Lily Conerlly [sic]
>
> PS. Excuse writing as I am not very good at it dear.

The next letter shows an advance in affections:

> Dearest Patrick
>
> Well dear I received your letter this morning and of course I was very pleased. The weather here is awful the wind is howling and it is raining so you can quite understand I am as fed up as you dearest but never mind we shall soon see each other again shant we honey. You write in your letter you will be back on Wednesday well dear as soon as you arrive will you please phone me as I shall not leave this address by then. Well Patrick it must be awful at Brighton and I think it would be far better for your health if you returned home dont you. Well you write to ask me if I go into the Queens well I am the first on [sic] in and the last one out but I expect you are having a few drinks where you are as I know you are awful fond of it aint you, and dear someone told me there were some nice *girls* at Brighton.

The letter ends:

> Bye Bye Your with lots of love Lily.
>
> PS Look after yourself darling.

The last letter is full of excuses:

> Dearest Patrick,
>   You must excuse me for writing this in pencil but we havent a
> pen in the house and I am in a hurry to mail this to you. Well dear
> I suppose by this time you are finished with me and you do not
> wish to see me again but you must quite understand after living
> with someone ill one gets very tired and I asked the maid in the
> house if she would call me at four and she left it until five so you
> can quite see by the time I was washed and dressed it was nearly
> six so I thought you wouldnt wait until then so I did not come
> down and Patrick I havent had anything to eat all day not even a
> cup of tea so you can see how I feel dearest. I will leave it to you
> after reading this letter to see if you still want me and if you do
> meet me on Tuesday at 5.30 same time in Rayners and I shall not
> fail you this time we can spend a little longer together then dear.
> You can phone me up before to tell me if you like dear. Well dear I
> trust you will excuse me again for the pencil and not coming I
> remain
>   One who loves you
>   Lily X X X X X X X X

This bears a close resemblance to the letter written by Jenny in
The Midnight Bell after she had failed to keep an appointment
with Bob:

> Dear Bob
>   No doubt by now you are through with me as I did not turn up
> today but Bob it was not my fault dear. You must excuse pensil as
> I have no pen. Well dear you must understand it was not my fault
> as I was out all that night before and did not get in till half past 4
> in the morning and overslept myself until it was too late to meet
> you and I have not had anything to eat all day dear as I have no
> money.
>   Well Bob it was not my fault and if you are not through with
> me perhaps you will meet me on Friday Bob will you I will be at
> the Green man at 3 and hope you come along there I will be there
> erlier if you like I hope you will let me hear.
>   Please excuse pensil and not turning up
>   yours truly
>   Jenny Maple.

If Patrick's fictional account of the affair is to be believed, Lily led him a merry dance of frequently missed dates, unpaid debts, unreturned phone calls, and vague inconsequential promises to give up the game and get a 'proper job'. He remained in thrall to her for many months, although assuring Bruce in October: 'Don't worry about my Esther Ralston prostitute. I've cut her out long ago.' But he was still in touch with her more than two years later when Bruce returned from Barbados and was introduced to the object of obsession, whom he found 'very pretty' and unostentatious in appearance, dress, manner and speech. By then Patrick's fever had passed its peak. While it was at its height, friends like Charles Mackehenie and Michael Sadleir could only shake their heads and watch it burn itself out, consuming Patrick's health and bank balance in the process. Unsurprisingly, Bruce took Patrick's part in his judgement of the affair, accusing Lily of playing hell with Patrick's tender feelings, taking all and giving nothing, making and breaking appointments as the whim (or the exigencies of her trade) moved her and reducing him to a condition oscillating between exaltation and despair. Patrick's older and wiser friends cynically advised him that the best way to rid himself of his debilitating obsession was to sleep with Lily like any other punter. But this contradicted his chivalric code and he preferred instead to alternately roast masochistically in the heat of ecstatic love and freeze in inexplicable rejection.

Looking at the affair from Lily's viewpoint, her behaviour becomes not only excusable but fully explicable: to her Patrick must have seemed an intense and unstable puzzle, blowing hot and cold in her pursuit; sometimes overwhelming her with romantic protestations far removed from the realities of her existence and sometimes giving her stern moral lectures on the iniquity of selling her body. In truth there was never any real chance of the relationship reaching a satisfactory conclusion: convention, class and a thousand other difficulties barred the path to true love. There was no common ground and eventually Patrick realised the futility of his passion, as is shown in *The Midnight Bell* when Bob asks himself,

Why had he pitted himself against all the accepted facts?

Any fledgling could have told him from the first what he was now learning with such cost and pain – that women of the streets were of and for the streets, and that love of such was inconceivable – unnegotiable – mere despair and degradation. She had even told him so herself when he first knew her. And yet, like a child of 18, he had thought that in his own case it would be different.

The ending of the affair left Patrick emotionally and physically exhausted. For the rest of 1927 he was able to do little more than see *Twopence Coloured* through the press to publication and contemplate his loss. But when in the following year he had recovered sufficiently to contemplate the experience more calmly he was ready to begin writing the large project he had already outlined to Bruce. It was to be a trilogy of novels chronicling the lives, not of his middle-class peers with whom he had dealt in his first three books, but of the dispossessed, the lonely, needy, sad yet oddly noble legion who thronged the bars and tea-houses of the twenty thousand streets of London he had come to know so well.

12

The Midnight Bell

EARLY IN THE NEW YEAR OF 1928 Patrick wrote to Bruce, humbly excusing himself for his failure to communicate frequently or fully enough over the previous six months. He made no attempt to explain his all-consuming involvement with Lily, contenting himself with heavy hints and an assurance to assuage Bruce's pathetic complaints that he was being edged out of his brother's life:

Dearest Ecurb,

I have just had your last letter – the one dealing mostly with my remissness in correspondence. Let me now say that if I once started to think about this I should go mad, and the only thing to be done is to think and say no more about it, but to get ahead with my weekly letter as though there had never been any stoppage.

You not necessary to me! My God, I don't think there has ever been a time when I needed you more. And the terrible thing is that it is utterly impossible to *begin* to tell you about it. I see now that there will have to be sides to my life over here which will have to remain absolutely in the dark until we meet again. Only by writing all day and all night could I tell you anything that wasn't teasing and unsatisfactory.

So it'll have to be left. Don't think from this that I'm in any trouble. On the contrary I now have my life under the most extraordinary control, and am going right ahead.

141

I don't smoke, don't drink, don't do anything that I shouldn't; and I can now say that a new and harder and firmer gospel is creeping up to replace the extremes and slight hysterias of my old.

Patrick expanded on his maturing plans for his next novel, *The Midnight Bell*:

My present object is to harness my old enormous gusto to my new vehicle. And that brings us to the next book – which is rather ticklish. The only book of importance on my horizon now is my prostitute one – but I don't think I can undertake this at once. For one thing it requires as much study as an Elmer Gantry or M. Arrowsmith, and for another I've just finished a 130,000-word novel and I want a rest. I'm therefore going to do two books this year. I'm going to be slowly constructing the prostitute one, and writing another *short* one for publication.

The short one, I think, shall be about a pub. What a miraculous opportunity for reaping my wild oats! If ever a man knew the atmosphere and life and ethics of these places it's me. And what an opportunity for my own particular brand of fun! Drunkenness. I should be able to write a rollicking little masterpiece.

Patrick stuck to this with remarkable fidelity – he did indeed go on to write both books, in the order he planned; the 'pub' book became *The Midnight Bell* and the 'prostitute' one *The Siege of Pleasure*, telling the early life-story of Jenny Maple. The trilogy that became *Twenty Thousand Streets Under the Sky* was completed with the publication of *The Plains of Cement*.

On 17 January, Patrick wrote another 'excuses' letter to his brother, profusely apologising for not having sent a promised parcel of books to the beleaguered Bruce, lonely in Barbados, and starved of reading material:

I'm terribly sorry about my slackness. I wish I could write decently now, but just at the moment I've got a splitting head-ache (owing to a new pair of spectacles) and I'm in the throes of a diarrhoea which is making me feel very sick ...

Worried by Patrick's physical condition, and anxious to get

him away from Lily, London, and its manifold temptations, Nellie packed her son off for a restorative holiday in Hove, where he took a room in Brunswick Terrace, hard by his old childhood home. On 4 February he wrote to announce his safe arrival and the start of work on *The Midnight Bell*. Two days later he was reassuring her as to the improvement in his health. But, unbeknownst to Nellie, Patrick was continuing to correspond with Lily (her teasing letter about Brighton girls dates from this holiday) and a week later the tug of London had become too insistent to resist. On 12 February he declared himself restored – physically, mentally and morally – and ready to return.

For once, Patrick's promises that he would turn over a new leaf, become a new man, and generally embark on a healthy and sober life seem to have been partially fulfilled over the next five months. Although his besotted obsession with Lily continued, he also got down to writing his novel, completing it by June, when he again sat down at his typewriter and wrote to Bruce:

> My dearest Ecurb,
>   At last I write again. If you knew all I've been through since I last wrote, I daresay you'd find some excuse, but really, when you come to think of it, there can never be any excuse for not writing. People say that they have not the time, but that's all nonsense, for they could easily take an hour out of their sleep if they wanted to.

Patrick admitted that the completion of the novel had been followed by more backsliding:

> When I got my book delivered – I straightway fell into worse horrors than the one I had escaped. For not only did I have a terrible bout of smoke-inhaling: I also ran into a terrible drinking mood, and got myself into a fearful state of depression. Which state of depression could only be alleviated by further smoke, and further drink – which was followed by a worse depression still.

Then, accompanied by the urgent caveat 'Not a word to Mummie', Patrick revealed that he had fallen back into the clutches of Lily:

In which phase I entered upon the most *devastating* love affair that a man could be called upon to suffer. I can't begin to tell you about this. It's all too involved, and incomprehensible and scandalous. I can only say that I have been truly obsessed and have suffered agonies. I cannot definitely say that it is over yet. But it may be, and at least it worries me no more.

Then followed a prolonged meditation about another, and similarly ruinous addiction:

My present worry comes from quite a different source. I am trying to give up smoking.

Smoking, really, is the root of all my troubles. It makes me want to drink, and the more I drink the more I smoke, and then I get into that terribly nervous state of body and mind, in which it is utterly impossible to conduct such a thing as a love affair peaceably and without agony.

Patrick made clear that he placed his commitment to writing above all addictions and was determined to break the bonds of his enslavement to lust and tobacco:

Now in so far as all love is, and must be, to the philosopher, of secondary importance, if I cannot have a love affair peaceably and without agony, I *cannot have one at all*. In other words, if my sentiments are for one moment going to interfere with my efficiency as a writer, then I must evade my sentiments by flight from the one who inspires them.

A few days later Patrick wrote from a new address, 50a New Cavendish Street, W1. There were compelling reasons for the move: Patrick probably wanted to be closer to Lily in her West End haunts and he felt a need to escape his mother's insomnia and stifling watchfulness. But there was another motive: Bernard Hamilton, increasingly enfeebled, had moved back to the family home from his Bayswater hotel so that he could be cared for by Nellie. The burden of the presence of his increasingly invalid parents was too much for Patrick to handle on his own (Lalla had also moved away again), royalties were rolling in from his first three books, and he could well afford the small but comfortable apartment from where he wrote to Bruce, inviting his brother to join him when he returned from Barbados.

In July Patrick took another trip to France in the company of Michael Sadleir and Martha Smith. Describing this to Bruce he let loose an extraordinarily vindictive diatribe against the country and its people:

We went to Paris, Autun, ... Dijon and Auxerre. Paris I think is the *filthiest* and most *loathsome* city in the world. I absolutely hate it from every point of view. I have ... a list of the things I hate about it.

1. The dirty, filthy smell of the place – the cheap restauranty omeletty Highlifecigaretty *stench* which greets your nostrils at (and between) every corner.

2. The Revolting advertisements of Savon Cadum with which the whole place is plastered – a picture of a lewd fat smiling baby (do you know it or remember it?).

3. The peeling, grey, debauched rottenness of the slummier quarters.

4. The obscene, gurgling language, which I *can neither speak nor understand*. And when they hear you fumbling with it they haven't one eighth of the sympathy which an Englishman would have for a Frenchman in the same predicament. They look angry and indifferent.

5. The Americans. Everybody will tell you that Paris is completely spoiled by the Americans. Well – if it is spoiled, what is the use of going there?

6. The French.

7. The hashed, buttery cooking – invented for a people with enervated appetites which require tickling and are absolutely opaque to the subtleties of plain food.

8. The coffee complex. I cannot digest coffee, I loathe French bread, and so I feel slightly sick for the rest of the day.

9. The horse traffic. There are six times as many horses on the road than in London, and the whole air is singing with the crack, crack, crack of infinitely longer and more vicious whips. I nearly went mad when I first woke to this fact at first, but on closer inspection I found that the animals were being tortured only about a quarter as much as they appeared to be. That is bad enough. And even if they were not being tortured at all, the

hideous delight with which these foreigners (I use the word advisedly) flourish and play about with the instrument is enough to send one into a madhouse.

10. The noise. The amount of cobbled stones and drays, and incessant sharp shriek of the taxi horns.

11. The fact (this is an unreasonable objection, but none the less real for me) that all the traffic is going the wrong way and much too fast.

One might be tempted to take this jet of vitriolic spleen as a satire on the xenophobia and Francophobia traditionally associated with the most blinkered and stodgy Englishman – a sort of anachronistic *Sun* leader column – were it not all written deadpan: Patrick unfortunately leaves us in no doubt that the rant is to be taken seriously. Given his frequently expressed horror of 'abroad' in later years, it is perhaps not surprising to see such sentiments set down so early in his life, but it is nevertheless disturbing, albeit hilarious in its po-faced seriousness. For an Englishman to criticise French cooking is laughable indeed and it is an interesting commentary on Patrick's perversity that the very sights and smells which draw the English across the Channel are the ones that so repel him. The origin of this attack may have been a passionate reaction to the fleshpots of the city where Bernard Hamilton had mis-spent so many of his days; but there is also a contradiction, if not flagrant hypocrisy, in this chronicler of London's low life so vehemently denouncing the sins of France's capital city.

By December Patrick had finally brought himself to speak freely about Lily and his long infatuation:

That, indeed, was terrible, though I am as free as air now. I am so free that I can talk about it without a tremor. I am dying to tell you the story, and *what* a story it makes! I shall tell you all one day – of Lily Connolly (but *she* thought it was spelt Conerlly), the mad harlot from Ipswich – of Priscilla, the wearied courtesan who had seen the Isles of Greece – and of Joan, the red-haired whore of Soho. And how I had tea with them all on a foggy day in a filthy little room at the top of a house in Bolsover Street – just opposite Great Portland Street station ... they all three slept in the same bed, and syphilis was in the air. Not that there was any air, or anything but the heavy odour of carbolic soap, gone bad ... And yet I couldn't run away. I got into brawls at restaurants, and fights in the street, and fell amongst thieves in Soho dens. You will never believe it. And yet, when you hear my story, you will not be able to detect one psychological flaw in my behaviour. You would have done exactly the same yourself, and so would anyone of lively temperament. But I've lost my taste for low life permanently, and thank God I'm out of it all.

All the incidents Patrick mentions find their way into *The Midnight Bell* whose main protagonist, the barman Bob, is, despite his supposed working-class persona, as much an autobiographical portrait of his creator as Anthony Forster or Master Wildman. But, fortunately for his readers, Patrick's claim that he had lost his taste for low life was very premature.

Discussing the novel he had made of his experience, Patrick made his now standard claim that his new book was

> ... streets ahead of what I've done before ... Its background is taken from what I have sketched, perhaps rather exaggeratedly, above, and it has gathered to itself, quite unconsciously, the theme of which all really great novels are composed. There is only one theme for the Hardy-cum-Conrad great novel – that is, that this is a bloody awful life, that we are none of us responsible for our own lives and actions, but merely in the hands of the gods, that Nature don't care a damn, but looks rather picturesque in not doing so, and that whether you're making love, being hanged, or getting drunk, it's all a futile way of passing the time in the brief period alloted us preceding death. It is all, of course, profoundly true, and bears no actual relation to life whatsoever. It is merely the portentous dirge of the poet mind – it being the poet's business to put into words the universal wail of humanity at not being able to get everything it wants exactly when it wants it. Everybody knows, in his heart of hearts, that it's a first-rate existence if only one or two things would go right.

Patrick indicated that *The Midnight Bell* was different in style as well as substance from the novels that had gone before:

I have developed a lot of new theories about writing and style, the latter having acquired a weird penchant for short sentences ... Also I never try to get effects, except in comic writing. My maxim is to *see*, relate what you see, and your effects will come.

He disclosed that he had dropped the device of his beloved, but much-criticised Komic Kapitals, adding,

Vision and imagination are the things, and they arise from stored observation ... If your vision and feeling are clear, they will transcend mere prose. I am far from being through yet, but my navigation is finished and I am riding home on the waves of the story. I hope to be done shortly after Christmas.

Patrick concluded his letter with a forgivable boast about the hype *Twopence Coloured* was getting in America:

We learn in the *New York Eve. Post* that 'Hamilton writes from 6 to 9 in the morning, has breakfast, and continues until 1 or 2 in the afternoon.' Also that 'Hamilton's hobby, after work hours, is to explore London on a push bike.'

He closed:

Be sure of your success and mine. Only work like an extra special maniac in the next year, so that we can meet each other with a real gleam of achievement in our eyes. I have all sorts of irons in the fire, and I hope to be famous before I meet you ...

Prophetic words, for Patrick was indeed to be a celebrity within a few months. In a PS he added, 'I hope this letter doesn't sound pompous or silly,' and assured Bruce, 'in all the world I love you best'.

The Midnight Bell was published in June 1929. It was at once evident that Patrick had written a superb novel and one that marked a huge stride forward in maturity, technique and the handling of his subject matter. Out of an experience that had shattered his physical health and psychological stability, he had fashioned a powerful work. As he had told Bruce, his style was natural and masterly. He dispensed with the special effects that had marked (and sometimes marred) his earlier novels. His use of short sentences and chapters, the employment of dots and dashes drive the narrative forward with an urgency matching the desperation of Bob's plight as he plunges ever-more recklessly into the quagmire of his erotic obsession. The novel demonstrates, too, Patrick's knowledge of the geography of London and a close familiarity with the drab pubs and dank rooms in which the characters act out their minor tragedy. It is, in short, a book that any author could be proud to have written, especially one only twenty-five years old.

There are no time-wasting preliminaries or prologues: we are swept at once into the life of the Midnight Bell – a typical central London pub off the Euston Road – and introduced to its regulars, stock Hamiltonian bar-room philosophers; and to its staff, the barmaid Ella, who nurtures an unrequited passion for the barman, Bob, whose fate is sealed when the street-walker Jenny Maple strolls into the saloon.

Bob is ostensibly a working-class man who harbours secret dreams of becoming a writer. Upon meeting Jenny he is at first amused, then fascinated and finally, as the plot moves to its conclusion, hopelessly and fatally enslaved. At first he imagines he can control his passion and dictate the terms of the relationship, but he is swiftly disabused. With a perfect control of material in art that so chaotically overwhelmed him in life, Patrick builds the edifice of the mausoleum that will entomb Bob, brick by deadly brick, under the jealously disapproving eyes of Ella. Jenny's control gradually becomes absolute, but with Bob's increasing servitude she is ever more elusive and maddening, until, seeking some scapegoat to blame for his self-imposed torment, Bob turns the focus of his self-hatred on Jenny's profession:

> What a filthy crew. They were all the same. But retribution fell on them. Yes, they got what was coming to them. There was, after all, a God. They rotted in their own sins and diseases. God was just and good. He loved God. He was on the side of God. They rotted in their own sins and diseases. In the meantime it would be best to get drunk.
> He did so.

Here is a first glimpse of a trait that was to grow increasingly strong in Patrick's later fiction: the idea of punishment and revenge. It is a sinister quality, particularly when, as is often the case, it is directed against women. The sheer hatred which he evinces towards some of his more malevolent creations reveals a most unattractive side of Patrick, and he seems to take a sadistic delight first in the long-drawn out torturings of his 'good' characters by the bad; then in the unpleasant fates that sometimes, but not always, overwhelm the perpetrators of the original evil. The tormenting of the murder victim's parents and friends in *Rope*; the exquisite mental torture of Mrs Manningham by her husband in *Gaslight*; the sufferings of George Harvey Bone at the hands of Netta and the violent vengeance that he wreaks upon her in *Hangover Square*; the petty malice served up to Miss Roach by Mr Thwaites and Vicki Kugelmann in *The Slaves of Solitude*; and the wicked machinations of Gorse against his female victims in Patrick's last three novels all demonstrate this tendency. It is a world in which everyone is either a torturer or a victim – and in some cases both.

But however much he may despise and insult prostitutes, Patrick/Bob is forever at the mercy of his tender instincts, and compassion is always close to the surface: when Jenny/Lily for once turns up to an appointment on time, his rancour dissolves into touching concern and love:

> 'How are you tonight?' he said.
> 'Well,' she answered, 'I'm not very well, s'matter of fact.'
> 'Oh dear. What's the matter?'
> 'I got a pain in my side. It ain't half bad.'
> 'Oh dear. Well we'll get you something for it.'
> He was sure she loved him. She was in pain and she came naturally to him ... waiting trustfully three minutes before the time of their appointment. He couldn't think what all the fuss had been about – why he had got raging drunk on her account the night before. He had merely been insultingly rude to her, and they had quarrelled. Now she came quietly back to him – as to reality.

But of course this happy state cannot last.

Jenny teases and frustrates Bob to distraction until eventually his tolerance snaps. In a marvellous chapter, Patrick describes how he goes on the mother and father of all benders, is robbed in a Soho dive and ends up spending the night in a doss-house. Then comes the morning after; Bob staggers blearily into the dawn and from Westminster Bridge he surveys the river, which in turn suggests the sea:

> The sea! The sea! What of the sea?
> The sea!
> The solution – salvation! The sea! Why not? He would go back, like the great river, to the sea! To the sea of his early youth – the mighty and motherly sea – that rolled over and around the earth!

There the novel ends, with Bob resolved to literally drown his sorrows and cleanse his soul of its poisonous fascination for Jenny by going back to the sea – the womb-like 'motherly sea' that also suggests the scenes of Patrick's 'sea of his early youth'. It is not, perhaps, the most convincing of conclusions, but Patrick then stands back from the drama and, in arguably the most optimistic, life-affirming passage he would ever produce, he absolves Bob of his weakness:

> For there is this about men. You can embitter and torment them from birth. You can make them waiters and sailors (like Bob) when they want to be authors. You can make them (as Bob and most of them were made) servants of their passions – weak – timorous – querulous – vain – egotistic – puny and afraid. Then, having made them so, you can trick them and mock them with all the implements of fate – lead them on, as Bob was led on, only to betray them, obsess them with hopeless dreams, punish them with senseless accidents, and harass them with wretched fears. You can buffet them, bait them, enrage them – load upon them all evils and follies in this vale of obstruction and tears. But, even at that, there is yet one thing you cannot do. You can never make them, under any provocation, say die. And therein lies their acquittal.

The Midnight Bell was instantly recognised by critics, reviewers and Patrick's peers and seniors as not only the most impressive novel he had written, but an important new work. The *TLS* declared,

> Mr Hamilton holds his reader by his accomplished writing, his gift for realistic portraiture, his pitiless refusal to cast any befogging glamour over what can only be falsely romanticised, and, not least, by his ability to make the least of his characters real personalities, and to make their personalities the motive forces of his story.

The novel's power is drawn from the intensity of the experience which inspired it. Some critics may regard its scope as limited but they might agree that as an authentic study of infatuation *The Midnight Bell* is almost unmatched. It is a ghastly anatomy of humiliation that anticipates and in some respects is superior to Patrick's later work. It is more true to life than *Rope, Gaslight* or *Hangover Square*, with no lurid murders to cap the plot; instead it describes ordinary people living ordinary lives. The quality of the novel derives from the strength with which Patrick renders their suffering.

When *The Midnight Bell* appeared in June 1929 there was good reason for the critics and the public to take more notice of Patrick. For, in the interim, he had scored one of the most stunning theatrical successes of the decade with his play, *Rope*.

13

Rope

THE CONCEPTION AND WRITING OF *ROPE* are shrouded in mystery. If Patrick described it in letters to Bruce, none of them have survived. The first we hear of it in the brothers' correspondence is an ecstatic telegram in May to Bruce in Barbados, coming after months of apparent silence:

> Play enormous success your schoolmastering days are over writing weekly henceforward Patrick.

According to Bruce's subsequent account, *Rope*

> ... may have been written before the Lily affair had fully expired, for Patrick was still living an irregular life; much in the West End, and in and out of cinemas, pubs and cheap restaurants. Later indeed he told me that almost the whole first draft of the play had been scribbled on old envelopes and odd scraps of paper either in saloon bars or in small Lyons teashops.[1]

Bruce stated baldly that 'the well-known starting point of the play was the famous Leopold–Loeb case in America'[2], but in his preface to the published version of *Rope* Patrick explicitly denies this:

> It has been said that I have founded *Rope* on a murder which was committed in America some years ago. But this is not so, since I

153

cannot recall this crime having ever properly reached my
consciousness until after *Rope* was written and people began to
tell me of it.

He repeated this denial at the end of his life, telling Angus
Hall that *Rope* had been conceived as early as 1922 – two years
before the Leopold and Loeb murder. But while Patrick may have
thought he was being entirely honest in disavowing any such
link between life and art, the circumstances of the play are too
similar to those of the *cause célèbre* to leave room for much doubt
that, consciously or unconsciously, murder case and murder play
are intimately connected.

Nathan Leopold and Richard Loeb were two students at
Chicago University, both brilliant, spoiled scions of wealthy
Chicago Jewish families.[3] They were able, gifted, popular and
seemed to have the world at their feet; they were also bored.
Early in 1924, having fallen, like Patrick, under the influence of
Nietzsche's *Thus Spake Zarathustra*, they began to think of themselves as 'Supermen', far above the common herd in intelligence
and ability, and despising the laws, codes and customs of their
caste and society. (They were also lovers.) From this theoretical
standpoint, they progressed rapidly towards the conception and
implementation of a plan for a perfect murder. Their crime is
often called a 'killing for kicks', but more properly it seems to
have been coldly conceived and calculated as a demonstration of
their superiority to a society they despised. Their victim, chosen
at random, was Bobby Franks, a child cousin of Loeb. They had
intended to strangle him, each holding one end of a rope (the
method used by the killers in Patrick's play), but their plan began
to go wrong as soon as they had enticed the little boy into their
car. The child began to scream and Leopold killed him in the
back of the speeding vehicle by bludgeoning him with a cold
chisel. Their Nietzschean vanity began to dissolve before the
reality of their crime. Beginning to panic, they dumped the body
in a culvert on some waste ground, having stripped the corpse
and poured acid on its face to hamper identification. The young
killers then made a threatening phone call to the boy's parents
and sent them a typed ransom demand for his safe return,

knowing he was already dead. Their stupidity was as breath-taking as their cold cruelty, for they had left a series of clues which would have put the most plodding of policemen hot on their trail. Leopold had dropped his spectacles by the culvert where they had so inexpertly hidden the body. Loeb's family chauffeur spotted the pair cleaning bloodstains off the car's interior – Loeb lamely claimed that he had spilled some red wine – and finally the ransom note was matched with Leopold's typewriter. They were arrested, and having sworn to stick together in their denials, broke down at once and made separate confessions blaming each other for the crime. Feeling in Chicago ran high against the privileged young killers and it seemed certain that they would be condemned to death. But family money bought the services of America's celebrated defence lawyer, Clarence Darrow, and a combination of his eloquence and the evidence of psychiatrists caused them to be given life sentences instead.

Such were the bare facts behind Patrick's play. He borrowed for his killers, Brandon and Granillo, Leopold and Loeb's cold arrogance and Nietzschean pretensions; their intended method of murder; their drawn-out teasing of their victim's parents; their close connection with the victim; their blunders; and their gradually escalating panic and fashioned these raw materials to the needs of the stage to make a taut and chilling thriller.

The play opens with the murder itself, carried out in the darkness of a Mayfair flat. Brandon and Granillo – by implication, homosexuals – bundle the body of their friend Ronald Kentley into a large chest. They then prepare to hold a supper party, with the sandwiches laid out on the lid of the chest. Their guests arrive, including, with a macabre touch, the father of the deceased who has come to buy up Brandon's library. Last to arrive is Rupert Cadell, a disabled war veteran and something of an intellectual mentor to the two murderers. Almost at once, Cadell is suspicious, noticing that Granillo still has Ronald's theatre ticket sticking out of his pocket while denying that he has been near the theatre in question. When the other guests leave, Cadell makes an excuse to return and confront the killers. His first action is to give an exposition of his own nihilistic/Nietzschean philosophy, but when he forces open the chest and is confronted with the end result of this amoral standpoint, his humanity is outraged. He denounces the killers, and summons the police.

Once again Patrick called upon his sister's help in getting the play staged. Lalla showed the script to the producer Reginald Denham who arranged for it to be given a try-out Sunday night production by the Repertory Players company at the Strand Theatre on 3 March 1929. The success of this encouraged him to mount a full-scale production at the Ambassadors' Theatre on 25 April. Present on this occasion was Lalla, Mummie (in tears of delight) and a grumpy but proud Bernard. *Rope*'s reception was ecstatic. Denham pushed his young author on to the stage to make a speech of thanks to the applauding audience. The play ran for six months; its small cast and single set made it a profitable production and, for the first time in his life, Patrick made a considerable sum of money. It was a goose that continued to lay golden eggs for the rest of his life – in 1960 he told Bruce that worldwide royalties from *Rope* were still flowing in at the rate of some fifty pounds a month and, a year later, just before his death, Patrick made a similar boast to Angus Hall:

> He lifted the lid of a large, sombre chest [Shades of Rupert Cadell!] and pointed to the dozens of unopened press cuttings envelopes that lay inside it. 'Behold my income,' he said apologetically. 'I never read them but they're all reviews of *Rope* and *Gaslight*. There isn't a week goes by without someone somewhere in the world staging my plays. They've given me a modest income for many years now, and I need never work again.'[4]

Patrick's increased income resulted in a change of lifestyle. From now until his final collapse in the 1950s, he was always seen in perfectly tailored dark suits and hand-made shirts and shoes. There were other immediate fruits of success to be savoured: Denham whisked him off to Italy to stay at a villa near Portofino; and he indulged in a brief half-hearted love affair with an actress in a bid to banish the still-haunting image of Lily.

In the same preface in which he defensively denied pinching the idea for *Rope* from the Leopold and Loeb case, Patrick also made an unnecessary and somewhat shamefaced apologia for the play to the 'highbrow' readers of his novels:

> I should like to say that *Rope* is not intended to be a highbrow play – and that, supposing my ordinary writing to be designated as highbrow, then it bears no relation to the rest of my writing.

Patrick also took a stand against some critics who had pronounced the play morally disgusting:

> I have gone all out to write a horror play and make your flesh creep . . . If I have succeeded you will leave the theatre braced and recreated, which is what you go to the theatre for. But when *Rope* is accused of delving into morbid psychologies and so forth, of being anything but a sheer thriller, of being anything but a De Quinceyish essay in the macabre, I am at a wretched loss.

Perhaps Patrick felt a touch of guilt at the sheer scale of his popular success. Like many writers of novels and plays, he rated his fiction higher than his dramas, but *Rope* is, on a purely technical level, so skilfully constructed and paced, that there was certainly no reason for its author to feel ashamed. On a deeper level there is much more to *Rope* than meets the eye.

In an essay entitled 'The Strange Case of Patrick Hamilton' published in the *TLS* just after the Second World War, a critic puzzled over the fact that Hamilton's two stage thrillers had given him a much more serious and weighty reputation than that normally awarded to authors in the genre. From this the *TLS* deduced that the craftsmanship of the plays concealed a deeper core of meaning beneath the sensational subject matter: 'For serious studies in the more popular perversions will never fail to fascinate, yet there is plenty of evidence that Hamilton's plays penetrate a little further.' Considering *Rope*, the writer attributes to Patrick that almost uncanny power of anticipating the *zeitgeist*, not just of his era, but of the next. Writing at the end of the 1920s, Patrick sensed what the 1930s would bring in terms of fascistic, Hitlerite violence:

> Looking at it now it possesses an almost historical interest . . . a

few years later London was made very acutely conscious of a
gang of young men with the highest social pretensions and an
almost mystical pursuit of violence. By the late 30s most of them
were in gaol after being caught for various robberies, usually with
violence. The chief character of *Rope* and principal villain,
Brandon, is most carefully described in the stage-directions as
'plainly very well-off ... with clear blue eyes, a fine mouth and
nose and a rich, competent and really easy voice ... with the
build of a boxer.' The type is only too recognisable and its importance and role in Europe at that time was greater than that of
amateur cracksmen. It was very fortunate that in this country
Mosley never attained the social importance to attract the Mayfair
toughs, whose spiritual home was clear enough. This play then
was rather more perceptive than the average, and even in 1929
perhaps the audience felt a disquiet which, if inspired by seeing
the play, certainly went beyond its story. Sensitive writers were
beginning to feel similarly though few saw the implications ...
and Hamilton at least showed himself in touch, if unconsciously,
with the prevailing social currents.

Written in the aftermath of the Second World War, the *TLS* piece
spotlights one of the themes that runs through all Patrick's work:

> The implicit attitude of the play, however, is more interesting
> than its prophetic qualities. It is lifted quite out of the ordinary rut
> of thrillers by the tremendously strong indignation against
> violence and cruelty that runs through it. This is very rare as
> either violence is minimised in English detective drama and the
> emphasis is on the intellectual fun of spotting the crook or, as the
> American influence grows, it is shown for its inherent sadistic
> excitement ... Of course *Rope* was intended to be and remains a
> thriller, not a piece of social reporting. But whether the author
> was conscious of it or not, his social sensitiveness had invested
> the thriller form with more than its usual significance. And he has
> shown himself at least concerned for human values and able to
> feel passionate indignation at their denial.

This seems a highly perceptive piece of criticism, though the
article's author was even more accurate than he could have
guessed. It is an axiom of psychology that those who have strong
or extreme feelings that are socially unacceptable repress them so

deeply as to appear to hold diametrically opposite positions. Thus, on a vulgar level, chairmen of moral purity committees can turn out to be secret voyeurs; vicars molest choirboys; schoolmasters and scout leaders can be sadists and paedophiles; animal liberationists bomb human babies; pacifists are violent in their denunciations of war, and so on. So it was with Patrick Hamilton: alongside a strong sadistic streak lay rationalist pity and compassion. This was why he could so convincingly represent Rupert Cadell *and* Brandon; George Harvey Bone *and* Netta; Ernest Ralph Gorse *and* Esther Downes. The tension between these two poles of his personality is the current that gives his writing its power to shock. His contemporary George Orwell again provides an interesting parallel: he too possessed a strong sadistic and authoritarian side – his first job was as an Imperial Policeman where, he confessed, his deepest desire was to drive a bayonet deep into the guts of a Burmese Buddhist priest. Later, sharing a flat with the writer Rayner Heppenstall, Orwell mercilessly beat him up. It was precisely his awareness of this dark force within himself that made Orwell such a reliable barometer warning against the power-worshipping totalitarian violence of the times in which he wrote. If Orwell contained Winston Smith and O'Brien, so Hamilton contains Bone and Gorse, both victim and executioner.

The fact that *Rope* became a steady source of income for Patrick was also due to the professionalism of its original production in which Brian Aherne and Ernest Milton played the principal roles of Brandon and Rupert Cadell. Milton, grateful to Patrick for providing such a plum part, became a firm friend, as did Reginald Denham, who in deference to the young playwright's stage experience, allowed him a much greater hand in the production than would normally have been given to a fledgling dramatist. The result was the success of the London stage season – only the grouchy *Observer* critic, St John Ervine, who had turned a blind eye to the merits of *Outward Bound* and was thus something of a bane to the Hamilton family, withheld his voice from the chorus of critical acclaim. In the year of *The Midnight Bell* and *Rope* Patrick had the world at his feet. But the decade, and with it his own life, was about to turn.

14

Lois

PATRICK'S CABLE REPORTING THE SUCCESS OF *Rope* came at the right time for Bruce. The Head of his college in Barbados had already offered to release him from his three-year contract six months early so that he could return to Britain with a young white Barbadian woman, Aileen Laurie, with whom he had fallen in love. Aileen was going to London to study at the Royal College of Art and Bruce also now wanted to participate in Patrick's success. In addition, he had completed a detective novel and Patrick's promises that he could help get the book published clinched the matter. He and Aileen booked passage on a banana boat and arrived at Avonmouth in mid-September 1929. He was encouraged by a letter from Patrick, written from his Italian holiday, glorying in his success:

Dearest Ecurb,
   I have money! I am making from £30–£40 a week now and the future potentialities are enormous! How can I begin to describe to you the *uncanniness* of my success? It is all a strange Byronic dream. For it is not only the money – it is *fame*. And by this I do not mean petty notoriety – but the real article – fame! I have done exactly what Noel Coward did with *The Vortex*, I am known, established, pursued. The world, truly, is at my feet. You, reading a few notices over there, cannot possibly imagine what has happened.
   And all through *Rope*. It is all too funny. I think it's deserved,

though, as the play is really well written (a thing almost unknown in the theatre).

When Patrick met his brother's train at Paddington, the first thing Bruce noticed about him, after an emotional embrace, was his changed appearance: Patrick looked much older. His brown hair was thinner, his face bore the marks left by experience, suffering – and perhaps dissipation. His fingers were stained yellow with nicotine and his youth seemed gone. Prosperity had brought changes in his brother's dress and demeanour. His single best suit which Bruce thought had set off his tall, slim figure, had been replaced by a black pin-stripe cut to the latest fashion. He wore a black felt hat and his shirt, tie, socks and brilliantly polished shoes had clearly come from the smartest outfitters. The modest Bruce felt outshone by the splendour of his younger brother's apparel.

Patrick was introduced to Aileen – a relationship not destined to prosper – and then the brothers adjourned alone to a nearby pub where Patrick began to fill Bruce in on his lean and fat years. They then repaired to Chiswick, where Nellie welcomed the prodigal home. Bruce found his father sadly fallen away to a shuffling figure in a dressing-gown. Bernard had recently returned from the last of his many foreign jaunts, to Greece, and had made a pathetic effort to renew his sexual life with Nellie (after a quarter of a century of conjugal separation), but now it was to be all downhill for the O.D.

A prophetic book, 'The United States of Europe', having failed to find a publisher, Bernard, had turned to writing another opus about the queens of England; but his mind, as well as his body, was failing and he could make no headway. An unfortunate incident while dining with his daughter at the Trocadero restaurant hastened his demise. Bernard lit a pipe and, when told that smoking was forbidden, defiantly retained the offending but unlit article in his mouth. The manager was summoned and brusquely ordered him to remove it, at which Bernard lost his temper and muttered an insult about 'damned Jews' (the Trocadero was owned by the Lyons family). At this he was abruptly ordered to leave and hustled out. He slipped and fell in the hallway and though he recovered partially from the injury he was never able to walk properly again.

Bernard's family were helpless witnesses to his decline. Through his study door they could hear the muffled tapping of his typewriter as he tried to complete his book, but all too often came curses and the tearing of paper. Then one morning he came to the dining-room table, put his head in his hands and moaned, 'I can't go on with it.' Nellie suggested a fishing holiday to restore his vitality. With his manservant, Sutherland, Bernard was duly packed off in a hired car. But they were back in a few days. The trip had been a fiasco. Fishing was simply beyond Bernard's failing strength. It was clear that he could no longer be accommodated at Burlington Gardens and a room was found for him in a home for ex-officers in Westbourne Terrace. Before leaving, he reluctantly gave Nellie powers of attorney to administer his financial affairs which, upon examination, were found to be in a sad state. The O.D. had entirely run through his fortune, and was, in fact, deeply in debt to his bank. The only thing to do was to sell the Chiswick house, which at the onset of the depression made a derisory £900. Bernard's substantial library was hastily sold to a second-hand book dealer for a fiver, and Nellie decamped to stay with her sister and Frank Bridger in Hove.

Bernard begged Bruce to bring him his old army revolver and ammunition so that he could end the life that he found insupportable. Bruce was willing to give this quietus, but was overruled by the rest of the family. When the ex-officers' home closed down, Bernard was removed to his final resting place, a nursing home run by Catholic nuns in Ealing. Here, confined to a wheelchair, the O.D. enjoyed the start of his final summer in 1930, taking pleasure in being wheeled around the grounds when his family paid their duty visits. Although only sixty-seven, his memory was failing and he had to give up playing cards and reading. His only pleasure left at the end of a life devoted to hedonism was looking at the cartoons in *Punch*.

Bruce's last meeting with his father was in keeping with their lifelong relationship: the O.D. was delirious and raving about the mountains of Canada, but he was aware of his son's presence and begged him not to leave. When the duty sister finally ordered him away, he was pursued by Bernard's voice, bellowing for him to return.

Bernard died on 1 July 1930.[1] All the family were summoned to the bedside, but Patrick was the only one to arrive in time to find his father alive and the O.D. died clasping his younger son's hand. The cremation took place at Golders Green. At a funeral party held in Lalla's flat, Nellie gave way to tears, but Patrick sternly rebuked her, telling her that as it was the event she had been awaiting for years she should not pretend otherwise. Bruce disagreed:

> I think here he showed a failure in imagination. How could Mummie help thinking back to young and hopeful days when Bernard had been at his best, and she had looked forward to making something good of her marriage?[2]

Now it was too late.

Lalla's life was as convoluted as ever. H r four-year involvement with a married man having petered out in mutual recriminations, she promptly began a similar relationship with an ex-colonel working as a stockbroker. Given Patrick's known distaste for both colonels and stockbrokers, the relationship unsurprisingly did not meet with his approval and Lalla began to see more of her other brother. She warned Bruce not to take Patrick's wild promises of finding him a congenial job in England too seriously and the two of them began work in adapting a play that Bruce had written while at university. This collaboration, *The Home Front*, was staged at Birmingham Rep under Sir Barry Jackson and later given a London production by Sir Cedric Hardwicke.

Lalla's warning that Patrick would prove powerless to land Bruce a job proved well-founded, but he did do his best to boost his brother's career. He had passed the manuscript of Bruce's first novel, *To be Hanged*, to his own agent, A.M. Heath, who placed it with Faber. The exciting news was conveyed to Bruce, who was holidaying in Hove, in Patrick's usual slightly mean-minded way, reminiscent of the manner in which he had withheld the news of Bruce's success in the comic competition of their boyhood. Patrick came down from a trip to London and, with a mournful look, intimated that the book had failed to find a publisher. Eliciting a disappointed reaction from Bruce, he then broke into a grin, put his arm round his brother's shoulder and exclaimed, 'They've taken it, old boy, they've taken it!'

Patrick himself was going through a creative block. Desperate to follow up the success of *Rope* with another hit play, he tried to settle down to work on two or three different ideas. He was hampered by his own continuing literary lionisation with its concomitant heavy drinking. His current favourite cocktail was the fashionable Gin and Italian, although he sometimes drank beer laced with gin or his usual staple, scotch. After two holidays with Bruce – in Devon and Hove – which he paid for, Patrick rented a flat in Hatfield owned by the star of *Rope*, Ernest Milton. It was extremely cold and Patrick found the atmosphere of Milton's study, decorated entirely in black, unconducive to creative labour. However, he did succeed in finishing another dramatic thriller, *John Brown's Body* which, like *Rope*, had a single try-out in London. The plot centred around a scientist driven to murdering a detestable man who had tried to destroy years of work on a research project. The scientist eventually commits suicide, leaving the completion of his work to his son with the words, 'Let us replenish the scattered ranks of facts and advance upon eternity.' If this single surviving line is any indication of the play's overall quality it is small wonder that the reviews were bad and that no West End management was tempted to risk a production. It seems that both Patrick and Constable were aware that the piece fell below his usual standards, for *John Brown's Body* was never published, and, like *The Procurator of Judea*, his dramatic adaptation of an Anatole France story, the manuscript has disappeared.

Soon after his father's death, Patrick met Bruce for one of their regular sessions in a London pub with an unusually preoccupied air. Eventually he admitted why: he was to marry in a few weeks' time. Nellie learned of the nuptials in an extraordinary *post facto* letter from Patrick, written from the Mayfair flat he had taken to begin his married life, 52 Upper Berkeley Street:

My darling Mummie – I am writing this to tell you that I have at last done what you, in your wickedness, have known all the time I probably would do – *married*!

My sweet one – I thought it best not to tell you about this until it was a *fait accompli* – as it could only fill you, and every one, with distress and doubt for me.

But I am terribly happy, and *madly* in love, and I swear you will eventually be glad.

Sweet one – this is why I have been a little *distrait* lately – and I want to write and tell you that no woman on earth can come between me and my love and adoration of yourself. My love for you has been going on for twenty-six years and will never, never, abate. I shall never wander away, or regard you as any thing but the first and loveliest woman on earth. I mean this, my own.

I will try to get down to Brighton as quickly as possible, and tell you all about it. It has all been such fun. I am *incredibly* happy – touch wood.

Give my love to Godmother. You will have something to talk about – won't you!

All my love, my sweetest darling, Your doting Patrick.

Patrick knew that his marriage would cause ructions amongst his unusually close-knit family. Mummie would have to be appeased and Bruce was fearful that the change in Patrick's life would adversely affect their relationship. Despite his own matrimonial hopes, Bruce was shocked at the news, recognising, despite all Patrick's reassurances, that he would no longer be at the centre of his brother's life.

Among the excuses offered by Patrick for his sudden step were that his life had got out of control; his continual meetings with people with whom it was necessary to maintain good relations, almost always accompanied by drinking, were threatening to disrupt and destroy his capacity for work. For eighteen months he had produced nothing apart from the moribund *John Brown's Body*. In Bruce's words, 'What he needed was a home, to which he could return as to a secure companioned base instead of to a lonely cave.' There were more positive reasons, too, for wedlock. Although both Patrick and his bride, Lois Martin, were on the rebound from unhappy love affairs, there was a strong bond between them, and if this lacked the wild passion of Patrick's infatuations for Maruja and Lily, there was some hope that steady affection would form a more firm basis for a successful marriage.

But doubts persist. If Patrick had been as 'madly in love' as he claimed in his letter to Nellie why had he not even bothered to mention the name of his bride to her? We know, too, that he wanted at first to have an affair with Lois but she, bruised by her recent unhappy experience with another man, rejected this, offering Patrick a straight choice between marriage and platonic friendship. In addition there is the strange fact that in the letters he continued to write to Maruja, he referred to Lois as 'My first wife', implying that Maruja, if she were ever to be free, would be his next.

Lois Marie Martin was, at twenty-nine, three years older than Patrick at the time of their marriage. Of Irish stock, she was the daughter of a Cardiff doctor. Fair-haired and delicately pretty in her youth, she was later to tend towards dumpiness. She had come to London to study at the Royal College of Music and was an excellent pianist. She also studied shorthand and typing and supported herself after graduation by secretarial work, becoming a senior secretary in the City. Her business abilities were to prove of great service to Patrick and from the beginning she took over the management of the professional side of his writing, keeping it in good order until their estrangement when he began to suffer tax troubles as a direct result of the loss of her firm guiding hand.

If Lois laid down conditions for their marriage, Patrick, too, had his requests: he asked her to promise that he could continue to meet family and friends with the freedom he had enjoyed as a bachelor, without automatically bringing his wife with him. Lois gladly gave her consent to this arrangement and, unlike most similar promises on the eve of marriage, faithfully adhered to it.

Patrick had first met Lois at a party given by J.B. Priestley at his Hampstead home in Well Walk. They married on 6 August 1930 at Brentford register office, Patrick giving his profession as author. His best man was not Bruce but Sutton Vane. The newly-weds then departed for a fortnight's honeymoon in Brittany.

Sleeping together for the first time they discovered to their dismay that they were sexually incompatible. We can only speculate as to what the trouble was, although Bruce insists that it was 'a matter neither of frigidity on her part nor impotence on his, but one of those physiological incompatibilities that have wrecked or embittered so many marriages'. Mutual recriminations resulting from frustration on one side and mortification on the other made the first weeks of the marriage miserably unhappy and Patrick, unsurprisingly, took to the bottle.

By Christmas Patrick was openly admitting his troubles to Bruce, describing his marriage as a failure and discussing the possibility of divorce after a decent interval. But Bruce soon came to suspect that this was letting off steam and found to his surprise, when visiting the couple at their new flat, that the atmosphere was peaceful and soothing. A physical sense of calm seemed to emanate from Lois, her piano playing appeared to delight her husband and she was tolerant and understanding of his all-too-frequent drinking bouts. Patrick decided to give the marriage a try after all and began to write the second novel of his London trilogy. He called it *The Siege of Pleasure*.

15

Accident

ALTHOUGH PATRICK BEGAN WORK ON THE novel in London, he soon discovered that life as a literary and theatrical celebrity was something of a hindrance to productivity. The drinking jag that had commenced at the time of his affair with Lily had never really abated; if anything it had been boosted by his bitter disappointment over his marriage. Although the book he was writing would be short – barely one hundred pages – he found to his dismay that he could make no headway with it and came close to despair. It was Lois who suggested a solution. She persuaded Patrick that it was hopeless for him to attempt to go on with his writing while living in London; the temptation to drink to excess was ever-present and for the first time in his life his health was beginning to suffer. Lois proposed that they should clear out and move to the country, where he could complete the book in peace and restore his shattered nerves. Patrick had the sense to accept the wisdom of her advice, only stipulating that their chosen retreat should be close to the sea. At the recommendation of some friends of Lois they journeyed to the village of Burnham Overy Staithe, a tiny fishing and sailing hamlet in a secluded corner of north Norfolk. Here they stayed for a fortnight in a cottage before setting out in a hired car on the serious business of house-hunting.

They explored the whole coastline of Norfolk, Suffolk and Essex before deciding that nowhere suited them more than the place they had started from; and so they took a long lease on 'Harbour View', the cottage where they had been staying, and moved in.[1] Patrick hinted at the privations of country life in his first surviving letter to Bruce written from Norfolk, 'The rooms also, apart from two disadvantages, namely draughts and spiders, are nice.' Bruce lost no time in hurrying up to see his brother in his new surroundings, undeterred by the more explicit warning:

> I am longing to see you again. I think you will enjoy yourself – though you must realise I live very crudely here. I am not ordering a taxi from the station here, and you will therefore have 'many miles on foot to fare' (with me) before actually becoming brimful of the friendliness which in a little cottage you will find – friendliness, but no lavatory indoors, nor much in the way of utensils to eat your food with.

When Bruce arrived, he found Patrick had not been exaggerating: there was no bathroom, the outside lavatory was fifteen yards away, the sole source of water was a well with a hand-pump, and the fireless rooms were deathly cold. 'Harbour View' was the middle cottage in a row of three, one end being kept for guests and the other occupied by the landlady, Mrs Bird, a busy and cheerful woman who did her best to make up for the lack of creature comforts.

Burnham Overy Staithe was a small community largely comprising of Norfolk fisherfolk during the winter, when the sailing fraternity and charabanc-borne trippers had left. There was (and is) just one Post Office-stores, and a single pub, The Hero, named after Norfolk's most famous son, Horatio Nelson, who had been born a few miles down the road at Burnham Thorpe and who had got his first glimpse of the sea and ships in the harbour at Overy Staithe. But the pub was out of bounds to Patrick who, under Lois' watchful eye, was struggling fitfully to keep to his self-imposed regime of abstinence from alcohol as he laboured on *The Siege of Pleasure*. During breaks from writing, Patrick took some much-needed physical exercise, going off alone for long walks over the surrounding marshy pastures, or through the sand dunes along the harbour creeks. He came to love the flat, bleak and sombre landscape, particularly in winter when the biting cold winds, whipping in from the North Sea, buffeted the solid walls of his cottage and gave him a cosy illusion of security and contentment. Under these influences his mind returned, for the first time in many years, to poetry. He planned a long poem in Horatian metre modelled on Marvell, on the theme of a ghostly wanderer, returning to Norfolk after an absence of a millennium to find his fate waiting for him in the unchanging face of his native land. But when he came to pick up his pen, Patrick found that the practice of poetry had entirely deserted him, and he dropped the project after half a dozen lines. His poetic muse was never to return.

Patrick passed most of 1931 at Overy, with frequent trips to London to meet up with friends and publishers and, unbeknownst to Lois, to drink. In one letter arranging a fraternal meeting in April he told Bruce, 'I propose getting a trifle drunk, but without committing street-breach.' There were other diversions to be found amidst the temptations of the twenty thousand streets; as a result of a 'passade' with a prostitute, Patrick contracted a dose of the clap that could not be concealed from Lois. This resulted in an understandable *froideur*, noted by Bruce when he spent a fortnight with the couple in the early summer at the Downs Hotel in Hassocks. A few weeks later Patrick told his brother:

> I have had a sudden feverish spurt of work, and have finished my book! I am hoping that it may have succeeded as a kind of *tour de force* – by which I mean that it certainly has not succeeded as a well-constructed or well-written book. It will take a terrific time to revise and this I am going to do at my perfect leisure.

Patrick relaxed a little after completing *The Siege* and for the remainder of the year occupied himself with projects of less pressing urgency: reading Sidney Colvin's life of his old hero, Keats; tinkering with his poem; adapting *Rope* for a radio broadcast in the New Year; and, as a favour to his brother, revising the dialogue of a third-rate Elstree studios filmscript for a fee of £200 – his first venture into the world of the movies.

Patrick had also done his best to make good his promise to find Bruce a job. He had pulled strings at his agents, Heath's, and had got them to create a position for Bruce as the head of their drama department; this was a new departure for the agency and indeed for Bruce, who proved wholly unsuited to the task. Almost his only success in several months of work was the film-script farmed out to his own brother, and he swiftly quit the post. In his spare time Bruce had written his second detective novel, *Hue and Cry*, which had been rejected by his first publisher, Faber, but was accepted by the Collins Crime Club. Once again Patrick, who extravagantly praised the novel as 'an outstanding achievement', saw their literary careers and life-courses marching in tandem. With his usual excessive optimism he wrote:

> I believe that this moment is the gravest and most portentous in both our lives. After a nerve-wracking, ill-adjusted, wretched early youth, we at last know the ropes. I think we should bless our past miseries, as they have reversed the process common to men in general. The more I read the more I am impressed by the wild and lovely happiness which has been the outstanding feature of the youngest days of most men – from Keats and Wordsworth to Gladstone. Then the sourness and horror has come. Well, we have got all our sourness over at the beginning, we have already battled with and been tortured by the monsters – we know what to expect from them, where we are with them, and how to evade and live tolerably in their company. Hereafter let us see if we can be *statesmen* in the dubious and shifting policies of Life. The days of floundering and uncritically experiencing are over: now is our chance to take charge of ourselves, and with what gifts God has granted us we should be able to give a not ignoble performance, in or outside the light of fame.

Patrick was not to know that fate was soon to deal a sour and totally unexpected blow that was to shatter his optimism for ever.

In October Bruce joined him at Overy for an extended stay. Bruce has left an account of the weeks they spent together which, suffused in the afterglow of nostalgia, and with the hindsight of what was to come, take on almost unbearable pathos:

After breakfast until half-past-eleven or twelve we would work or attempt to work, then, with Lois accompanying us on most days, we would walk to the sea. On the way, we amused ourselves by playing a kind of football golf ... when we reached the sands, we might walk for a bit more or throw catches to one another. I cannot exaggerate the exhilaration of these glorious mornings in so pure and keen an atmosphere. The sun seemed to be always shining, and although by evening a strong wind usually rose, I can hardly remember a rainy day. We all reached a pinnacle of physical well-being hardly touched before or after. Even when winter had fully arrived there was no change in either our routine or our clothing, and we did not feel the cold as an affliction.

Lunch was at one-thirty, and here too a fixed routine presently developed; a Bradenham ham followed by a port-treated Stilton with Bath Oliver biscuits. We never found the fare monotonous.

Afterwards it would be chocolate, cigarettes, reading and usually sleep, comfortably snuggled ... in the deep Manor chairs Patrick had bought. Mrs Bird bustled in with tea at four, and presently we might go for a walk, but before or after a light eggy supper there was no lack of indoor diversion. There was the wireless, a valve set whose batteries had to be watched, games of patience or tiddlywinks, at which Patrick developed astonishing proficiency and played with a jocular parade of championship ceremony – and talk, talk, talk. We never ran dry, and really recaptured the utter intimacy of our adolescence. And I gratefully realised how much of it was due to Lois, and her quiet unobtrusive management of the small household difficulties that arose.[2]

Patrick had so much improved, physically and psychologically, during his months in Norfolk, that Lois reluctantly raised her absolute alcohol ban. Patrick and Bruce were permitted to have a pint of bitter at the famous Lord Nelson pub in Burnham Market, during long weekend hikes that took in a traditional tea at Wells-next-the-Sea, and another beer halfway home at the Ostrich.[3] Here Lois would play the out-of-tune piano while the brothers watched the eccentric landlord, who had the odd but endearing habit of chewing the leaves of his aspidistra plant.

At Christmas 1931, leaving Bruce behind to savour life in Overy alone, Patrick and Lois left for London to stay with Lalla at her flat at 134 Earls Court Road. Soon after his arrival Patrick became embroiled in the sort of controversy that has become familiar to us today, but which was then, in the infancy of broadcasting, something novel.

Val Gielgud, the dynamically energetic head of drama at the BBC, had decided to give his radio production of *Rope* an unofficial pre-transmission hype by issuing a statement, in the form of a three-minute warning talk, that the play might prove strong meat for some listeners. He advised his audience to 'Send the children to bed and lock granny in her room'. Gielgud followed up this opening shot by having the *Radio Times* publish a leader repeating the warning. He then sat back and awaited the inevitable press reaction.

It was not long in coming. The ultra-conservative *Morning Post* was the first fish to rise to Gielgud's carefully cast fly. Under the headline 'Bringing Horrors to the Home' the *Post* thundered:

Many playgoers who are also listeners-in are expressing understandable astonishment that *Rope*, the clever but gruesome play by Patrick Hamilton ... should have been chosen for reproduction on the British Broadcasting Corporation's Daventry National programme next Monday.

The paper then quoted an unnamed correspondent who was duly 'disgusted':

I am surprised to see that the BBC are proposing to broadcast that disgusting play, a psychological study of two neurotic youths who murder a harmless companion, put him in a chest, and subsequently hold a cocktail party in the room, some of the party sitting on the chest.

The play had a successful run – there is, of course, a section of the public which enjoys the degenerate; no one wishes to interfere with their pleasure. It is, however, quite another matter to broadcast this sort of stuff into millions of homes.

The correspondent continued, in familiar vein:

Surely we have enough horrors already in the daily papers – outrages and murders of little girls – and the broadcasting of this sort of thing only encourages the morbid tendency which leads to these crimes. I submit that the BBC is making a gross misuse of its powers.

That same afternoon, the London *Evening Standard* joined the furore with an ironic pro-Patrick piece headlined 'Not Disgusting'. The paper quoted Gielgud, doubtless chortling inwardly over the success of his publicity ploy:

There is nothing disgusting or gruesome about this play, [but] it would have been unfair to broadcast it without letting people know in advance what they were going to hear. For example it might not be the most suitable thing for patients in hospital.

The diligent *Standard* reporter even sought out Patrick himself for his comments on the controversy:

The idea of the play is murder as a fine art. It is less gruesome than the average stage thriller. A murder certainly happens, but the listener learns the fact only by suggestion. If the BBC warning makes people think that they are going to hear something disgusting, they will be disappointed. I wrote it as a 'thriller' but some people seem to be taking it seriously.

The *Standard*'s rival, the London Evening *Star*, devoted a leader to the subject the same night, coming down on Patrick's side against the would-be morality censors:

Complaints are being made on the grounds that it is too gruesome and unpleasant. The BBC has already warned listeners that the play is a 'shocker'. Those who do not want this sort of excitement can always switch off and leave the others to their enjoyment. If the BBC is to make progress, it ought to be given a free hand and not be intimidated by minorities. Otherwise it will become a mere purveyor of the lowest common denominator in amusement.

The next day, on the eve of the broadcast, the *Sunday Times* reported that a right-wing pressure group, the British Empire Union, had lodged a protest with the BBC. It read:

While not questioning the 'cleverness' of the play or the undoubted dramatic ability of the author, we consider the broadcasting of a play of this description cannot but encourage in unbalanced and degenerate minds that morbid tendency which leads to the crime depicted.

On 18 January, the day of the broadcast, the *Morning Post* returned to the fray, reporting that the BBC was persisting with the broadcast in the teeth of 'a number of protests from various bodies and individuals throughout the country'. Endeavouring to stoke the fires of public outrage, the *Post* had rung hospital authorities which, it said, 'although not taking an active part in the protests, betrayed some concern. It was generally stated that, although no general censorship existed in the hospitals and nursing homes, anything of too gruesome a character was switched off.'

Delighted by the bogus demons he had raised, Gielgud broadcast *Rope* to the eagerly listening millions, with Ernest Milton recreating the part of Rupert Cadell in which he had triumphed on the stage. It was by far the largest audience any work of Patrick's had yet reached. The verdict of the critics the next day was overwhelmingly favourable: W.A. Darlington in the *Daily Telegraph* said he had switched on his loudspeaker with a lively sense of anticipation, and had heard an excellently produced and acted play which never lost its grip for a second. He concluded that the protests against *Rope* were unjustified.

Only the *Morning Post* and the *Daily Mail* continued to deprecate the broadcast, the *Mail* assembling an array of small guns to pepper the play including Sir William Gentle, ex-Chief of Police in Brighton, a well-known neurologist and the West Midlands Coroner.

Excited by the new fame he now enjoyed, Patrick met Bruce in Lalla's flat for lunch on Sunday, 24 January. Bruce recalled that Patrick was on top form and, though he did not say so, one of the things they must surely have discussed was Patrick's article that had appeared that morning in the *Sunday Referee* headed, 'The Author of *Rope* discusses Real Drama', and which set out Patrick's views on thrills and thrillers. Before parting the brothers made an arrangement to meet the following morning at the Temple tube station to go and listen to some cases in the nearby Law Courts: it was an appointment Patrick was destined not to keep. In his piece in the *Referee* Patrick posed the question – 'Should thrillers thrill?' concluding that the word 'thriller' had been rendered meaningless by overuse and suggesting that his own type of thriller was a legitimate form of entertainment, indeed a serious work of art:

> For the true thriller, after all, is something which can be traced back, like poetry, to the childhood of both the race and each indi- vidual, and ... is really nothing but the grown-up sequel to the fairy-tale. This is the final proof of its harmlessness. Let the squeamish consider the appalling drama and horrors of, say, an ogre consuming daily the thumbs of little children! Or of a little girl making the slow realisation that her grandmother is not her grandmother at all, but a wolf ... And yet in childhood we pestered our mothers and nurses to repeat and pile up those delicious horrifications, and they considered it the most gentle and health-giving bedside transaction to comply.

Fortified by this answer to his critics, Patrick sallied out into the Earls Court Road that Sunday evening for a short stroll before the seven o'clock opening time at his local, The Pembroke. He was accompanied by Lois and Lalla. They turned into Logan Place, a narrow street without pavements leading west off Earls Court Road, when a car, emerging from Lexham Gardens on the opposite side of Earls Court Road, in the words of a witness, 'leapt into the street like a slap in the face.' Patrick, who was walking alongside a wall on the north side of the street abreast of Lois and Lalla, was struck and carried along for several yards before being thrown off the bonnet into the road. The young driver stopped and asked, 'What's all this?' then, catching sight of Patrick lying bleeding on the ground, cried, 'Oh, my God!' and broke down in tears. A policeman was soon on the scene, and an ambulance arrived shortly after and conveyed Patrick to the nearest hospital, St Mary Abbots, in nearby Marloes Road.

Patrick was fully conscious and in obvious shock, assuring all and sundry that he was 'Perfectly all right' despite his obvious multiple injuries. On examination, these were found to be a compound fracture of the left arm above the elbow, a compound fracture of the right thigh and wrist and multiple contusions and lacerations, most seriously to his face and head: his forehead had been deeply gashed and his nose almost torn off.

He was dosed with morphia and as soon as he was asleep, Lois and Lalla set off on an unsuccessful mission to locate Bruce who had gone to see a Marx Brothers film, *The Coconuts*, in Victoria. The next day, as arranged, Bruce was waiting for his brother at the Temple when an agitated Lalla appeared and told him about the accident. They took a taxi to the hospital with Lois, where they found Patrick awake and full of bravado about the accident. Bruce blanched and almost fainted at the sight of his brother's fearful injuries. He was swathed in bandages and his broken leg was suspended from a stretching mechanism known as the 'Balkan beam'. Bruce left the hospital and adjourned to an ABC café to try and eat some lunch; emerging, he bought a copy of the *Evening News* and found that Patrick's accident had made the front page: 'Playwright injured' – 'Very serious condition of the author of *Rope*.'[4]

Understandably alarmed by the paper's report, Bruce flung it away with a cry of despair and hastily retraced his footsteps to the hospital where he insisted on seeing the ward sister and demanded to know whether his brother was going to live or die. She was able to reassure him that, while Patrick remained on the danger list, he was recovering well from the shock and there was every chance that he would pull through.

The Hamiltons formed an anxious roster to mount a vigil at Patrick's bedside, taking turns to be with him from early in the morning until late at night. During the crisis, Lois' gentle ministrations became indispensable to Patrick and from this time on, until after the Second World War, Bruce never heard him speak of divorcing her again. Bruce, as long as there remained any chance that Patrick would succumb to his injuries, was almost beside himself.

He rented a room near the hospital and soon contrived to share some part of Patrick's sufferings. By his own account, Bruce, who had always been prone to nightmares and sleepwalking, 'probably springing from some forgotten childhood trauma', retired to bed one night after an unusually heavy supper cooked by Lalla. In the early hours of the morning 'impelled by the terrors of heaven knows what dream', he jumped out of bed, smashed the window of his room, and woke up standing on a flimsy balcony forty feet above the West Cromwell Road. His cries for help were eventually answered by his landlord, who pulled him back to safety through the shattered window. Suffering from superficial cuts to his hands and feet, Bruce was taken by ambulance to none other than St Mary Abbots hospital, where, his wounds having been stitched and dressed, he was placed in the bed next to Patrick! Bruce asked himself the obvious question of whether the incident was psychologically prompted, but left the answer open:

> All I knew is that I had long been subject to nightmares, though never yet to one of such terrifying violence, and that although sure that the fundamental cause was cumulative anxiety about Patrick, that was as far as I could take it.

Bruce managed to extend his hospital stay for a fortnight, the final week of which was spent, thanks to the indulgence of the tolerant hospital staff, in a two-bed ward with his beloved brother. He was in seventh heaven to be in such close proximity to Patrick for the first time since the shared bedroom of their boyhood. Patrick, by contrast, was almost continuously in severe pain which he endured with considerable fortitude. He came under the care of an ex-army doctor, a Major Sinclair, with a brisk, no-nonsense attitude to which Patrick responded unexpectedly well. A personal friendship was formed (Patrick invariably hit it off with his physicians) that was reinforced when Sinclair cured Lois of colitis. Eventually, still seriously ill, but off the danger list, Patrick was moved from the hospital to a nursing home at 99 Cromwell Road, where Sinclair continued to treat him.

One day Bruce (who had moved to digs in Hove to recover from the depression which had followed the trauma of the accident and its aftermath) was ordered out of Patrick's room during one of his weekly visits. Sinclair, with the traditional reassurance that, 'This will hurt you more than it hurts me', applied hard manual pressure to Patrick's sinuses, through which pus from his suppurating wounds was draining. Bruce heard an agonising scream from his brother, but soon after Patrick told him he was feeling much better. It was the turning point. Soon he was discharged from the nursing home and went to convalesce with a wealthy former employer of Lois in Hereford Square.

Patrick never completely recovered from the physical and psychological scars left by the accident and Bruce believed that he escaped death only because of the high level of physical fitness he had, through rest, exercise and fresh sea air, managed to achieve in Norfolk, coupled with his relative sobriety and high morale. All this had been destroyed at a stroke. Physically, he was left with a withered left arm and a stiff leg that considerably hampered his mobility. In addition his face was permanently scarred, and his nose, despite plastic surgery, was left as an unsightly blob. Patrick, always highly conscious of his appearance, now became obsessively and morbidly sensitive. Friends who knew him in later life uniformly reported that his facial scars, although instantly noticeable, were not grotesquely disfiguring; but nothing that they could say could convince him that he was not a hideous cripple. The carefree and even cocky self-confidence that had come with the success of his early novels and *Rope* vanished, to be replaced by shyness and introversion. From now on, when in company, he was no longer the extrovert, but the man on the margin, silently glowering and acutely self-conscious. Patrick himself was well aware of the changes in his personality and physique that the disaster had wrought: he referred to his accident, only half-jokingly as 'When I was killed', and there is little doubt that he saw it as the watershed of his life, far more psychologically wounding than even his involvement with Lily had been. That Patrick did no significant new work for two years after the accident has been attributed by many to its consequent trauma. Priestley certainly thought so, writing:

> If he has not yet had the very big public he deserves, I think it is because the motor-car that knocked him down ... seriously

injuring him so that he could not work for two years, chose its moment to strike with diabolical precision. At that time, his popularity was rapidly growing; and he himself was obviously in fine creative vein, a young artist quickly maturing. Few novelists could have had a more bitter stroke of bad luck.[5]

Claud Cockburn, the closest friend of Patrick's middle years, reached the same conclusion:

> A person of an earlier age would have held that Patrick, so good-looking, so enormously talented, must have been the victim of an envious spirit determined to lay him low. Suddenly in the forefront of successful playwrights, Patrick ... was put out of action at the very period when, at least from a material point of view, action might have been expected to be most productive.[6]

Cockburn went on to blame Patrick's decline into 'lethal alcoholism' and his premature death on the accident, but this is far too simplistic. It is true that his injuries may have accelerated his boozing, but he was already inclined to drink heavily, and alcohol plays a prominent part in almost every book he wrote. It is also true that the accident played a part in bringing the seeds of his bleaker visions into full flower, but we know that those seeds had been planted far earlier. Bruce Hamilton confirmed that his brother's subsequent lack of productivity was not due solely to the accident. He had already showed a disinclination to settle down to hard and sustained creative work in London and Norfolk, and the accident provided a convenient, if legitimate, excuse to continue his idling. From now on Patrick's inspiration came more slowly, drawn from deeper and darker wells in his psyche. His first youthful flourish was over, and he was to produce his finest writing in the face of the alcoholism that increasingly threatened to destroy him. In retrospect the accident may be seen, if not as a blessing, heavily disguised, perhaps as a disaster which enriched his work. As an Arab proverb has it, 'The blow that does not kill me makes me strong.'

The legal aspects of the accident were resolved simply and speedily. Although the policeman who had attended the scene told Lalla that the young car driver, Graham Branch, had been stinking of gin, Branch was not charged with drink-driving, but driving without due care and attention and fined five pounds after lamely explaining that he had not realised that Logan Place was a road without pavements. The magistrate expressed surprise that Branch had not been charged with dangerous driving, a fact darkly attributed by Bruce to the influence wielded by his wealthy family.

After his recovery Patrick sued for damages and the case came before Mr Justice du Parcq early in 1933. Patrick was ably represented by Charles Doughty KC and went into the witness-box to give his account of the accident and his injuries. He was scrupulously honest in not exaggerating the effects of his wounds and was complimented by the judge on the 'immaculate fairness' of his evidence. As a result his award, £6,000, was somewhat less than he had hoped for, but was still a very large sum by the standards of the time. Patrick gave Bruce a gift of fifty pounds to compensate his brother for the anguish he had suffered on his behalf, before departing with Lois to recuperate in Italy and Greece. He also added a road accident to the final draft of *The Siege of Pleasure* before the book was published late in 1932. In this episode he equated the emotional damage done to him by Lily with the physical bloodshed wrought by the car that had knocked him down, by making Jenny – the central character and 'victim' in the book – an accessory to, and almost an accomplice of, a drunken driver who runs over an innocent man. It is a vividly realised scene:

> And then, intoxicated with wine and speed together, and with the wind tearing at her face and round her ears, an insane and uncontrollable impulse surged into Jenny's soul. She stood up like a fury. She screamed.
> 'Step on 'er!' she screamed. 'Step on 'er! *Step on 'er!*' And then 'Look out for the bike! *Look out for the bike!*'
> But it was too late. With a grating noise and a thud, a man and his bicycle were hurled helplessly against the side of the car, and left behind in the darkness.

Unsurprisingly Patrick returned to the theme of the accident that dogged and haunted his life later in his work; his second

radio play, *To the Public Danger* (1939), commissioned by Val
Gielgud at the request of the Home Office as part of a road safety
campaign, was an account of the carnage caused by drink-
driving, made all the more graphic by its author's suffering.

The Siege of Pleasure, despite the difficulties Patrick had experienced during its composition, is a minor masterpiece. The novel
begins and ends with the predicament of three elderly people
living in a large house in Chiswick in the post-war years who are
feeling the effects of 'the servant problem' just when they are at
their most vulnerable: decrepit, lonely and dreading the onset of
senility. Patrick treats their difficulties with compassion, and
with an unflinching honesty all the more remarkable because the
trio are an unmistakable portrait of Mummie, her sister and the
dying Bernard during their declining years in Burlington
Gardens. Bruce remarked:

> What Mummie thought about it is a mystery, for neither she nor I
> ever raised the subject, but she was far too intelligent not to
> understand the use that had been made of her, and I believe too
> large-minded to feel distress.[7]

With the arrival of Jenny in the household to replace their
slatternly char Mrs Brackett, Patrick permits the old people the
illusion that they have found a 'treasure' of a servant. Alas for
their hopes! After just a day's employment, Jenny is drawn into a
drinking bout with a fun-loving friend, Violet, and three casual
male pick-ups. Patrick takes us all too convincingly through the
painful process of intoxication as Jenny is persuaded to have just
one glass of port and then another. Before our eyes she changes
from the demure, respectable servant who 'knows her place' to a
bold, careless, selfish slut who casually casts off her consumptive
admirer, Tom, and throws in her lot with her new car-driving
fast set. It is also a strong portrayal of the corrupting power of
drink:

> What if she had had a bit too much to drink – what if this was a
> wild piece of folly, and she had to go back to her dreary routine in
> the morning – what of it? She was happy, she was immensely

and wildly happy, that was all that mattered. You had to enjoy yourself once in a while – didn't you? . . . And a rich man around her little finger! If she didn't celebrate tonight she never would, she might write herself down a little prude for ever. Of course she'd have another drink. She liked drink. She'd have as many more as she wanted. At last she was abandoned. She was going to have some pleasure for once. Pleasure – that was the thing – pleasure for once!

In the course of a single night Jenny is swept off her feet and carried across social barriers through which she can never return. She rides in a car for the first time in her life which kills or injures a passing cyclist; dead drunk she spends her first night in the flat of a strange man (one from the mysterious upper classes to boot); ashamed the morning after, she nonetheless allows herself to be revived with her first whisky and decides not to go back to her skivvying. Bereft of their 'treasure', her employers are left alone to face their mortality:

> Thus they talked, and flattered themselves with hopeful thoughts, and went to bed once more unconscious of their long-drawn-out sorrow and helplessness. And so they would go on and on, day after day, and perhaps year after year, in the same tormented way – and never, oddly enough, have anything but a kind of horror of the thought of the day when they would not be able to get up and go on, but would have perforce to lie and be patient, and then, all of a sudden, while all the world moved and suffered around them, become startling waxen images which did not move or suffer.

There is a kind of ambiguity at the heart of the novel. For Patrick tells the story of Jenny's 'fall' from domestic service to another sort of servitude – of the streets – from the standpoint of a nineteenth-century Christian moralist. But he does not approve of Jenny's former status either and we are left with his pity for her inescapable lot. She is condemned to act callously because the world is cruel to her, but the fate of her aged betters is almost equally unenviable; to be human is to suffer and to cause suffering. Jenny cannot understand Tom's love for her because she herself is incapable of love. Such is her tragedy and, Patrick implies, the tragedy of humanity. There is no escape; and only partial redemption can be achieved through the absurd humour of human behaviour (Jenny's pick-up splashes in his bath 'like a freshly captured seal') which mitigates against the universality of pain.

PART IV
1932–1941

16

Marx Mad

THE SIEGE OF PLEASURE WAS GREETED by the critics with the sort of praise that was now becoming the customary reaction to a new Hamilton work. The *London Mercury* proclaimed it 'most polished and finished' and the *Sunday Times* called it 'a small gem of a thing ... There is to be another book about *The Midnight Bell*. When that has been written and printed with the two stories about Jenny, it will be seen that Mr Hamilton has done a very big thing.'

Patrick's handout of fifty pounds had not alleviated Bruce's perennial problem – what was he to do with his life? He was now past thirty, his second novel, *Hue and Cry*, had not sold well and he had given up the third book he had been writing after the interruption caused by Patrick's accident. Apart from his years in Barbados he had failed at every job to which he had turned his hand. In desperation he decided to try his luck as a translator and began to learn Russian with a view to tackling contemporary Russian literature. While Patrick was touring Greece and Italy with Lois, Bruce departed for Passy in France where he arranged to live with a White Russian family to improve his knowledge of the language. Back in England he took lessons from an émigré girl who was an ardent supporter of the Soviet system and the always suggestible Bruce was stirred to sympathy for the young Soviet state. Already something of a radical, he began to study propagandist works such as John Strachey's *The Coming Struggle for Power* and *The Menace of Fascism* which depicted contemporary world history as a simple struggle between good – represented by Stalinist Communism – and evil – Fascism, and its abetter, capitalism. (Strachey was perhaps not the most reliable political guide – his mercurial career veered from Mosley's New Party to Communism, before he came to rest as a minister in Attlee's post-war Labour Government.)

Bruce told Patrick of his new-found enthusiasm and found a ready response. Patrick was now back at Overy, trying, without much success, to get going on the final novel of *The Midnight Bell* trilogy, which he wanted to call *Time, Gentlemen, Please,* and then, after discovering this title was already in use, *The Black Dispenser.* He finally settled on *The Plains of Cement* shortly before the book appeared in 1934. His new London base when he was in town was a pub/guest-house catering to literary types, the Wells Hotel, in Well Walk, Hampstead. Here, in the spring of 1933, he encountered the young novelist Arthur Calder-Marshall, who had just arrived in London.

Calder-Marshall, tired of teaching after coming down from Oxford, had published one novel and was about to embark on a second and had come to London to widen his experience.[1] On the advice of the bibulous critic John Davenport, he had decided to take a room in a pub in order to draw on live material in the saloon bar. He had settled on the Wells, a friendly house owned by a large elderly lady named Ma Mickle, who had run a gin palace in the Edgware Road and had taken on the Wells in her retirement. For three-and-a-half guineas a week, Ma Mickle provided her literary guests with four square meals a day and rooms with views south across London. On his first evening at the hotel, Calder-Marshall eagerly descended to the lounge bar at six o'clock sharp. Despite the early hour, two people had beaten him to it. Disregarding the quiet, undistinguished figure sitting scribbling in a shadowy corner whom he thought was a commercial traveller writing up his notes, Calder-Marshall's attention focussed on a very impressive-looking man standing at the bar. This person, a bearded giant in shirt-sleeves and waist-coat, produced a pewter quart pot which Ma Mickle filled with mild. The giant threw it down his throat without swallowing and demanded a refill. Calder-Marshall thought he must be a sculptor but he turned out to have the dubious honour of being the last leech-gatherer in London. Calder-Marshall continued to ignore the recluse in the corner and it was only when he went upstairs for his evening meal that the commercial traveller reappeared with his wife and revealed himself to be Patrick. When Calder-Marshall started to enthuse about *Rope,* he found to his surprise that Patrick appeared rather ashamed of the play and Lois wanted him to be quite clear that it had been written purely in order to make money. Lois, speaking across a silent Patrick, recommended Calder-Marshall to read Patrick's novels of which until then he had been unaware. He got the impression that Lois was more of a secretary, who did all the selling of his work, than a wife. Patrick seemed reluctant to talk about his writing and the obsessive theme of his conversation was still his accident, which he told Calder-Marshall had made him 'hideously ugly', although the younger man assured him that this was not so.

A fierce argument then broke out between the two men over their respective attitudes to Nazism. Hitler had come to power only three months before, but Calder-Marshall had been made aware of the menace of the Nazis as early as 1931 when he had visited Germany in the company of his fellow Oxford student, Stephen Spender, and had seen the power and violence of Nazi demonstrations on the streets. At the time, the world Communist movement was adhering faithfully to Stalin's line that the real enemy was Social Democracy, or 'Social Fascism', and the German Communists had even formed a tactical alliance with the Nazis against their common enemy. Calder-Marshall found that Patrick was adhering strongly to the Stalin line in dismissing Hitler as a strictly temporary phenomenon. Talk became no easier when the subject of psychoanalysis was raised. Despite his early interest in Freud, Patrick now totally rejected analysis, ostensibly on orthodox Marxist grounds. Calder-Marshall, however, got the strong impression that his real reason was that there was something sexually wrong between himself and Lois which he expiated by a total absorption in Marx who, Patrick insisted, 'had got everything right'.

By September 1933, Bruce was sufficiently enthused with the idea of the Soviet experiment to make arrangements to go to Russia to see it for himself. He booked an Intourist ticket to Leningrad and was waved off at Hay's Wharf by Patrick, who expressed sorrow that he wasn't able to accompany him. For three months Bruce lived illegally in a Moscow flat, paying his hosts in hard currency, but failing to make much progress with his Russian studies or finding the journalistic employment he had hoped for. His experience of Soviet life was somewhat dis-illusioning. Moscow in winter is no place for rosy idealists at the best of times, but in the days Bruce was living there the Stalinist terror was beginning and even a foreigner could hardly fail to be aware of the pervasive atmosphere of fear. He endeavoured to drop hints in his letters home, but could not be specific, causing his brother to complain of his vagueness. Patrick, for his part, was plunging into full-blooded espousal of Communism and a rigorous study of Marxist texts, as a letter to Bruce from Overy on 25 September makes clear:

... one thing I do ask you to assure me, in your next letter, in no uncertain terms. (a) that you are *liking* Russia and (b) that your premature enthusiasm for it has not been dimmed. Let me know this, and I shall ask no more, but wait in patience till we meet.

My own enthusiasm remains unabated. I plunge further in every day – and am *really* becoming more informed. I have *Das Kapital* up here with me and to my *joy* am finding it within my grasp – *well* within, though it is hard work at times.

In a study of Marx I am finding that my brief excursions into philosophy are standing me in good stead – enabling me to get the real hang of the meaning of dialectical materialism and the actual philosophical and historical basis of the whole show. This thing *means* something to me. It is not a *game* – like all my other romps – it is my *vocation* – however humble the part I play. It is not only my *religion* – it is my *hobby* – the *details interest* me – in the same way that stamps interest a philatelist. For this reason I am in a position to *master* it – as I mastered novel writing.

This is the realisation I have had since I last saw you. And another thing I have realised is the enormous extent to which the rotting intelligentsia over here are entering by the same doorway. When you get people like Middleton Murry (*Middleton Murry*!!) writing 'anyone who has really surrendered themselves to Marx's great work *Das Kapital* ... knows to what company he belongs. He belongs to the great company of the Hebrew prophets – of whom the most universal was Jesus', it makes you sit up. I am of course Marx-mad at the moment – regarding Lenin as [a] sort of Luther in the Marxist Reformation...,

A month later, Patrick was still labouring away:

I am still sweating (a terrible task) at *Kapital* now. But I am *winning* and *thrilled* by every word of it. *What* a book!

In the same letter he reported the purchase of a parrot to keep him company in Norfolk. The creature, which he christened 'Quarles' – his nickname for Michael Sadleir – had been his third bird. The first one had been disappointingly silent; the second, by contrast, had let out '*horrifying* screeches', but Quarles was a total success. Patrick reported that he was using another slice of his compensation damages to buy 'Harbour View' and the guest cottage from Mrs Bird. He also asked Bruce to procure him a bust or death-mask of Lenin to furnish his study. (His increasing Communist fervour even caused him to rename his parrot 'Pollitt' – after the party's General Secretary.)

Patrick's conversion to Marxism was of course typical of middle-class intellectuals of his generation. The carefree spirit of the 1920s, which had tried to bury the trauma of the Great War in a decade-long party, had gradually given way to a more serious and earnest generation at the country's major universities. Marxism became not just fashionable, but almost *de rigueur* amongst progressive circles at Oxford and Cambridge, and the leaders of Britain's tiny Communist Party (and, of course, the Soviet Comintern) adopted a deliberate strategy of recruiting the brightest and best brains to their cause; for they would be the country's future rulers.[2]

Their message fell on fertile ground. The political and economic situation, nationally and internationally, favoured radicalism.

The worldwide depression had flung millions on to the dole and the predominantly conservative regimes of the democratic world seemed to have no idea of how to climb out of it. In Germany, Italy and eastern Europe, Fascism was rampant, but the governments of Britain, France and the United States appeared to regard Hitler and Mussolini as convenient bulwarks against the menace of Bolshevism. Against this background, it was small wonder that some of the most generous and idealistic young scions of the ruling class espoused Marxism. To some – including Patrick – the doctrine appeared to offer a scientifically based replacement for the religious faith of their fathers' generation. To others, the romantic appeal of revolutionary Leninism was the main attraction, with Moscow glittering in the distance as the new Jerusalem. Bruce commented:

> It was a thing so general in that period that I am by no means ashamed of my feeling that, with all its imperfections and teething troubles, the Soviet Union might be pointing to the whole western world a way out of its apathy, defeatism and political cynicism. I clung to the hope long after it had ceased to be easily tenable...[3]

Patrick, of course, was to cling even more tenaciously to the dogma, and for far longer than his brother. Bruce likened his brother's new-found political faith to a religious conversion: after losing his formal faith while a boy, he had found another, but equally strong, secular creed. Once convinced by Communism and its utility for humanity's welfare, it was psychologically impossible for Patrick to abandon it. He was determined to allow no one to undermine his convictions: indeed, he held that anybody expressing the smallest doubts and reservations was living in a state of wilful ignorance.

Although Bruce was the acknowledged agent in his conversion to Communism, Patrick had paid homage to Moscow some time before. In an article in the *Evening World* on 3 March 1930, entitled 'The Faith of a Modern Young Man' Patrick had proclaimed a philosophy that lay uneasily between his former Nietzschean enthusiasms and Marxism:

I do passionately believe (and this is the first time I have properly divulged this secret) in mankind as a whole, and in a splendid and limitless destiny for the race.

I think it is muddle-headed to argue whether any good will ever come of this world. We are in the childish habit of regarding good as a phenomenon which will or will not occur. The briefest analysis will reveal that it is nothing of the sort. The truth is that no good will ever be done until someone *does* it (the realisation of this profundity is the secret of the success of such people as Mussolini and Lenin), and it is in the hands of anybody so inclined to do what he is fitted to do towards bringing about what he desires.

Now that he had found a faith, Patrick clung fast to it, for fear, perhaps, of falling into the abyss should he lose hold. He expressed his dogma with a fanaticism that alarmed Bruce:

He was *not* tolerant; his need was for absolute dogma, with any falling away among the elect felt as a betrayal. His hatred of bourgeois politicians of all parties, but particularly Labour, became extreme, almost venomous. So also of Christianity – though not Jesus – and he called himself a militant atheist. I am sorry to express my belief that he might, given the opportunity, have become a persecutor; and I am not sure that it was not possible to trace the tendency in the lines of his beautifully shaped mouth, and perhaps in his eyes.[4]

Why, given this commitment, did Patrick not follow many of his contemporaries into the Communist Party itself? One of his left-wing friends of the later 1930s, Kenneth Robinson (later Minister of Health in the Wilson Labour Government, and subsequently Chairman of the Arts Council) said simply, 'He was not a joiner.'[5] As Burgess, Blunt, Philby and Maclean disguised their Marxism from their family and unenlightened friends, so Patrick hid the flame of his new faith from those whom he knew would be unsympathetic, even when they were as close to him as the apolitical Michael Sadleir. A moderate socialist friend like J.B. Priestley was unaware of the passion of Patrick's politics and after his death Priestley wrote that he had turned to Marxism and Soviet Russia 'without any

great conviction or passion'.[6] But to those he thought
sympathetic, like Claud Cockburn, Patrick wore his politics
openly.

As well as the external reasons turning Patrick leftwards in
1933, there were, perhaps, other motivations for his new faith.
Patrick shared with a number of his literary contemporaries the
incubus of an over-bearing authoritarian father: George Orwell
had the gruff Mr Blair, armoured in tweed and always saying
'No'.[7] He pleased him by enlisting in the Imperial Police, but
when his father died he discarded his name and became a
radical, a tramp and a writer. Christopher Isherwood described
how his conflicts with his military pater, Major Bradshaw-
Isherwood, led to rejection, exile, name-change and homosexuality.[8] Arthur Calder-Marshall came to dread his father,
away governing India: 'He was a castrating sort of man';[9] while
Malcolm Lowry's life as sailor, hobo, remittance man, writer and
alcoholic on a scale even more gargantuan than Patrick was a
sort of continual child's shriek of rage against his businessman
father's bid to channel him into the ways of bourgeois respectability.[10] Patrick, similarly afflicted, reacted and rebelled in
similar ways.

But it was his other parent who was in Patrick's thoughts as
the year 1933 ended. In late November he wrote urgently to
Bruce, who was pausing in Estonia on his way back from Russia,
asking him to hurry home as Mummie had to have an urgent
cataract operation in three weeks' time, but was too nervous,
restless and sleepless to undergo the ordeal.

The last Christmas the younger Hamiltons would spend with
their mother was celebrated in Lalla's flat in Willow Road, off
Hampstead Heath. Lois had gone to her parents in Cardiff, so an
unencumbered Patrick was able to join Nellie and his siblings for
the festive season. Before the New Year Patrick and Bruce took
the opportunity to renew their links with Charles, Maruja and
Josefina Mackehenie, who were in London with other expatriate
Peruvians. Early in 1934 the brothers left for Overy with Lois,
leaving Nellie – still apprehensive over the coming operation –
with Lalla. A few days later they were listening to a concert on
the radio when a telegram arrived from London:

Come immediately Mummie very ill Lalla.

Patrick and Bruce set out on the wearisome train journey to London, not arriving until after midnight. They found Nellie in a terminal coma. Lalla told them that the night before her mother had pinned a note to her bedroom door asking not to be disturbed as she had taken a draught of Medinal and wanted a good night's sleep. Lalla had strongly suspected that she was attempting suicide, but felt she could not impede Nellie's deep wish for death. She had delayed entering the room until the afternoon when she had found Nellie unconscious, with a note by her bed saying that at her age (seventy-three) she could not face an operation and having seen her children set on their way, had no purpose in living longer. Patrick and Bruce collapsed in bed to try and snatch some sleep, but within half-an-hour were roused by a nurse and told their mother was sinking. They saw her die and then all three Hamiltons kissed her forehead in a final farewell.

An inquest returned a verdict of suicide due to temporary insanity, and Mummie was interred in Highgate cemetery. Patrick seems to have taken the death of his mother with surprising equanimity; he was soon back at Overy, making arrangements with Collets to subscribe to various Marxist journals, and telling Bruce that he was working hard at *The Plains of Cement* in order to finish it by the spring. The task over, he departed in May for a holiday in Greece and Capri, pronouncing 'Athens a bore – Parthenon a bore, Corinth, Marathon, all bores, *club* bores', but the Greek people 'extremely charming and intelligent – haters of the French.' In June he was back at Overy, swimming, golfing and on the wagon: although confessing to one lapse 'into naughtiness'.

Bruce had evidently broached the idea of returning for a holiday with Aileen to her native Barbados, after the couple had become formally engaged during the winter. Patrick approved, 'I think you are very wise to get what fun you can,' while adding, ominously and presciently, 'Not too bad a place to be in when the war comes either.'

Isolated in Overy, Patrick felt cut off from the hurly-burly of

London life and politics, and had to rely on Bruce, who was acting as an observer for the Civil Liberties Union at Mosley's Fascist rallies, to keep him abreast of events. Writing to acknowledge receipt of the Communist Party's journal *Labour Monthly* and a clutch of other Marxist magazines Patrick wrote naively:

> What delights they are! Needless to say, I propose to contribute to all regularly ... and really believe that one may have found some form of adult replica of the weekly bliss of the *Magnet* or *Gem*!

On more personal matters, Patrick offered some advice to his brother, who, despite his forthcoming betrothal to Aileen, had been smitten after meeting Maruja's younger sister Josefina. Possibly jealous, Patrick let out a spurt of uncharacteristic spleen at his old friends:

> With regard to the Mackehenies ... Take the word of a ten-year-old campaigner in that direction that they are – though a *fascinating*, agreeable, amusing and extremely *friendly* family – in the long run utterly self-absorbed and *unreliable*. Moreover the girls are extremely *stupid* and *immature* – in fact I should say *backwards* – a veneer of Paris–London sophistication not having really affected the good old imprisoned Shavian type one hears about. For this reason one could waste more time with them than one might with half-a-dozen other women, and so I should advise you quietly to let the relationship drop or wither.

Bruce receded and in December 1934 he married Aileen. Patrick – who had never liked Bruce's beloved – took the news on the chin, treating the newly-weds to a slap-up lunch at the Ivy restaurant. While he was afraid, as Bruce had been earlier, that marriage would get in the way of their exceptionally close relationship, he need not have worried. Bruce, despite a long and happy marriage with Aileen, always put Patrick's interests before those of his wife. Patrick's invitations to stay at Overy never included Aileen, a fact that she bitterly resented: nevertheless Bruce, like an obedient dog, always responded to them. More intimately still, Bruce obeyed Patrick's injunctions not to have children. As he admitted, 'For this ... I must bear the guilt.' Bruce explained that his precarious economic position, plus the influence of earnest entreaties from Patrick that he should not risk an utter loss of independence, made him insist on the use of contraceptives for five or six years and, later, an abortion. After that, precautions were finally abandoned, but no conception resulted.

After a honeymoon in the Channel Islands, Bruce and Aileen began their married life in a Pimlico flat, before taking an idyllic cottage deep in the Dorset countryside. Patrick's refusal to let Aileen have any sort of access to his life bred bitter dislike, but Bruce remained impervious to her protests:

> Perhaps I should have stood on my dignity, and refused to go by myself [to stay in Norfolk]. But I was not prepared to foresake all others, virtually to give up Patrick to save Aileen some mortification.

17

Twenty Thousand Streets

*T*HE *PLAINS OF CEMENT* WAS PUBLISHED in 1934 and in it a return is made, both chronologically and thematically, to the territory of *The Midnight Bell*. If the original *Midnight Bell* was Bob's book, and *The Siege of Pleasure* told Jenny's story, then *The Plains of Cement* reveals, with great pathos, not just the story, but the very soul of Ella, the pub's barmaid. She is one of the most convincing, and certainly the most sympathetic, of all the characters Patrick created.

All through the novel there are echoes of the first book in the sequence, but this time events are seen through Ella's eyes; with the pub as the backcloth to the action, she emerges as the central figure. There are only distant hints that Bob is undergoing a similar crisis, as we are led through Ella's agonies as she resists, succumbs to, and eventually rebuffs, the importunings of the absurd yet sinister Eccles. If Ella is an acute piece of characterisation, then Ernest Eccles almost matches her, taking his place in the proud line of middle-aged to elderly male monsters which begins with Mr Spicer in *Craven House* and reaches its zenith in Mr Thwaites of *The Slaves of Solitude*.

Patrick weaves a complex and colourful tale around Eccles' siege of Ella using a dialogue (foreshadowing that of Harold Pinter) which although difficult to reproduce in short sections, perfectly conveys the inconsequentiality, *non sequiturs* and outright lunacies that punctuate and make up much of ordinary conversation. At the end of their first encounter, Ella finds herself having accepted Eccles' invitation to the theatre:

> They remained, however, despite the private nature of their common commitment, wrapped in the deepest mystery to each other. So uncanny, grotesquely adjusted, and obscurely moti-vated are the parisitisms and coalitions formed by the small fish in the weird teeming aquarium of the metropolis.

Later, in a book written when Patrick's Marxism had all the enthusiasm of recent conversion, comes the novel's only ex-plicitly political passage. Ella is visiting her mother – a tired, exploited drudge living in a dim Pimlico tenement, and married to a monstrous husband. Patrick describes Ella's morose step-father:

> A saddler by trade, he had been, before and just after the war, 'in his own way'. The laws governing the benign progress of capital, however, had by slow and painful methods pinched and thrust him from the ranks of the petty bourgeoisie into the ranks of the proletariat, with the result that, instead of being 'in his own way' he was now in almost everybody's way, and a misery to himself. Always a sour-tempered man, a staunch conservative in politics, and something of a snob, instead of having sheltered himself with any form of philosophical encrustation, his fall from private ownership obviously yet rankled and gnawed at him day by day, and hour by hour. There was nothing doing in his line, and he made a few unhappy shillings every week by cleaning the brass, and sweeping the floors, and snatching up the empty glasses of the more fortunate in a large public house round the corner. A false and humiliating occupation indeed. There was thus much to excuse him, but not enough to account for his invincible and chronic silence and savagery, which he wreaked upon his wife, and which arose, perhaps, less from sheer distress than from a vindictive sense of vanished superiority. Ella, uncomprehending of social causation, saw no excuse.

Rarely does Patrick state so directly what is implicit throughout his work – the suggestion that it is society and circumstance that moulds the individual. It is a statement of Marxist determinism which allows its author to broaden and extend his sympathy to embrace even his nastiest creations. We even feel a twinge of pity for the ghastly Eccles when he confesses, crudely and haltingly, that he too is a victim of the isolation and essential loneliness that is the fate of everybody in an atomised society. Patrick presents people as suffering from anonymous social and economic forces that they are powerless to understand, let alone control, as they are ground into dust in the cement wilderness of the hooting, heartless city.

Ella's ideal man is Bob, whom she loves dumbly but devotedly; but he, unknown to her, is wrapped in the toils of his obsession with Jenny and immune to her devotion. So they go on, in mutual misapprehension, until Eccles is cajoled into first a half-hearted declaration of love, then a proposal of marriage, so vaguely made that Ella is unsure whether she had heard him properly. But as his persistence begins to wear her down, Eccles becomes ever more odiously overbearing, revealing his true colours as a lecher and exploiter who wishes to add Ella to his list of chattels.

Christmas comes – the same Christmas that sees the crisis in Bob's pursuit of Jenny – and the stories that have been running parallel now threaten to collide. Chapter 54 of *The Midnight Bell* begins, 'They had a splendid Christmas Day at the Midnight Bell'. Chapter 31 of *The Plains of Cement* starts identically. Cooped in her attic room, a heartbroken Ella, on a sudden impulse, writes to Eccles rejecting him finally and forever, but does not post the letter. She is now alone, bereft of comfort, having lost all but her dignity:

> It is a sad pass when a solitary young woman in London is so low in spirits and miserable in her thoughts that she decides she must buy herself some sweets and go by herself to the pictures and sit in the gloom, to hide from the roaring world, and try to divert her mind from its aching preoccupations by looking at the shadows. You will sometimes see such lonely figures, eating their sweets and gazing gravely at the screen in the flickering darkness of picture theatres, and it may well be that they are merely other Ellas, with just such problems and sorrows in their grey lives as hers.

Driven out of the cinema by troublesome children – who in this, as in most other Hamilton novels, seem to be excluded from his sympathy, being presented as meddlesome and vindictive little beasts – Ella struggles into the wet streets, harried by her misfortune. By chance she meets Bob, but it is a brief salvation and Patrick allows the pair just enough time for a few awkward apologies and a couple of kind intimacies before they make their farewells forever. Before parting, Ella gives Bob her letter to post. Then it is back to the bar, putting a brave face on it, chaffing and flirting with the customers in the same old way; but at about half-past ten that night, John, the new waiter at the Midnight Bell, hears the barmaid weeping.

So Patrick leaves Ella to her fate. Despite his professed Marxism, a more ancient and grimmer truth breaks through the novel's apparent moral structure: the sheer sorrow of existence. Patrick does not evade this, nor pretend that it is other than lonely and frightening to be alive. Again what redemption there is lies in the humour and humanity with which we face up to our insignificant position in the universe, and the stoic dignity with which we hold up our heads under the random blows of chance.

The completion of *The Plains of Cement* closed the second phase of Patrick's literary career. His first three novels had introduced a fresh young author, colourful, humorous and sharp, if nothing out of the ordinary, but the trilogy forced a reassessment of a writer altogether deeper and darker than that.

Early in 1935 Constable brought out all three London novels in one volume with the title *Twenty Thousand Streets Under the Sky*, prefaced by an admiring introduction by J.B. Priestley. The best of modern critics have by and large upheld the judgement of Patrick's contemporaries. In his introduction to a new paperback edition of the trilogy in 1985 Michael Holroyd praised the novels' authenticity, and elsewhere Doris Lessing compared Patrick to Dickens and Orwell, whilst making the distinction that what Orwell described from the outside Patrick Hamilton viewed from within.

18

The Age of Anxiety

PATRICK REMAINED IN NORFOLK THROUGHOUT 1935, fitfully working on a new play which, in fact, was destined never to be performed. The idea for it came to him when he saw the film of Eugene O'Neill's *Strange Interlude*. In his conception, a voice, amplified through loudspeakers, would give expression to the real thoughts of the chief character, utterly differently from the lines he spoke on the stage. The plot was a murder story, described by Bruce as 'exciting and suspenseful but not specially venturesome'. Despite a continuing creative block, Patrick managed to complete a typescript, but he was not satisfied with the result and he handed the project over to his brother, hoping that with his experience of writing crime fiction and drama he would be able to make something of it.

Bruce rewrote the play as a straight thriller, without the vocal gimmick, taking the result up to Overy for his brother's approval. But Patrick had lost interest and the project fizzled out.

A more fruitful idea that Patrick got from Bruce formed the germ of *Gaslight*, which he got down to writing some three years later. Bruce's novel *To Be Hanged* gave him a notion of the dramatic possibilities that could be evoked in a room at night being brightened or darkened by the rise and fall in gas pressure as someone left or entered another room. When Patrick broached the plan to Bruce, his brother, with typical selflessness, told him that he had no copyright on the idea and gave him *carte blanche* to develop it.

Patrick continued to plough dutifully through Marxist texts. He pronounced Henri Barbusse's hagiographic *Stalin* 'extremely interesting, but emotional and not very intelligent'. His copy of *Lenin*, by the British Communist Party's chief ideologue, R. Palme Dutt,[1] is heavily underlined in the early pages, but unmarked for the rest of the text, indicating that Patrick probably failed to finish the book. Heretically, he enjoyed Trotsky's *History of the Russian Revolution*, although at this time the former Bolshevik hero was being ostracised by orthodox Communist parties around the world.

Political disagreements were beginning to surface between the brothers, with the amiable Bruce holding to a more moderate socialism than Patrick, whose theoretical commitment to the Communist cause became ever-more extreme. Patrick tried to paper over these gaps:

> I hope that you were not affected by our disagreement prior to your departure. Our trouble is that we are so *paralytically* close to each other in all matters that the *minutest* divergence has the appearance of being a 'stupendous gulf', particularly under the magnifying influence of beer – the neurotics' microscope. But we should not allow this: no doubt there are thousands of things we could disagree about if we set our minds to it, and disagree permanently. But the fun and love which exists between us arises from the vast arsenal of things which we *do* agree about, and so let us just run away from all else.

Despite his efforts to mend and patch his squabbles with his brother, Patrick was forming other friendships of which Bruce knew little or nothing. This compartmentalisation of his life was to become an increasing feature of Patrick's world and, although they occasionally overlapped, he took great care to keep his political, literary, social and drinking friends apart.

One new relationship started in the early 1930s was with Dick Clancy, an insurance broker in the City, whose father had handled Patrick's insurance claim after his accident. Dick, who had served as a Captain in the army in the First World War, was politically on the Left, and formed an instant bond with Patrick.

Under Patrick's influence, Clancy moved rapidly from socialism to full-blown Communist commitment, as Patrick told Bruce:

> Dick Clancy as a Marx–Engels–Leninist–Stalinist is an absolute miracle! If you could only hear this ex-captain talking in his cottage! His theory impeccable, and with a nose and vituperation for Trotskyists unequalled anywhere! By the way I have no doubt now that Trotskists [sic] of any sort are *the* sods nowadays – replacing even the [Ramsay] Macdonalds in filthy humbug and invidiousness.

A couple of years later, Clancy introduced Patrick to his new business partner, Kenneth Robinson, who recalled, 'We clicked straightaway ... because he was such a charmer, a delightful companion.'[2] Robinson remembered Patrick as 'a good straight Marxist', like himself a fellow-travelling anti-Fascist and critic of the 'wet' Labour Party. Levity of the kind enjoyed by Patrick and his friends was discouraged by the party faithful; another fellow-traveller, the sculptor Jason Gurney, compared any attempt at humour at party meetings to 'farting in Church'.[3] Robinson recalled:

> We had a little joke, the three of us; Richard and I were in the City, we were all three left-wingers, and Patrick and Richard used to play golf together. He inscribed my copy of *Impromptu in Moribundia* The First Manifesto of the CBGS – the City Bolshevik Golfing Society. He and I qualified on two counts, Richard on all three.

There is a strong hint here that Patrick did not take his politics unduly earnestly and had something of a dilettante approach to Communism. Almost unbelievably, at the height of the Spanish Civil War – a heroic cause that was wringing left-wing hearts and minds around the world and which Patrick himself followed from afar with great interest and sympathy – he could write to his brother in 1938, reporting a plan to go on a walking tour to Spain with Charles Mackehenie, 'who was very keen on the idea, and, in view of the political situation over there, predicts that we might both be swept to supreme power!' Patrick was too frivolous to be a good Communist. It was not that he was hypocritical in his professions of Communist convictions, but that his whole approach to the study of Communism was a sort of gentlemanly game, an intellectual equivalent, perhaps, to his passion for golf, or, in his own words, 'My hobby'. Such amateurism in his political engagement was understandable, given Patrick's isolation from political struggles in the cities. His involvement was second-hand via book parcels from Collet's and the London Library. However this attitude was something of a luxury in the face of the ever-more threatening international situation and the polarisation of domestic politics, and soon, Patrick came to feel that he was missing out on great events; he began to think of moving from Overy to take a closer interest and a more personal part in political life, as the world accelerated towards war.

Events in Europe were even more gloomy and depressing than at home; the Nazi regime, having established firm internal control in the years 1933–36 (in the process eliminating the once-mighty German Communist Party), turned its attention abroad having occupied the Rhineland. In Spain the election of a Republican Government was followed by a military coup, the division of the country into two armed camps and the outbreak of civil war. British Communists put themselves at the head of the 'Aid for Spain' campaign, and Patrick lent his own support to the cause. He was visited by Ted Willis, then a young left-wing firebrand, who found him 'A thin almost mournful man, unhappy and disgruntled.'[4] Nevertheless Patrick wrote out a cheque for £100 to help the campaign for Spain – a large sum in those days.

But amidst this public turmoil, Patrick's inner life once more plunged into the shadows. He had again fallen obsessively in love. The new object of his affections was a young Irish actress, Geraldine Fitzgerald, who had made a name for herself in the theatre in her native Dublin, and come to London in the mid-1930s to expand and extend her career. They had met through sharing the same theatrical agents, Linnit, O'Brien and Dunfree, whose principal, Bill Linnit, had become one of Patrick's greatest friends, and a close confidant and adviser on affairs of the heart.

Matters followed the same course as they had with Lily Connolly ten years before; only this time Patrick was no longer a headstrong youth, but a married man in his thirties, and Miss Fitzgerald was no Lily, but a rising young star in her own right. It was possibly for this reason that Patrick felt unable to declare his passion openly, and seemed content at first to meet Geraldine socially during his descents on London. She for her part was happy and flattered to be a friend of the renowned author of *Rope*. So things remained for some months, but when Patrick discovered that Geraldine was engaged to be married to another man, his attitude and behaviour towards her underwent a dramatic change.

Geraldine had always been a little perplexed and awed by Patrick. She knew of his growing fame as a writer and when with him was convinced that she was in the presence of genius, but his inner life was a mystery to her (shades here, perhaps, of Mr Eccles and Ella) and he carefully concealed the fact that he was married. But once he found that she was attached to another man he seemed to undergo, in her words, 'a kind of breakdown'. His behaviour towards her became disturbing and vaguely menacing. She became aware that meetings with her fiancé in her London flat were sometimes observed by Patrick, who would ring to ask if the man was still with her. At other times the phone would ring, and the person on the end of the line would not speak when Geraldine answered. Though she had no proof that the mystery caller was Patrick, she strongly suspected it was him. On other occasions she would observe Patrick standing alone in the street opposite her apartment, watching the windows. Geraldine became so disturbed and frightened by this threatening conduct that she sought out Bill O'Brien, who suggested that she should leave her single flat and seek shelter in the company of others, adding that Patrick could be capable of doing her actual physical violence and might even go so far as to kill her. Without further ado, Geraldine took his advice. She left the flat and went to live on a houseboat moored on the Thames with other members of her family, taking care that Patrick did not discover her new address. Soon after, she left London to seek her fortune in Hollywood, where she achieved stardom in *Wuthering Heights,* alongside Laurence Olivier and Merle Oberon, and playing Mrs Woodrow Wilson in the film of the President's life. Patrick was left to lick the wounds of his unrequited love, but the obsession with Geraldine remained.

During his eighteen months in Dorset, Bruce had been hard at work writing and had published two further novels. The first, *Middle Class Murder*, became his most successful thriller to date; it was translated into several languages, adapted by Lalla into a stage play, and also produced on Britain's infant television service as one of the first dramas to be televised by the BBC. His next book, *Rex v. Rhodes* was written during what he described as his 'near-Communist phase' and dealt with the trial of a political assassin. On the strength of this relative success, Bruce felt that he had earned himself a holiday, sailing for Barbados with Aileen in December 1936.

He enjoyed his return to the island, renewing old friendships and making new ones, and he and Aileen entered one of the happiest periods of their life together; she with her painting, and he with writing a new book, *Traitor's Way*, and learning to drive. (Simultaneously, Patrick was attempting to master the same skill in Norfolk. Despite his unhappy associations with cars, he managed to pass his test on his second attempt.) In the autumn of 1937 Bruce heard from Patrick that he was to spend some weeks in the United States that winter, and wanted to visit Barbados before returning to England. Despite his dislike of foreign travel (recent holidays had been confined to a quick trip to Dublin, possibly in pursuit of Geraldine, and a tour of the Scottish Highlands in Keats' footsteps, in the company of Lois and Lalla), Patrick had several pressing reasons for wishing to visit the USA. He was, despite political anti-Americanism, beguiled by the Hollywood image of the country and wanted to see it for himself and he had also been in touch by phone with Alfred Hitchcock about the possibility of writing a film script. 'Hitch' had long been an enthusiastic admirer of *Rope*, whose blend of the sadistic and the macabre suited his own tastes perfectly, and had a long-term ambition to direct it on the big screen – something that was to be finally realised after the war. Patrick had, at Hitchcock's request, sent him a film treatment of the radio play he was writing for Val Gielgud, *Money with Menaces*, but nothing came of this project. In addition Patrick wanted to look up Charles Mackehenie, who was currently attached to Peru's Washington embassy. Last, but by no means least, was the hope of meeting Geraldine again. Lois, who was to accompany Patrick on the trip, was fully aware of her husband's obsession, but bore the affliction with her usual patience and tolerance, while feeling sure that he would turn back to her in the end.

Patrick and Lois sailed for the States at the end of September and based themselves in New England, where they stayed with an American couple, the Feurhakes, whom they had met on holiday in Greece. Fuelled by his obsession with Geraldine, Patrick's drinking had again hit dangerous new heights and he found Mr Feurhake's intake of a single afternoon highball with a little wine at dinner somewhat constraining. He hit upon the subterfuge of smuggling whisky into the house, hiding it in his bedroom, and making continual excuses to retire for clandestine nips.

They visited Washington, where Patrick renewed his friendship with Charles; and spent some weeks in New York, where Patrick managed to engineer a dinner with Geraldine and some mutual friends. Geraldine found him much like the Patrick she had known at the outset of their friendship: kind, considerate and gentle, and full of contrition. He told her that he had completed a play – *Gaslight* – that was bound to be a sure-fire hit on both sides of the Atlantic, and he even went so far as to offer her the full American rights for it, by way of recompense, so he said, for his unforgivable behaviour towards her in England. Geraldine declined the offer, because she 'did not want to be beholden to him', but they parted on the best of terms.

Patrick wrote to Bruce from the Barbizon Plaza Hotel on 24 October, telling him that he had booked a passage on a boat sailing to Barbados on 10 November. He said he was enjoying New York tremendously despite the expense. Lapsing into American slang he spoke of 'having enough dough' and 'counting every cent' as he rode the subway. He added, 'the weird thing is that I am really doing some *work*; also I'm *dead* sober and really have high hopes that this trip is going to shake me out of my rut and start afresh [sic].'

As it turned out Patrick's visit to Barbados was little short of disastrous. The island's climate was at its worst – humid, enervating and oppressive – and Patrick, who always suffered badly in the heat, had found the slow voyage south from New York almost unendurable. He only possessed one lightweight tropical suit, a cast-off given him by Charles in Washington, where he had suffered a foretaste of misery in the sticky late summer weather. As his habitual dark and heavy clothes were totally unusable, this suit soon became very dirty, but Patrick refused to wear anything else.

The house that Bruce and Aileen had rented for Patrick and Lois in Bridgetown was a little way from the beach, in a particularly stuffy low-lying district. In addition to these miseries, the quartet did not harmonise well, with Patrick's antipathy towards Aileen barely hidden and Lois' constant namedropping of her grander friends irritating Bruce and Aileen. Aileen herself, Bruce reported, was sometimes 'gauche and offhand', and Bruce was the uneasy middleman who attempted to keep the peace. It must have been a relief all round when Patrick decided to cut short the visit after about a month and sail home to England, leaving the Ford that they had bought to visit the higher parts of the island as a present for Bruce. Unavoidable discomfort continued on the voyage home and they had such a rough passage that they felt obliged to remain in their port of landfall, Plymouth, for several weeks in order to recover from seasickness.

But, in spite of the unhappy way in which it had ended, Patrick's vacation does seem to have had the desired effect of shaking him out of the rut into which he felt he had fallen in Norfolk. He instantly set about making arrangements to leave Overy for good, renting furnished rooms in a house at 8 Keble Road, Oxford, as a base from which to look for a permanent home. He wrote to Bruce in February 1938, saying that he was 'seriously thinking of settling down here' and reporting that he was hard at work on a new book, of which he had shown his brother the opening pages in Barbados:

... getting up at six in the morning again, and ploughing ahead with *Moribundia* which is none too easy at the moment.

There was also an attempt to buck Bruce out of what seems to have been some political backsliding:

> Spain looks nice at the moment – doesn't it? [The Civil War still had more than a year to run before Franco's final victory, and Patrick was referring to a short-lived Republican success.] At the moment my optimism in this matter is showing signs of being justified. Rest assured that my general optimism will *also be justified*. One of the more disquieting features of my strange, strange trip abroad was the fact that I found both you and Charles in the political *doldrums*!

In fact, Patrick and Lois were unable to find a suitable house in Oxford and, extending their search farther afield, hit upon a flat in Henley-on-Thames that suited their requirements. Forge House in Hart Street was very spacious and soon, thanks to Lois' touch, turned into a most comfortable home; it was to be Patrick's main base until after the war. Patrick found Henley, with its languid Edwardian atmosphere, the ideal place to live out of London; quiet, but not as remote and out of touch as Overy had been. By the summer of 1938 they had settled in.

They were soon visited there by Bruce, who had reached another career crossroads. None of his novels had proved as financially rewarding as he had hoped. The most successful, *Middle-Class Murder*, had, with its stage and television spin-offs, made him £300, but none of the others had made more than £100. His meagre inheritance from Mummie was rapidly dwindling and, cheap though life was in Barbados, it was clear that he would have to find a job. He was offered a senior post at Harrison College, the school where he had previously taught on the island, but before deciding, he made up his mind to go to England to have one more shot at establishing himself in some alternative position. Once again, he was heavily influenced by Patrick who was set against any permanent return to Barbados. Patrick made a considerable effort to keep his brother in Britain. He and Lalla arranged for George Warden, a friend who ran an advertising agency, to lunch with Bruce with a view to him testing the congeniality of the advertising world, but the meeting came to nothing. Finally, Patrick offered to keep Bruce and Aileen out of his own pocket until he either achieved success as an author or found a rewarding job. This entailed an outlay of between £200 and £300 a year, which, considering Patrick had not yet started to make the big time with *Gaslight*, would have been a considerable financial sacrifice. Bruce was moved by his brother's suggestion, but felt too proud to accept it.

The offer illustrates one of the most appealing sides of Patrick's convoluted character – his generous open-handedness. It was not a thoughtless, spendthrift trait, for it cost him much – and not just financially. Years later he told Bruce, 'People think that if you're well off, throwing the stuff around right and left means nothing to you. But it *does*. And it *hurts.*' Bruce believed that Patrick's exceptional generosity was only partly a pleasure and that it was also a masochistic self-denial, made as a propitiatory offering to the gods.

Finally, and reluctantly, Bruce made the decision to accept the job at Harrison College and return to Barbados in September 1938. With war fast approaching, he did not know when he would see his homeland again and so he asked Aileen to sail to England for his last two months in the country, to accompany him in a final nostalgic wallow in the sights and sounds he might never experience again. Bruce bought a new Morris car and the couple set out on a series of journeys around the length and breadth of Britain. Among the places they visited with resonant Hamilton associations was Hove, where they were entertained by Frank Bridger. Bruce also fitted in a couple of private expeditions alone with Patrick. One was to see a professional golf match-play championship at Oxhey; another was a jaunt covering family haunts in south-east England – Waldershare in Kent, where their father had spent his childhood, the village of Charing near Ashford, where Patrick had stayed with actor friends during the height of his *Rope* success and, finally, St Leonards, where they had spent their youthful holiday in the company of Nurse Swain and her husband. Already it seemed like a lifetime ago. Finally, Bruce loaded up the Morris and drove with Aileen to Dover, where they embarked for Barbados. He was not to see England – or Patrick – again for more than seven years.

19

The Road to War (Impromptu, Gaslight, The Radio Plays)

PATRICK'S OBSESSION WITH GERALDINE FITZGERALD, WHILE wreaking havoc with his inner life, seemed to kick-start his creative drive, just as his pursuit of Lily had done a decade before. Despite renewed heavy drinking, he succeeded in shaking off the torpor that had lain upon him since his accident and the completion of *Twenty Thousand Streets*. In the years 1936–39 he managed to write the experimental novel, *Impromptu in Moribundia*; an attempt, only partially successful, to bring Marxist methods into his fiction by departing from his naturalistic mode and creating a dystopian work in the tradition of *Gulliver's Travels*, *News from Nowhere*, *Erewhon* and Huxley's *Brave New World*. These years also saw the completion, staging and filming of his second great theatrical success, the classic Victorian melodrama *Gaslight*; and, in another departure, the writing and broadcast of his first two radio plays, *Money with Menaces* and *To the Public Danger*. In addition he conceived the idea for what is arguably his greatest, and certainly his best-known, novel, *Hangover Square*, the inspiration for which arose directly from his unrequited passion for Geraldine Fitzgerald. In short these were highly productive times for an artist beset with private dreams and demons, writing in a world lurching inexorably towards catastrophe.

210

The earliest fruit of this fecund period was *Money with Menaces*, written in 1936 at the request of Val Gielgud, and broadcast on 4 January 1937. Gielgud was trying to interest serious writers in the possibilities of radio as a new dramatic medium and, after the success of the broadcast of *Rope*, Patrick was a natural first target for his considerable powers of persuasion.

For his theme, Patrick chose one of his pet obsessions: revenge. The play deals with the torment meted out through the course of a long afternoon to Carruthers, a powerful newspaper owner, by an anonymous telephone caller who implies that he has kidnapped Carruthers' daughter. After forcing the tycoon to undergo a series of humiliating manoeuvres to raise a ransom, the caller reveals his identity – Stevens, a schoolfellow of Carruthers whom the latter had systematically bullied at school:

Yes, torture him. Physically, mentally, publicly, privately, without mercy and without cessation tortured him – day in and day out, week after week, term after term, and year after year. Well, this is Stevens speaking, and now he is torturing you.

In the end it turns out that the child has not been abducted at all, but has been safely playing with a neighbour. The play works well as a tense radio drama, a medium that, as Gielgud noted, Patrick instantly mastered. It is remarkable for its use of the phone as an instrument of torture, a technique Patrick had used in *The Midnight Bell* and was to repeat, with more maddening and intense effect, in *Hangover Square*. Its theme of obsessive revenge possibly bears out Bruce's feeling that, given the opportunity, Patrick would have made a zealously vindictive police chief in a Stalinist state.

Patrick's next endeavour was a most unusual piece of work, the novel *Impromptu in Moribundia*; a cross between a satire of contemporary trends in capitalist society and a hellish vision of the future. Usually careful in concealing from his public an open profession of his Marxist credo, here Patrick openly proclaimed his disdain for the British *modus vivendi* in a way that let his highly distinctive sense of humour and his whimsical imagination have full rein. In the novel the land of Moribundia stands as a symbol for England in the inter-war years. Here the comfortable complacencies of his upbringing and the redundant pretensions of the ruling class stand exposed in all their smug and blinkered stupidity. The novel takes the form of a trip to the planet Moribundia by a visitor from Earth. In a highly significant scene, the traveller immediately finds himself watching the very game of cricket immortalised by Sir Henry Newbolt, in his poem 'Vitaï Lampada' ('Play up! play up! and play the game!'). For Patrick, these values of Imperial, Edwardian England still inform society in the 1930s and are leading it, as Edwardian England was led, into the disaster of war. It is the generally assumed common sense of the English, their pragmatic, no-nonsense insularity, that is their downfall:

> ... the land in which the ideals and ideas of our world, the
> striving and subconscious wishes of our time, the fictions and
> figments of our imagination, are calm, cold actualities.

The bulk of the book is taken up with Patrick's poking of fun – with a grimmer underlying purpose – at one of the major innovations of the 1930s: the all-pervasive intrusion of advertising, with its mindless, catchpenny slogans, into the mass consciousness. Patrick saw that the language of the adman was corrupting the vocabulary of the people, conditioning them into becoming the slaves of 'admass' society. He illustrates this by the graphic device of making his Moribundians think and talk in clichés which issue from the top of their heads in bubbles, like characters in a comic. The world of advertising is satirised by literally transposing the adman's images into the workaday Moribundian world. Thus people walk around with dripping taps on their faces instead of noses and martyrs to indigestion have a stomach-full of little devils, prodding their bellies with toasting forks.

Patrick portrays the class-ridden society of Moribundia divided into strict castes: the working classes, who think and behave as the patronising middle classes believe them to do:

buying grand pianos to 'improve' themselves, then promptly smashing them up for firewood; keeping coal in their baths and, above all, knowing their place. In strict Marxist terms, Patrick believes the workers are brainwashed into enduring their condition by the propagandist ploys of their rulers, who also manipulate the lower-middle class, 'little men' of Moribundia, all identically uniformed in bowler hats and suits, all thinking and acting in conformity to rigid codes of behaviour. They are the foot-soldiers of Fascism. In the novel's climactic scene, the little men chase the narrator out of Moribundia for daring to question their narrow-minded, *petit-bourgeois* norms:

> Instead of the harmless, helpless, friendly, tolerant duty-doing little business men ... I saw cupidity, ignorance, complacence, meanness, ugliness, short-sightedness, cowardice, credulity, hysteria and, when the occasion called for it ... cruelty and blood-thirstiness. I saw the shrewd and despicable cash basis underlying that idiotic patriotism, and a deathly fear and hatred of innovation.

Patrick mercilessly lambasts the conservatism of little, middle England with his satire upon the ruling Moribundian ideology of 'Unchange'. Moribundia 'was ideal because it could not change: it could not change because it was ideal'. It follows that the revolutionary doctrines of Communism and Marxism, palindromed in Moribundia as 'tsinummoc' and 'tsisxram', are the mortal enemies of the Moribundian status quo; the contemporary Utopia, 'Ehtteivosnoinu', is its idea of Hell.

Patrick also uses the novel as a vehicle for his uncomplimentary views of contemporary writers. Those exhausted volcanoes of turn-of-the century gradualist Fabian Socialism, Shaw and Wells, are lampooned for accepting honours, titles and favours from a corrupt society that they attacked in their early works; and the masters of modernism 'S.T. Toile', 'Ecyoj', 'Yelxuh' and 'Ecnerwal' are belaboured for their inner preoccupations, which take no account of the social reality around them:

> They are for the most part hopelessly and morbidly turned in

upon themselves, and sterile in consequence. But where else are they to turn save upon themselves? In a world which is unchangeable and inexpandable, where is there to gaze save inwards? ... Obviously, in doing so, they must become self-conscious to an ever more tormented degree, and paralysed for effective action accordingly. Finally, a stage must be reached when the mind can only look at ever-receding reaches of the mind, and an art on the border line of madness or idiocy must be reached ... For these reasons art, literature and poetry in Moribundia take on a more and more painfully subjective aspect, more and more the character of meaningless masturbation, there being no future which they can fertilize.

The form of the novel owes most to two twentieth-century works on the borders of science fiction and satire: H.G. Wells' *The Time Machine* and Elmer Rice's *A Voyage to Purilia*. From Wells, Patrick derives the 'Asteradio', the device the narrator uses to travel to and from Moribundia; and the attack on the narrator by the 'little men' closely parallels the assault by Wells' 'Morlocks' on the protagonist in *The Time Machine*. Elmer Rice was a Communist sympathiser who wrote *A Voyage to Purilia* in 1931, soon after a disillusioning experience as a Hollywood scriptwriter. We know from Bruce that Patrick had read and admired the novel and took from it the central situation of a man catapulted through space to a world that was a distorting mirror of the society he had left behind. The climactic scenes of the two novels are nearly identical, with the narrator of *Impromptu* fleeing pursued by an enraged mob of monarchist Moribundians, while the protagonist in *Purilia* is seen off by a clergyman and his congregation.

Satire, to be effective, must aim its sights at specific targets, and this Patrick had certainly done. The 1930s was the age of the political novel, and Patrick responded to the pressure of his time with an interesting and innovative departure from his usual fiction. For an avowed Marxist, *Impromptu* was quite daring in that it ignored the norms laid down for Communist writers by Stalin's literary apparatchik, Zhadnov, who extolled as a role model the 'heroic tractor driver' school of 'Socialist Realism' – then the only style permitted to Soviet writers, and thus to orthodox Communists the world over. British literary Communists largely eschewed this bogus proletarianism and tedious worker-hymning in favour of more adventurous routes employing allegory and even surrealism such as Rex Warner's *The Aerodrome* and *The Wild Goose Chase*, Edward Upward's *The Railway Accident* and Ruthven Todd's *Over the Mountain*. *Impromptu* was a significant contribution to this literature. Commercially, however, the book was a flop. The critics were not enthused, sales were poor – this sort of innovation was not what Patrick's public expected of him – and the novel was never reprinted. From the perspective of the 1990s it looks impossibly dated.

Impromptu was Patrick's greatest commercial failure, the work which immediately followed it, *Gaslight*, was to be, along with *Rope*, his biggest success, and the work by which he is probably best known to the public today. The play was written concurrently with *Impromptu* – and first presented to the public at the Richmond Theatre on 5 December 1938 in a production by Gardner Davies who, since Reginald Denham was about to depart to the United States, was to be Patrick's closest friend in theatrical circles until his untimely death. The play soon transferred to the West End, where it enjoyed a successful run at the Apollo Theatre – which was crowned by a visit from King George VI and Queen Elizabeth; with near-unanimous critical praise (with the usual exception of the *Observer*), it became the event of the London theatrical season. After a six-month run, the play was staged at a small theatre in Los Angeles with financial help from Denham. Under the title *Angel Street* it transferred to Broadway where it enjoyed a huge money-spinning success, running for four years and making Patrick a very wealthy man.

The play's plot is too well-known to need more than a brief exposition: it is set in a gloomy, mid-Victorian middle-class house where Mr Manningham, at first sight a straightforward paterfamilias of the period, holds his wife Bella and his two female servants in a conventional patriarchal tyranny. It soon becomes clear, however, that Manningham is playing a sinister game; trying, in fact, to drive his wife insane by a series of fiendish tricks. For example, he secretes his own possessions in her work-basket and then accuses her of stealing them; she has no knowledge of these thefts but, confronted by the mysterious presence of the missing items among her own things, is driven to accept them as her own misdeeds, and thus as the actions of a madwoman. Her sanity, and her life, are saved just in time by the arrival of Inspector Rough, a good-hearted detective, who reveals that her husband is a bigamist and murderer (were the audience expected to hiss at this point?) who – and here the mechanics of the plot begin to creak a little – killed a rich but harmless old woman in the same house twenty years before in the expectation of stealing her valuable jewels. Manningham failed to locate the jewels at the time, but has returned to the scene of his crime (here the creaking becomes deafening) in order to recover the proceeds of his foul deed at leisure. To make Manningham's villainy consummate, Patrick has him kissing the housemaid, in the best – or worst – traditions of melodramatic stage roguery. However his evil designs are foiled by Rough, who confronts him with the evidence of his crimes before handing him over to a pair of policemen for justice to take its course.

Several qualities lift *Gaslight* out of the rut of run-of-the-mill pastiche Victorian melodrama and explain its enduring success as a play and film. Lacunae in the plot apart, the writing is tight and tension builds effectively. *Rope* had proved Patrick's skill as a thriller writer and Victorian London with its fogs and muffin men provides an atmospheric setting. However the play's stroke of genius is that which Patrick borrowed from Bruce: the central device of the heightening and lowering of the gaslight as a signal of the villainous Manningham's approaches and departures. This symbol of the ebb and flow of excitement, the encroachment of the forces of darkness upon those of light is the touch of magic that ensured success.

There are many interesting aspects to the play's text that have echoes and resonances in Patrick's life. There is the familiar sadism in the refined mental cruelty that Manningham practises on his distraught and helpless wife; the way he plays on her exposed nerves, giving that extra little twist to the rack to prolong and heighten the agony. There is the fear of the dark, which, as we know, had its roots in Patrick's own childhood.

Bernard Hamilton, Patrick's father, pictured with the monocle he wore for effect, and in the barrister's robes in which he never practised. (*Estate of Bruce Hamilton/Aileen Hamilton*)

Nellie Hamilton, Patrick's mother. (*Estate of Bruce Hamilton/Aileen Hamilton*)

The Dale House, Hassocks: Patrick's birthplace. (*Estate of Bruce Hamilton/Aileen Hamilton*)

The Hamilton children (*left to right*): Bruce, Lalla, and Patrick (aged 6). (*Estate of Bruce Hamilton/Aileen Hamilton*)

First Avenue, Hove: the street where Patrick grew up. (*Author's collection*)

Holland House School, Hove
(*Claudia Richardson*)

Patrick in his twenties. (*Aileen Hamilton*)

First love: Maruja Mackehenie at the time she met Patrick. 'Sweet was the word for her face', *Monday Morning*. (*Maruja Mackehenie*)

Charles Mackehenie in the uniform of the Peruvian diplomatic corps. (*Maruja Mackehenie*)

Success: the prosperous young author of *Rope*. But bad habits were already
setting in – note the nicotine-stained finger. (*Estate of Bruce Hamilton/Aileen Hamilton*)

Bruce Hamilton in his twenties. (*Estate of Bruce Hamilton/Aileen Hamilton*)

Lalla Hamilton. (*Estate of Bruce Hamilton/ Aileen Hamilton*)

The first productions of *Rope* (1929) *above* and *Gaslight* (1939) *below*. (*Mander and Mitchenson*)

Lois Martin, Patrick's first wife. (*Estate of Bruce Hamilton/Aileen Hamilton*)

Michael Sadleir, Patrick's friend, editor and publisher. (*Constable & Co*)

Claud Cockburn, comrade, crony and most influential of Patrick's friends. (*Communist Party Library*)

Patrick in the 1930s. The scars of his 1932 accident are clearly visible. (*Estate of Bruce Hamilton/Aileen Hamilton*)

Geraldine Fitzgerald, the unwilling love object of Patrick's middle years and the model for Netta in *Hangover Square*, pictured in her Hollywood role of Mrs Woodrow Wilson. (*Pictorial Press*)

Patrick the dandy: pictured in his apartment in the Albany by Bill Brandt
for a feature in *Harper's Bazaar*, 1947. (*Mrs N. Brandt*)

'La', Lady Ursula Chetwynd-Talbot, Patrick's second wife. (*Lady Audrey Morris*)

An uncharacteristically cheerful Patrick towards the end of his life. (*Estate of Bruce Hamilton/Aileen Hamilton*)

'Martincross', the house at Sheringham, Norfolk, which was Patrick's last home and where he died. (*Claudia Richardson*)

Bruce, Patrick's most loyal and devoted admirer, pictured a few days before his death in 1974, clutching his brother's books.
(*Estate of Bruce Hamilton/Aileen Hamilton*)

There are the familiar figures of the bullying, overbearing male head of household and the counterpart of the put-upon suffering female, who have their origins in Bernard and Nellie Hamilton. Finally, and perhaps most disturbingly, there is the re-appearance of rope (used to bind Manningham at the end of the play) and Bella's vengeful exaltation in the humbling of her husband. As a counterpoint to this cruelty, there is a good dollop of sickly sentimentality to sugar the pill, with the figure of Rough as that by now extinct stereotype, the good and saintly policeman:

> You shall have your Devonshire cream, my dear, and you shall have your fresh air to bring the sparkle back into your eyes.

Of course, no work by Patrick would be complete without a reference to drink, and in *Gaslight* he gives a heavy hint as to why he himself was becoming so reliant on the false comforts of the bottle:

> MRS MANNINGHAM: What medicine is it?
> ROUGH: You shall sample it and see. You see, it has been employed by humanity, for several ages, for the purpose of the instantaneous removal of dark fears and doubt. That seems to fit you doesn't it?
> MRS MANNINGHAM: The removal of doubt. How could a medicine effect that?
> ROUGH: Ah – that we don't know. The fact remains that it does. Here we are. (Produces what is obviously a bottle of whisky.)

Amidst all the excitement surrounding the success of *Gaslight*, Patrick scored another hit with the broadcast of his second play for radio, *To the Public Danger*, on 25 February 1939. It was written at the request of Val Gielgud as part of a Home Office road safety campaign and amounts to a re-run of the accident scene in *The Siege of Pleasure*. *To the Public Danger* is a straightforward propaganda piece warning against the fatal dangers of drink-driving. One odd contradiction that seems not to have occurred to Patrick is the contrast between the praise that he heaps on the magical powers of scotch in *Gaslight* and his warning against its hideous perils in *To the Public Danger.*

Patrick revelled in the new wave of popular acclaim that his drama successes brought. After his first radio play he told Bruce:

> My wireless play was a smash hit – the greater part of the press saying that it would be a model for all future wireless plays, and making a most unexpected fuss about it ... and a terrific amount of letters from unknowns everywhere.

Gaslight also brought in, along with the money, a deluge of praise from Patrick's public and peers:

> I had a wonderful letter from the author James Bridie about this play, who said if [R.L.] Stevenson had been alive today he would have loved to have written it – this pleased me enormously ... Also got colossal praise from Noel Coward! Ivor Novello!! All the authors are mad about it.
>
> I seem to be taking an enormous interest in myself as a writer! – a new departure! But I must say that all these things happening at the same time have given me an enormous fillip, and for the first time in years I really feel like doing some work. I certainly think that with this sudden burst I am now what you might call 'known' by reading and theatre-going people – in fact I think I can very nearly say, paraphrasing Keats, 'I think I shall be among the English writers while I live.'

But while Patrick was enjoying the fruits of success, the world was stumbling towards war. In the same letter (April 1939) he commented:

> The war? ... Certainly one *wants* it to come, in a way – as the slow fascisisation of Europe is proceeding, [Franco's forces had triumphed in Spain only weeks before] and the gangsters *might* be able to direct it against [the] USSR before falling out [among] themselves. But I somehow don't believe they'll get away with it, and if I *had* to bet on it I should say that there will be one fairly soon.

At the time Patrick wrote this letter, war was just four months away. He occupied the nervous months leading up to the outbreak of hostilities, like many other people, with restless, almost distracted activity. There were golfing weekends at Brighton and Broadstairs with friends like Bill Linnit and Dick Clancy, and fevered discussion with Kenneth Robinson and other left-wing friends as to the correct line to take when it became clear that war was only weeks or months away. There was great confusion among British Communists and their allies as the choice was ever-more starkly revealed – whether to fight for what they saw as the decayed and corrupt corpse of capitalist Britain against the greater evil of Fascism and Nazi Germany, or whether to cry 'a plague on both your houses' and take no part in the coming conflict in the expectation that Fascism and capitalism would destroy each other, leaving a purified world to fall gratefully into the arms of Soviet-Stalinist Communism. The choice became uncomfortably plain at the end of August when the news burst upon the world that Stalin and Hitler had signed a surprise non-aggression pact, giving the Führer a free hand to destroy Poland and, later, the Western democracies. Kenneth Robinson was with Patrick the day the news was announced:

> It was a bombshell. We just did not know what to do. But I remember that we all welcomed a statement by Harry Pollitt, the General Secretary of the Communist Party, that we must now fight a war on two fronts – one against Nazi Germany, and one against the Establishment in this country.[1]

Pollitt, however, was overruled by other members of the party's Central Committee who insisted on the imposition of the Comintern line dictated from Moscow that the war was an imperialist quarrel and that workers and Communists should have no part in it and should indeed sabotage the war efforts of their own countries. These and other tensions led Patrick to fall back into his old habits and indulge in frenetic drinking. As usual he strove to reassure a worried Bruce that he was being a good boy and behaving in an abstemious manner, but what he considered his relative abstinence gives an insight into just how deeply he was now in thrall to alcohol:

The first thing in your letter is about the drinking situation, and on this head you will be surprised and pleased to hear that I have been *absolutely wonderful*!! I *had* to be so efficient in the mornings that I just didn't *dare* to over-indulge, and drank much less than when I was idle. I have about 4 or 5 double whiskies every night ... I *always* have a meal in the evening ... I am actually planning to do a lot of work in the next year!

Though there is some excuse for Patrick's intake in that this was obviously a period of universal strain and that he did have a considerable professional workload – he did indeed succeed in doing an immense amount of work over the next year – there is little doubt that it was during these nerve-wracked months that his drinking passed from the state, in Claud Cockburn's words of 'quite normal heavy drinking' into actual alcoholism. And, despite numerous good resolutions, and periods of abstinence the slide was to be irreversible.

20

Hangover Square

THROUGHOUT 1939 THE TIDE OF PATRICK'S success swept on remorselessly. The broadcast of *To the Public Danger* was followed by a renewed avalanche of fan mail – but also a considerable number of hate letters from the lunatic fringe of the motoring lobby, who saw the play as a hysterical blast against their god-given right to drive how they liked, and as fast as they wanted.

Hardly had these echoes died away when the press announced that the Anglo-American Film Corporation was to turn *Gaslight* into a movie, to be filmed at the Elstree Studios. In the same month *Rope* was accorded the honour of a BBC television production, broadcast from Alexandra Palace on 8 March. Produced by Dallas Bower, the cast included Ernest Milton playing his old role of Rupert Cadell, and the young Dennis Price in one of the smaller parts. Bower, owing to the necessity of keeping the murder chest continually in shot, filmed to the capacity of his cameras in takes lasting as long as ten minutes – a technique that was to be copied by Hitchcock after the war when he came to film the play.

Patrick would make regular journeys to London to meet Bower and friends such as Gielgud and Priestley. Although he sometimes stayed at the Savile Club overnight, Patrick usually took a room at a superior guest-house run by a Miss Cooke near Sloane Square. The money he was now making would have enabled him to afford more luxurious accommodation, but the old call of the lodging-house was too seductive to shake off. Patrick needed a London base because, in a moment of weakness, he had agreed to take on the job of theatre editor for the weekly *Time and Tide*. This review was an idiosyncratic journal, owned by the wealthy aristocrat, Lady Rhondda, and used by her primarily as a vehicle for her strongly anti-Nazi views and as a platform for a variety of political and literary writers representing a wide spectrum of opinion, whose only common links were their opposition to the appeasement policies pursued by the Chamberlain government. Quite why Patrick agreed to this irksome task is a mystery; he certainly did not need the money. Perhaps he saw it as a way of keeping in touch with theatrical people, or possibly he needed an excuse to escape from the cloistered calm of life with Lois at Henley in order to plunge into the rackety world of literary and drinking London that he loved so much.

At any rate, he soon realised that the move had been a mistake. His appointment was announced in May, but by July his name had disappeared from the list of editors. His contributions were undistinguished; the journal did not allot much space to the theatre and it must have been a relief when he used a request by Lady Rhondda to 'puff' a play which he disliked as an excuse to resign on a point of principle. He had loathed the work – sitting through dull plays – and found association with the other press degrading.

The final weeks of peace seeped away in an atmosphere of tension and crisis. In July Patrick told Bruce:

> Time rushes by with such mad swiftness nowadays that one can hardly look round before a fortnight has gone. I think it is this incessant air of crisis that causes this – one can settle down to nothing – nothing which will serve to mark the passage of time – one is just waiting from weekend to weekend for something to happen.

Patrick was suffering from haemorrhoids and, as if he did not have enough trouble, his sister's love-life was again causing him and Bruce acute anxiety. After a series of doomed relationships with married men, Lalla had finally taken a second plunge into matrimony with a wholly unsuitable partner, Bertie Meyer, a widower many years older than herself who had actually been a friend of Bernard Hamilton. Meyer was a man of many parts, a theatrical entrepreneur, a sometime owner of the Bell Hotel in Tewkesbury and a farmer in Kent. The marriage was soon on the rocks and Patrick, with typical generosity, offered his sister money and a refuge in Henley should her domestic life with her new husband prove insupportable.

Patrick was also trying to lure Bruce back to Britain from Barbados, using as bait the money he was making, and he wrote renewing his offer to support his brother financially. But with war imminent, Patrick also sounded a note of caution:

> Have you much nostalgia for England? The point is, there is no sense in your coming back possibly to get conscripted if you can get out of it by staying there ... England is very unpleasant, more and more fascisised – what with ARP [Air Raid Precautions], territorials, militiamen, and advertisements of uniform-makers in the papers. Also one is almost expecting an air raid any moment – and if there's no air raid there's worse – another betrayal.

Writing just weeks before the announcement of the Nazi–Soviet pact, Patrick sympathetically analysed Stalin's dilemma, as he was wooed by diplomats from the Axis and the Allies:

> The best thing that can possibly happen now is a war *without* Russia – and I think this at the moment is what she wants to achieve. She has never been in so strong a position diplomatically as at the moment, and if she can bring off an embroilment of the bourgeois powers and keep out of it herself, she certainly will.

With the German threat to Poland growing daily more menacing Patrick asked:

> Can Chamberlain betray Danzig? I don't see *how* he can, but he has such power and resources as a traitor ... I wonder what they'll find written on Chamberlain's heart when he dies!

Having secured his Eastern front by his pact with Stalin, Hitler invaded Poland on 1 September and two days later Britain was at war. On 8 September Patrick wrote to Bruce:

> Well – we're off now! and so history marches in the way you and I know it must ever since 1933. Apart from all the horror and bloodshed and misery which lies ahead I suppose one should be relieved, as Hitler and his pals are now going to get it in the neck.

After warning Bruce that letters from henceforth would be subject to censorship, Patrick said that his contribution to the war effort so far had consisted of 'running material necessities' over to Aldershot, where Dick Clancy, who had been called up, was stationed before being shipped to France:

> Last night we arrived there just in time to see the King inspect them in a car! . . . an extraordinary situation when two weeks ago one was lunching peacefully in the City! after it we went and had a few drinks and tomorrow we will see him [Dick Clancy] for the last time. I can only give you a few other impressions in a news-reely way. Evacuation of children to Henley – all went very smoothly – like an extraordinary sort of Easter outing – for some reason we have not yet got a mother and child billeted on us, although they had been arranged for by the authorities.
>
> Black-outs at night wonderfully complete – incredibly dark – Henley seeming to be rather romantically a mediaeval town in the night.
>
> In day time Henley High Street like Chiswick High Road, owing to London evacuees all speaking Cockney.
>
> Went to London two days after war commenced – town rather like a London Sunday – barrage balloons as you approach town from a distance by car like little bugs in the white bed of the sky – you look up and slowly become aware the sky is thick with them! As you come nearer them they have a wonderful sort of Wellsian impressiveness.
>
> Soldiers everywhere, of course, and singing the 1914 tunes – 'Tipperary', 'Pack up your Troubles', etc. – Everybody carrying a gas mask – first air raid warning day before yesterday, 7.30 AM lasting till 9 – unable to take it at all seriously, and went out and bought a paper during it! – which other people were doing too.
>
> I don't believe there's any likelihood of raids here at *this* phase

of the war. It'll come *later*, if at all. All the same one is inclined to look up at passing aeroplanes, and to imagine noises one hears are the beginnings of warning sirens. The weather is glorious! One simply can't believe anything has started!

Once the shock of the declaration of war had passed, the country quickly settled down to surprising normality. The lack of fighting after the lightning German conquest of Poland contributed to the feeling of being somehow in limbo and this phase, the phoney war or the 'bore war', was to last until the Nazi invasion in the West in May 1940. Patrick's next letter to Bruce, in October, was full of grief at the death of Gardner Davies, the producer of *Gaslight*, at the age of thirty-two. Life was otherwise almost exaggeratedly dull apart from a few inconveniences, 'not all of which are inconveniences at all – such as the black-out and fewer cars on the road'. Patrick began to consider writing a new novel, but was unsure about how to start. He toyed with the idea of writing a three-volume Victorian thriller *à la* Wilkie Collins, his current enthusiasm. He was concerned, too, that whatever he wrote would be defined in terms of the war – which could be expected to change mores and attitudes in society significantly. He did not want a new novel to become instantly dated. However the book that he actually did undertake would not be a pastiche Victorian triple-decker, but one firmly set in the neurotic months leading up to the war, *Hangover Square*.

Writing on 30 November with a touch of smugness, Patrick congratulated himself on his abilities as a political prophet:

I am beginning to regard myself as an absolute *oracle* in world affairs! Since you left, all through Munich, right up to September I have made one correct forecast after another. I forecast the absence of air raids, the deadlock on the Western Front, the fate of Poland ... and now, today, I am proving marvellously right about Finland. (Russia has just broken off diplomatic relations) [As a prelude to its disastrous winter war with the Finns].

All these forecasts may just be luck, but I think they derive from increased knowledge plus the ability to look at things realistically, and not News Chronicly and New Statesmanly and Vernon Bartletty and all the other wish-fulfillers. How these crack up in the sterner pressures of wartime!

To this I stick through thick and thin – Hitler's power is on the *decline*, however long he may take in going. The arrangement he made with Russia was a terrible *symptom of weakness* from which there is no sort of recovery in the long run.

On New Year's Eve he reported that he had started work on 'a lightning novel – a Blitzy Novel!' This was the first mention of *Hangover Square*, though, at 100,000 words, it was hardly to be a 'lightning' novel. Depressed by snow, freezing cold and a toothache, the turn of the year found Patrick in a melancholy mood. Despite the predictability of events, this did not lessen their grimness; the fact that they almost certainly meant the end of life as Patrick and Bruce knew it. Optimism that a different, better world would emerge from the war was, however, some consolation. A long, hard winter followed. Patrick failed to finish his novel by his birthday target, and on that auspicious date (he was thirty-six) wrote to Bruce. He complained that he found idleness all but intolerable, but writing increasingly tough. Like many solitary workers he missed the stimulus of having other people around. Escapism, giving up everything but golf, reading and sleep, was out as he had to keep in touch to earn a comfortable living. He also reported that he had adhered for a week to a new regime, which varied his day and minimised opportunities for drinking. Patrick's letters throughout his life are full of such good resolutions, new routines and regimens, and replete with vows to stick to them. Knowing the dissolute side of his life, such boy scout-like self-homilies might make us smile. But we should remember that there was also a self-disciplined artist lurking within the same body as the hard-drinking, roistering Hamilton.

In April he wrote to Bruce that his new novel was a sort of thriller, to be called *Hangover Square*. This inspired title had been slopping around Patrick's mind since 1938, when he had joked to Bruce about 'taking a walk around Hangover Square'. Its theme, too, had been with him since the same date; as Geraldine Fitzgerald instantly recognised when she read the book, it is a fictionalised account of Patrick's passion for her.

Patrick had begun writing the novel on Christmas Day 1939,

and the story begins on Christmas Day 1938; we are immediately introduced to its hero, George Harvey Bone:

> Thirty-four, tall, beefy ... He had a fresh, red complexion ... His eyes were big, and blue and sad and slightly bloodshot with beer and smoke.

Bone is going through one of his 'dead' moods. He has suffered from these phases all his life, but lately they have been getting worse:

> It was as though a shutter had fallen. It had fallen noiselessly, but the thing had been so quick that he could only think of it as a crack or a snap ... Life, in fact, which had been for him a moment ago a 'talkie', had all at once become a silent film. And there was no music.

Bone does not know it, but he suffers from schizophrenia and when this 'shutter' falls, he knows what he must do – 'he had to kill Netta Longden'. Netta is the beautiful but worthless object of his dog-like, but potentially homicidal, obsession:

> Netta. Nets. Netta. A perfectly commonplace name ... But because it was hers look what had gone and happened to it! He could not utter it, whisper it, think of it without intoxication, without dizziness, without anguish. It was incredibly, inconceivably lovely – as incredibly and inconceivably lovely as herself. It was unthinkable that she could have been called anything else. It was loaded, overloaded with voluptuous yet subtle intimations of her personality. Netta. The tangled net of her hair – the dark net – the brunette. The net in which he was caught – netted.

The wordplay and repetition here convey the mental thrall in which Bone is held. But his dreams – to take Netta away from the corruption of Earls Court to rural bliss with him on a Sussex farm – are hopeless and absurd. To Netta, the aspiring actress and socialite, Bone is merely a butt for jokes, and (because he enjoys a small private income) a convenient cash cow to milk for drinks and meals. He is the ungainly, lumbering Fool at her feast.

Although he drinks with Netta's loose-living Earls Court set, he is not a part of it, and at times he is able to step outside the confines of his obsession to judge and condemn these people: 'Drunken, lazy, impecunious, neurotic, arrogant, pub-crawling cheap lot of swine – that was what they all were.'

Through the distorted prism of Bone's vision, Patrick expresses the prejudices of 'old money' (as represented by his hero's private income) against the vulgar, *nouveau riche* lifestyle of this saloon-bar set:

> They would get the shock of their lives if they knew how he could see through them at times – how transparent they were, for all their saloon-bar nonchalance and sophistication. He could see through them and, of course, he hated them. He even hated Netta too – he had known that for a long time.

Although Bone's Earls Court is a private hell, his actions are played out against the background of a wider world marching into its own inferno of madness and violence. And, in his sane and sober moments, he is dimly aware that Europe's crisis, like his own, is heading towards a climax. To him Netta and her most constant admirer, Peter, stand for Fascism. Patrick identifies their vicious amorality with appeasement of Hitler and fundamental principles of evil. At the end of his life, he told an interlocutor:

> What I was trying to present was a 'black' social history of my times. There were so many 'white' portraits of the Twenties and Thirties that I wanted to show the other side of the picture. After all, those were the decades in which Hitler rose to power. No one that I read was writing anything about him and the evil he represented.[2]

Not for the first time in his fiction, private bad behaviour stands for public vice. Patrick the novelist becomes Patrick the moralist:

> But now ... according to Netta and Peter, there wasn't going to be a war at all ... But he wasn't such a fool here, either – he could see ... with what facility they turned their ignominious desires

into beliefs. *He* hadn't fallen for all this 'I think it is peace in our time' stuff. But they had – hadn't they just! They went raving mad, they weren't sober for a whole week after Munich – it was just in their line. They *liked* Hitler, really.

Bone is not so easily hoodwinked, knowing:

> Munich was a phoney business. Fine for an Earls Court binge, but a phoney business, however much you talked ... All grinning, shaking hands, frock-coats, top hats, uniforms, car rides, cheers – it was like a sort of super-fascist wedding or christening. (Peter, of course, *was* a fascist, or had been at one time – used to go about Chelsea in a uniform.)

On one of the rare occasions when Bone persuades Netta to come on a dinner date with him, it is clear at once that she has an ulterior object in view – she wants to make contact with influential people who can help her in her theatrical career. As for Bone, he is merely her tool. Sure enough, upon reaching the restaurant, they run into a famous theatrical agent, Eddie Carstairs, of 'Fitzgerald, Carstairs and Scott'. In the name 'Fitzgerald' Patrick drops a heavy hint as to Netta's real-life identity and 'Fitzgerald, Carstairs and Scott' is clearly modelled on the theatre agency O'Brien, Linnit and Dunfree.

Bone is driven to a rare rage:

> All at once he was in a fury ... She had just brought him here so that she could see a man, a bloody theatrical manager: she had taken his money, she had taxied, wined and dined at his expense: and now the man had gone, she was going too ... He felt he could smack her face: he felt he could kill her.

Bone's anger has the effect of bringing on one of his schizoid 'dead' moods in which Netta ceases to be the *femme fatale* who is driving him to distraction, becoming merely a vague nuisance who has to be eliminated.

Occasionally, Patrick steps outside the claustrophobically confined world of his characters to evoke the false calm of the last summer before the war: such a lyrical scene comes when a

friend of Bone, Johnnie Littlejohn, strolls through Leicester
Square on a bright warm afternoon:

> Now it had been warm and fine like this for three weeks without
> a break ... In the thick green of the trees the birds screeched and
> sang above the subdued thunder of the traffic. In the middle of
> the square the effigy of Shakespeare stared greyly out ... A
> pigeon had alighted on the head of the poet, who seemed
> watching the red coat ... of the man who cleaned shoes on top of
> the Men's Lavatories. Fine, fine, fine ... Blue and sunshine every-
> where ...
>
> > Fine for the King and Queen in Canada ...
> > Fine for the salvaging of the *Thetis* ...
> > Fine for the West Indian team ...
> > Fine for the IRA and their cloakrooms ...
> > Fine for Hitler in Czechoslovakia ...
> > Fine for Mr Strang in Moscow ...
> > Fine for Mr Chamberlain, who believed it was peace in our
> > time – his umbrella a parasol!
> > You couldn't believe it would ever break, that the bombs had
> > to fall.

Patrick uses contemporary news stories (a Royal Visit to Canada;
the sinking of the British submarine *Thetis*; the West Indian
cricket tour; an IRA campaign with bombs left in station cloak-
rooms; Hitler's occupation of the rump of Czechoslovakia; and
Chamberlain's half-hearted bid to secure an alliance with Stalin)
to illustrate the illusory nature of peace and the roar of coming
war. That Patrick was not alone in perceiving the fragility of the
peace beyond a typical English complacency is evidenced by the
uncanny similarity of this scene to the passage in *Homage to
Catalonia* in which George Orwell describes his homecoming
from the Spanish Civil War:

> Down here it was still the England I had known in my childhood:
> the railway cuttings smothered in wild flowers, the deep
> meadows where the great shining horses browse and meditate,
> the slow-moving streams bordered by willows, the green bosoms

of the elms, the larkspurs in the cottage gardens; and then the huge peaceful wilderness of outer London, the barges on the miry river, the familiar streets, the posters telling of cricket matches and Royal weddings, the men in bowler hats, the pigeons in Trafalgar Square, the red buses, the blue policemen – all sleeping the deep, deep sleep of England, from which I sometimes fear we shall never wake till we are jerked out of it by the roar of bombs.

The appearance of Johnnie gives Patrick a chance to demonstrate that Bone's view of Netta and Peter is in fact objectively accurate. For if Bone is a schizophrenic, his balance hopelessly distorted by his obsession for Netta, then Johnnie's point of view is that of an undisturbed observer. He too looks at the Earls Court set as they really are, and he does not like what he sees:

He didn't like the look of the man at all. He did not like his general carriage, his fair, cruel face, his fair guardsman's moustache, his eccentricity of dress, his hatlessness, his check trousers and light grey sweater with polo neck ... And he did not like the look of the girl very much better. She was decidedly attractive, he saw, but in an ill-natured, ungracious way ... This girl wore her attractiveness not as a girl should, simply, consciously, as a happy crown of pleasure, but rather as a murderous utensil with which she might wound indiscriminately right and left.

When Johnnie accompanies George and Netta on a West End binge, Patrick takes the opportunity to show why in the novel he quoted *Roget's Thesaurus* on the word 'drunk', for which there were forty synonyms, each with a different shade of meaning (tipsy, maudlin, dead drunk, etc.). Drunkenness, to the sober, seems monotonously similar and drunks are notorious for being prize bores to all but themselves. But to the practised Patrick, drinking, like every human experience, was enormously complex, and the process of getting drunk was different for every drinker:

Soon the time came to order more drinks and it became clear to Johnnie that they were all going to get drunk. He came to this conclusion with a certain amount of gloom, as he always did nowadays, but he realised philosophically that on this occasion it was more or less a practical necessity. His friend George was in a state of happiness he could not spoil: the girl, previously hostile, had become mellow and friendly, and he himself was elated and talkative. So, at a given moment, he resigned himself to the joys of alcohol, wisely telling himself that if there was to be a hateful and repentant morning after the night before, he would at least see that the pleasure of the night before was not marred by the hatefulness of repentance – so that the night before and the morning after, the one in its pleasure, and the other in its pain, might, from the true perspective of a long-distance view in time seem to cancel each other out.

It is noteworthy that Patrick both praises the joys of alcohol and also equates it with 'excess and sin'. At this stage in his life, the joys still outweighed the dangers, but the balance was fragile.

For Bone, alcohol is the vehicle that transports Netta from her usual state of callous cruelty into a friendly and mellow human being. But the reprieve is a short one – soon she is back to her usual self; contemptuous, mocking and humiliating him in front of Peter, with whom she collapses into bed. Bone's loneliness becomes apparent once more. We have to imagine Bone as Patrick, locked out of Geraldine's flat as she met her fiancé, just as the hero of *Hangover Square* is locked out of Netta's life with his own hopeless, unrequited love. But who was Netta? Leaving Bone's disordered and confused mind, Patrick gives us a glimpse of the real woman behind her mask. This is one of the high points of the novel; chillingly, Patrick unveils the object of Bone's passion in her true colours:

> Netta Longden thought of everything in a curiously dull brutish way, and for the most part acted upon instinct. She was completely, indeed sinisterly, devoid of all those qualities which her face and body externally proclaimed her to have – pensiveness, grace, warmth, agility, beauty ... Her thoughts, however, resembled those of a fish – something seen floating in a tank, brooding, self-absorbed, frigid, moving solemnly forward to its object or veering slowly sideways without fully conscious motivation.

Netta's passions are similarly fishlike – cold-blooded and negative – she dislikes her relative poverty and her sordid Earls Court existence, and she is looking for an easy escape route, preferably via the studio couch and a figure like Eddie Carstairs. In the meantime she contents herself with the loathsome Peter; his attraction for her lies in a blend of snobbery and the violence of Fascism:

> ... a feeling for something which was abroad in the modern world, something hardly realised and difficult to describe, but which she knew Peter could discern as well as herself ... It had the same stimulus and subtle appeal for her as the fact of Peter having been in jail. It was not the avowed ideology of fascism. She was supposed to dislike fascism, to laugh at it, but actually she liked it enormously. In secret she liked pictures of marching, regimented men, in secret she was physically attracted by Hitler: she did not really think that Mussolini looked like a funny burglar. She liked the uniforms, the guns, the breeches, the boots, the swastikas, the shirts. She was, probably, sexually stimulated by these things in the same way as she might have been ... by a bull-fight.

It is not Netta the woman who stands in the dock, but Netta as symbol and representative of an entire class and a way of life that is sweeping the world. She and Peter are coupled, not by the mutual attraction of man and woman, but by a shared enthusiasm for the perverted tendencies of the times they live in. Patrick endows them with the familiar totems of his disdain: Peter with his small moustache, his blackshirt bully-boy persona, his record as a thug and car-driving killer; Netta with her indolence, her lack of pity, her casual duplicity and above all perhaps, her brazen sexuality. But Patrick goes beyond these two individuals to encapsulate a whole class in his indictment. In this sense, *Hangover Square* is a major advance over *Twenty Thousand Streets* where Jenny and Mr Eccles were laughably loathsome in themselves, but were no physical threat to anyone. Peter and Netta are in another league entirely; despicable, certainly, but also deeply dangerous because the attitudes they represent have already undermined, and threaten to overturn what Patrick understood as the civilised decencies of life: democracy, culture and common humanity.

Patrick was writing *Hangover Square* under the shadow of the seemingly unstoppable advance of Germany and Nazism; 1940 was Hitler's *annus mirabilis* when his armies overran Norway, Denmark, the Netherlands, Belgium, Luxembourg and finally France, leaving Britain in desperate isolation facing the Nazi juggernaut. Little wonder, then, that the novel's underlying theme is the search for a human metaphor to express the sickness that in Patrick's view underlay the whole course of the twentieth century. He followed the Marxist line that Fascism was the last gasp of capitalism; the final attempt by the bourgeoisie to preserve their power against the inevitable triumph of socialism and the working classes. He therefore identified the petty bourgeoisie, from which Netta and Peter sprang, as the enemy. There is an element of personal snobbery here, a relic of Patrick's establishment background, for he had assimilated his parents' contempt for those 'in trade' and despite his own financial success was still embarrassed by the vulgarity of money-making. Bone, as we have seen, also looks down on the new money represented by Peter and Netta. So Patrick had compelling private, as well as political reasons, for making the stagnant pond of Earls Court a microcosm of political decadence, mirroring the ideological conflicts of the world at large. Bone, Peter and Netta may be minnows, but the forces that motivate them are the same as those that actuate the sharks in wider waters.

Patrick uses the last half of *Hangover Square* to tip his characters down an ever-steepening slope towards extinction. Twice the action shifts from Earls Court to Brighton, where Bone succeeds in luring Netta, in the expectation, if not of enjoying the kind of dirty weekend traditionally associated with the resort, then at least of spending a few days alone with her.

Alas for his hopes. When Netta arrives, she is in the company of Peter, and also of a stranger, picked up on the train, who is yet another Fascist, and with whom she promptly goes to bed; a tortured Bone in the room next door hears every sound – the splash of whisky into tooth glasses and the inadequately suppressed laughter and murmuring of Netta and her new conquest.[3] The strain drives Bone into another schizophrenic fit, during which he resolves anew to kill Netta and Peter, and actually visits them armed with a golf club, intent on braining them both, but at the last minute he snaps into reality and backs down.

Once again in his 'right mind' he resolves to make a clean break with his way of life and gives notice at his Earls Court hotel. But there is one last betrayal still to come. Netta shatters all his good resolutions by sending for him in her hour of need (she has flu). Then, having nursed and cared for her, Bone gets her to agree to come away with him to Maidenhead, the idyllic destination of his fantasy throughout the book.[4] To Bone's disordered senses Maidenhead represents a paradise:

> Maidenhead, peace, the river, an inn, a quiet glass of beer, and safety, utter safety ... the river in the sun, in the shade of the trees, his hand in the water over the side of the boat, the sun on the ripples of the water reflected quaveringly on the side of the boat, his white flannels, tea in a basket, the gramophone, the dank smell at evening, the red sunset, sleep!

But there is to be no peace in a world rushing into war – August is over. Hitler has invaded Poland. And Bone has reached the end of the tether that ties him to Netta.

Casually, she reneges on her promise to go to Maidenhead, and departs again, instead, for Brighton; hot on the trail of Eddie Carstairs. Bone, believing that she has gone away with his friend Johnnie Littlejohn, follows her to expose her duplicity. As the novel comes to its crisis, Bone lapses in and out of his schizoid states with bewildering rapidity, so that by the end, it is difficult to discern when he is sane and when not. He carries out the murder of Netta and Peter in his final 'dead mood' but by then it hardly matters. The war is going to make killers and victims of everyone, and Bone's private homicide and suicide are swallowed up in a larger genocide. Returning from Brighton after a final redemptive reprieve, during which Eddie and Johnnie stand him drinks and roundly curse Netta – '*that* bitch' – Bone makes his way to Netta's flat and drowns her in her bath, before smashing Peter's skull with his golf club (a typically perverse touch by Patrick, making the instrument of one of his great pleasures into a murder weapon). As a counterpoint, Neville Chamberlain's voice is heard on the radio, announcing the outbreak of war. Still in a trance, Bone binds the scene of the crime in cotton thread:

> It was all threaded together.
>   All the threads were gathered up. The net was complete. The net. Netta. Netta – the net – all complete and fitting at last.

Bone walks to Maidenhead alone but the reality in no way ties in with his dreams:

> Maidenhead was no good at all ... It was just a town with shops, and newsagents and pubs and cinemas ... He had made a mistake. In fact he could hardly recognise it. It had let him down, like Netta. But as there was no Maidenhead, there was no anywhere, and he had got rid of Netta and Peter, and now of course he must get rid of himself.

He checks into a hotel, writes a confused note to the coroner attempting to explain his actions and, fortified (of course) by a bottle of whisky, turns on the gas in his room.

It took Patrick fourteen months to write the novel, but on 19 February 1941 he told Bruce that it was complete and a month later it was delivered to Constable:

> It is a long book (over 100,000 [words]) and, you will be pleased to hear, in *my* opinion *extremely* good! It's unambitious, a sort of 'thriller', but I have a feeling that, in its own *métier*, its the best thing I've *ever* written!

Sadleir also thought it Patrick's best book, though its author briefly wavered in this judgement when the first reviews were only lukewarm. However Patrick's initial impression was borne out as more notices trickled in. The *New Statesman* was enthusiastic and the *Times Literary Supplement* agreed:

Mr Hamilton has an experienced way with the sordid and the gruesome ... he hits off very accurately the seedy bohemianism of life on the hard, frozen plains of Earls Court.

But the book's sales really took off when the doyen of critics, James Agate, gave over the whole of his column in the *Daily Express* to praising it as:

... the best study of a trull since Shakespeare's Cressida ... Don't gulp this: ration yourself to fifty pages a day, and make it last the week.

Patrick was exultant, writing in November that the first edition had gone so quickly that the book was out of print for several weeks (this was partly, too, owing to wartime binding and paper restrictions) and that he was unable to get copies himself. He was buoyed up by the almost entirely favourable press reception the book received, and felt that, almost unwittingly, he had been drawn by his subject matter into producing his best work:

Oddly enough I did not intend it to be a good book, writing it almost for 'fun'; but it did get hold of me in a remarkable way, and the leading character, George Harvey Bone, is, I think, quite a *creation* – and I'm not sure it's not my best.

Patrick's achievement has been compared to that of Isherwood, Scott Fitzgerald and Graham Greene – novelists who create myths of social decay out of an individual crisis. In this novel, more successfully than any other, the lives and dilemmas of his characters reflect their times; Bone's personal tragedy is a microcosm of the greater threat to civilisation posed by the war. Here again it seems impossible to avoid comparison with George Orwell, whose novel *Coming Up For Air*, published in 1939, has many parallels with *Hangover Square*. There is no evidence that either writer ever met, or was even aware of the other's existence, but apart from sharing similar geographical and social backgrounds both seem to have the uncanny ability to sense and

voice the prevailing *zeitgeist*. Orwell's George Bowling, like
George Bone, is aware of the coming war, seeing visions of
bombs demolishing the peaceful streets of England. Like Bone
his thoughts are played out against the background of newspaper posters screaming about ''orrible' murders, and crises in
some 'faraway country about which we know nothing'. Like
Bone, Bowling is possessed by a dream of his past life as a
pastoral paradise, to which he wishes to return to escape the
humdrum present. And like Bone, the return, when it comes,
brings only bitter disappointment and disillusion.

In J.B. Priestley's words, Patrick has:

> ... a suspicion of society from which his chief characters are
> exiled. It is a deep feeling that there are no real homes for his
> homeless people to discover. It is a growing despair that dreads
> the way our world is going.[5]

Despite Patrick's Marxism, Priestley seems to be correct in his
belief that this despair was not merely the result of political–
economic opinion, but an instinctive abhorrence of modern
urban life. A youthful acquaintance of Patrick at that time, the
Communist poet Arnold Rattenbury, viewed the book similarly,
adding that *Hangover Square* caught the quintessence of the late
Thirties – the period from Munich to the outbreak of the war,
when Auden's 'low, dishonest decade' ended and even the most
purblind of Chamberlain's Conservatives saw that conflict could
not be avoided.[6] *Hangover Square*'s characters are in this limbo,
enacting their fatuous, futile rituals of drinking and hangovers,
hangovers and drinking. It has to be ended, and the most perceptive character among them – it is Patrick's comment on the
twisted times that a madman is more sane than those who are
ostensibly normal – is the Samson who pulls down the pillars of
the intolerable *modus vivendi*. The novel is interspersed with
epigraphs from Milton's 'Samson Agonistes', underlining the
image of a strong though blind man who wreaks revenge both on
a woman and a society.

But *Hangover Square* goes beyond mere social commentary. A
resonance also lies, as always in Patrick's best work, in its roots

in the author's own life. Bone parallels his creator in both his hopeless infatuation and even more destructively, as Bruce noted, in his drinking:

> I have to admit that although I fully recognised the terrible concentrated power of the novel there were aspects of it which disquieted me. If Patrick had been a stranger my admiration would, I think, have been unqualified. My uneasiness arose from the circumstance, perceptible increasingly in his fiction ... from the time of *The Midnight Bell*, that this novel was saturated, almost drowned in drink; the governing condition of its little world. What sort of life, I asked myself, must my brother not now be living to be impelled to explore, with such awful percipience, every shade, every nuance, every degree in the process of getting intoxicated and sobering up?[7]

PART V
1941–1948

21

Darkness

PATRICK DID NOT LET UP IN his creative burst despite the huge effort he had put into *Hangover Square*. In March 1941, just days after delivering the novel to his publishers, he told Bruce that, to fulfil a promise to his agent, Bill Linnit, 'I am going to try and write a sort of high-brow "Cloak and Sword" – just as *Rope* and *Gaslight* were high-brow thrillers'. In May, this conception had become more exact:

> Now that I've finished *Hangover* I have got to get down to a play, and am having the effrontery to try and write a *historical* melodrama! – about an imaginary imprisoned Duke in France of [the] later sixteenth-century – Henry [III of France], Guise, Navarre period. What a nerve! I doubt very much whether it'll come off, but I'll try and finish it, as I've got to write a play.

Bruce, who had a more professional interest in the discipline than his brother – he was to be awarded a doctorate by London University for a thesis on aspects of Barbadian history – had grave doubts about whether Patrick had sufficient knowledge of the historical background to write such a play in a convincing context, but when he came to read the finished work, all such

241

fears were assuaged. *The Duke in Darkness* is the most unfairly underrated of all Patrick's dramatic works. The fact that it flopped commercially when first produced (and has not often been seen since) has obscured the play's real qualities. It is, firstly, much more than a 'cloak and sword' melodrama. Behind his blades and ruffs, Patrick wrote a play dealing with the most fundamental questions – freedom, friendship and individual loyalties balanced against the good of the community or a political cause. Above all it is a parable on the Nazi occupation of France. Written at one of the darkest moments of the war, with Europe having entered a seemingly endless night of tyranny and with Hitler's armies at the gates of Moscow, it proclaims Patrick's faith in the ultimate victory of human values over the inhumanity of Fascism.

The play is set in the castle of the Duke of Lamorre at the time of the French wars of religion in 1580. Lamorre has kidnapped and incarcerated his rival, the Duke of Laterraine, together with his faithful servant Gribaud, for sixteen years. But when the play opens, Laterraine's plans to escape and lead his (Protestant) cause to victory over the forces of obscurantism, reaction and Catholicism, are about to reach fruition. The major flaw in the escape plan is the mental condition of Gribaud, who is cracking under the strain of his imprisonment. A further thread that Patrick weaves into his plot is the fact that the Duke is feigning blindness to make his captors believe that he too is broken and incapable of effecting his escape.

At last, and after much soul-searching, the Duke consents to have the by now hopelessly insane Gribaud poisoned in order to give himself a clear run to freedom, and thus enable him to improve the chances of universal liberty.

The play's Marxist message approves the Duke's reluctant realisation that the life of one individual cannot bar the path to the achievement of the general good. Logically, Patrick sternly demonstrates, sentimental ties of love and loyalty must sometimes be set aside in the interests of the inevitable triumph of progress over reaction. This may even involve, in the most extreme circumstances, in Auden's phrase, 'The conscious acceptance of guilt in the necessary murder.'[1] The cause of the people comes before bourgeois nicety.

Patrick explicitly admitted the play's political roots when visited by an admiring Arnold Rattenbury while he was staying at the Savoy Hotel. Rattenbury was attempting to secure Patrick's agreement to print extracts from the play in the Marxist journal *Our Time*. He recollected:

> In great pain at that time, he was drugged and propped up in bed when I called on him as messenger-boy from the office ... Given his condition when I saw him and my unimportance, he said very little I can remember – except once. I had mumbled something about my sense of wonder at his play. 'So you noticed?' he said, straining forward from the pillows. 'There, the Duke's speech, at the top of the page – there – it's a paraphrase of Lenin's "One Step Forward, Two Steps Back",' and then sank down again into stupor.[2]

The scene that Patrick adapted from Lenin occurs when the Duke confronts his captors to denounce the reaction they represent and to foretell the eventual victory of the people:

> You are condemned to death by the people, however long the sentence is delayed, and however long and cruelly the battle is waged. And then the people will be the world, and the world all the people – and the world will be its fair self, not the wild arena of slaughter, devilry and misery it is now.

The dramatic skills which Patrick employed in *The Duke in Darkness* are quite as formidable as his encapsulation of its optimistic political message: the idea of a man shamming blindness to lull his enemies into a false sense of security had been with him since the early 1920s when he had mentioned it to Bruce on a Chiswick walk. And in the character of Gribaud he had written one of the most difficult stage roles ever created: the young Michael Redgrave grasped its possibilities when he snapped up the role for the play's première in September 1942 at Edinburgh's Lyceum Theatre and it transferred the following month to the St James's Theatre in London. Redgrave also directed the play, which had Leslie Banks in the part of the Duke. Despite this star-casting, however, the reviews were decidedly mixed, as Patrick ruefully reported to Bruce, 'Some rave, some ferociously anti', and the play was taken off after a two-month run. Patrick was philosophical and attributed its commercial failure to the fact that the cast was exclusively male, a defect also blamed by Redgrave himself.

The political optimism of *The Duke in Darkness* reflected Patrick's posture during the war, an attitude he was to resolutely maintain in life and work as long as hostilities lasted; but it also seemed to conceal a deep-seated and worsening malaise, as Bruce, reading between the lines of his cheery wartime letters, perceptively noticed,

> ... it was the product of an act of will at least as much as of conscious reasoning. It would be an exaggeration to call it whistling in the dark, it was pursued too consistently and too strenuously for that. Nevertheless his high spirits, his fun, his resolute refusal to believe that evil could finally prevail, were one side of a medal whose hideous reverse he would rarely permit himself to look at, deliberately thrusting it as deep as he could into his unconscious mind. And this had been true, though more perceptibly at some times than at others, since his boy's anguish when first confronted with the idea of eternity; but it was in his later years that the turning of his thoughts away from it became more marked. That was why the war, in this one respect, was actually good for him. His time was so filled with work, business insisting on his attention, a vivid rackety social life among friends, and the exigent demands for sleep made by an exhausted body, that he seldom had time or leisure to contemplate 'the horror of the shade'. And the habit of rejecting this contem-plation became finally a fixed purpose, though one only to be maintained at a heavy cost; nothing less than the gradual ruin of his health.

Patrick's letters from the early and middle years of the war give a good idea of the hectic activities with which he stuffed his days and nights, keeping the darkness at bay. In April 1940 he wrote:

> I have been having a rather good time recently – though quite

mad ... The high shots of this mad period included a weird sort
of *millionaire's fortnight*, in which I went away in a huge Rolls
Royce with Bill Linnit to Bournemouth and mingled with the
forty women composing the cast of *The Women*! – which was
immediately followed by staying at the *Savoy Hotel*(!) with Dick
[Clancy] on leave (he insisted on it and paying)! – all of which,
both with B.L. and Dick, was mixed up with a great deal of super-
golf played on super-courses with *caddies*!

The following month, on 11 May, Hitler launched his devastating
blitzkrieg on France and the Low Countries, and within days, the
German armoured columns had sliced through the French
armies and the British Expeditionary Force and were at the
Channel ports.

On 3 June, while Britain struggled to evacuate the survivors of
the BEF from the beaches at Dunkirk, Patrick wrote from his
Henley backwater:

I'm just stuck down here writing and watching the war! It's got
going now all right! ('Navy fights to save last thousands' is the
headline in today's *Daily Mirror*) I am terribly worried about
Dick. They say four-fifths of the BEF has got back, but we haven't
heard from him. If we don't hear in a week's time I should think
almost certainly it will mean that he is killed or a prisoner.

Patrick had been working on a dictionary of significant dates in
world history by way of relaxation from the strain of writing
Hangover Square. He had shown the draft to Clancy during their
jaunt at the Savoy:

I made a little compact with him. It was, that if he was killed I
would dedicate that book ... to him. Alternatively if I was
bumped off he would finish it or get it finished and dedicate it to
me! I should now like to add this – if *both* of us are bumped off,
will *you* please finish it, and dedicate it to both of us! I may add
that I don't anticipate getting bumped off at all! But with the war
almost certainly coming to this country one begins to think about
such things, and I should like to leave this little perpetuation of a
friendship. [The book was never finished.]

It was at this inauspicious moment in the war that the Anglo–American Film Corporation chose to release their movie version of *Gaslight* to the public. Directed by Thorold Dickinson, who had made his name with a documentary on the Spanish Civil War shot largely in the front-line trenches before Madrid, the film starred Anton Walbrook and Diana Wynyard. The verdict of the press was mainly favourable and all the papers commented on the freedom with which Dickinson had extended the claustro-phobic atmosphere of the drawing room to take in the whole of Victorian London in the 1880s, complete with a recreation of Pimlico Square with its hansom cabs. Even Patrick was reason-ably pleased with his first – and happiest – experience of the liberties which the cinema was to take with his work.

> On the day Belgium capitulated I was in town seeing the trade show of the *Gaslight* film! The story was *incredibly* ballsed up and ruined, but actually the production and technique was excellent and Anton Wallbrook gave a really first-class performance. On the whole, the thing wasn't too bad.

By the time he next wrote to Bruce, in July, his agonies over Dick Clancy had at last been laid to rest. Clancy returned safely and Patrick had even played golf with him. The state of the war, however, was still grim: Britain, under the premiership of Churchill, now stood alone. On 3 July, the day that Churchill demonstrated his ruthless will to continue the battle by ordering the Royal Navy to attack the fleet of his erstwhile ally, France, Patrick reported:

> ... we're *still* waiting for the real trouble to begin over here. It will do so all right – very, very soon now, I think.

If Patrick's prophetic abilities deserted him here, he was not alone. Virtually the whole nation believed that a German invasion was imminent, and that the battle for France was about to transfer to Sussex. Patrick was phlegmatic about the situation:

> ... impossible to convey in a few words how really *extraordinarily* calm and philosophical one is about the whole business over

here. The belief in one's star, the feeling that *somehow oneself* is coming out all right, quite absurd as it is, is deeply rooted in human nature, and keeps everybody going in a wonderful way. Then there is (to me at any rate) a sense of *interest* and *excitement* which keeps one going – aeroplanes, tanks and troops going through the streets – here is a sort of nightmare *stimulation* of the faculties. What I am trying to say is that one is not (as one would have imagined) in a blue funk and miserable: one is, at present any rate, quite composed and just about as happy or miserable as one always was.

However, despite this reassurance, Patrick had built up a supply of Medinal (which of course had killed his mother) for him and Lois to use in case of a successful German invasion.

By the time of Patrick's next letter, in October, the Battle of Britain had been fought and won, not on the beaches and fields, but in the skies over southern England. The threat of invasion temporarily postponed, the Germans turned their tactics to trying to break the British will by bombing London and the other major cities. It was the beginning of the Blitz:

It's most immediate effect has been to bring up the population of Henley from 7,000 to 17,000! – and nearly always there is someone staying in the flat – including complete strangers who are given a bed for the night. There is not an inch of room in the town – the place is a sort of Palm Beach! This does not mean that the place is *completely* immune from the enemy: the sirens go every night, which is a bloody nuisance because Lois has to be out on her ARP – she drives an ambulance – and stand by till the all-clear which often doesn't come till dawn. Then bombs *do* drop, but so far more than a mile away, and *always at definite objectives.*

Patrick reported on a recent visit to London:

I went up to the front line ... last week, and was made a little sick by the wreckage – Oxford Street, Lewis' gone, Peter Robinson with huge chunks of white pillars lying in Oxford Circus (as though Samson had been having a go at it) a huge building completely gutted in Gt Portland Street.

By the way, the bombing, so far, though indiscriminate in effect is not so in intention – you will notice that the above mentioned are all aimed at the BBC.

It's all a nightmare and *not* a nightmare. At one moment you're really rather appalled and scared, at the next you're cracking jokes in a pub serenely oblivious that there's a war on.

Communist sympathies notwithstanding, Patrick joined in the prevailing Churchillian patriotism.[3] As Hitler tightened his siege of the British Isles, U-Boats began to take their toll of Allied shipping in the Atlantic and among the casualties were apparently several letters from Patrick to Bruce, for in January 1941, Patrick puzzled over the fact that his brother had not been receiving his recent correspondence and concluded, 'there can be no doubt that some have gone to the bottom'. Bored by Henley, Patrick reported that his only sight of the war came when he travelled to London for a few nights:

> ... with all this misery and peril around one I feel one ought to carry on as far as possible *as one did before* – and so I have had my share of the Blitz. This frightens one *amazingly* little – indeed with a few drinks inside one, not at all.
>
> The trouble with this war over here for the huge majority of civilians is not the *danger* – but the bloody *inconvenience* and *boredom* – the restrictions, the black-out, the travelling, petrol, posting and telephoning difficulties.
>
> One other *dreadfully* boring thing about this war is other peoples's stories of their bombs, etc. There are a terrible amount of bomb-braggarts, and it now almost become a tradition amongst well-behaved people not to mention their own bombs, however severe. And certain wags go about wearing little badges on their lapels, reading 'I am not interested in your bomb story' or 'My bomb was bigger than yours' or 'For sixpence I will listen to your bomb-story'!

By February 1941, the tonnage of Atlantic convoys sunk by the Germans was beginning to show up in severe rationing. This deprivation was alleviated when Patrick's American friends, the Feurhakes, 'rather sadly and sweetly (imagining we were starving, I think) sent us a bundle of tinned butter and things!'

The next month Patrick reported that he had been called up for a medical examination by the authorities and had been given a Grade Three categorisation, or declared unfit for active military service – presumably because of his accident injuries, and short sight.

By May the strains of a year under siege were beginning to tell. Patrick explained to his brother the rudiments of his stoical philosophy for riding out the times.

In these incredible days there is only one bird to emulate – one wiser by far than the owl – the *ostrich*. If one ceased for a moment to be ostrich-like, if one started to think about anything, one would go mad ... As I see it, either this war goes on indefinitely, or there is the wrong sort of peace, which will mean intensified fascism over here, which will mean incredible misery for people like us. But I may be wrong and wonderful things may happen in our own lifetime.

These blitzes in London are bloody. One goes up to town and wades through glass-strewn streets and rubble-blocked ways and still-smoking buildings to one's destination, wondering whether it will still be there – and the phones being out of order causes incredible anxiety generally. But again it is *astonishing* how quickly the town pulls round, and establishes a new *modus vivendi* in a few days. People, of course, are 'wonderful'. What one can put up with when one has to! ... Constables has been hit about but still stands – having had two remarkable escapes when houses next door have been demolished ... But I still meet Martha and Michael in Gordon's wine house and drink sherry! And I still play golf with Bill Linnit!

On 22 June 1941 the Germans invaded Russia. It was the turning point of the war. After a year's exhausting struggle, Britain was no longer alone in resisting Hitler. Stalin's hopes of playing off the Fascist against the capitalist powers collapsed and he was soon fighting a desperate battle for sheer survival. The Communist Party policy promptly switched back to all-out support for the war and on 15 August Patrick wrote to Bruce, '... the Russian business, has knocked everything else out of one's head – one just holds one's breath and can think of nothing else.'

As he watched while his beloved Stalin slugged it out with Hitler
– a feeling he described as 'the horrible sense of being shut
outside the room during the bloody birth and climax of history' –
changes had been happening in Patrick's life. Following his army
medical he had been summoned to see a conscription clerk:

> ... who asked me what I was. I said a writer, and he replied that if
> I could write a good hand I might be very useful. Extremely
> farcical, but as it looked as though I might have to spend the rest
> of the war licking stamps and addressing envelopes in Reading I
> wisely pulled some strings. Got Bill Linnit to talk to Basil Dean,
> who saw me and gave me a job on ENSA! I don't have to do very
> much at present (I write the chat linking up the songs in ENSA
> broadcast half-hours) but it means going up to London a lot.

The Entertainment National Service Association was the
brainchild of Basil Dean, a theatre producer who had organised
concerts for the troops in the First World War. At the outbreak of
the Second World War, Dean determined to oppose the authorities' tacit policy that theatre should go dark for the duration.
Dean, a man of formidable energy (and egotism), fought a one-
man battle to convince the bureaucrats that the arts could be
valuable morale-boosting weapons of war. After a bruising
struggle, he got his way: ENSA was established in the Drury
Lane Theatre, from where Dean sent out his army of thespians to
make the nation laugh, sing and dance. Soon the troupe were on
the road staging lunchtime sing-songs in factories which were
broadcast by the BBC. This is where Patrick's 'links' came in.
Later he was somewhat ashamed of his absurd contributions to
the war effort, telling Bruce that he felt he had touched bottom as
a writer when he found himself having to write a link between
'My Blue Heaven' and 'Tea for Two' that ran, 'But it isn't the
blueness but the twoness that matters...'

A compensation for Patrick was that his London work gave
him more chances to deepen his acquaintance with Claud
Cockburn. He also persuaded Constable to give Cockburn a £100
advance for his autobiography, at a time when Cockburn was in
dire financial straits after the closure of *The Week*.[4] (This was not
an act that made him popular with the publisher's accountants,

though, for the book was not completed until twenty years later.)
Cockburn's forceful personality soon established a sway over
Patrick, who was flattered by his new friend's enthusiasm for his
work.

All his adult life, Patrick had been in search of a father-figure
to replace Bernard's crushing influence, even though he had
consciously rejected such domination in early manhood. The first
person to fill this role had been Carlos Mackehenie, whose
worldly persona had enchanted Patrick during the 1920s. With
Carlos' departure the role had been taken over first by Michael
Sadleir, and then by Bill Linnit, whose services were valuable
both in business affairs – he was the moving spirit behind the
triumph of *Gaslight* and the less successful *Duke in Darkness* –
and in more personal matters. Linnit, with his access to young
and attractive actresses and his air of the elegant boulevardier
suffering from an excess of *ennui*, had the broad experience
which Patrick needed when he came to confess his turmoils and
tribulations over Geraldine Fitzgerald. Linnit's advice was to
take affairs of the heart more lightly. Not every romance, he
counselled the love-lorn Patrick, need be a grand passion and it
seems pretty certain that he subsequently acted as a sort of
upmarket procurer for Patrick, effecting introductions to young
women who would understand his complex needs and not be
averse to satisfying them. This, at any rate, seems to have been
what Bruce believed:

> It was this friend who, almost hypnotically, pointed the way to a
> sexual life more satisfactory than Patrick, hitherto subject to an
> excess of diffidence, had ever before enjoyed. He taught him the
> technique of a self-confident approach, and how to exploit it;
> also, at least equally important, the art of seeing a sexual
> adventure as a *passade* rather than a passion. For this, Patrick,
> profiting in an entirely practical way, was infinitely grateful.

If there is something distasteful in this picture of a cynical,
middle-aged man coldly plotting the love-life of his client, it
should be remembered in Linnit's defence that it was the consequence of an approach from Patrick, who doubtless spilled a tale

of woe regarding his loveless – or at least sexless – marriage. Indeed, reading Patrick's wartime letters, one could almost forget that he had ever married, so little mention is made of Lois. Bruce, however, brushed the omission aside:

> There is nothing significant about this. It is just that her position as the creator and manager of Patrick's domestic background at Henley, and often as hostess to his friends, was taken for granted. I do not mean that he failed her in either affection or gratitude, although she must often have been lonely when he was away on his own in London, and at times, when he was at home, tried hard by his behaviour in his periods of heavy drinking. His failure to write much about her was really a question of wives not being 'news' in the normal terms of our correspondence; except when Aileen was laid out with pneumonia I wrote as little to him about her. My impression about Lois' experiences and feelings at this time is shadowy. I know that she made friends in Henley, that she turned herself into an excellent cook; and I am quite sure that she engaged in active and useful employment which filled her solitary hours. Certainly, and particularly in the periods when London was not subject to attack, she sometimes accompanied Patrick there; but he never mentioned it. I think that her war experiences must have been relatively lacking in the factitious [sic] stimuli of excitement, danger – and hard liquor; and been a great deal more bleak than his own.

Bruce's attitude to women is evident. Lois is consigned to the role of a mere homebody; cooking, cleaning, making the Henley domicile a fit place for her husband to receive his friends when he is at home, and alone in his absence while he happily drinks and philanders the war away in London, enjoying, as an additional bonus, the vicarious thrills of the Blitz. No doubt the honest Bruce was totally unaware of the condescension implicit in his description of Lois' war; for him, as always, his brother could do little wrong. Of course an even more overt 'sexism' pervaded Patrick's entire life. It is notable that *none* of his friendships were with women: despite all the sympathetic portrayals of them in his fiction, he was at heart a man's man. Women were good for the kitchen and the bedroom, but they did not really belong in the pub and club. His only serious relations with women, apart from his mother, were on a sexual level. It must be accounted something of a tribute to his powers as an observer and an artist that despite his misogyny Patrick was able to render such insight and sympathy to female characters in his fiction.

There was one level, however, on which he was unable to connect with Bill Linnit, as he had been unable to connect with Michael Sadleir – politics. It took the advent of Claud Cockburn into his life to fill this gap.

Cockburn was born, like Patrick, into an upper-middle class family that was to become steadily more impoverished.[5] This establishment background and journalistic talents won him a foreign correspondent's job on *The Times*, but he converted to Communism and under the pseudonym Frank Pitcairn became a writer for the party newspaper, the *Daily Worker*. A natural conspirator with an unrivalled flair for propaganda, his searing (but frequently mendacious) reports from Spain drew the wrath of Orwell, for Cockburn made no bones about letting the truth stand in the way of a good story when it might result in favourable publicity for the cause. Cockburn justified his lies by claiming that they served the party of progress, but the anarchist in him enjoyed the whole process of telling whoppers for its own sake.

Returning from Spain, he founded his own private newsletter, *The Week*, a trail-blazing publication which purported to give 'the news behind the news' but owed many of its scoops to the Editor's fertile imagination. The main targets of the paper's invective were the Chamberlain Government and its flabby appeasement policies, and Cockburn coined the phrase 'the Cliveden set' to describe the circle of pro-Nazi Tory politicians and socialites who allegedly met at Lady Astor's country home near Henley to plot their schemes. Cockburn obediently followed the party's *volte face* after the Hitler–Stalin pact and in January 1941 Churchill's Government felt obliged to ban *The Week*, along with the *Daily Worker* itself, for its anti-war activities.

Patrick had been introduced to Cockburn through the unlikely agency of Willie Gallacher, Britain's sole Communist MP and a militant teetotaller as well as politician. Patrick had

told Gallacher that he wanted to do something in the cultural
sphere for the Communist cause without having to actually join
the party. Cockburn commented:

> He had never been a Communist. As a passionate anti-fascist
> with a world reputation ... he was constantly approached by
> what the Americans call 'Front' organizations. However, the
> thought of joining anything made him shudder. The notion of
> just having his name listed as one of fifty vice-presidents of
> something, even though assured that he would never have to
> attend a committee or other meeting, brought on a terrible attack
> of agoraphobia.[6]

Gallacher offered to introduce Patrick to other writers serving
the party and brought him down one day to the *Daily Worker*
office in City Road. Cockburn recorded:

> Always panic-stricken at the eleventh hour by the prospect of
> any new human contact, and on this occasion additionally terri-
> fied by horrid visions of a couple of grim-minded pamphleteers,
> ever alert to chloroform and pierce with deadly pin anything
> looking like an intellectual butterfly, Hamilton – as he told me
> afterwards – actually considered deliberately falling off the tram
> before it got to our office.[7]

As an alternative escape, Patrick briefly contemplated dashing
into the local pub to fortify himself for the ordeal. But his guide
was the ardently 'dry' Gallacher and so he did not dare make the
suggestion. Patrick's fearful visions were realised. In an atmosphere of general embarrassment, Gallacher introduced Patrick to
the staff. Cockburn wryly commented, 'Gallacher's idea of an
introduction was to say, "Well, there you are. All intellectuals
together," and then stand back, smiling benevolently and waiting
for us to get on with it.'

Fortunately for Patrick the staff of the paper were obviously
busy and Cockburn cut the appalling encounter short by
suggesting that they should meet again a few days later.
Shepherded by Gallacher, Patrick tottered thankfully out,
resolved, at that moment, to cancel the appointment as soon as

possible. He felt he had already had one narrow escape, and that his nerves would hardly stand a longer session, consisting probably of a discussion of the Novelist's Duty to Dialectics or something of the kind, washed along its course by draughts of tea.

On the tram back to Westminster, Patrick discovered that he need not have worried. Gallacher said meditatively in his powerful Scots accent, 'You know, it's a very funny thing about those two men, Cockburn and Holmes. They're fine lads, fine writers. They've both of them given up a lot, a whole lot, for the sake of our paper. And yet, would you believe it now, they *drink*.' Patrick let out a yelp of mingled surprise, pleasure and relief, which Gallacher took for a very natural cry of disappointment and dismay. 'Like fishes,' added Gallacher.

Patrick decided to keep his date and a few days later met Cockburn in a pub near the office. They hit it off so well that they were twice admonished by the barmaid for laughing too loudly and disturbing the regular customers. This set the tone for the friendship between the two men. Cockburn, with his outgoing, powerful personality, was undoubtedly the senior partner in the relationship: this influence was most obviously demonstrated in their politics, for he was even more widely read in Marxist works than Patrick, and his combination of a seemingly infallible knowledge of the sacred texts with his adventurous life of action proved irresistible. (On one occasion, Cockburn even got Patrick out distributing Communist leaflets in the City Road, although a convenient flying-bomb raid soon caused them to seek shelter in the local pub.)

Not forgetting the original purpose of their meeting – Patrick's desire to place his literary talents at the service of Communism – Claud did procure for his friend for a short while the unofficial post of play-reader to the Soviet embassy, advising the Russians on what British works would be ideologically suitable for translation and distribution in the USSR.

This is not as eccentric as it sounds. Britain, from mid-1941 to the end of the war, passed through an unprecedented phase of enthusiasm for all things Russian. After Hitler's attack on the Soviet Union, Churchill led the way by swallowing his lifelong anti-Bolshevism and welcoming Britain's new ally with open arms. There was a rush of relief that the country was no longer alone in fighting Nazism and Tory politicians rubbed shoulders with Communists on platforms up and down the country to raise support for the desperately hard-pressed Russians; ENSA staged a 'Salute to the Red Army' which filled the Albert Hall; crusty reactionaries like Lord Beaverbrook wore themselves out in campaigns to open a Second Front to relieve the pressure on Russia; and 'Uncle Joe' Stalin became a figure comparable to Santa Claus in benevolence. For the moment, Patrick was swimming with the popular tide. In Cockburn's company he shed his shyness and diffidence and opened up on every conceivable topic from socialism to sex – two subjects, in fact, which were uppermost in his mind in the latter years of the war.

Though Claud Cockburn was very sympathetic to Patrick, some of his Party comrades were less so. One was the formidable Bill Rust, Editor of the *Daily Worker*, and Cockburn's friend began to come under the scrutiny of this functionary's cold eye. He did not like what he saw. A rumour reached Rust that Patrick had had some past connection with a Fascist organisation, or at least had travelled in such company. Cockburn believed this absurd story owed its origins to the accurate depiction of the Fascist mentality in *Hangover Square* but, however it began, it was disturbing to the party bosses, who feared that he might have taken a viper to his bosom. Rust, who doubled as the head of the party's Cultural Division on the strength of his fondness for attending the first nights of West End shows, was deputed to investigate the claim and cross-questioned Cockburn.

Referring to *Hangover Square*, Rust said that it was the general opinion of the comrades that nobody could possibly reproduce so exactly the manners, speech, outlook, and behaviour of a Fascist who had not been or did not have the most intimate connections with the Blackshirts.

> It took a number of uproarious and deeply sympathetic meetings between myself [Cockburn], Patrick and several party leaders to convince them that fascism for Patrick was the embodiment of all that he most hated.[8]

One wonders whether it ever occurred to Patrick or Cockburn, while they were laughing this matter off, that had Rust actually had the political power they were labouring to give him and the party, the consequences of such suspicions could have been much more serious.[9]

It was Cockburn who referred memorably to Patrick's 'bat's wing ear':

> Just as some people can listen to a voice once and an hour later mimic it perfectly, so Hamilton could listen, without even seeming to listen, to a half-hour's conversation going on at the other end of a bar and afterwards not only reproduce its content and cadences, but intuitively deduce from it the whole nature of the talkers.[10]

When standing with him in a London bar Claud would often be astounded to have their conversation suddenly interrupted by Patrick suffering from what seemed to be a minor convulsion or rictus:

> Seeing my astonishment he would say, 'But, my God, didn't you hear what that man said: don't you see the sort of thing he is up to? God help us.'
>
> The man in question, with his back to us, was probably seven or eight feet away but Patrick had not only heard what he said but actually interpreted it. Two or three times I rather meanly tested him on this by waiting until he had left the pub and scraping acquaintance with the stranger. On each occasion the man's opinions proved to be precisely what Hamilton had deduced.[11]

Claud's observation was reinforced by his wife Patricia, who agreed with her husband that many of Patrick's problems could be attributed to his painful shyness.

> I have heard many people described as 'shy' – usually as an excuse for some sort of boorishness. Nobody, I used to think, knew what shyness could really be until he had met Patrick Hamilton. But in his case the word, so far from describing any kind of boorishness, indicated a sensitivity towards other human

beings which for him frequently produced actual pain. I believe when he was very young this sensitivity had been an almost continuously painful liability. With great deliberation he turned it into an asset.[12]

Under the combined influence of alcohol and Claud's close companionship, Patrick confided many of his most closely guarded secrets – particularly those to do with sex. This was usually a taboo subject in Patrick's correspondence with Bruce; caution about the prying eyes of the censor, together with an understandable apprehension that one of their wives would chance upon the missive, probably made them both careful. But once, when he was safely away from Henley and writing on a train, Patrick let the mask slip a little. On 6 June 1942 he hinted to Bruce that amid his hectic social life he was conducting some amours. From this suggestion, and other vague references, Bruce deduced,

> that he attained maturity in his sex life during the war ... he had never appeared to show the diffidence or inhibitions that were for so long damaging to myself, the besetting fancy that one was uniquely unattractive to women. But he often told me that he was every bit as bad ... Practically, since the failure of his marriage to bring sexual satisfaction, he had, as before it, to go with tarts; not however very frequently and usually when tight.

If sexual maturity consisted, in Bruce's view, in resorting to prostitutes while drunk, one wonders by what curious means he measured Patrick's sexuality. In private conversations with Cockburn, Patrick confirmed that he frequented prostitutes – particularly those who had no objection to indulging his penchant for tying them up preparatory to engaging in various sado-masochistic games and rituals. This comes as no surprise to any student of his work: sadism, cruelty, ropes, tying, confinement and restraint are a regular feature of his published writings from *Rope* itself down to the home-made rope by which the hero makes his escape in *The Duke in Darkness*, and beyond to the ever-more overt bondage scenes in *The West Pier* and his last novel, *Unknown Assailant*. Cockburn also averred that one reason

for Patrick's low output during the 1950s was his second wife's
fear that he was giving away too many secrets in his books,
regarding his own sexual tastes and proclivities.

One fairly obvious reason for Patrick's behaviour is attested to
by both Bruce and Claud (who agree on little else when inter-
preting Patrick's curious personality): the conviction that,
especially after his accident, Patrick felt he was simply too ugly
to have any hope of having a successful relationship with
ordinary, respectable women. His bruising experience with
Geraldine Fitzgerald can only have confirmed his conviction that
he was the Beast to her Beauty and we have Geraldine's own
testimony from her recollections of Patrick's conversation that he
was 'absolutely obsessed with prostitutes'.[13] Patrick must have
felt much happier in the unsentimental relationship of a tart with
her punter. It gave him unquestioned power over his partners for
they were paid to ignore the ugly scars on his face and allow him
to enact his domination fantasies. He made no secret of these
feelings to understanding male friends like Cockburn and Bill
Linnit (it was the latter's partner, Bill O'Brien, who, it will be
recalled, warned Geraldine Fitzgerald that the urbane, literary
Patrick could also be capable of outbursts of sadistic, violent
rage).

Patrick's understanding and fear of the Fascist mentality
derived from self-knowledge; he knew that all men hide the
capacity for such irrationality. He concealed his own fascination
for cruelty well, but as he grew older, and the depredations of
alcohol on his mind, body and character were to become more
pronounced, his inhibitions fell away, and the dark side of his
psyche was to draw him down.

22

Victory – and Defeat

I N JUNE 1942, WITH THE USA having joined the war, and the tide turning irrevocably in favour of the Allies, Patrick cheerfully wrote to Bruce, boasting of the continuing success of *Gaslight* in the States where, as *Angel Street*, it was minting money for its author. He rejected a proposal from Bruce to meet in America:

> Alas, it is, I fear, impossible. I daresay one *could* wangle it for a week or so – but one couldn't stay longer because one is known nowadays and one would be accused of running away – and rightly. It's funny how one *doesn't* want to run away.

On Christmas Eve 1942, with the German Sixth Army besieged at Stalingrad, and the corner of the war definitely turned, Patrick began to look forward to seeing Bruce again. He reported that he was

> very well and annoyingly busy ... writing a book – after Burton's *Anatomy of Melancholy* – called 'The Anatomy of Hypocrisy'. You can see the possibilities. I don't know if it will come off or come to anything.

However, Patrick's productivity was brought to a sudden halt by the onset of a mysterious illness in early 1943. Probably induced by a combination of circumstances including the wear and tear on his nerves caused by the war and his frenetic workload, plus his disappointment over the relative failure of *The Duke in Darkness* and his heavy drinking, the malady laid him very low. (It was almost certainly this illness that he was suffering from when seen by Arnold Rattenbury in the Savoy Hotel.) But by September 1943, as he told Bruce, he was out of the woods:

> I am fine now, but I had a beastly time, feeling utterly unable to move, unable to eat, and running a temperature all the time. It was put down to a sort of permanent flu, and I was given M & B [A newly-discovered antibiotic 'wonder' drug] without the slightest effect, and at last I went to a London doctor, who said it was due to glands (due to overwork and overdoing it generally) and he treated me and I got well. In addition I came out in a most awful way in spots, but that also is cured.

Patrick reported that he was busily working on a new play, again set in the Victorian era. It was about a sadistic governess and reintroduced Inspector Rough of *Gaslight* in an episode set earlier in his career. However, none of Patrick's friends who read it were enthusiastic. John Gielgud evidently shared their misgivings for he turned down the chance to produce it. Among the doubters was the influential literary editor of the *Listener*, J.R. Ackerley, then acting as play-reader to Robert Donat, actor-manager at the Westminster Theatre, to whom the script had been sent. Ackerley, in his customary caustically honest fashion, tore the play to shreds in his report; pointing out the many holes and inconsistencies in the plot, and finally pronouncing the whole, 'Maddeningly repetitious . . . piffle.'

It must be said that the critics are right. Patrick, whether due to illness or exhaustion, had produced a piece of unconvincing second-rate work which deserved its subsequent failure. After the originality of *The Duke in Darkness* he had reverted to a melodramatic mechanical formula, in an attempt to reproduce the success of *Gaslight*, but returning to the same territory with considerably less conviction.

The play was written under the title *Ethel Fry* but eventually produced as *The Governess* and it deals with the machinations of the eponymous governess, one Ethel, who, motivated by sheer wickedness, kidnaps a child from the upper-middle-class household where she works. Her devilry is frustrated through the intervention of Inspector Rough, thanks to Ethel's tortured charge, Ellen, who exposes what has been going on in a prolonged piece of somnambulism.

Though deplorable as theatre, the play is not without interest for a student of Patrick's psychology, for it shows several of his usual preoccupations and obsessions. There are, for example, echoes of his childhood in the night-light which feebly illuminates the children's room. There are traces of his father in the 'John Bull-like' figure of the household paterfamilias, Mr Drew; and of his mother's sleeplessness in the child Ellen. There is also evidence of his increasing interest in punishment, evil and cruelty in the vicious torturing of the child.

Irrespective of its merits or demerits, Patrick could not have written *The Governess* at a worse moment when considering its chances of commercial success. The London theatre, under the blows of the Blitz and the black-out, had ground to a virtual halt; and there was a severe shortage of actors, as many had by now been called up. By August 1944, having tried in vain to get it staged, Patrick was describing the play as 'dead till after the war'. The following year he did manage to mount a production at Glasgow in February with Flora Robson in the main part. The rest of the casting was a serious problem and Patrick began to regard the play as a distraction from writing novels.

The Governess played a number of dates in the provinces and Patrick faithfully followed it around the country, suffering endless delays and frustrations en route, at the mercy of the war-disrupted railways. When, after the war, it finally arrived in London with a short run at the Embassy Theatre, the play's moment, if ever it had one, had passed; and most critics agreed it was over-contrived and poorly structured.

In addition to his other duties, Patrick took on the onerous task of firewatching during air-raids, for which he had to travel regularly to London; and he was still putting in a regular two days a week at ENSA, where Dean had prevailed upon him to become Editor of the Service's internal newsletter, the *ENSA*

Record. The bulletin interspersed statistical tables of plays and concerts with amusing articles and humorous stories from camp and factory. Fortunately for Patrick, publication was halted after only two issues on the orders of a bureaucrat bearing the delightful title of Paper Controller, who deemed that the *Record* was squandering too much of the precious commodity. Patrick was then appointed to ENSA's advisory council for drama, chaired by John Gielgud, and also including Edith Evans and Emlyn Williams, as well as his own actor friends Leslie Banks and Diana Wynyard. Never a committee man, Patrick must have been relieved that this august body rarely, if ever, met.

His commitments in the capital, however, were growing too frequent and pressing for continued commuting from Henley to be practical, and so, on Bill Linnit's advice, he acquired a permanent London base at the elegant Piccadilly apartment block, the Albany. The Albany had originally been the town house of Byron's mistress, Lady Caroline Lamb, and the poet himself had once lived there. This fact must have appealed to the romantic in Patrick, as did the clubbable, literary associations of the place: Gladstone, Macaulay and Lord Lytton had all owned apartments in the Albany in their time, and until the First World War there had been a ban on women. By the time Patrick moved in, his 'Albanian' neighbours included Terence Rattigan, J.B. Priestley, and the actresses Edith Evans and Cathleen Nesbitt. Patrick reported the acquisition of his flat to Bruce in somewhat shame-faced terms, justifying his extravagance by the need to be in London and the difficulty of having any sort of night-life if one was living in the suburbs.

Relapsing into his usual state of vagueness about his wealth, confident that with so many of his works running, repeating, or reprinting, he was in the money, Patrick reported:

> *Angel Street* still runs, and so I'm still doing finely for money – though one has not the slightest idea what one is worth – because income tax is an imponderable factor. I see to it that I put by more than half I get into a separate tax account, and just hope for the best. But I am spending quite a lot, so if you are hard up and want some, *do* let me know, my dearest Ecurb.

I don't see much of Claud Cockburn nowadays, because I *daren't* drink on his scale! Did I tell you of the *spectacular* drunks I had with him down at Henley?

In December 1943 Patrick had begun work on a new novel, but by April 1944 this had been completely abandoned due to 'an *indescribable* amount of work, rush and worry – in fact my life has been a complete shambles, intellectually and emotionally'. Not surprisingly, the inevitable confession followed that he had resorted to drinking excessively. By May the novel had been resumed and the smell of victory was in the air. With D-day only a month away, the country was awash with GIs:

> I am again in a train – in a [com]partment with some American soldiers, who are screaming the place down. With all the good will in the world, I must say these allies of ours are a dreadful nuisance socially – they are absolutely everywhere – like locusts – and they are at last getting on everyone's nerves – poor things.
>
> There is a great air of tension everywhere – the Second Front may have started up before I write again.

It had. On 6 June, Allied forces invaded Normandy; but there were plenty of kicks left in the Germans, of which one particularly nasty one was the flying bomb. On 22 July Patrick wrote:

> People are taking them rather badly, I think, they are not as bad as the last February blitz (and of course nothing *approaching* the first blitz) though a nuisance because they go on in a desultory way day and night. Claud Cockburn has been bombed out and is now in my flat in Albany.

Patrick insisted that he had been 'off the booze completely for a whole month', apparently on medical advice, but added ominously, 'I am allowed to go back tomorrow.'

Despite his travails, Patrick said he was still 'pathetically striving to get my novel done – but find this practically impossible'. In November he revealed the title of the book he had been labouring over:

> I am trying to write a long novel called *The Slaves of Solitude*. Do

you like this title? I do. It is for a long, and would-be important book, remember.

With the liberation of France and Belgium turning into a long slogging battle, Patrick looked to the Eastern Front for salvation. At last, in the spring of 1945, that deliverance came about and by September the war had ended with the dropping of the two atomic bombs on Japan. At home a Labour Government under Clement Attlee had been swept into power with a landslide majority. But the coming of peace brought no respite to a war-weary Britain. Rationing was actually expanded to cover more items and, under the cold austerity programme of the Chancellor, Stafford Cripps, the coming of socialism seemed to a shivering population less the dawn of a new Jerusalem than the arrival of a new ice age. Abroad, 'our gallant Russian allies' had changed overnight to their old familiar guise of 'the Red menace'. The invention of the atom bomb, coupled with the dreadful discoveries of the Nazi death camps, seemed to herald a nadir in human bestiality. It was far from being the brave new world that Patrick had hoped to see emerge from the carnage of the war.

On top of all these public troubles there was a private grief to be borne. Patrick broke the news to Bruce in October that Lalla had been forced to undergo a mastectomy after she was diagnosed with cancer. In November, Patrick wrote again with the result of Lalla's post-operative pathologists' report, declaring the operation a success – and giving Lalla a ninety per cent chance of complete recovery.

Lalla had had a lousy war. Her husband's inexplicable decision to sell up his hotel in Tewkesbury and move to a loss-making farm in Kent, had brought them both financial ruin and considerable danger. She had endured the Battle of Britain, fought in the skies above her home, and the fall-out from the London Blitz. In addition, her marriage itself had proved a disastrous failure. Although Bertie Meyer was honest, well-intentioned and devoted to his wife, these qualities had proved rather too much of a good thing: Lalla felt herself constricted, a virtual prisoner of her husband. For long periods she was forbidden to see Patrick, and Bertie had sought to extend his control to every area of her life. Moreover Lalla's acting career, already in decline when she married, had come to a complete halt. This was largely owing to her own fastidiousness about the parts she was prepared to accept; like many beautiful women, she found it hard to acknowledge the fading of her physical charms. At the age of forty she turned down a role in the successful play *Dear Octopus*, written by her friend Dodie Smith, because it did not square with the image she still had of herself as a young and glamorous woman. Her life became a hell of nagging rows with her over-protective husband, exacerbated by increasing financial constraint and hardship. In desperation she, like Patrick, turned to the false comfort of the bottle. Her cancer capped this dreadfully unhappy situation.

Bruce arrived back in Britain from Barbados in January 1946 and almost at once Patrick revealed that the optimistic noises he had made about Lalla's prognosis were a smokescreen; in fact the doctors had told him privately that the chances of the cancer recurring within three or four years were more than fifty per cent. If that should happen, their sister could not expect to survive.

Apart from his natural worry over Lalla, Bruce's homecoming after an absence of seven years was unhappy and disquieting in other respects, principally regarding Patrick. Bruce found his brother little changed physically – perhaps a touch thinner, but still exquisitely dressed and very much his charming, humorous old self. It was only when Patrick took him down to Henley for a ten-day stay that he began to notice disturbing signs of the malaise beneath his brother's urbane mask.

Outwardly everything was completely normal. Patrick had arranged to give his brother all his time, and together they explored the streets of Henley, and made what brief car trips they could under the restraints of severe petrol rationing. One such visit was to nearby Reading, a wholly unremarkable town of which Patrick had become, for some reason, unaccountably fond. (It was to be the locus of his penultimate novel, *Mr Stimpson and Mr Gorse*.) Another local jaunt was to Goring-on-Thames, where, safely out of Lois' earshot, Patrick told his brother some details of his amorous adventures in the intervening years. For the first time, Bruce learned of the seriousness with which his brother had taken his passion for Geraldine Fitzgerald. Patrick also told him of an affair that was to have even more devastating consequences for his life – with an aristocratic writer named Lady Ursula Stewart. He implied that this relationship was over, but, in fact, it was merely dormant.

Bruce's leave in England passed peacefully enough, with visits to Lalla and Frank and regular work on his PhD at the Public Record Office. He took a room in Earls Court, as a base, where Aileen joined him in July. Another extended visit to Henley followed, and it was on this occasion that he began to notice the surfacing of tensions which, in the first flush of happy reunion, he had previously overlooked. One evening, Patrick, with a few drinks already under his belt, proposed an outing to a nearby country club. Lois demurred, saying that she had already started cooking dinner. To Bruce's consternation, his brother let fly with a sudden torrent of noisy abuse, and stormed out of the house (with an obedient Bruce trotting at his heels). It was clear to the elder Hamilton that such scenes were by no means a rarity.

Another disturbing portent was that Patrick had lost his enviably easy facility for writing. He had been struggling with his new novel for two years, and he still had not managed to complete it. Writing was no longer the sheer joy it had been in his youth; it was more of an irksome chore, only to be attempted, in Bruce's words,

> ... after painful screwings-up to the sticking place. And he was to become ever more distressfully aware of how he was dissipating his time, his health, his gifts – failing, at a vital and favourable phase of his career, to consolidate, enhance and put beyond question his already high reputation as an author.[1]

The main cause of this failure, of course, was drink. Although Patrick seemed superficially well able to cope with his high alcohol intake and his robust constitution appeared undamaged, he was uncomfortably aware that all was not as it seemed. He had been consulting a Harley Street physician who warned him that from an insurance point of view he was ceasing to be a 'good life'.

Observing Patrick at close quarters, Bruce made a careful calculation of his daily intake. While at home he would get through more than one bottle of whisky a day. Outside, this high consumption became gargantuan, with at least four double whiskies downed in the morning, and eight to ten glasses in the evening to round things off. On average, Bruce decided, Patrick was knocking back a little less than three bottles of Scotch per day. His only regular meal was lunch and this was merely 'blotting paper' to enable him to drink more. Bruce worked out that his brother was spending something in the region of £2,000 a year on drink; in addition to this heavy outlay, he chain-smoked Players untipped cigarettes, and paid a hefty mortgage for his Albany chambers. Transport tore another hole in his pocket – he often commuted between Henley and London, and when in town, travelled by taxi rather than by tube. Patrick's conscience was troubled by his dissipation, but he would console himself by feeble devices such as quoting the instances of writers who had 'ruined' their talents, not by dissolution, but by absti-nence – Swinburne being his favourite example. Another rationalisation was to pose the question: 'Who are the three biggest drunks at the Savile Club?' When his name did not figure in the list, he appeared satisfied that his own drinking was still within reasonable bounds. Reluctantly, Bruce was driven to the conclusion that drink had warped his brother's moral fibre as well as his physique. He had allowed himself to fall into a state of self-delusion that would have been foreign to him in his clear-eyed youth.

Other instances of unhappy character changes noticed by the punctilious, but possibly over-puritanical, Bruce, were Patrick's habit of lavishly over-tipping those who did him small services: taxi-drivers, porters, barmen and waiters. Bruce, ever eager to see both sides of the matter and to give Patrick the benefit of the doubt, conceded that his brother's generous nature may have accounted for this, along with some sense of guilt about his own wealth, and an idealistic wish to do his bit to level social inequality. But his main conclusion was that Patrick was trying to buy himself the favour of those he patronised, and that they repaid his gratuities with something approaching contempt.

Bruce detected a similar fault when Patrick was with his bosom friends, particularly Claud Cockburn. He noted with dismay that his brother, who had always been the most prominent in any given group, was willing, even keen, to give the premier position to Cockburn. On one occasion, what Bruce saw as Patrick's fawning to his friend provoked a serious row between the brothers after the first night of *The Governess* at the Embassy Theatre; Bruce, possibly jealous of Cockburn for usurping his previously unquestioned role as Patrick's chief confidant, accused his brother of 'making a drunken ass of himself'.

Despite these ructions, the brothers managed to mend their fences in time for Bruce to enjoy an idyllic summer. Inevitably Brighton proved a lure for them, this time because Lalla's stage adaptation of *Craven House* was being shown at the Theatre Royal. This afforded an occasion for a full-scale Hamilton family reunion involving Patrick, Bruce, Lalla and their spouses, as well as Frank Bridger. A few days later the brothers attended one of the final performances of the great George Robey at the Brighton Hippodrome. The comedian's career was in sad decline and, given second billing, he was reduced to a pathetic Archie Rice-style appeal for the audience to take pity on 'your old red-nosed comedian'. Patrick was touched by the sad spectacle and made a point of going backstage with Bruce after the show. They found Robey sitting disconsolately in his dressing room, lamenting his performance and the half-hearted applause that had greeted it. 'They don't want me any more,' he told the Hamiltons, an assertion which Patrick strenuously denied, assuring the old man that he was as good as he had ever been.[2]

In August, Bruce and Patrick went away together to Norfolk, where they spent a week in the small town of Holt, making expeditions in Patrick's Ford to the surrounding countryside – including Burnham Overy Staithe (where Bruce was amused to see the conspiratorial lengths to which his brother went in order to avoid being recognised by the villagers). They also got in a few rounds of golf on the windswept links at Sheringham, the small seaside town that was to be Patrick's final home. During this holiday, Bruce noticed that Patrick was subject to severe nervous stress. This manifested itself both in feelings of claustrophobia and agoraphobia. Patrick was unable to walk for more than a few minutes in Norfolk's wide-open countryside without being overcome by unbearable tension and the same feeling, he told Bruce, overwhelmed him when on the Underground, which accounted for his only being able to travel by taxi when in London.

While Patrick was suffering the miserable effects of writer's block, his brother was enjoying what would prove to be the pinnacle of his own literary achievement. Having completed his PhD thesis, he gave his full attention to the publication of the two novels he had written in Barbados during the war. The first was *Pro*, a novel with a cricketing theme which, thanks to Patrick's help, was sold by Heath's to the Cresset Press and published to considerable acclaim and high sales. This success was followed up with *Let him Have Judgement*, a crime novel involving a judge accused of murder, which did well in both Britain and America, where it was published under the title *Hanging Judge*. The actor Raymond Massey later adapted it for a West End stage production.

Possibly urged on by the example of his brother's efforts, Patrick gritted his teeth and knuckled down to finishing *The Slaves of Solitude*. Bruce was able to read the typescript before he left for Barbados; but before doing so he penned an entry in his journal which summed up all his growing doubts and dismays about Patrick, and his dark forebodings for the future. It is a formidable document which lists the faults and forces, which, in his view, were to be Patrick's undoing as a man and writer. It is also uncannily prophetic:

As I see them at the moment, these are the chief points – (A) That his life, conditioned by continuous drinking and half-business and half-social contacts, is filled by small things and subject to senseless extravagances. (B) That the effect of this life is to coarsen his sensibilities, because in a multiplicity of personal relations he has to apply rough and ready second-best solutions to irritating and mostly unnecessary day-to-day quandaries; and insincerity, often taking the form of excessive flattery or fulsomeness, has become habitual. (C) That the standards of an intelligent clubman, which at present seem to be his own, are not compatible with the proper use of his powers of noble, even if sometimes fanatical thinking. (D) That his anxiety to justify or avoid discussion of his conduct *in detail*, however much he courts condemnation of it *in general*, together with his frequent and almost too dutiful or expiatory performance of good works, without faith, show that, far from being a frank hedonist he is not, in rejecting a reasonable mode of life, achieving harmony on any level. (E) That his life, as well as being too stimulating, is too cushioned; that he makes use of Lois, and of his money (in the form of an ignoble habit of paying his way out of trouble) to save himself minute awkwardnesses, inconveniences and discomforts of the sort it is proper a person should face, in an unworthy and damaging way; and that this, as well as his proneness to meaningless gestures, shows a high degree of nervous tension. (F) That the answer obtained by adding together his drinking, his social preoccupations, his imperfect sincerity, the want of large-ness in his existence, and the absence of real liberty and repose, either external or internal, seems to be a great danger of loss of creative power. I suspect that the range of subjects he can effec-tively use in such a way as to exploit his full powers is steadily narrowing (though till I have read *The Slaves of Solitude* this can only be a provisional opinion); that no work really large in conception and strong in execution can emerge from his present background; that he is certainly capable of short bursts of bril-liance, but they are not good enough; that even if he is capable of more than occasional brilliance it still should not be good enough for him to be a master in a small field, in which alcohol is a first condition of life; and finally, that salvation cannot come by such expedients as retiring to write a novel in bed in six weeks (with little or no whisky), but only by an *inner* rejection of false ideas of living. This would lead to a quieter pattern of outer existence, in its turn permitting the recovery of the desire for that prolonged and intense concentration which used to lie behind his work. (G) That there is the final danger of both physical breakdown and financial failure; and it would be very terrible if the two came together.

Though prefaced by the assurance that nothing Patrick could do could diminish the love Bruce felt for his brother, and disfigured, by his own admission, with more than a touch of smugness and resentment at Patrick's financial success, this is a powerful summary of the flaws that would destroy his brother's talent, and eventually devour his life. Both processes would be much longer in duration than Bruce feared; indeed, Patrick still had much of his best work ahead of him, but there is little doubt that the process of gradual dissolution was already in motion, and Bruce had every justification for his disquiet as he set sail for the Caribbean again.

23

The Slaves of Solitude

THE COMPLETION OF *THE SLAVES OF SOLITUDE*, early in 1946, had cost Patrick dear. It says much for the deterioration of his previous powers of concentration, that he was only able to finish the book by taking to his bed in Henley. Starting when he awoke, only breaking off for breakfast and lunch, brought to him on a tray by the ever-loyal Lois, he laboured steadily each day until five or six o'clock. It was only then that he allowed himself the necessary luxury of his daily drink, walking alone to the pub or the grand Phyllis Court Hotel.

Bruce, knowing the parlous condition his brother was in, feared the novel would demonstrate a marked falling-off in Patrick's gifts. But when he read the book in proof, he was delighted to discover that his pessimism was misplaced. *The Slaves of Solitude* is one of the high points of Patrick's achievement as a novelist and, along with its wartime twin, *Hangover Square*, is considered by many to be his masterpiece. The two novels are very different, reflecting the changed conditions in which they were written. If *Hangover Square* is a novel of crisis, with its drama reflecting the wider tragedy of a world stumbling toward the abyss, then *The Slaves of Solitude* is a novel of survival. Set in 1943 it deals with the ordinary lives of little people bobbing in the wake of the war. There are no murders, no suicides, and if there is madness, it is only the generalised, genteel insanity of the human condition as experienced by a

273

small nondescript group, transformed by Patrick's art, to a status of almost tragic grandeur.

Apart from the human characters, there is one other 'personality' that dominates the novel – the war itself. It may be offstage, but it is always in the background: a growling, grim presence, infecting and darkening the lives of those whom it holds as slaves in thrall. Claud Cockburn remarked how the novel deliberately and 'blatantly' personified the war:

> Dozens of books, good and bad, were of course written with the war as a background, as a factor, or as a general condition like the weather. In Hamilton it assumes a more active and malign role, something rather more than human, yet affecting human life like the devil in a morality play.[1]

Another looming, inhuman figure is the city, London, from which the novel's heroine, Miss Roach, is fleeing as the book opens:

> London, the crouching monster, like every other monster has to breathe, and breathe it does in its own obscure, malignant way. Its vital oxygen is composed of suburban working men and women of all kinds, who every morning are sucked up through an infinitely complicated respiratory apparatus of trains and termini into the mighty congested lungs, held there for a number of hours, and then, in the evening, exhaled violently through the same channels.

Miss Roach is a shy, put-upon spinster in her thirties but who manages to retain a fierce inner integrity. A slave of solitude, certainly, but nevertheless still possessing a spark of hope that some circumstance will rescue her from the fate of the other maiden ladies who are her fellow guests at the Rosamund Tea Rooms – the café turned boarding-house where she lives in Thames Lockdon. This is a riverside town, which, as Patrick explains in a prefatory note,

> bears a rough geographical and external resemblence to Henley-on-Thames. The Rosamund Tea Rooms, however, resembles no

boarding house in this town or in any other, though it is hoped that it resembles in some features every small establishment of this sort all over the country.

In other words, we are back in familiar Hamilton territory – the world of the shabby suburban guest-house – and find ourselves amid a cast of characters bearing all the author's typical hallmarks; homeless, ageing, lost, lonely and timid, clinging to their last shreds of gentility and self-respect. Marooned by the war which has uprooted them all, Miss Roach shuffles blindly through the blackout, barely understanding the world in which she finds herself a stranger:

> Immediately she stepped forth into Thames Lockdon (which itself was not even permitted to be Thames Lockdon, all mention of the town having been blacked out from shop-fronts and elsewhere for reasons of security) the snubbing began with:
>
> NO CIGARETTES
> SORRY
>
> in the window of the tobacconist opposite.
> And such was Miss Roach's mood nowadays that she regarded this less as a sorrowful admission than as a sly piece of spite...

Among the guests at the Rosamund Tea Rooms there is one man who does not share the meek passiveness of the other residents. Mr Thwaites, malevolent to the point of evil, deeply sinister and yet comically absurd, is one of the greatest of Patrick's creations. He is an old bully who delights in torturing everything from flies to humans and even the very language he speaks. He manages to incorporate the sadism, snobbery, small moustache and Fascism of Peter in *Hangover Square* and the booming pomposity and antiquated Edwardian linguistic fruitiness of Mr Eccles in *The Plains of Cement* and indeed Bernard Hamilton himself. The only brake on Mr Thwaites' total dictatorship of the Tea Rooms is the timid resistance of two other guests, Miss Steele and Mrs Barratt, who usually take Miss Roach's side when his attacks on her become too violent:

'I Keeps my Counsel,' said Mr Thwaites, in his slow treacly voice. 'Like the Wise Old Owl, I Sits and Keeps my Counsel.' Miss Roach, shuddering under this agonisingly Thwaitesian remark – Thwaitesian in the highest and richest tradition – knew well enough that there was more to follow. For it was a further defect of Mr Thwaites that when he had made a remark which he thought good, which he himself subtly realised as being Thwaitesian, he was unable to resist repeating it, either in an inverted or a slightly altered form. He did not fail to do so on this occasion.

'Yes,' he said, 'I keeps my Counsel, like the Wise Old Bird . . . I Happens to keep my Counsel . . . I Happens to be like the Wise Old Bird . . .'

And in the silence that followed, broken only by the scraping of soup-spoons on plates, the whole room, with all its occupants, seemed to have to tremble in hushed reverence before the totally unforeseen and awful Bird which had materialised in its midst – its wisdom and unearthly reticence . . . Miss Roach guessed that honour was now satisfied, and that this would be enough. It was not, however, enough. With Mr Thwaites nothing was ever enough.

'I Hay ma Doots, that's all . . .' said Mr Thwaites. 'I Hay ma Doots . . .'

(He is NOT, thought Miss Roach, going to add 'as the Scotchman said,' is he? SURELY he is not going to add 'as the Scotchman said'?)

'As the Scotchman said,' said Mr Thwaites. 'Yes . . . I Hay ma Doots, as the Scotchman said – of Yore . . .'

(Only Mr Thwaites, Miss Roach realised, could, as it were, have out-Thwaited Thwaites and brought 'of Yore' from the bag like that.)

Desperate to escape the stupefying ennui of the lounge, Miss Roach flees out into the evening and the womb-like embrace of the cinema. The next evening, returning to her room after her day's work, she is invited out by Lieutenant Pike, one of the American soldiers infesting Thames Lockdon, who has been billeted at the Rosamund. Astonished but flattered by this unaccustomed display of male attention, a flustered Miss Roach allows herself to be swept off and into the unfamiliar ambience of a pub.

Despite her realisation that the Lieutenant's prime quality is his inconsequentiality, in her solitude Miss Roach allows herself to be kissed, and within a few weeks is thinking of Pike as 'her' American and visiting pubs and cinemas with him as though she had been doing so all her life.

Miss Roach's other lifeline in her loneliness is a German girl, Vicki Kugelmann, stranded, for unexplained reasons, in Thames Lockdon, and shunned by most of the population. She is not such an obvious villain as Mr Thwaites, but there is something about her behaviour that gives away her real character, that of a heartless opportunist. Every detail about her, from the habit of tapping non-existent ash from her cigarette, to her outmoded and too-perfect English, is tellingly etched. Perfect, too, is the sinuous loathsomeness of her machinations; the way in which, under a mask of friendship, she uses the kindly Miss Roach as a bridge, first to enter the closed fortress of the Rosamund Tea Rooms and, once installed, to muscle in on her relationship with Lieutenant Pike, and finally to turn against her benefactor in cahoots with the appalling Thwaites – who, for all his stated xenophobia, is her willing ally in motiveless malice.

Apart from these precise delineations of character, there are passages in the novel that bear out Claud Cockburn's contention that Patrick 'was aware of and, so to speak, harassed by the full meaning of every English word which obtruded on him, long before it ever dared to escape his head onto paper.'[2] Cockburn compared his friend to Joseph Conrad,

> who suffered the same pressures precisely because English was not his native language. Though nobody could have been more English than Patrick, his sense of the language, so much more acute than that of most of his countrymen, sometimes almost suggests that he is not a natural English writer.[3]

Such a passage, which helps to make *The Slaves of Solitude* so compelling, marks an otherwise inconsequential scene in which, typically, the characters are quite alone, unconsciously revealing themselves in action. The residents of the Rosamund wake in their rooms to face another day:

The feeling of the morning after the night before is not a sensation endured by the dissolute only: every morning, for every human being, is in some sort a morning after the night before: the dissolute merely experience it in a more intense degree. There is an air of debauch about tossed bed-clothes, stale air, cold hot-water bottles, and last night's cast-off clothing, from which even the primmest maiden ladies cannot hope to escape. Sleep is gross, a form of abandonment, and it is impossible for anyone to awake and observe its sordid consequences save with a faint sense of recent dissipation, of minute personal disquiet and remorse.

Patrick has the knack of showing the skull beneath the skin; he sees both the beguiling cosiness of boarding-house life, the 'racks of toast and plates of porridge', and, as revealed in a brutal paragraph, the inescapable fact of human mortality:

When he at last came out the other elderly guests were already setting about their business – the business, that is to say, of those who in fact had no business on this earth save that of cautiously steering their respective failing bodies along paths free from discomfort and illness in the direction of the final illness which would exterminate them.

The male counterpoise to the malevolent Thwaites at the Rosamund is Mr Prest, a faded star of the music halls. But although Prest is the recipient of that sentimental regard bestowed by Patrick on any and all characters associated with his own memories of his happy youth in the theatre, he does not escape the pervading miasma of sadness tinging all the denizens of the Rosamund:

He was ... a miserable man – his sense of failure and futility showing in his demeanour. He had, in fact ... an air of having been battered silly by life, of submissiveness to events, of gentleness, of willingness to please, of dog-like gloom and absent-mindedness as he floated through the day.

When Vicki Kugelmann takes her place in the Rosamund, she

is an instant hit with the other guests. Only Miss Roach, her supposed friend, is disturbed by the proprietorial air with which she moves in and becomes 'quite one of the circle', charming even the monstrous Thwaites. The unholy alliance between Vicki and Thwaites grows apace; they have many features in common: a shared secret Fascism and an admiration for Vicki's 'poor country', Nazi Germany, and a similar penchant for archaic language-torture. Vicki has her dated 1920s slang: 'Can I make a cocktail, or can I make a cocktail? Uh-huh! Oh Boy! Wizard!' and Mr Thwaites his pseudo-mediaeval anachronisms: 'Certes, the damsel doth not offend the organs of optical vision. Moreover she hath a way with her, withal.'

But, good, bad or merely absurd, all these slaves of solitude are heading in the same direction:

> She [Miss Roach] was aware, all over the countryside around, all over the country, cars were racing along with just such noisy loads to just such destinations. If it wasn't Americans, it was Poles, or Norwegians, or Dutch, and if it wasn't singing it was sitting on each other's knees, and whatever it was it was drinking and drinking and screaming and desperate.

Quiet desperation, silent screaming, and above all, drinking: a sad and accurate piece of authorial self-portrayal.

Having surrendered the field (and her lieutenant) to Vicki, Miss Roach gives way to a bitter, racist hatred of her serpentine rival. In Miss Roach's mental fulminations against the 'German fascist character' and 'Teutonic arrogance' Patrick's own prejudices are writ large. We have already seen his dislike of France and the French; in his later years this disdain was turned against Germany and the Germans, as witnessed in a letter written in the late 1950s when he told Bruce, 'All I know is that an enormous amount of Germans are *bad* – racially bad – incurably bad.' Going on to compare the German Chancellor, Konrad Adenauer, with the US President, Dwight Eisenhower, he added, 'Now the Americans are *not* racially bad. Compare Mr Eisenhower with Dr Adenauer. There is nothing *evil* in Mr E – there is every sort of evil in Dr A.' Bruce commented:

> His hatred of Germans ... had become almost pathological:
> practically of the common 1914 brand ... I gave it up, forbearing
> from the cheap rejoinder of asking him to consider the proven-
> ance of the name Eisenhower. Nor what exactly he meant by the
> American 'race'. Patrick had fallen into a sort of blind, irrational
> mystique, from which he could no more be moved than a Funda-
> mentalist or a Jesuit Father of the older variety; and I never felt
> more remote from him than over this subject.[4]

What Bruce did not mention was the whole question of how
Patrick's racial judgements squared with his avowed Marxist
outlook, nor the irony of him condemning Germans for being
'racially bad' because of Nazism.

Mr Thwaites conceives a sort of dribbling, senile passion for
his soul-mate Vicki, to which she plays up in a coquettish way.
Perceiving the rift that has opened up between Vicki and Miss
Roach, Thwaites proceeds to explore the wound, continually
contrasting Vicki's sexual charms with Miss Roach's spinsterly
wrinkles and maidenly plainness. The nastiness between the ill-
matched trio reaches a climax after a particularly gruesome
Christmas. Mr Thwaites, slobbering after Vicki in a way reminiscent of the senile lechery of Bernard Hamilton, becomes ridiculously drunk and reveals that Vicki has been spreading
poisonous rumours that Miss Roach has been sexually
corrupting a seventeen-year-old boy, with whom she has struck
up a casual and wholly innocent friendship; goaded beyond
endurance by his innuendoes and by Vicki's increasingly open
sympathy for Hitlerism, Miss Roach, blinded by anger, pushes
Mr Thwaites over on the stairs. At about the same time, she
learns from Mr Prest that the other man in her life – Lieutenant
Pike – has been building up a reputation all over the Thames
valley for proposing marriage to a string of girls. It appears to be
the nadir of fortune for Miss Roach, but all at once, things start to
look up.

Miss Roach's push is the cathartic act that dispels the clouds
lowering over the Rosamund Tea Rooms. Within the space of a
few pages, Mr Thwaites is taken ill with peritonitis and swiftly
expires. At the same time, another death, that of an aunt,

provides Miss Roach with a financial windfall and an escape route away from the suffocating constraints of the lodging-house. For the first time in her deprived life she decides to spoil herself and takes a room at Claridge's in London while she looks for new accommodation. Before leaving, she exacts a sweet revenge on Vicki – who, bereft of Mr Thwaites' support, is sent to Coventry by the other guests – by making sure that the German woman learns of her good fortune.

There only remains, it seems, a sentimental touch to make Miss Roach's triumph complete. It comes in the form of what Patrick, who had used the device in his early novels, liked to call 'a country dance' – a simple, life-affirming scene designed to round off the book and leave his readers well satisfied with a traditional happy ending. This heart-warming episode comes when Miss Roach, finally liberated from the trials and terrors of the Rosamund Tea Rooms, goes to London where her boss, Mr Lindsell, has booked her a luxurious hotel room. Before checking in, she keeps a date at a theatre in Wimbledon, where the kindly Prest has landed a part in a pantomime. The old comedian gives the performance of his life: 'Somehow his triumph seemed to be Miss Roach's triumph as well, and her heart was lifted up with pleasure.'

If *The Slaves of Solitude* were merely a sentimental novel, Patrick could have ended the book here, on this high point, with Miss Roach victorious, her sufferings redeemed and her enemies routed: virtue rewarded and vice punished. But he was too honest a writer for that, and, in a moving coda, he creates a more convincing conclusion. This is an ending in which, by impli-cation, we are left in no doubt that there are no genuine happy ends in this world; that life goes on, neither tragically nor trium-phantly and that the human condition – sad, funny and above all, lonely – is merely to be stoically endured:

Then Miss Roach – this slave of her task-master, solitude – had to choose which bed she was going to sleep in, and chose the one nearest the window, and then got into bed and stared at the ceiling, and then decided that they were heavenlily comfortable beds anyway and that was all that mattered, and it was lovely and quiet and that was all that mattered, too ... and so everything was all right, in fact very nice.

And then she realised that it would be a bad thing if she didn't have a good night as she had to be up early in the morning looking for somewhere to live, and then, of course, she had to go to the office, because Mr Lindsell had said, 'See you tomorrow', when he had left her ... and then this thing, and then that matter, and this thing again, until at last she put out the light, and turned over, and adjusted the pillow, and hopefully composed her mind for sleep – God help us, God help all of us, every one, all of us.

24

Hollywood and Hitchcock

THE RECEPTION OF *THE SLAVES OF SOLITUDE* was gratifyingly ecstatic. Patrick received accolades from senior critics like Richard Church, who wrote in *John O'London's Weekly*:

> Mr Hamilton is a literary artist of fastidious skill. His prose is admirable ... What Baudelairian flowers of beauty it produces. Mr Hamilton is a poet in that kind.

To this praise was added the admiration of writers of his own generation, like Anthony Powell, who called the book 'Absolutely up to date in subject and manner' and John Betjeman, who was attracted by a fellow connoisseur of the curious and offbeat in English life: 'I think Mr Hamilton is one of the best living novelists and that this is the best book he has yet written.'

Despite, or perhaps because of his success, Patrick's finances had been getting increasingly tangled since the early war years. Like many of those who can afford to, he found dealing with money distasteful and his comparatively privileged background, coupled with his early financial success, had bred an attitude in which he assumed that money would always be readily available. When it was not, he was forced to consult the first of a succession of accountants in a bid to restore his depleted coffers and beat off the demands of the Inland Revenue. One of these firms, Waters and Co. of North Cray in Kent, wrote to the BBC in

October 1941 asking for the details of fees paid to Patrick during
the previous tax year during which *Rope, Gaslight, Money with
Menaces* and *To the Public Danger* had all been broadcast or
repeated on the radio. A Corporation bureaucrat in the accounts
department replied that fulfilling the request was impossible,
'owing to the amount of clerical work involved.' By March 1943,
it seems the muddle had been sorted out, for Patrick wrote to the
ever-parsimonious Corporation mildly complaining that he 'was
surprised to learn I only got thirty guineas' for *Gaslight* – and
pointing out that he had received fifty guineas for the previous
broadcast of *Rope*. Unsurprisingly, owing to Patrick's increasingly chaotic existence, his financial problems were never to
be satisfactorily resolved, and although he never wanted for
whisky money, the repeated demands of the Revenue were
to be a source of nagging worry to him for the rest of his
life.

The final years of the war and the immediate post-war period
saw Hollywood's recognition of Patrick's works in the form of
three full-length features, the first of which was *Gaslight*. The
1940 British film had been bought subsequently by Columbia
pictures and then sold to MGM, who committed the unforgivable
crime of destroying it and burning copies of every print they
could find in order to clear the path for their own re-make. It was
one of the greatest acts of vandalism in cinema history, and hit
Patrick hard. But if he was upset by the destruction of a work he
had approved, MGM's version appalled him: titled *The Murder in
Thornton Square* it was a prime example of Hollywood kitsch.
Starring the veteran matinée idol, Charles Boyer, as the evil
husband and a new discovery – Ingrid Bergman – as the tortured
wife, with Joseph Cotten as the suspicious policeman and Angela
Lansbury as the maid, the movie blithely ignored Patrick's story
line and obliterated the atmospheric seedy Victorian gaslit world
in favour of a high society setting. Under the direction of George
Cukor, the film would have been competent enough if it had
even had an original screenplay, but as a transcription of the
subtleties of Patrick's drama, it was a lamentable disaster. British
critics groaned at such gaffes as two-horse hansom cabs, and
twee touches such as Dame May Whitty chirruping 'Good

Morning' to her garden crocuses in a cod Cockney accent. To accommodate Charles Boyer's saturnine looks, a large section of the film was even set in Italy.

If this movie was an unintended horror, 20th-Century-Fox's version of *Hangover Square*, released the following year, 1944, was a deliberate devastation of Patrick's novel. Elspeth Grant in the *Daily Sketch* summed up the general reaction:

> I extend to Mr Patrick Hamilton, a writer I much admire, my deepest and sincerest sympathy for all that Hollywood has done for him (no matter what he received for the film rights), what Hollywood has done for his enthralling story *Hangover Square*: Hollywood *has* done for *Hangover Square*.

Fox's treatment of the novel was not so much a mutilation as a mass murder – and, indeed, a mass murderer was what they made poor George Harvey Bone out to be. The part of Bone was played by a young actor, Laird Cregar, who, enthusing over the novel, had drawn its attention to Fox, only to have the story snatched away and turned into a travesty. In the hands of the film company the plot was twisted out of recognition – the setting was transposed to the turn of the century, giving a fog-swirling *Gaslight II* effect. Like the film of *Gaslight*, the social milieu was raised from its sordid Earls Court setting and wafted into the fragrant reaches of upper-class Edwardian society. Bone himself was turned into a composer of classical music who, in his schizoid moments, butchered and burned all those who crossed his path. Netta, after strangulation with a thuggee cord, was immolated on a Guy Fawkes bonfire, and the lonely Maidenhead room where the hero took his life became a concert hall where he was incinerated during his final performance. Cregar was so mortified by the part he had played in this farrago that, according to his co-star George Sanders, his distress was a major factor in causing his death from a heart attack at twenty-seven, before the film was released in Britain.

Most of the British critics emulated Elspeth Grant's pity for Patrick. James Agate, who had so raved over the original novel, proclaimed the movie,

> A masterpiece turned into rubbish. The film ... has almost
> nothing to do with Hamilton's novel. Only the title and the
> schizophrenia remain ... Apart from one tiny shot, no drink is
> consumed and everybody in the film might be teetotal. The
> atmosphere of that kind of saloon bar which reeks of fug and
> fumes is at no time suggested, nor is there any hint anywhere of
> that hangover which thickens every page of Hamilton's master-
> piece of frowst. In a word, this is the worst betrayal of a first-class
> novel that I ever remember, and I advise readers who have seen
> the film to compare it with the admirable original...

The film critic of Patrick's old paper *Time and Tide* said he had
watched the movie 'with mounting fury', while other reviewers
used words like 'emasculated' and 'Hotchpotch' to describe what
Hollywood had made of Hamilton. As for Patrick's own reaction,
the press reported that he was 'not anxious' to see the film. He
was privately, according to Bruce, very angry about the fiasco
and bitterly disappointed.

Perhaps hoping for third-time lucky, but probably interested
mainly in the money, Patrick gave the go-ahead for Alfred
Hitchcock to film *Rope*. He was also asked to write the screenplay
himself, and may have naively imagined that this would give
him a measure of control over the resulting film.

Hitchcock had been an admirer of Patrick's work for years,
and the film had finally become a practical proposition in 1944
when Hitchcock visited wartime London and discussed with the
producer Sidney Bernstein the possibility of filming successful
stage plays. One of the attractions of Patrick's play for Hitch was
the fact that its small cast and single set made for a very in-
expensive production. When he first conceived the idea, his plan
had been to film the entire play in a single gigantic take – thus,
hopefully, reproducing the theatricality of the original – but
although this revolutionary scheme had to be modified, Dallas
Bower's prototype pre-war television version of *Rope* had proved
that it could be shot in long ten-minute sequences, and this was
the method that Hitchcock adopted when he came to make the
movie in 1948.

Patrick was called in to produce a preliminary script treatment
with Sidney Bernstein at Elstree in the summer of 1947. A

chauffeur-driven limousine called for him regularly at Henley to drive him to the studios, but being a novice, Patrick found the work and the studio atmosphere something of an ordeal and when it was over wrote to Bruce:

> S.B. is a most *delightful* man but a *slave-driver*! ... Released from this strain I am afraid to say I took to heavy drinking for three weeks. The result of this was that I contracted ... 'alcoholic gastritis' – a not very bad, but nagging pain in the tummy. So I decided on a nursing home, both to cure this and completely knock off drink. Out in a few days ... I mean to use this rest as a starting point for a long, long wagon, so have no fears for me.
>
> Doing *Rope* was exciting as well as exhausting. In colour, if you please! – and all indoors with five rooms – a Hitchcock stunt. The camera, like an invisible man, simply walks about the flat (or rather apartment, because it has been translated into American) and sees and hears everything. Never done before, and so, as you can imagine, a difficult job for an inexperienced screen writer.
>
> Under my contract I can be called upon to do another six weeks – either here or in Hollywood – I hope to Heaven here. I am paid £300 a week for this – apart from the £3000 I get for the film rights.

When Bernstein returned to Hollywood, Patrick's treatment was delivered into the hands of a second scriptwriter, Hume Cronyn, who rewrote the plot, giving the Rupert Cadell character an anguished guilt over having led the boy murderers astray with his teaching of Nietzsche. Hitchcock himself, as Cronyn recalled, was preoccupied with the revolutionary techniques he was about to use:

> It was written to be shot in those tremendously long takes, and I think he found that fascinating – he was always intrigued by the innovative. But I think that sometimes this led him astray where the narrative was concerned. He became so fascinated with the images that sometimes the direct line of the story got lost and there would be some awkwardness in the dramatic construction.[1]

Behind Cronyn's back, Hitchcock brought in a third writer, the young dramatist Arthur Laurents, to write the film's dialogue.

Warned by Bernstein that every line of *Rope* had to be 'a pure gem' as it was his first co-production with Hitchcock, Laurents produced the finest draft he could manage and then left for the Christmas holiday. When he returned to do the rewrite, he found that Hitchcock had inserted some of the original play into the text, and made other adjustments – such as slipping in a typically personal line when the character played by Joan Chandler says, 'Ah, Yes! Ingrid Bergman! She's the Virgo type – I think she's just lovely!' (Bergman was the director's current sexual obsession.)

Hitchcock also made more explicit the homosexual bond between the two killers which had been only unconsciously present in Patrick's original play. Laurents commented:

> We never discussed the homosexual element of the script, but Hitchcock knew what he wanted to be able to get away with. He was as intrigued by the varieties of sexual life and conduct as he was by the varieties of movie-making methods – in fact, he was like a child who's just discovered sex and thinks it's all very naughty. It was obvious to anyone who worked with him that he had a strong sense of sin, and that whether he was a regular churchgoer or not, his Victorian Catholic background still affected him deeply.
>
> He might have been indirect in dealing with sexual things in his films, but he had a strong instinct for them. He thought everyone was doing something physical and nasty behind every closed door – except himself: he withdrew; he wouldn't be part of it.[2]

It is not difficult to see what it was in Patrick's work that so attracted Hitchcock. The 'master of the macabre' was of the same generation, and imbibed the same ethos of sexual repression and guilt in his infancy that had crippled Patrick's childhood. Like Patrick after his accident, the fat, toad-like director fancied himself too physically repulsive to engage in 'normal' sexual relations with women, but had a strong sexual drive nonetheless. His sense of sin drove this instinct into his subconscious where it festered into a fascination for sado-masochism that uncannily echoed Patrick's characteristic concerns. Director and writer shared a certain misogyny, inextricably linked with a tendency to idealise and worship the untouchable goddesses who emerged from Hollywood. Hitchcock's sado-sexual obsessions for his blonde stars such as Ingrid Bergman and Janet Leigh are well documented and he also had a penchant for bondage; witness the clanking fetters with which Madeleine Carroll is encumbered in *The Thirty-Nine Steps*. With both men, this perversion became increasingly explicit.

The interest that Patrick had evinced in the sex symbols of the cinema had by no means evaporated with age; during the course of his work on *Rope* he had been introduced to the actress Paulette Goddard, a former wife of Charlie Chaplin, and reported to Bruce:

> Have had one very thrilling experience. Did you know that Paulette Goddard was my dream-girl? (Mary Pickford – Esther Ralston quality)? Did two and a half hours drinking alone with her at Claridge's – by alone I only mean in a bar alone – but that was good enough. But then, again, where does it get you?

Although there were more meetings, in Patrick's case, the answer was nowhere at all. In a virtual reprise of his experience with Geraldine Fitzgerald, Patrick made a love-sick fool of himself, pestering Paulette for more intimate assignations, until, exasperated by his importuning, she rejected his advances and returned to Hollywood, where she met and married a very different writer – Erich Maria Remarque. Poor Patrick was left alone to lament his loss, albeit not for long.

Back at the Warner Brothers studios in downtown Burbank, the cast of *Rope* were assembled. Hitchcock had originally wanted Cary Grant for the role of Rupert Cadell, with Montgomery Clift as the first murderer, Brandon. Both actors were unavailable, so he settled for James Stewart as Cadell and cast two young unknowns, John Dall and Farley Granger, as the apprentice murderers. Despite setting the movie in the States, he gave the cast a strong British bias by assigning two of the more important minor roles to a brace of stalwarts from the London theatre – Sir Cedric Hardwicke and Constance Collier.

James Stewart was very much a second choice. The actor had been out of circulation during the war years, when he had been serving his country as a USAF pilot, and was not thought to be good box office. Despite his reduced star status, Stewart's services did not come cheap, and his $300,000 salary – $200,000 more than had originally been offered – accounted for a substantial slice of the $1,500,000 the film eventually cost to make. In the event, casting him proved to be a major mistake. Stewart had made his name playing middle-American heroes; the role of the subtle, intellectual and morally ambiguous Cadell was a piece of casting against type that did not work, despite a perfectly competent performance. But this was to be the least of the problems that beset the filming of *Rope*.

When the cast gathered for the first script read-through in January 1948, it at once became clear that they were unhappy with Hitchcock's plan to film the drama as if it were on stage. The constant presence of the camera amongst them, as it weaved its way from cue mark to cue mark, upset and unnerved the actors, who were already uncomfortably aware that their lines would have to be word perfect on the first take – re-shooting an entire ten-minute reel being a prohibitively expensive business. But, despite all precautions, a whole scene was ruined more than once by a missed line, a camera bumping a table, or a wrong cue. The nerves of the cast became progressively more frayed. Eventually James Stewart exploded, sarcastically suggesting to Hitchcock that he junk the idea of making a movie in favour of turning the studio into a theatre and inviting in an audience for a live performance. 'The really important thing being rehearsed here is the camera, not the actors,' he fumed. Hitchcock himself was wryly amused by the mutiny, observing of Stewart, 'He couldn't sleep nights because of the picture. It was the bewildering technique that made him worry.' In retrospect Stewart felt that his qualms were justified by the finished film. He recalled:

It was hard to see how the picture was going to work. We had a lot of rehearsal, but the noise of the moving walls was a problem, and so we had to do the whole thing over again for sound, with just microphones, like a radio play. The dialogue track was then added later. I think he [Hitchcock] realised later that giving up the device of the cut was giving up the tool for pacing, for impact. It was worth trying – nobody but Hitch would have tried it. But it didn't really work.

Other technical problems bedevilled the filming. For his first colour movie, Hitchcock insisted that he must see all the rushes in colour, an untried and hideously expensive demand but one which was justified: a cyclorama of the New York sunset skyline, achieved with the aid of 8,000 bulbs and 200 neon signs, proved on viewing to be a rancid orange, requiring the re-shooting of five of the film's eight reels and doubling the shooting time of the whole movie. However, despite all these setbacks the film was completed in a brisk eighteen days, and Hitchcock then got down to the editing.

The film version of *Rope* is certainly more *grand guignol* than Patrick's original tense thriller. The movie opens violently with the strangulation of the victim by a rope held by both killers, seen in gruesome close-up. Not content with this, Hitchcock larded the script with heavy-handed jokes such as 'Knock 'em dead!' and 'I could strangle you!' *Rope* was released in August 1948; reviews were mixed, and public acclaim muted. Hardly anyone noticed Hitch's daring ten-minute take techniques and the experiment must be deemed a failure. Patrick's own reaction was one of predictable rage:

> I was heartbroken by the film of *Rope*. I had thought that working with Hitchcock was going to be heaven, and put everything I knew into it. However, he utterly rejected my script, got someone else to write it, and finally produced a film which I think (and all intelligent friends agree) was sordid and practically meaningless *balls*.

John Russell Taylor, in his biography of Hitchcock, wrote an appropriate requiem for *Rope*:

> Maybe it was Hitch's curious denying himself of cutting, the very resource which had always meant most to him in the cinema.

Maybe it was the deadening effect of the limitations of sound this kind of shooting involved – it was so meticulously disciplined, with all the furniture, props and camera carefully muffled so that the sound track could be recorded directly with virtually no need for looping dialogue. Or maybe it was just that the project so long planned had finally gone cold on him ... for whatever reason, *Rope*, despite its gimmick value and some effective moments, which earned its money back with a modest profit, seems strangely flat and ponderous, all played at a uniform pace which kills most of the excitement and suspense built into the subject matter.[3]

Although he never admitted it publicly, Hitch himself realised the film was a flop and never permitted it to be re-shown in his lifetime.

In London, Patrick reluctantly attended the launch party for the British première. Disliking the finished version of the movie, he felt that, as usual, he had been bribed into getting involved by a mixture of assurances that his text would be adhered to and threats that if he did not take part, his script would be mangled by lesser writers. As it was, he feared he had had the worst of both worlds, with his name on the credits of a picture which bore little relation to his play. This impression was reinforced by conversations he had at the party, when various guests asked him, by implication, how he had come to be involved in such a travesty. Depressed, he drank more than was wise and, as the afternoon wore on, an idea came into his befuddled mind that was to have momentous and disastrous consequences. Like many men before and since, he staggered to a phone; intent, in his alcoholic misery, on reactivating an affair, previously broken off, but which his desire for uncomplicated and uncritical human comfort now drove him to revive. In retrospect, he must have asked himself a hundred times how different things might have been if the lady concerned had not been at home and he had merely made his way back to the Albany alone to sleep off his depression. But, unfortunately for him, she was in.

PART VI
1948–1962

25

La

IT IS UNCLEAR WHEN OR HOW Patrick first met the woman who, despite her title and multiplicity of surnames, was known to close friends simply as 'La'. Bruce believed that the ill-matched pair first became acquainted before the war when Patrick was asked by a mutual friend to give a pre-publication opinion of what was to be her most successful novel, *The Gentlewomen*. This cannot be correct since *The Gentlewomen* was published by Macmillan in 1952 – some four years after their reacquaintance following the *Rope* party. But however it happened, their first meeting, according to Patrick's later account, had resulted in some mutual attraction and a little 'dalliance'; perhaps this had been one of the 'light amours' referred to in one of his wartime letters. The affair, such as it was, had been allowed to die a natural death because Patrick had realised that it had no future and that he was making a fool of himself. Then, after several years of mutual non-communication, Patrick had acted upon that fatal, alcohol-inspired whim.

Born Lady Ursula Chetwynd-Talbot, La was four years younger than Patrick, and was several strata higher than he in the social scale. Her ancestor, John Talbot, the first Earl of Shrewsbury, had died fighting the French at Castillon, the last

293

battle of the Hundred Years War. A later earl had been one of the original members of the Cabal Government during Charles II's reign, and the family had continued to hold sway on its estates along the Welsh Marches.[1] La's father, Viscount Ingestre, died of pneumonia before acceding to the twenty-first Earldom, which passed to her younger brother, John, who was still a child, on the eve of the First World War. Her mother, Lady Winifred Paget, left a young widow with three daughters and a son, had married Richard Pennoyer, an American diplomat, in 1917 and La had passed an unsettled childhood at a succession of foreign postings.

This background had deeply marked La, a shy and sensitive child, leading her to become timid, highly strung and self-conscious to a degree, prone to bolt from the balls and parties to which her imperious mother directed her in the hope of landing a marquis, or making some equally suitable match. Elegant rather than beautiful, La had inherited the characteristically long and shapely legs of the female Talbots, as well as a prominent nose which was less comely if equally striking – a defect which she remedied with a cosmetic operation in the 1930s. Like Patrick, she was tall and almost painfully thin, stately in carriage, and worried to the point of obsession about correct appearances. She also had a jarringly high-pitched voice. As a fellow novelist, her observation of foibles was almost as acute as Patrick's. Her sister Lady Audrey Morris recalled:

> She simply didn't care about whether people saw her staring at them. She would stare intently at whoever or whatever took her interest and make no bones about it. She'd take in every wrinkle and eyelash in a person and wouldn't look away until she'd finished. And you could almost hear her listening to people's dialogue.[2]

La's nervous personality was always on the lookout for slights and affronts, and she seemed to derive a certain satisfaction in creating her own domestic crises if real life failed to provide them. Fortunately for her, the future was to be richly endowed with drama and passion, and she was to need no factitious stimulation.

The artistic side of her character initially manifested itself in a talent for both interior design and flower arranging. (She wrote a column on these subjects in *Country Life*.) Like Patrick in his later years, she was inclined to take to her bed for days or weeks at a time when the trials of life became too much. And like him, her personality seems a curiously contradictory one – aristocratic yet Bohemian, ordered yet passionate, controlled and hysterical. A sympathetic critic, Polly Devlin, wrote:

> Perhaps the act of writing relieved the obsessive internalised passions and pressures of her nature. Certainly there is a strong undercurrent of passion and rage flowing in her books which rarely bursts through.[3]

La's early marriages were as eventful and dramatic as her later union with Patrick. Her first husband, Hector Stewart, shortly after they married in 1930, remarked suddenly one teatime that he was going to drop his cup and within three days was dead of a rare nervous paralysis. La waited twelve years before plunging into matrimony again, this time to a cousin of her first husband, Lieutenant-Commander Michael Stewart. Although this wartime union (1942) formally lasted ten years, it seems to have suffered the fate of so many other marriages contracted under the pressure of the times, and died naturally soon after it was made. (La and Stewart remained on friendly terms after her marriage to Patrick, and it was on his recommendation that Patrick was referred to the first doctor to make a sustained attempt to cure his alcoholism.)

Whatever the state of their previous relationship, by the time Patrick made contact again in 1948, both parties were ready for a fully fledged fling; on the very first evening of their reunion, as he told his brother subsequently, 'there certainly was unequivocal love-making'. This one-night stand led to another, and then another, until finally, in January 1950, he was brought to the point of considering his first separation from Lois. Preceded by a series of unexplained silences in his correspondence, coupled with heavy hints about 'tensions' in his life too complicated to explain by letter, he finally broke the big news to his brother:

Although everything is *wonderfully* well at the moment [An invariable sign that things were far from well] I have been through a really *dreadful* time ... Although extremely amicable with Lois (and seeing quite a lot of her) I am now separated from her and living with *another*! This sort of thing may seem to be a more or less easy thing to accomplish, but, believe me, it is *not*! The transitional stage was *awful* – the seriousness of the situation becoming more and more apparent to Lois, and the quarrels becoming deeper and deeper, longer and longer, hideouser and *hideouser*. And, on top of this, illness all round, and myself drinking like a *fish* in order to keep myself going. But at last the proper break has been made and I am better than I have ever been in my life (at any rate since Norfolk days), and *working again*, and hardly drinking at all, at a tiny little house rented at Hove (46 Hove Street, you could almost put all of it into my sitting-room at Albany.) The character of 'Another' can again of course not be gone into by letter. I can only say that she is by no means a glamour girl – mature (forty-two) – thin (extremely) – and extremely nice and polite and shy to meet. And practically a tee-totaller, you will be glad to learn! Also been married twice, and is still married! ... The point, really, though, is that I have been made sexually happy for the first time in my life, and do only hope that merciful providence will make this amazing turn in my life one which will bring about *renewed productiveness* and complete freedom from the bottle, which will now, I trust be *my* slave.

In spite of this seeming confession, Patrick remained curiously unrevealing about his new domestic arrangements in his correspondence and only when Bruce protested were titbits of information reluctantly disgorged. Later, Bruce heard, via Lalla, the real name of Patrick's beloved:

I was fascinated by Lalla having mentioned to you the decidedly irrelevant fact that L.T. is 'titled'! Yes – she is – but neither of the Mr Stewarts were. She is the sister of an Earl (Shrewsbury) and this means that it is one of those titles which you carry about with you whoever you marry. (Thus, she was Lady Ursula Stewart when I first met her). The *names* this woman has had! ... Now she is hovering between Laura Talbot, Lady U.S. and Lady U.H.!

> Absolutely fantastic – you should see the variations in names
> when she gets a large post.

The facetious, almost shamefaced way that Patrick refers to La
and her title raises the question of other possible motivations for
their union, beyond the sexual satisfaction openly admitted by
Patrick; old-fashioned, unadulterated snobbery almost certainly
played its part.

Delighted that a decision of sorts, however forced, had been
reached in his emotional imbroglio, for a brief period Patrick
allowed himself the delusion that the change in his personal
circumstances meant that matters would henceforth run
smoothly:

> ... my strange triangle is, I *believe*, working out better for all
> three, than if it had never occurred. *Touch wood*. I see a lot of Lois,
> and hope to see a great deal more of her in the autumn.

The turmoil in Patrick's personal life was reflected by
upheaval in his domestic arrangements; the Henley flat and the
Albany apartment were both sold, and for a short while before
moving to Hove, Patrick repaired to the Isle of Wight, where,
influenced by Priestley, who had also purchased a property near
Ventnor, Patrick believed he might find a safe haven from the
storms and stresses of the outside world. It was not to be, and
within a few months he reported:

> The Isle of Wight was a *disaster* – climate, people, length of
> journey from London, and a million other things it would take too
> long to go into. Result – I am selling it (at an unpleasant loss) and
> am back where I was. All the bore and hard work of moving in,
> and now all the ditto of getting out – though, of course, the main
> burden fell on Lois.

Troubles for Patrick never came singly, and during his six
months on the island, he was involved in another road accident.
Always an erratic driver, he had been negotiating a bend and,
hugging the side of the road too closely, had ended up in a ditch.

He and Lois suffered severe bruises and were lucky to escape
without more serious injury.

Patrick and Lois moved back to the Thames Valley to the small
town of Whitchurch, taking a mews cottage that they named,
with a wistful look back to previous London opulence, 'Albany
Stables'. Leaving Lois here, Patrick took off to Hove with La, but
by January 1951, he was again living with Lois at Whitchurch. So
began a pattern that was to endure for the next decade, until
Patrick's final decline and death:

> My P.L. [Private Life] is in about as great a muddle as it possibly
> could be. After the Hove experiment I find that I can neither go
> *forward* or *back*. I know now that I simply cannot abandon Lois.
> Whatever my *inclinations* (which are curiously mixed) my *con-
> science* would not allow it. Twenty years of marriage creates an
> unbreakable bond, and to throw her out of my life utterly would
> be too cruel – out of the question. On the other hand I am *equally*
> bound by my *conscience* to 'Another' . . . Now not only am I bound
> by conscience to L.T. – I do not think I have the strength of
> character to give her up. And so this most disturbing, unnatural
> double life has to continue. All three of us are behaving very well
> and calmly – but the situation is at times (not at others) what is
> called 'impossible'. It is also amazingly expensive.

A letter from June 1951 gives some indication of the 'impossibility' of Patrick's domestic life:

> I am myself having a *very* peculiar time at the moment! L.T.
> (whom I still adore and who *couldn't* be a nicer character) hits me
> over the head with trays and dials 999 to have me removed by the
> police! Lois, on the other hand, behaves *immaculately*! So what *is*
> one to do!

Patrick had fallen into the familiar trap of having the two
contradictory sides of his nature catered for by two women. The
placid Lois, with her genius for domestic harmony and her long-
suffering patience with Patrick's drinking, offered peace and
tranquillity but also boredom and frustration. The highly strung
La provided excitement, violence and sexual relief. There was

also, of course, the opposing attraction of habit, his two decades of marriage to Lois, versus the social kudos of having an earl's sister as his mistress. It is not altogether surprising that Patrick took refuge in the bottle. For the time being, however, he claimed to be deriving a perverse pleasure from the problems he had brought upon himself:

> ... about three weeks ago, I had a sort of revelation – a sudden one as I lay in bed at seven in the morning ... I can only say that a sort of voice (my own) said to me:
> '*Difficulties* and *disasters are* life. That is why life is such fun.'
> ... It has helped me *incredibly*. Over things like money and tray-hitting at any rate.

As if the tribulations of his own life were not enough for Patrick to cope with, he also had, almost alone, to deal with the final illness and death of his beloved sister Lalla.

Lalla's long and sad decline had begun with her operation for breast cancer. Although she apparently made a full recovery from the surgery, the disease had not been eradicated, but had only gone into remission. Coupled with this, the privations of the war years, the unhappiness of her marriage, worsening financial hardship and continual heavy drinking had undermined both her physical resistance and her temperament. She became shifty, snappy, and perpetually difficult to those who knew and loved her, trying Patrick's patience up to and beyond breaking point.

In 1947 her husband Bertie, having failed disastrously as a farmer, had reverted to his former career and taken a job as a front-of-house theatre manager in Newcastle-upon-Tyne. Lalla had joined him there, but the attempt to patch up the marriage was a failure, and she was drinking to the extent that a spell in a nursing home was required. In March 1949 Patrick wrote to Bruce:

> My dear boy, this problem just goes on and on ... One can only hope that it is a change of life and that somehow this will at last settle down. I don't really think that B. ... is really the trouble.

There would be some other man and some other emotional complication even if she left him.

In August 1949 there was an ominous development: Lalla had a fall in a hotel room, apparently caused by a blackout. As she recovered in hospital, the doctors warned Patrick that such blackouts were a common symptom of brain tumours, indicating a possible recurrence of the cancer.

After her discharge, Lalla settled down in a cottage near Newbury where Bertie visited her at weekends. She relied on him, Patrick, and the wealthy Frank Bridger for financial support, but most of her money went on gin. After one drunken binge too many, the reclusive Frank turned her out of his house, and she tapped Bruce for a 'loan' of fifty pounds. When Patrick heard of this, he revealed the true state of affairs, warning that Bruce would never get the money back:

> ... in lending her money, you are not really helping a distressed sister – you are just pouring *gin* down her throat. The time has come when I simply *must* speak candidly to you about this *wretched, miserable* character, whom I would give anything on earth to help if I could.

Patrick explained that he had spent several hundred pounds on trying to alleviate Lalla's plight, before coming to the same conclusion as 'the most *generous* Frank' had earlier – that Lalla's remittances had to be kept within reasonable bounds:

> I have, therefore, while *trying* to be generous, taken a more evasive attitude lately – withheld or delayed this 'Gin-Geld'.

Patrick appealed to Bruce to join him in trying to control their sister, who he claimed had become untrustworthy and treacherous in her gin-sodden condition.

It is clear that Patrick did feel a sense of guilt and shame over Lalla's sad state, though it is equally obvious that he had done all he could to help her. The guilt probably stemmed from his awareness that he too was as deeply in thrall to alcohol as Lalla.

The difference between them, however, was that he could afford to slake his thirst, while she could not.

In 1951 fate intervened to bring an end to a hopeless situation. One morning, Lalla found herself physically incapable of getting out of bed. A recurrence of cancer in the bones was soon diagnosed and she entered a nursing home, not to emerge alive. Her doctors told Lalla that she was suffering from 'rarefied bones', a euphemism that seemed to satisfy her; and, Patrick assured Bruce, once in the nursing home and free from external worry, she entered a more peaceful state of mind:

> When I last saw her she was *amazingly* well. She told me that at the moment she had *absolutely no pain* and was sleeping *excellently*. Her brain and whole manner were as good as they were when she was in her 20s – better in fact ... She has now no idea (it seems to me) either that she is dying, or that cancer has recurred. This is strange with so shrewd a woman, but there you are.
>
> I may *conceivably*, in the future, let her know that she is dying, but (on everybody's advice) must never let her know that it is from cancer. People (particularly women) apparently *hate* such an idea. (I don't quite know why – I wouldn't mind, would you?)

Patrick was never called upon to perform this distasteful duty.

Lalla spent her last days lying in the dark, drugged with morphia. Patrick's feelings were mixed as he watched his sister dying:

> My own conscious mind is, of course, rejoicing at seeing the end in sight – but down in the subconscious there is great distress – a misery that haunts one all day.

At the end of the month, Bruce received Patrick's cable announcing Lalla's death; her final collapse had come so quickly that he had been unable to be with her at the end. Foremost among the memories and reflections crowding Patrick's mind at his sister's internment were intimations of his own mortality. The shipwreck of Lalla's life was altogether too close for comfort.

Nearing fifty now, and feeling himself running out of creativity, his personal life was in chaos and he knew he was as hopelessly addicted to alcohol as his sister had been. Patrick could be forgiven for viewing the future with a chill shiver on that cold autumn day in the Hampstead churchyard.

26

Mr Heath and Mr Gorse

PATRICK'S FINAL WORK, THE TRILOGY OF novels dealing with the criminal career of the charming con-man and killer Ernest Ralph Gorse, had been brewing in his mind for years before he began to put his ideas on paper. A fascination with the criminal mentality, exemplified in *Rope*, had been with him since the very start of his writing career and his contact with Claud Cockburn had directed that interest into the particular form of the confidence trickster. Patricia Cockburn recalled how her husband and Patrick would collect newspaper clippings about the exploits of notorious con-men and planned to collaborate on a book about them, to be entitled *Larceny in the Blood*.[1] That particular project never got off the ground, but his enthusiasm stayed with Patrick, and the immediate postwar years brought a real-life villain to his attention who seemed to personify the two faces of crime that most interested him, those of the sadistic psychopath and the con-artist.

Neville George Clevely Heath was born in 1917 in Ilford, into a lower-middle-class suburban London family.[2] He was brought up in Wimbledon where he was educated at a mixed Catholic convent school, before going on to Rutlish, a minor public school at Merton. At an early age, while still at the convent, he exhibited a propensity for sadistic behaviour towards girls. Heath grew into a prepossessing adolescent — tall, athletic, with wavy golden hair, blue eyes and square-jawed manly good looks. But beneath this exterior there were disturbing signs of what was to come – he was expelled from Rutlish for thrashing a girl in the classroom. This and similar incidents were hushed up and passed off as exuberant horseplay, but a local MP, Evelyn Walker, who knew the family and tried to take the boy in hand, reported failure: the young Heath, he said, although an extremely charming lad was also an 'impossible, fantastic liar' who had a disturbing penchant for stealing girl's handkerchiefs. Leaving school at fifteen without enough qualifications to further his education, Heath was forced to take a menial job as a packer in a textile warehouse. But he saw himself transcending this grey world. The life he mapped out was one of fast cars and pretty girls, of easy money, expensive clothes and louche nightclubs. He affected the dress and the public-school accent to go with the image, sporting a tweed jacket, Oxford bags and a pipe clamped firmly between even white teeth in a smiling mouth. More than a few young women fell for the romantic facade, without questioning too deeply the shabby reality that lay beneath. Heath's reading reflected his unsalubrious tastes, his staples being Parisian pornography and 'hard-boiled' American crime fiction. His favourite 'respectable' writer, however, was none other than Rupert Brooke, a figure who, he proclaimed – as had Patrick at a similar age – was indubitably the finest English poet since Shakespeare.

In 1935, on his eighteenth birthday, he said goodbye to textile packing and applied for a commission in the RAF. Passing successfully through the RAF College at Cranwell, Heath was made a Pilot Officer and posted to Duxford near Cambridge. Here nemesis caught up with him. He was popular with his colleagues, most of whom came from a wealthier background than his, and he endeavoured to emulate their high-living, free-spending ways in the pubs and hotels of Cambridge. As treasurer of his squadron's sports club, he cheerfully bankrolled his activities by embezzling the funds. This activity only came to light when he was posted to Mildenhall as a fully fledged pilot. Knowing discovery was at hand, he deserted and returned to the embrace of his loving mother at Wimbledon, where he was arrested some weeks later by the RAF Police. While awaiting court-martial, he compounded his offence by stealing a fellow officer's car, but despite this he escaped being cashiered and was merely dismissed from the service.

With his flying career over, Heath now reverted to his true *métier* as a criminal swindler, and apart from the war years, lived out the remaining decade of his life on the wrong side of the law; getting by on his wits, his charm and the gratuitous gulling of his – sometimes willing – victims. His favoured technique was a fraud known as 'ear-biting', which involved ingratiating himself with wealthy young women to the point of a formal engagement. He would then run up huge debts, sometimes of thousands of pounds, relying on his unfortunate fiancée's family to settle the bills in order to keep her name from being dragged through the courts. The technique rarely failed (similar 'simultaneous engagements' were contracted by Lieutenant Pike, the feckless anti-hero of *The Slaves of Solitude*).

Heath became a familiar figure in the pubs of Fleet Street and the bars and seedy hotels of Kensington and Notting Hill, where his military uniforms and bearing and his embellished accounts of his wartime activities found a ready audience. (He was even photographed shaking hands with the Prime Minister, Clement Attlee, after bluffing his way into the VIP room at Twickenham rugby ground.) But something had occurred in the dark under-currents of Heath's psyche that was to have fatal results for him, and for two women who crossed his path.

The first victim was Margery Gardner, a divorcee, and, like Heath, a habituée of the seedy drinking clubs that had sprung up in wartime London where lonely and rootless men and women could meet and pair off. Margery was a confirmed masochist whose need to be bound and beaten conformed exactly to Heath's taste. The couple made no secret of their fondness for flagellation, but perhaps under the influence of liquor or the unnerving experience of his active service during the war, Heath's inhibitions seem to have gone haywire, and on more than one occasion, the staff of a London hotel were summoned to his bedroom by the screams of a woman in pain. Undaunted by these experiences, Margery agreed, in June 1946, to go again with Heath to his room in the Pembridge Court Hotel, Bayswater.

Here she consented, not only to be pinioned and flogged, but also to be gagged; a serious miscalculation, as Heath, in a paroxysm of lust, forced her face into the pillow and suffocated her. He also bit her body and violated her with the riding crop he had used to beat her. After the murder, Heath betook himself to Bournemouth under his last alias – Group-Captain Rupert Brooke. Here he picked up a young girl, Doreen Marshall, took her to a lonely chine, stripped her and stabbed her to death, just hours before he was arrested for the murder of Margery Gardner. The Old Bailey jury refused to accept Heath's plea of insanity and he went to the gallows with a display of bravado, describing his execution in RAF slang as a 'one-way op' and telling the warder who poured him a last whisky, 'Make it a double'.

The story of Neville Heath's life and crimes, luridly reported by the popular press, made a deep impression on Patrick. The man seemed to him to sum up all that was most rotten about England. With his absurd public school and militarist pretensions, his penchant for fast cars and 'popsies', as he called his women, he might have stepped out of one of Patrick's own novels. But it was in the darker side of Heath's criminal psyche that Patrick saw parallels with his own disturbed personality and it is easy to imagine him thinking, 'There but for the grace of God ...' as he read of Heath's fetish for bondage and flagellation. Thinking back to his encounter with Geraldine Fitzgerald and his frequent recourse to prostitutes prepared to indulge his own sadistic fantasies, it is little wonder that Patrick the writer saw in Heath the criminal echoes that were worryingly familiar.

In the summer of 1950, three years after Heath's death, and just when his affair with La was reaching its height, Patrick wrote the first novel in the Gorse trilogy, *The West Pier*. The book was completed in the same concentrated, almost frenzied burst of activity that had finally given birth to *The Slaves of Solitude* and was delivered to Constable in October that year. Patrick told Bruce of the grand conception behind the novel and its successors:

The West Pier ... is the first of a series in which a really wonderful monster of a villain appears. This character will be taken up in later books – the whole series covering a period from 1912 to the present day. The villain will at *last* get his deserts ...

It is obvious from the outset of the novel that the book is an account of Heath's development grafted on to Patrick's early life. The dates and the setting of the novel are autobiographical, the incidents and description of the protagonist – from the name onwards (Gorse equals Heath) – are Heath's. We first meet the boy Gorse at a small private school in Hove: Rodney House is a precise portrait of Holland House, down to its location next to the County Cricket Ground and the boys' green-capped uniform. An early hint of Gorse's later sexual development comes in the first pages when he leaves a small girl tied to a roller in the County Ground. Saved from the consequences of this action – as Heath was often miraculously preserved – by the unwillingness of the authorities to believe such a well-brought-up boy capable of evil, the young Gorse goes on to his first truly criminal act: the cruel and elaborate parting of a good-hearted, working-class Brighton girl from her meagre savings. The main body of the novel retails this plot in chillingly convincing psychological detail. Patrick establishes the young Gorse as evil in embryo, complete with the tell-tale moustache:

> His reddish moustache improved him. It largely succeeded in removing what had been so noticeable in his face as a boy – that expression of smelling something nasty immediately underneath his nose ... He had even acquired a sort of dashing charm.

Having drawn his charmer, Patrick proceeds to tease out the villain's intricate swindle as Gorse first ensnares the naive Esther and then accomplishes her downfall. The spidery care with which Gorse draws the innocent fly into his web well illustrates a curious central truth about con-artistry – that it is very hard, painstaking work, requiring a skill and energy which if harnessed to good rather than evil might make the con-man an artist of another sort; a positive, rather than a negative force. But Gorse's positive qualities – his forceful leadership, his self-confidence and ingenuity – are merely a patina overlaying a meanness of spirit and a petty wickedness which remain un-explained.

A common criticism of the Gorse trilogy is that, having set out to dissect the progress of an Iagoesque villain, Patrick contents himself with describing Gorse's actions and their effects without exploring their motivation. Why does Gorse torture people who may be silly, naive or grasping, but are essentially harmless? Unlike his contemporary, Graham Greene, Patrick lacked the Catholic faith that underpins the other great novel about evil deeds in Brighton, *Brighton Rock*. Pinkie's crimes can be partially explained by Greene's belief in original sin and the fall of man. Patrick's explanation of Gorse's motives, such as it is, remains political and psychological.

Although Patrick did his best to answer his critics and provide some account of the genesis of Gorse's nature in the subsequent novels of the trilogy, the motiveless nature of his evil hangs enigmatically over all three books. J.B. Priestley branded the Gorse trilogy, 'a bad idea anyhow', and added, 'Hamilton no longer had the creative energy to bamboozle us into believing it was a good idea'. There is more truth in the second part of this statement than in the first for there is no reason for thinking the nature of evil an unfit subject for a novelist. The fact that few English writers have attempted such an examination and that even fewer have succeeded, makes Patrick's efforts appear courageous at the very least. The most memorable representations of evil in modern literature have come from writers whose lives and culture have been intimately connected with the sort of turmoil and collapse which inspire society's dark forces: Dostoevsky's pre-Communist Russia; Kafka's pre-Nazi central Europe; Céline's wartime and Fascist France. English literature, deriving from the relative stability of British society, has largely remained more provincial. Certainly in the postwar years its most complacent, pipe-and-crumpets quality was exemplified by Priestley himself. Little wonder that the bard of small-town Bradford was unable to understand his friend's desire to get to grips with such an un-English theme.

In *The West Pier* the scale of Gorse's misdeeds is more villainous than monstrous; defrauding a shop-girl of a few pounds cannot be presented as wickedness on a heroic scale. The interest of the novel lies in the meticulous examination of the entrails of Gorse's nefarious scheme. In Walter Allen's words:

> Hamilton gives us an almost clinical description of Heathmanship in action; and this defines both the fascination of these novels and their limitations.[3]

The fascination, of course, lies in the insider's view of the criminal mind at work; the limitations, that Gorse is no Himmler or Genghis Khan, merely a small-time crook about his shady business.

Gorse is not merely one-dimensional, however. There are plenty of laughs along the way to be had from both him and his victims, as for example in his Thwaitesian deforming of the English language:

> This was of a fearful Wardour Street, Jeffrey Farnol kind – packed with 'Thous't', 'I would fain', 'Stap me', 'Beshrew me', 'A vast deal', 'Methinks', 'Albeit', 'Where-anent', 'Varlet', 'Knave', etc. – a style commonly used, for reasons hard to ascertain, by people either with very naive or very unwholesome minds. But the mind of Ernest Ralph Gorse was by no means naive.

And there is a charmingly Hamiltonian touch; an excessiveness when compiling lists, as in his roll-call of the various sorts of food staining the pages of a pocket edition of Wordsworth. This is a return to the over-gilding of the lily which typified Patrick's early work, condemned by Priestley as 'too determinedly facetious', by Walter Allen as a 'tendency towards a ponderous irony', but defended by Patrick himself as, 'the delight in the odd, longer word instead of the direct, simpler one – the long (and at times purely facetious) construction instead of the natural one . . .' By now, it must be assumed, his loyal readers found these conceits less an annoyance than a familiar touchstone to be recognised with affection.

Patrick was living with La in Hove Street, very close to the pier itself (then still a thriving pleasure-dome, unlike the sad, broken skeleton it is today), while writing *The West Pier* and the book gives off, like a blast of sea breeze, the exhilaration he felt from rediscovering the old stamping-grounds of his childhood. It is a novel of place, and its author was writing about the locations he loved best; his old home in First Avenue, his old school, the County Cricket Ground, the two piers, the Metropole Hotel, Brighton station: 'Funny', as he put it to Bruce, 'how one always comes back to Brighton.' This familiarity seems to justify at least a part of Graham Greene's tribute to the book, 'The best novel written about Brighton'.

The mechanics of the plot are straightforward. Gorse and two ex-school chums, Ryan and Bell, are holidaying in Brighton just after the Great War. On the West Pier they pick up the pretty Esther and her plain friend Gertrude after some banter and wordplay involving the bookish Bell and the resolutely philistine Gertie. 'It is intensely difficult to believe that sane young people ever talked like this. They did, however. Furthermore they undoubtedly still do. Let the unbeliever sit on piers in the evening, and eavesdrop,' comments the novelist, giving us an insight into his working methods.

Gorse perceives that an attraction is growing between Ryan and Esther. He resolves to destroy their relationship and by a clever combination of making up to Esther himself and writing poison postcards warning the couple off each other, drives a wedge between them. Learning that Esther has, though desperately poor, managed to save the tidy sum of sixty-eight pounds he compounds his mischief-making by tricking her out of it, persuading her that she can part-buy a car with him. He establishes his credentials as a man of means by treating her to cocktails in the Metropole, and flashing a ring embossed with a bogus family crest. Having fleeced Esther he drives off into the future with 'a set, ugly, hard, more than ever satanic expression ... as he sped ahead – sped ahead to London, and to his very curious destination in life'.

Apart from the relishable character of Gorse and the sad Esther a large part of the book's poignancy lies in its depiction of lesser figures such as Esther's father and grandfather who are put-upon, sickly railway porters – a Marxist view of the insulted and the injured – and the ugly ducklings Bell and Gertrude, secretly longing for sexual fulfilment but destined to remain frustrated.

Michael Sadleir at Constable adored the novel when Patrick presented it in October 1950:

Dear Hen. I admire your book beyond measure. It is a triumph of deceptive simplicity, of mosaic-like construction, of laugh-aloud fun flickering over an abyss of infamy. What a *horror* Gorse is! ... The ingenuity with which out of perfectly ordinary – indeed trivial – material you have devised the web of villainy, prevented the victims stumbling on the truth – and all with a cast of five people and within the space of a square mile – is masterly. And of course the funny bits ...! Farnol Wardour Street; the life of a railway porter; the lamentable condition of Bell's copy of Wordsworth ... oh, lordy, I became quite weak. I find this a ravishing book.

When *The West Pier* was published in August 1951, reviews were widespread and favourable. The novelist L.P. Hartley enthused in the *Sunday Times*, 'The entertainment value of this brilliantly told story could hardly be higher.' Only Bruce was guarded in his praise; while recognising the novel's powerful and moving passages he found it a great disappointment. His complaint was that Patrick had failed to explore or explain the roots of Gorse's villainy. He also felt that Patrick had lost the exuberance evident in his earlier novels.

Patrick, however, sent his brother an ecstatic account of the book's reception, as though to reinforce his faith in a project whose wisdom he had already come to doubt. He reported that the *TLS* had given it a full page and the BBC a half-hour talk. He declared that it was as if he were of the popular and literary stature of Hemingway or Maugham.

But beneath this boasting, doubts lingered: Patrick complained that his press acclaim, though gratifying as far as it went, had been somewhat muted, as if suspending final judgement until the completion of the Gorse sequence, and he had misgivings about having announced the book as the first of a series. The enormity of the task he had set himself also worried him. He felt that he had a formula for a 'Human Comedy' without being sure that he had the ability to make the most of it. Pathetically, he asked Bruce for his fullest encouragement. His brother obediently complied with high praise for the book, making an effort to disguise his lukewarm feelings about it ('it was out of the question to be cruelly candid') and giving only the mildest criticisms. This in turn led to a letter of self-exculpation from Patrick in which he answered his brother's muted criticisms point by point. To Bruce's contention that Esther Downes was not fully realised, Patrick responded that he considered her 'the best and most pathetic character he had ever constructed' and revealed that he had intended to bring her back in a later book – until persuaded by Michael Sadleir that such a perfect being should be left as she was. On the character of Gorse himself, Patrick admitted that getting to the root of his creation had stumped him:

> I will *never* get really into his skin and have told the reader as much – 'It is extremely difficult to guess what goes on beneath the surface of their minds. It is only from their surface behaviour, and surface utterances, that the depths can be dimly understood or estimated.' In other words it is impossible to tell (it is for me at any rate) what really goes on in the heads of the criminal-maniac, Brides-in-the-Bath-Smith, Ronald True, Neville Heath, Haigh, etc.-type. They are, I think, sort of *somnambulists*. They live in a sort of dream – an evil dream.[4]

Underlining the personal significance of the signet ring Gorse uses as a prop to dupe Esther, Patrick wrote:

> What would have been fatal would have been to have the name Hamilton as the family name. For some reason one must *never*, in fiction, use one's own name – not even for the name of a grocer over the way. Why is this?

How far Bruce was justified in regarding *The West Pier* as a disappointment must remain a matter of debate. If the book never quite reaches the standards set by *The Slaves of Solitude* or *Hangover Square* it still contains moments of dark hilarity and considerable pathos and certainly there is much in the whole trilogy to appeal to contemporary taste, weaned on the black comedies of Joe Orton and Amis *père et fils*.

Bruce's negative reactions to the Gorse saga are understandable: his own literary tastes were genteel and middle-brow, and it might be expected that he would react with distaste to the exploration of a figure as irredeemable as Gorse. On a personal level, he was peeved and distressed by Patrick's decline into alcoholism. Likewise he disapproved of his liaison with La, and took Lois' side in the battle between the two women. He may have felt it was time to take his successful younger brother down a peg or two by a barrage of rather nit-picking complaints about minor inaccuracies in his portrayal of life at Holland House. Whatever his motives Bruce was subsequently remorseful, feeling he had failed Patrick at the critical moment and, typically, blaming himself for not being supportive when, with his brother's personal life in chaos and with growing doubts about his failing powers, such support was needed most.

Early in 1952, Bruce, on leave for six months from his academic duties in Barbados, arrived in London for the West End production of *Hanging Judge*. Patrick had booked him into the Great Western Hotel in Paddington, and telling him of this by letter warned,

> Be prepared for a shock when you see my face again after all this time! Although, I think, I'm amazingly young in general health and outlook, I haven't worn at all well in my face – which is terribly seamed and lined and makes me look a lot older than the 48 years I'll be in a few weeks' time ... Well, no more now, until we meet – except to say how *indescribably* I'm longing to see you!

Bruce, for his part, was as eager as ever to renew his intimacy with his beloved brother and watched impatiently from the hotel doorway for Patrick's arrival, little knowing that he was about to undergo what he described later as, 'the most horrible evening of my life'. Patrick was uncharacteristically late and Bruce soon discovered why. As he decanted himself from a taxi, Bruce took in his appearance: although immaculately dressed and slim as ever, Patrick's hair was in a state of 'almost bedlamite disorder'; his eyes were a little wild, and Bruce recognised his brother was already well-lubricated. They adjourned to the bar to split a bottle of scotch and for the first couple of hours all was satisfactory as Bruce described his life in Barbados and Patrick responded with news of his latest project, *The Man Upstairs*, and recounted with a certain lack of enthusiasm updated instalments of his domestic dramas with La. But the fraternal amity started to fray when they adjourned to a fashionable steak restaurant in Panton Street, and the talk turned to politics. Bruce, who had lost all his former illusions about the Soviet Union, mildly remarked that Russia, then in the last phase of Stalin's tyrannical rule, would make more friends internationally if she presented a less rigid face to the world: this infuriated Patrick, and his brother had some difficulty in pacifying him.

From the restaurant they progressed to a bar where Patrick was well known. He encouraged the barman, who shared with the Hamiltons an encyclopaedic knowledge of their favourite boyhood comics the *Magnet* and the *Gem*, to set Bruce an oral exam on the characters that formed the mainstay of Frank Richards' immortal works. Returning to the hotel, they broke into Bruce's duty-free whisky and Patrick became progressively more drunk and aggressive. They met an acquaintance who joined their attack on the bottle, and Patrick proposed that they should all recount their most embarrassing experience.

When Bruce failed to rise to this challenge satisfactorily, Patrick rounded on him angrily, demanding to know why he couldn't let his hair down. Genuinely embarrassed now, Bruce obediently retailed a truly humiliating recollection. After his friend departed, Patrick turned the full force of his alcoholic rage against Bruce, spewing out an incoherent stream of insults, of which the choicest came as he pointed to some brown freckles on his brother's hands, and shouted, 'Look at your hands! Look at your hands! I like my niggers black!' Anticipating an explosion that would cause an unbridgeable gulf, Bruce took advantage of his brother's blurred senses to hide the whisky bottle and when Patrick demanded another shot, refused to hand it over. In his father's best parade-ground staccato Patrick demanded, 'Give me that whisky! *Give – me – that – whisky*!' Fearing that the noise would rouse the sleeping hotel, Bruce weakly gave in, extracting a promise that Patrick would have just one more drink and then call it a night. Analysing the appalling performance after Patrick had left, Bruce speculated that Patrick's rage reflected a growing awareness that his elder brother no longer idolised him as he had in their youth, either for his politics or his writing.

There were other reasons for Patrick's resentment: his guilty awareness that his brother hated his excessive drinking and what it was doing to him, and, extraordinarily, Bruce's failure to match Patrick's own formidable boozing capacity: 'to me [Bruce] a physical impossibility, not, as I believed he supposed, a mark of disapproval'. All this, allied to the recent imperfectly concealed distaste for *The West Pier*, and old sores like Bruce's marriage and second extended spell in Barbados, combined to produce the eruption. By the time he had finished listing excuses for his brother's behaviour, it was Bruce who felt guilty.

It was typical of the masochistically mild-mannered Bruce that he should blame himself for his brother's outburst. Even after Patrick's death, Bruce remained his most devoted disciple and advocate. In Aileen's words,

> Next to Patrick, I counted for nothing. For Bruce, Patrick was always the spoiled little brother. His mother had said 'Look after Patrick, make sure he comes to no harm' and he did his best to do it.[5]

At his last meeting with Patrick, Bruce expressed the fear that he had been too censorious. 'My dear boy,' Patrick replied, 'you were never censorious.' But after Patrick's death, La maliciously told Aileen that he had neither loved Bruce, nor even much liked him.

There may have been an element of truth in this bitchy comment, despite the fact that it contradicts what La subsequently told Bruce directly; Patrick was a monumental egotist, and he probably saw Bruce, in his declining years, as a witness silently accusing him of his fall from youthful promise. It was Patrick's greatest tragedy however that he never really loved anyone, least of all himself.

27

Swan-song

THE MORNING AFTER HIS DISASTROUS HOMECOMING, Bruce met his brother again in the same Paddington pub to which they had repaired after his first return from Barbados between the wars. Patrick was subdued and suitably contrite about the previous night, saying he realised his behaviour had been 'absolutely mad'. After a couple of gins, Patrick took Bruce to the Savile Club where a group of cronies were assembled, including Val Gielgud, and later he escorted his brother to La's Chelsea flat for Bruce's first meeting with the new woman in his life. First impressions were not favourable:

> She was ... very thin and not beautiful; the nature of the sexual attraction she had for Patrick was far from clear to me. Her voice was high-pitched and nervous ... But she was composed enough, and, of course, extremely polite and good-mannered.[1]

Bruce, for his part tried to be polite and pleasant:

> But neither then nor thereafter did we succeed in coming very close together. We could never (as Lois and I could) say to one another, with the comfortable assurance of friendship, 'Don't be such a bloody fool, my dear.'[2]

Nevertheless, Bruce felt the meeting had passed off well enough, and at least (always his main criterion) Patrick approved,

316

showing little of the anxiety he commonly did when first bringing intimates together, and drinking very little. Bruce hoped that La might become an influence to Patrick's good.

Despite the surface cordiality, there was one tiny incident that stirred dark suspicions in Bruce's mind that Patrick's liaison with La was changing him for the worse and jeopardising the fraternal link between the Hamiltons: during the course of the evening, Bruce suggested that they might amuse themselves with an evening of music hall at the nearby Chelsea Palace theatre. There fell a leaden pause, which was ended by Patrick saying pompously, as though Bruce had committed some awful solecism, 'We don't care much for that sort of thing.' Bruce was astonished as his brother had always taken great delight in the warmth, vulgarity and absurdities of the music-hall stage. Was this new attitude, he wondered, a reflection of La's own snobbery and prejudice?

Bruce got the full flavour of Patrick's strange double life the next day when they travelled from London and La to Lois at Whitchurch. Bruce found Lois peaky and subdued, and clearly at pains not to irritate Patrick. At that stage, plans for divorce had been put on hold, and Bruce had the impression that Lois was trying to wean him away from La by providing the cosy background of domestic stability and comfort that had always been her main attraction for him. Patrick reacted to this mothering with barely suppressed fury, telling Bruce that Lois was menopausal and blaming her entirely for their marital breakdown. Anxious not to exacerbate Patrick's disturbed sensibilities, Bruce and Lois became allies in a tacit conspiracy to protect him from unpleasant realities, avoiding rows and arranging the domestic routine around Patrick's requirements. He was completing work on *Mr Stimpson and Mr Gorse*, the sequel to *The West Pier*, and for three hours each morning, Bruce and Lois would tip-toe around, while Patrick, using Lois' piano as a desk, laboured to finish the book. At noon Patrick knocked off and accompanied his brother on a short walk while Lois prepared lunch. Following a siesta, Patrick would either polish up his morning's work, or enjoy a solitary game of his own invention, a form of fives played against a corner of the garden walls. Evening drinking commenced at seven, followed by supper at eight-thirty. The piano would revert to its intended use for half an hour of soothing music from Lois, before Patrick retired to bed, fortified by a heavy dose of Medinal.

But this restful break was a short one and Bruce soon returned to London to supervise the stage production of *Hanging Judge* and to see his latest novel, *So Sad, So Fresh*, through the press, leaving Patrick behind to finish *Mr Stimpson and Mr Gorse*. Bruce had taken a room in Earls Court and once Patrick had finished the book and returned to La in London, the brothers often met up for a tour of their youthful haunts – notably the Courtfield pub opposite Earls Court station. Bruce found that Patrick was drinking far more in town than he had in the country, and seemed unusually depressed and introverted. He was especially dismayed to find that Patrick was indifferent to his own upcoming play and novel and was even uncharacteristically disheartening:

> It was almost as if he did not want [my own hopes] to be realised. I would not have thought much of this had not Frank [Bridger] told me how once when he had mentioned one of Lalla's plays or adaptations Patrick had said abruptly '*I'm* the only writer in this family.'[3]

Another irritating change in their relations was Patrick's new-found attitude to the aristocracy and the superior social circles in which he had begun to move. While still maintaining a good Marxist denunciation of the class in general, he seemed to Bruce to ingratiate himself unduly with those individual members of the upper classes he encountered in La's company. Likewise, he regularly patronised such upper-crust hangouts as Claridge's Hotel and an expensive hairdresser off the Haymarket, while still affecting to despise these status symbols. Bruce found this hypocrisy both baffling and annoying, but put it down to the influence of La to whom Patrick had become increasingly beholden since her divorce from her second husband had now reached the *decree nisi* stage. In despair, Patrick beseeched Bruce to advise him which way to turn, and when his brother counselled a reconciliation with Lois, replied that he was now morally bound to La. Seeing no reasonable way out of his impasse, Patrick was drinking more furiously than ever and, visiting Bruce in hospital after a minor operation, twice appeared in the ward incapably drunk and almost speechless. To the endless round of rows with La were added other worries: production of *The Man Upstairs* had been postponed indefinitely in the hope of getting Sybil Thorndike into the cast; a house briefly rented with La near Salisbury had proved unsuitable and hideously expensive; Patrick was having one of his by now regular run-ins with the taxman to the tune of a demand for £3,000; and finally he was expected to shoulder the costs of La's divorce.

In an effort to drum up some happy memories to take back to Barbados, Bruce proposed a short holiday in Brighton with his brother just before he sailed. Bruce's vision of nostalgically healthy walks amid the happy scenes of their childhood soon dispersed in the face of Patrick's restless lethargy and his magnetic attraction to the pub at opening time. The farthest Patrick could be persuaded to roam from their base at the Queen's Hotel was to nearby Hove, and the brothers spent most of their time in a hostelry where Patrick professed to be fond of the pianist. He nonetheless succeeded in annoying the man with too many requests to play 'These Foolish Things', a number which appeared to hold sentimental associations for him. Bruce fumed at seeing his brother spoken to with something like contempt by 'this seedy character', but Patrick didn't seem to mind. His retaliation, taking the form of an altogether excessive tip, neither went down well nor restored his dignity. Bruce was equally mortified to see the same barely hidden disdain on the faces of the waiters at the Queen's as he steered an intoxicated Patrick to the table for a reluctantly consumed late dinner. By the time he left England in December, Bruce was full of foreboding.

In the event, Patrick's hand was finally forced by the women in his life, and it was Lois, not La, who got her divorce through first; La's divorce was made absolute shortly after and Patrick moved into her cramped Chelsea flat, at the same time selling the house he had owned with Lois at Whitchurch. (She returned to Henley, where she remained for the rest of her life.) Patrick and

La were married in London soon afterwards.

The summer of 1953 saw the Queen's coronation, and Patrick exhibited a lordly disdain for the monarchist enthusiasm of the people; in a letter written on Coronation Day in June he told Bruce:

> Only by seeing could you *believe* what has been going on ... the seething, hysterical mobs which have been pouring daily into London to look at the decorations ... I was in all the blitzes during the war, and I stood up to them all with reasonable equanimity. This has really *terrified* me! ... And one is depressed as well as terrified. Nothing is worse for the soul, or can make one feel more *lonely*, than the knowledge that one is going against the masses (mostly Labour-voting, needless to say).

Patrick's alienation from the crowd only deepened the depression he had been suffering for months, and even the appearance of *Mr Stimpson and Mr Gorse* failed to lighten his load:

> My lack of peace of mind ... has been caused by sustained trouble in my public and private lives. The play [*The Man Upstairs*] in the most *torturing* way has *still* arrived at nothing. So has my private life – in an even more torturing way. About this, I propose, at the moment, to write nothing, because (1) *the least said about it the better*! and (2) I still have no *idea* where I am with it. Your guess would be as good as (probably better than) mine.
>
> However, I am manfully keeping my head above alcohol, in excellent physical health, and cultivating, not unsuccessfully, every ounce of self-negation there is in me.

Trying to jerk himself out of this slough of despond by a change of scene, Patrick, in a characteristically perverse move, temporarily left La and moved into a gloomy bed-and-breakfast establishment in Reading. This place, rejoicing in the grandiose title of the Café Royal, he had known since his Henley days – it presumably provided much of the atmosphere of the Rosamund Tea Rooms – and he professed himself delighted by his new surroundings, telling a young Henley friend that the view from his bedroom window over the Grand Union Canal reminded him of Venice. Reading of course, was the setting for *Mr Stimpson and*

Mr Gorse, whose critical reception he was anxiously awaiting.

The second novel in the Gorse sequence opens in 1928 with its anti-hero, a few years older than his incarnation in *The West Pier*, discovered in the saloon bar of the Friar in Reading.[4]

Gorse's chosen victim is the plummy-voiced, rabbit-toothed, genteelly foolish Mrs Joan Plumleigh-Bruce; a colonel's widow, dog-owner and servant oppressor. Gorse finds her at a loose end in the bar, waiting to hold court for her attendant Reading beaux, the stuffy estate agent Mr Stimpson, and the married but lecherous Major Parry. Gorse spots her at once for what she is: a snobbish, affected, and basically bone-headed fool, an ideal target for him to fleece of whatever wealth she possesses. Moving in with his usual oleaginous skill and deploying the weapons of an invented past as a war-hero and strike-breaker, Gorse soon succeeds in impressing the credulous woman and quickly goes for the kill. It is noteworthy that Patrick strives, in the novel's early pages, to counter the criticism that Bruce and others had made of *The West Pier* and makes some effort to explain Gorse's criminal motivation:

> The motives of such a criminal as Ernest Ralph Gorse are only partly commercial, and their criminal behaviour comes and goes in waves – waves which, nearly always, increase in volume and power.
>
> In years long after the events related in this book, people often argue as to whether Gorse (who was by then a famous figure) had 'any good' in him.
>
> He had not any sort of good in him. He might have been just conceivably, and in a manner, insane – but evilly so – not pitiably. In spite of his wordly astuteness, he may have lived, perhaps, like so many outstanding criminals, a sort of dream-life. But, even if this were so, the dream was evil.

Having made contact with his target, Gorse follows her home to establish the extent of her affluence, giving Patrick the opportunity to indulge in a few satirical thrusts at her suburban pretensions, and the class of colonial Conservatives living in what Angus Hall, writing of the Gorse novels, called 'the plains of pebble-dash':

These houses were squat, two-storied affairs, round-looking
because of their bow-windows on the ground floor, and with red-
tiled or green-tiled roofs.

Their fronts had all been most oddly treated. It looked as
though the builder had had some sort of infantile sea-side mania
for shingled beaches, and that, to indulge this passion, he had,
having covered the external walls with thick glue, used some
extraordinary machine with which to spray them densely with
small pebbles . . .

Mrs Plumleigh-Bruce's house, called 'Glen Allen', is as liberally
scattered with brass and silk inside, as it is littered with gnomes,
goblins and pebble patterns outside. However, Patrick's indictment of this suburban kitsch would perhaps have rung more true
had not he himself increasingly succumbed, in his life with La, to
the insidious charms of Plumleigh-Brucedom. Visiting Patrick at
his last home in Sheringham a few months before his death, a
pilgrimage inspired by his admiration for the Gorse books,
Angus Hall was appalled to discover that Patrick knew whereof
he spoke:

> It came as a shock to me . . . on reaching Hamilton's house, to find
> that he had a flat in just one of the derided 'Rossmores' or 'Glen
> Allens'. Due to the rain and the darkness, it was impossible to
> identify the figures studded around the garden, but Mrs
> Plumleigh-Bruce would have felt proudly at home.[5]

But at least Patrick would not have patronised his domestic
helps in the insufferable fashion Mrs P-B employs with her Irish
maid, Mary:

> She amused herself, in fact, by talking OIRISH. OIRISH may be
> considered as a language in itself, and Mrs Plumleigh-Bruce's
> OIRISH was, in a way, perfect – for it lacked nothing. It did not
> omit 'Bedad', 'Begorrah', 'Faith', 'Sure', or 'Entoirely'.

Having thus eviscerated Mrs Plumleigh-Bruce's tiny world,
Patrick turned to excoriating the fatuousness of her two
admirers. Her most ardent swain, Mr Stimpson, is the essence of

provincial mediocrity: mean, calculating, and blinkered, and whose creeping lust for Mrs P-B also extends to Mary. Then there is Major Parry, who spends his evenings attempting to emulate his success of two years previously when he had placed an armistice poem commemorating 'The Glorious Dead' in the local paper. In a richly comic passage Patrick pictures him struggling with another elegy:

> The Major, who was tired, and whose whisky (his fourth this evening) had slightly affected his brain, now dreamily – and because dreamily most ludicrously – began to extemporise.
>   'They are fallen, they are fallen, they are fallen,
> It really was most, *most*, most, *most* appallin''.
> Or:
>   'The slaughter, really *was* you know, appallin''.
> Then there was 'mauling'.
>   'They got an absolutely *awful* maulin''.
> Or:
>   'Those lads – good God – they got a frightful maulin''.
> And, of course, there was 'callin''.
>   'Can't you hear yet, their voices callin' callin'?'
> Or:
>   'Their sacrifice to Heaven high was callin''.
> There was, even, a treatment of 'stone-walling'.
>   'Grit, *grit*, pluck, *grit*! They *stuck* at it – *stonewallin*!'
> Or:
>   'On sticky wicket – there they were – stonewallin'!'

Oddly enough, this scene was one of the many things that Michael Sadleir disliked about the novel, nervously fearing that it might be resented if it were seen to be mocking Armistice Day.

But after this encouraging start, *Mr Stimpson and Mr Gorse* (a dull title, bafflingly substituted for the original *Signature to Crime*) gets bogged down into a long middle section of what Bruce aptly called 'plains of deadpan flatness' during which Gorse hardens his hold on Mrs P-B's interest by flattering her vanity, appearing to win money for her on the horses, and generally flirting his way into her affections without stooping to the unpleasant task of making love to her. At the same time he dishes his rival Mr

Stimpson by inveigling him into an alcoholic evening in London during which he succeeds in compromising the outwardly respectable estate agent with a prostitute. Having thus discredited Stimpson with Mrs Plumleigh-Bruce, Gorse further intrigues her by convincingly claiming kinship with a famous general, takes her to a London hotel, and makes a promise of marriage in exchange for a large sum of her money paid into a joint account. Needless to add he then decamps, leaving Mrs Plumleigh-Bruce the bitter taste of her stupidity. Patrick twists the knife by having Mr Stimpson marry Mary, thus leaving Mrs P-B deprived, at a stroke, of her reputation, her cash, her wooer and her maid. Humiliated, she leaves Reading to face a penurious old age in Worthing. Gorse, as at the end of *The West Pier* rides, or rather drives, off into the sunset to seek fresh widows and new victims. Patrick takes leave of him in a prophetic passage in which he sees a vision of England covered by cars. These machines are like a horde of giant beetles, an encroaching alien presence which gradually overwhelms and enslaves the men who have created them:

> Gorse, then, whose whole character and aspect, were, really, of a very beetly kind, knew as little of what he was doing as of where he was going. (In fact he ended up that day in a medium-sized commercial hotel in Nottingham.)
>
> Other beetle owners (that is to say, beetle-slaves) who overtook or met Gorse on his way, at least knew where they were immediately going, and had a very rough unconscious idea as to their ultimate destination on this planet. They imagined that they would one day, having worn their lives out in beetle-service, die, more or less painfully and slowly, in bed.
>
> And most of them did.
>
> But the red-haired Gorse – the reddish, reddish-moustached, slightly-freckled beetle-driver, driving slowly into the era of the all-conquering beetles, did not have even this trivial advantage in unconscious foreknowledge.
>
> For he was to die painlessly and quickly. And he was not to do this in bed.

For the first time in their long relationship of publisher and author, and as friends of more than thirty years, Sadleir hated Patrick's book. And he told him so:

> Candidly, I am gravely embarrassed what to say about *Signature to Crime* which, despite great technical virtuosity, gives an impression of petulance and of personal prejudices so peevishly overstated as to render the characters mere cockshies.
>
> This promises badly for the book's reception by critics and public. It will be thought disagreeable and unsympathetic, because there is not a tolerably likeable person in it. It will strike such reviewers and readers as do not relish your particular and highly individual brand of nonsense (and the notices of *The West Pier* showed that certain recalcitrants do exist) as laboured and facetious. Thirdly, sustained mockery and relentless scarification, dealt out by a novelist to characters whom he had purposely presented as grotesque marionettes, bring weariness to a reader and make him long for relief.[6]

Patrick must have been deeply wounded by these criticisms from his old friend, but he refused to substantially amend the book, which appeared much as he had written it. Nevertheless this point marked the beginning of the end of his friendship with Sadleir, a rupture made complete by the publisher's reaction to his last novel, *Unknown Assailant*, which, if anything, he liked even less than he had its predecessor. Bruce shared and echoed many of Sadleir's objections to the novel, again lamenting the lack of larks and laughs, as he had with *The West Pier*. Although he thought the car-clogged conclusion had the character of poetry and was a 'kind of chapter from a new "Book of Revelations"', he concluded that the novel as a whole was,

> pervaded by a sort of stylistic lifelessness ... the same sort of people are being written about as of old, but the appearance of spontaneity, of relish in them, is missing. Often, I cannot help feeling, Patrick was forcing himself to write. Love – love of exercising his craft – had been lost.[7]

But when the book was actually published, in August 1953, Sadleir's worst fears were not realised, and several critics praised it, including again John Betjeman, in the *Daily Telegraph*:

> *Mr Stimpson and Mr Gorse* so enthralled me that I dreaded
> reaching its end. Passing through Reading, where its ridiculous
> characters live, I looked out of the window at that red brick town
> and imagined Mr Stimpson and Mr Gorse propped up against a
> Tudor bar somewhere near.

There were favourable notices too from Peter Quennell in the
Daily Mail and from the *Spectator* and the *Sunday Times*. Despite
this acclaim, Patrick himself was uneasy, telling Bruce:

> In Mrs Plumleigh-Bruce ... I have written about a *type*, while
> completely neglecting to create an *individual* – the result being
> *lifelessness* and *unreality*.

More than a year after the novel was published, its faults still
nagged at him. Writing to Bruce in December 1954 he confessed
that he had neglected to send him a copy because he was afraid
of an adverse reaction, admitting:

> It is the one book of mine that Michael Sadleir hasn't liked, and,
> on the *whole*, cannot be called a success.
>   I myself am not really satisfied with it – but I *do* think it has
> countless 'patches of great brilliance' (to quote your expression
> about my third period). In fact I'm certain that these patches are
> as good as anything I've ever done ...

Patrick concluded with an even more pathetic plea than he had
made about *The West Pier*:

> If you *haven't* read it *please don't*. It'd be so much better to wait
> until I can *talk* to you. But if you *have* – then tell me,
>   *but*
> *don't* say anything discouraging about it!
>   Allude to it only *briefly* and, *even if you have to lie through your
> teeth*, agree with me that it has these 'patches of great brilliance'.

Patrick felt that his confidence had been further sapped by
Sadleir's reception and that his enthusiasm for the project was
seriously endangered. This feeling is reflected in the third, and

by far the least successful, Gorse book, his last completed work, *Unknown Assailant*. After this the series was finally abandoned, leaving Gorse dangling, though not from the noose which his creator had indicated was to be his ultimate fate.

Today critical opinion is inclined to judge the first two Gorse novels less harshly than Patrick himself did. The temper of the times has changed, and characters who struck Sadleir and Bruce as irredeemably unpleasant seem, in our less sanguine age, merely the sad face of corrupt humanity.

As summer turned to autumn in 1953, Patrick and La, more in hope than expectation of domestic bliss, began their married life in a small flat at 3 Hyde Park Gate Mews. Although the apartment was dark and gloomy, Patrick, with typical perversity, claimed to like this. The area had some distinguished inhabitants:

> I give them in their order of merit. (1) Epstein (2) Patrick Hamilton (3) Sir Winston Churchill ... his proximity may enable me to get rid of this place more quickly and on better terms.

Soon after moving into the new flat, Patrick broke a rib during a fit of coughing; but he turned this minor injury to advantage by using it as an excuse to withdraw from otherwise unavoidable social outings which he knew from experience would lead to more damagingly heavy drinking:

> I am really a new and different person. Above all, I am mentally so much calmer and this is a tremendous help in my private life with La. If only *one* party can keep calm, the really hideous hitting rows do not take place. Sharp words there must always be from time to time, of course – but that applies to any two people living together.

In this temporary phase of tranquillity Patrick returned with pleasure to former loves: reading and chess. Confessing that he had not read a book properly for three years, he extolled the delights of his father's old favourite, Sir Walter Scott, placing him just below Dickens among the great novelists. To these intellectual pleasures, Patrick added the physical exercise of his fives games, walks in Hyde Park and occasional rounds of golf. Domestic accord was assured by the absence of Lois, who had taken a six-month trip to South Africa.

But by the beginning of 1954, his precariously attained peace of mind had started to unravel. A golfing holiday at the Bell Inn, Hurley, near Henley proved catastrophic: thick frost made the ground too hard for play, and Patrick was driven to the hotel bar with predictable results. Additionally his financial position appeared precarious, with a writ being served on him by the Inland Revenue.

The post-war years had seen a changing of the guard among Patrick's friends. His wartime intimacy with Claud Cockburn had slackened and finally died with Cockburn's departure to a new life in Ireland. His growing estrangement from Michael Sadleir was matched by an increasing distance between Patrick and his other professional friend, Bill Linnit. But there were compensations: he had become acquainted with two of the grandees of English letters, Osbert Sitwell and Eddie Marsh, former secretary to Winston Churchill and devoted patron of Rupert Brooke. Patrick corresponded with both men, and visited them in their bachelor apartments in London. This new friendship with Marsh and Sitwell, both of whom were homosexual, was matched with a basically sympathetic attitude – despite its robust expression – towards homosexuality in his letters to Bruce. Commenting on a spate of homosexual prosecutions in 1954, Patrick remarked that one of the victims, Lord Vivian 'used to be a very old drinking chum of mine' and added:

> The police love to victimise any one well known ... Press and public too ... Here you have a perfectly ordinary young man (with a liking, no doubt, for Boy Scouts, Airmen, and other male whores) being fantastically pilloried – and convicted *on the word of the male whores.*
>
> In my tolerance for homosexuality I personally go further than the average civilised person, who is so often heard saying that it is all right provided 'they don't corrupt the *young*'. I don't see this. I don't think the young *are* corruptible. I think that homosexuality is something constitutional – you either have it or not –

I myself have had passes made at me as a boy, but they just didn't 'take'. And although, at Westminster I could (I now know) have satisfied these leanings in the case of one boy in particular – *still*, I'm sure, I'd never have acquired the habit.

In another letter, Patrick was more specific about his schoolboy sexuality. Recalling a contemporary at Holland House he wrote:

The boy certainly had charm and good looks. Those I remembered vividly enough to write about in the *W[est] P[ier]* ... I was never homosexual about him ... Willie Gray was my great pash in that way – and I got *him* badly. I also had a tiny feeling for ('Pivot-of-the-Team') Willoughby ... My pre-puberty homo-ism died with Grohner at Westminster, and will, I hope, never recur.

Patrick's greatest friend during this period, who remained close to him until his death, was the larger-than-life critic John Davenport. The two men shared a love of literature and an equal fondness for the pleasures of alcohol. Fellow members of the Savile Club, they also had mutual friends in Claud Cockburn and Arthur Calder-Marshall; their real intimacy began in the early 1950s, when they were neighbours in Chelsea and met frequently in the Builder's Arms pub. When Patrick and La were living at Hove, Davenport made occasional descents on their household which would frequently end in drunkenness and the need for subsequent apology.

Besides their shared fondness for the bottle, Davenport was able to educate Patrick in contemporary literary trends, which he had largely ignored during most of his writing life. As he admitted to Bruce,

The truth is that I have been ... absolutely *starved* of intellectual companionship, and it is *heaven* to have someone to talk to about literature and cricket.

J.D. – though at *periods* a heavy drinker and occasionally violent in drink – is, like yourself very much my intellectual superior ... It is glorious to have someone you can *learn* from. I think I told you I was very much off Claud Cockburn, whom I never see nowadays.

> J.D. has had exactly the same experience. He said the other
> day that both of us have 'had an intellectual love affair' with
> Claud ... Now both are out of love, and it is interesting to
> compare notes.

It is evident from Davenport's letters to Patrick that La feared the
unruly critic:

> Please give my love to Ursula and repeat that I am *not* a bad
> influence.

But Patrick's enchantment with his new mentor touched off
another sequence of blazing rows.

Despite Davenport's best efforts, Patrick could or would not
concede that there was any merit in English poetry after the
onset of the First World War; Eliot, Auden and their successors
were literally closed books to him. With occasional exceptions –
he returned Graham Greene's high regard – the same disdain
was turned on his other contemporaries. Novelists like Nigel
Balchin, then very popular, and the equally fashionable plays of
Terence Rattigan, were airily dismissed with no evidence that
Patrick had read or seen their works – although Rattigan had
been an Albany neighbour, and they had been at least on
nodding terms:

> Nothing will make me believe that T. Rattigan is really any good
> *ideologically*, but it is evident that he has a quality. And this
> quality, I should say, is basically a *constructional* one.
>   This business of *construction*, of which I had never thought
> before, was first pointed out to me by John Davenport ... J.D. ....
> swears that it is just this constructional quality which makes a
> writer. He says you can have all the profundity and/or brilliance
> in the world, but without this specific gift you get nowhere. I
> remember him saying to me, passionately, 'Ethel M. Dell is a
> good writer!' And I think he is right. Look, for instance, at Conan
> Doyle – intellectually near-puerile. But he had that constructional
> (or story-telling) quality which makes him not only gloriously
> readable, but nearly great. P.G. Wodehouse, too, perhaps. I don't
> think we'd revel so much in Bertie Wooster's verbal meanderings
> unless we had a story as well.

How Bernard Hamilton would have approved this curious praise of his old Hindhead friend Conan Doyle, and Dell, idol of the middle-class, middlebrow, reading public of Baldwinian England. Patrick was never an intellectual writer, but the growing conservatism of his tastes proved that he was in this, as in so many other respects, his father's son. Politically, he remained for the moment ostensibly Marxist. Speaking of the Victorian era, he told Bruce:

> From a certain point of view, what a *lovely* age that was! Darwin, Spencer, Huxley, Morris, Marx . . . He [Marx] *could* see the bloody struggle ahead. What he failed to see was that the bloody struggle was so horribly distant – that even people like you and I will not live to see its completion. It seems that capitalism is a sort of Rasputin, who, you'll remember, simply would not *die* . . . but at *last* he died – and so will capitalism.

This recalls a comment of Claud Cockburn, the man who did so much to renew and strengthen Patrick's almost desperate faith in the eventual triumph of Communism. Castigating Bruce's view that Patrick's Marxism was 'simply a form of escape to some kind of male security', Cockburn witheringly replied:

> It is never explained just how a philosophy of endless change, endless struggle, endless search for solutions to endlessly evolving new confrontations could be considered as any kind of escape to any kind of security.[8]

Cockburn claimed that Patrick's discovery and study of Communism was no escape. It was, rather, an attempt to find some explanation for the appalling condition of humanity – whether it be the poor at Hove, those in concentration camps or those suffering from the Blitz, English or German. Cockburn conceded that Patrick occasionally believed that 'the last fight' which was to bring an end to all these horrors was further than he had once fervently and absolutely hoped it would be. It took him some time to realise how long this was going to take, though Cockburn stated that he drew some comfort from an early theory of Lukács which postulated that the whole of the period was a form of prehistory and that real history was only just about to begin.

But without Cockburn's steadying influence at his side, Patrick's Marxism, from about the mid-1950s, began to seep away. There were many good reasons for this: Stalin died in 1953 and his successors began the gradual repudiation of his towering personality and ruthless policies. Reports of Khrushchev's speech to the 20th Soviet Party Congress denouncing Stalin and all his works filtered out to the outside world and Patrick felt curiously adrift, as though he had lost the anchor attaching him to the rock of his Marxist beliefs. His attraction to Soviet Communism had always been bound up with his liking for the image of Stalin the man, the fraudulent picture propagated by the Communist movement of a kindly Uncle Joe, the stern but loving father-figure who alone knew what was truly in the best interest of his people and party. Now all this was called into question: had Stalin really been a monster, he asked Bruce in anguish? Had Stalin's book, *Foundations of Leninism*, which Patrick greatly admired for its simple, unadorned style, been ghost-written by sycophantic hacks? Bruce sympathised with his brother's predicament, seeing that Patrick could not, at his age and in his condition, afford to ignore what he had invested emotionally and intellectually in Russia, nor to repudiate the teachings of the big Marxist–Leninist–Stalinist library he had accumulated and constantly studied:

> I do not think it is an exaggeration to say that this torturing problem was a powerful contributory cause to his final failure to come to terms with himself.[9]

Bruce insisted that his brother's political beliefs were not, as he wanted to believe, just a matter of cold analytical logic:

> Their basis was love. And he had to embody them in *persons*, to have faith in the rightness and goodness of *people* who had been and were pointing the way to a cherished future in which the lives of all men and women would, in the end inevitably, become cleaner, sweeter, more reasonable.[10]

Bruce saw clearly the misty romanticism of Patrick's politics:

> For the hope of this future he was indeed willing to accept
> present ruthlessness ... Always a lover of Shelley, he was really a
> Shelleyan, without the purposefulness of a man ever attempting
> to make his beliefs penetrate his personal life.[11]

In the end, Patrick fell back on another father-figure; the
image of the roly-poly peasant and man of the people portrayed
by Stalin's heir, Nikita Khrushchev. He justified with typically
Marxist dialectics his new allegiance to the man who was doing
his best to dismantle his hero's heritage, reasoning that while
Stalin's ideas and policies had been right in their time – a period
of perpetual wars and crises when the very survival of the Soviet
state had been at stake – they were no longer applicable in the
era of peaceful co-existence.

But this new enthusiasm did not endure: Soviet Communism
was increasingly revealed as intellectually bankrupt; the Korean
War, the Berlin crises; the ruthless suppression of popular anti-
Communist uprisings in Eastern Europe; and the apostasy of a
stream of fellow-travellers who had put their faith in
Communism before and during the war, all played their part in
sapping his faith, as did his own declining physical and mental
powers. There was, too, the powerful influence of La; this scion
of the old aristocracy could hardly look with favour upon her
spouse's identification with the struggle for world socialism. The
one consistency in his political position remained his hatred and
contempt for the British Labour Party.

The early 1950s saw the production of Patrick's final efforts as
a writer before his decline into alcoholic oblivion. First, in 1952,
came his third and last radio play, *Caller Anonymous* (originally
titled *Telephone Pest*), dealing with a woman terrified by an
obscene phone caller. A competent, but in no way distinguished
drama, the piece has the faults which marred his melodramas
Gaslight and *The Governess* – tension tautened until credibility
snaps and the familiar preoccupation with the refined
tormenting of a woman that betrays Patrick's own sadistic predi-
lections. There is too, a tiredness of language, a repetition of

redundancies like 'Well' before each speech, that reflects Patrick's own terminal weariness with words; downing the tools of his trade as though he was secretly aware that his job was done.

The obsession with evil evident in the Gorse books is revealed in the dialogue between the victim, Laura Jameson, and the policeman, Crewe, who is trying to track down her tormentor:

> LAURA: . . . But tell me, What's at the *back* of it all?
> CREWE: Now I don't quite follow you, Miss Jameson.
> LAURA: I mean what's his object. What's he *getting* at?
> CREWE: Well now – that really beats me – well as I know the type. What *is* a criminal – or a pervert – or a criminal pervert or whatever you like to call him – really getting at? All I know is that they just *exist*. Some little boys at school like tearing off the wings of flies or butterflies. And most of them get over it when they grow up. But some of them don't – unfortunately some people love cruelty for its own sake, to the end of their days . . . We'll never know their real motives. They probably don't know themselves.

In the play Patrick again raises his thesis that the sexual/criminal drives are fundamentally unknowable, buried deep in the darkest recesses of the mind. They occasionally break to the surface, not only in the individual criminal but also in a collective sense, as for example with Nazism.

His final stage play, *The Man Upstairs*, opens promisingly. A young electronics expert, George Longford, has rigged up a recording device, so that a friend can hear what goes on in his rooms from his quarters upstairs. Longford is visited by a menacing character, Cyrus Armstrong, who threatens his life. Armstrong is succeeded by a visitor claiming to be his mother who sends him home explaining that he is a homicidal maniac affected by phases of the moon; from this point on, the action deteriorates into incredible farce.

The most interesting scene in the play comes when Longford describes his views on world peace – echoing a similar speech in *The Duke in Darkness* in which the people are portrayed as the custodians of decency and goodness, led astray by their warmongering rulers. Patrick was writing shortly after the invention of the hydrogen bomb, when a third world war between capitalist West and Communist East seemed an imminent possibility: the passage has nothing to do with the play's plot, but serves to illustrate that its author was still faithfully upholding the current Communist line – that of a 'peace offensive' designed to hinder the West's rearmament against a perceived Soviet threat.

Despite its commercial failure, *The Man Upstairs* was published by Constable and attracted the attention of Orson Welles who wrote to Patrick in August 1956, expressing his enthusiastic admiration for the play and asking if he could make it into a movie. Welles revealed that he was a fan of everything Patrick had ever written adding, 'Only the last-minute defection of my leading lady, Miss Ruth Gordon, prevented me from acting in and staging the first American production of *Gaslight*.' Although Patrick rewrote the play with a view to an American production, nothing came of this promising project. Indeed failure now seemed to be dogging him.

In the spring of 1955 he managed to get his nerve up to begin *Unknown Assailant*. The circumstances of the writing of this sad little book explain something of Patrick's deterioration: for the first time in his career he did not directly write the novel himself, instead rapidly dictating it to a hired typist. The result was a disaster. The girl, as he told Bruce, was useless. Patrick had carelessly neglected to check what she was typing, and when he did, found it was 'practically *gibberish*'. The girl was sacked and Patrick resolved to type the book himself after all. He gave up quite quickly, but luckily La came to the rescue, taking Patrick's dictation 'beautifully'.

Patrick admitted that he was unhappy with *Unknown Assailant*, saying that it was neither up to the standard of *The West Pier* nor *Mr Stimpson and Mr Gorse*. Sadleir published it without enthusiasm and Patrick found their relationship more and more strained:

I can't *tell* you how depressing it is to have a publisher who does not *feign* to have the *smallest* enthusiasm about one's work. I know the Gorse books are inferior, but they're not as bad as all *that*.

Having an unenthusiastic and damping publisher is rather like having a carpenter compelled to use a hopelessly blunt saw. You begin to lose interest in your work, and consequently you do it badly.

Patrick complained that his old friend had become 'insufferably *rude*' and said he was asking his literary agent, Cyrus Brooks of Heath's to find him a new publisher. The request to Brooks, if it was ever made, was academic anyway; *Unknown Assailant* was the last novel he completed, and his writing career ended, as it had begun thirty years before, with Constable as his publisher and Michael Sadleir as his editor.

It is unfortunate that his sign-off came with such a thin (in every sense of the word) novel, but there is no gainsaying the fact that *Unknown Assailant* is the weakest piece that Patrick published. It is merely a reworking of the theme of *The West Pier* with Gorse, masquerading as the Honourable Gerald Claridge ('he had Harrow and Eton written all over him'), milking a pub barmaid, Ivy Barton, and her loathsome father, of a few pounds with his usual trickery and deceit. The starkest aspect of the novel is the fact that Patrick comes closer to revealing his own sexuality than ever before. The book begins with a newspaper account of one of Gorse's victims being left tied to a tractor in Norfolk (comparable to a scene in *The West Pier* during Gorse's schooldays), and concludes with Ivy undergoing the same ordeal, accompanied by some exculpatory authorial musings on the subject of bondage.

> Gorse, though normally rather sexless, had bouts of great physical passion, and when these came upon him he was mostly stimulated by what is (on the whole foolishly) known as a perversion.
>
> He liked to tie women up in order to get the impression that they were at his mercy, and he also liked to be tied up by women and to feel that he was at theirs.
>
> It is foolish to call this a perversion because, as every serious student of the general psychology of sex (who would be

supported by any prostitute, or keeper or frequenter of brothels) knows, it is merely a rather emphasised form of the sadistic or masochistic element underlying every physical relationship between man and woman or, if it comes to that, man and man, or woman and woman.

Gorse was, therefore, not to be blamed simply because of this so-called perversion. What made it objectionable in Gorse was the highly distasteful way he indulged in it. But then Gorse exhibited bad taste in almost everything he did.

Both this, and the ill-concealed relish with which Patrick describes the actual process of pinioning the unfortunate Ivy could hardly give a clearer indication of Patrick's own sexual preferences.

Patrick's erratic personal life continued throughout the mid-1950s, alternating between terrible rows with La and periods of relative calm. During one such truce he wrote to Bruce:

> I came to the decision [to marry La] with enormous suddenness – a Marxist dialectical leap – the change from quantity into quality – the *quantity* of misery, unfairness and damage the previous situation had been causing to *all three* of us *suddenly* making a real qualitative change in my attitude.
>
> So far it has worked admirably. We are *all* (and I genuinely believe I can include Lois) happier and straighter – in our own eyes and those of the world. (I don't know *why* the latter should matter, but for some weird reason it does.)
>
> After a really proper and long break from Lois, I am hoping to meet her next week. After that I hope to go and stay with her a lot ... One dare not hope for such a thing – but I *can* say that since marrying I have been building up *splendidly* on my renewed health and sobriety. You'd hardly know me.

But such illusory hopes were no sooner raised than dashed by a relapse into alcoholism, brought on, so Patrick claimed, by a disastrous visit to Lois. After this regression, La finally prevailed on a reluctant Patrick to seek medical help for his condition; persuading him to phone her ex-husband, Commander Stewart, another alcoholic, who had apparently been cured of his addiction by a Dr Dent. Stewart put Patrick in touch with Dent, and he made initial arrangements to enter a nursing home to take the same cure, but got cold feet at the last minute. He did, though, read Dent's book, *Anxiety and its Treatment – with Special Reference to Alcoholism* and this inspired him to attempt a whole host of self-help methods including visiting a hypnotist in a futile attempt at an auto-suggestive cure. Next Patrick read Aldous Huxley's *The Art of Seeing* and unsuccessfully tried the fashionable Bates method of curing short sight, which involved abstaining from wearing spectacles in order to exercise the eye muscles. Another bad habit – smoking – (he admitted to as many as seven cigarettes before breakfast) led to him taking up a pipe for a while. He said that he found even keeping it in his mouth unlit had a soothing effect on his nerves, similar to a baby's dummy.

However, all these patent remedies failed to reach the roots of his anxiety, which was exacerbated by a disastrous house-hunting holiday with La in Hunstanton. They had resolved to leave London for Norfolk, partly because the flat, though quiet and cosy, was cramped and inconvenient; partly owing to the difficulty of obtaining domestic and secretarial help; and partly because Patrick found the proximity of the Prime Minister a nuisance with 'cops lurking about'. What he called his 'Bounder's Relapse' (a reference to the title of Bruce's boyhood prize-winning story) into booze at Hunstanton was occasioned by the couple being marooned by a rail strike. They were obliged to hire a car at great expense in order to get home. This 'hellish' misadventure occasioned some political/social reflections from Patrick which clearly show his gradual drift to the Right:

> It is a singularly depressing, and I think rather muddled, strike. It has none of the *exhilaration* of 1926 [the General Strike]. And it will, I imagine, be betrayed in roughly the same way.
>
> Oh – how I *loathe* Labour leaders of all kinds. And yet the working-class is in a way to blame for falling for them. I have now had a feeling for a long time that the proletariat is as moribund a class as the 'aristocracy'. All they aspire to is getting a *television set*. And some of them, in the grimmest industrial areas, put up television aerials without having a television set! Just to pretend to the neighbours that they've got one!

It was to be but a short step from this middle-class recoil from the vulgarity of the working class to Patrick's declaration that he would vote Tory in 1959. The domestic ructions caused by the 'Bounder's Relapse' were also severe: La threatened to leave Patrick for good if he did not instantly undergo the Dent cure. He meekly agreed, and by the time Bruce arrived in England for another lengthy visit in September 1955, the treatment had begun.

28

Crack-up and Cures

PATRICK SPENT THE INITIAL STAGES OF the treatment in a nursing home, but by the time his brother arrived in London, he had left and was staying at the De Vere Hotel in Kensington with La, where a room had also been booked for Bruce. Patrick told his brother that the cure was hateful, but that he was gritting his teeth and meant to go through with it, promptly producing a bottle of sherry for Bruce as a demonstration that he could resist the lure of alcohol even when it was in front of him. After a couple of days at the hotel, Patrick and Bruce moved back into the Hyde Park Gate flat while La, no doubt relieved at handing over responsibility for supervising Patrick to someone else, went for a rest cure herself in a private hospital. For five or six days, closely watched by his brother, Patrick appeared to be well, though extremely nervous and restless. He dealt with this by going on long solitary walks through the London streets, while Bruce read at a local library. But getting Patrick to take his medicine proved to be an uphill struggle, which Bruce found like dealing with a recalcitrant child. The latter stages of the treatment primarily involved taking tablets of the sedative drug apomorphine three or four times a day and Patrick claimed they made him unwell, sometimes rejecting Bruce's insistence that he swallow the pills. At other times, Bruce suspected, he only appeared to take his medicine, actually concealing the pills by a sort of conjuring trick. As of old, Patrick would steer Bruce into a pub at lunch-times, insisting that his brother had a beer, while

340

he abstemiously sipped at a tomato juice. One day, making an excuse that he had to go to a chemist, Patrick left Bruce alone in the bar. When after several minutes he had not returned, Bruce went outside to look for him and spotted his brother further down the street, outside a different pub. Taxed, Patrick admitted that he had indeed slipped in for a quick one – and then confessed that he had in fact been secretly drinking whisky since before Bruce's return, sometimes in pubs during his walks, sometimes from a bottle hidden in his bedroom: the cure had failed.

Once the necessity of concealing his backsliding had gone, Patrick began to drink openly and heavily. Bruce was in despair, blaming himself for failing to control and dissuade his brother. La still lay in hospital, blissfully unaware of the disaster unfolding back at Hyde Park Gate, where Lois had been summoned in the desperate hope that she would manage to get Patrick back on the wagon. But her one attempt to restart him on the apomorphine ended in a monumental row and she returned to Henley. Bruce was left with the task of dealing with anxious inquiries from Dr Dent and John Davenport as to Patrick's progress; and finally to him fell the distasteful job of breaking the bad news to La. He did this during a respite, when Patrick, at his own suggestion, had left for another golfing break at Hurley in the hope that the open air and a return to a much-loved recreation would do something to restore his health and sanity. A letter from Bruce to Aileen in Barbados conveyed the desperation to which he had been driven by his brother's antics:

> The situation is, I am now in the house alone, and very relieved to be so. The cure has failed ... Since then things have gone from bad to worse. The climax came this morning, when I found him after my breakfast having started already, and having made a resolution to go to a place near Henley where he can get some golf. I had to see him off, pack for him, take him to the bank, put him on a train, practically out on his feet, though still able to talk. How it will end I can only guess – I fear he will either kill himself quickly or have to be placed under restraint. He seems to have become quite incapable of managing his own affairs. It is all complicated by the fact that at the moment (it may quite easily be

changed next week!) he has fallen in hate with his present wife. At present it looks as if he will go back to Lois, who seems willing to take him back again in spite of everything.

We have not quarrelled at all – I've seen to that; but after a few drinks he becomes quite intolerable – a bully, a braggart, and a bore. And almost cretinous. I know now that for practical purposes I have to write him right out of my life. You can imagine how distressing this is, though I have long feared that it was coming. But here it is – saving a miracle ... Anyway, now I am no longer an attendant in a mental home – and I assure you I shan't become one again ...

La took the news of Patrick's collapse on her aristocratic chin, refusing to blame Bruce, and, as soon as she came out of hospital, making arrangements to get Patrick permanently out of London. She contacted a man from Blakeney on the Norfolk coast who was going abroad and wished to let his house to suitable tenants. Within a few days an agreement was reached and La and Patrick departed, leaving a shaken but relieved Bruce with the responsibility of finding sub-tenants for the Hyde Park Gate flat until its lease expired. Having successfully done this, he took himself off to rented rooms in Barkston Gardens to await, with some trepidation, reports from Norfolk.

At first it seemed that the miracle Bruce had asked for had in fact occurred: Patrick's initial letters from Highfield House at Blakeney in early November were coherent, cheerful and reported that he was off the bottle and feeling better for it. He had bought a bicycle and was using it for exercise, along with a more eccentric method of self-improvement: barefoot walks on the wet lawn. Encouraged, but not over-optimistic in view of so many previous false dawns, Bruce accepted an invitation to spend the Christmas fortnight at Blakeney.

He was delivered to the house by his sister-in-law Joyce and her husband Edmund who, as he had feared, were offered whisky on their arrival. But Patrick appeared unperturbed by the sight and smell of scotch being knocked back under his nose, and told Bruce when they were alone that resisting such temptations was good for him.

The two weeks he spent with Patrick at Blakeney were, in Bruce's words,

> ... the last period of unqualified happiness I was to spend in close communion with my brother. It was all better, far better than I had dared to hope. Patrick looked well and was well. Whatever inner conflict may have been going on, he gave no outward sign of it. Temptation might not have existed, and of course, after the evening of my arrival, neither La nor I touched a drop of liquor. But, at this stage, I doubt if there would have been any risk if we had.[1]

Bruce allowed himself to be lulled into the cosy comfort of an English country Christmas, falling into an easy routine that recalled similar happy times at nearby Overy Staithe in the days before Patrick's accident, a quarter of a century before. Bruce obliged La by reading and making constructive criticisms of a novel she was working on (Patrick always contrived to avoid reading his wife's work), but the brothers were left alone together for most of the time. Patrick was doing no literary work, beyond a pastiche of some Tennyson, though he did talk of resuming the long Norfolk poem he had first contemplated at Overy. He occupied himself with practising and improving his already proficient shorthand, setting aside an hour around tea-time to do so – or expounding to a baffled Bruce the wisdom he found in a popular American corn-cob philosopher, Ralph Waldo Trine, author of *In Search of the Infinite*, (his book had been one of Mummie's favourites in former days at Kew). Bruce was perplexed by this new-found enthusiasm, regarding the absurd Trine as a thinker way below the level of Patrick's intellect. But as his brother continued to insist that his work held the key to the inward control and self-discipline he had long sought, Bruce did not pursue the matter.

During the day the brothers amused themselves by putting on the lawn, followed by coffee at eleven o'clock and a pre-lunch stroll into Blakeney. After lunch they would bury themselves in deep armchairs for a snooze before a roaring fire until they were disturbed by four o'clock tea brought in by La. The evenings passed with talk, reading, shorthand exercises and chess, rounded off with their usual eggy supper and bed. It was a quiet, innocent life, only disturbed by Patrick's annual tax demand from the Revenue (this time for £2,000). Bruce left for London early in the New Year, reasonably confident that if Patrick could sustain it, he had found a new stability.

Six weeks later Bruce was back at Blakeney for another ten-day stay, the last half of which he spent alone with Patrick after La had left for what were to become increasingly frequent solitary holidays (the effort of coping with Patrick, even during his better moments often proved too great for her highly strung nerves). Even before La's departure, Bruce sensed that all was not as well as it had been at Christmas. An underlying tension and the tell-tale signs of Patrick's restlessness were the ominous forebodings of another crisis. At first, superficially, things went smoothly enough. Patrick spent the mornings writing letters and even did some typing for Bruce. They resumed their previous routine of golf, walks, lunch and sleep. But around teatime, Patrick's restlessness became more apparent. Shorthand was abandoned, and it soon became clear that only a return to the bottle would calm his fraying nerves.

Gloomily, Bruce listened to the familiar arguments: now that he was 'cured', one or two drinks would do no harm; total abstinence was unnecessary and he could start a new life with a clean slate. Almost in despair, Bruce argued back, but in his heart he knew his protests were futile. He was certain that Patrick, as before, had anyhow begun to drink covertly. He gave in and agreed to have two whiskies with his brother: 'Thus did Patrick throw away what was, I believe, his last real chance.'

Back in London, Bruce saw Patrick fleetingly during a couple of visits he made to the capital. Although drinking, he appeared to be in control of himself and spoke optimistically of resuming work on a new book, outlining the plot of what sounded like another Gorse novel in which a Heath-like murderer plans his nefarious deeds in a country house modelled on Highfield. Apart from his objections to his brother wasting his talents, as he saw it, on this inferior theme, Bruce was also doubtful that he would be able to gather sufficient material holed up in his Norfolk retreat or boozing with his old cronies at the Savile. Outside his club, Patrick hardly ever talked to anyone except La, Lois, and Bruce himself.

Confirmation of Patrick's inability to work is found in a pair of letters he wrote to one of his closest Savile friends, Val Gielgud, at exactly this time. Gielgud had proposed that he adapt *Hangover Square* for a radio play. At first Patrick was fired with enthusiasm, telling Gielgud in a letter from Blakeney on 22 March 1956 that he found the project a fascinating challenge. But three months later he was having second thoughts; on 16 June he wrote again to Gielgud stating that he did not think *Hangover Square* lent itself to radio adaptation; the book's strength lay in its atmosphere and this could not be reproduced on radio:

> Although, of course, I could produce something, I know that I would not be happy about it, and would almost certainly be embarrassing you by offering it. So will you please forgive me if I abandon it? I needn't say how sorry I am for the bother I have given you in making this mistake.

At around this time a second dramatisation project mooted by Dallas Bower, also failed. Bower waited on Patrick with a typist in the full expectation of collaborating on a radio adaptation of *Rope*, but after a couple of sessions it became clear that the idea would not be realised. Making an excuse about 'taking his medicine', Patrick would retire to another room, returning with a tumbler of neat whisky and soon he would be drunk and speechless. The plan was abandoned.

The beginning of the climactic crisis of Patrick's life was now at hand. The opening scenes of his long agony were, appropriately enough, played out in the streets, rooms, pubs and County Cricket Ground of Hove. Bruce had arranged to spend his summer in the resort, in the same boarding-house in Cromwell Road where Lois and Patrick had enjoyed a convalescent holiday after his accident in the 1930s and he planned that Patrick should join him in August to watch some cricket. The brothers met at Brighton station and swiftly adjourned to a nearby bar. Patrick, who appeared upset, soon disclosed that he had had a blistering public row with La the previous night in a Cambridge hotel that ended with Patrick threatening to leave her. To his surprise and chagrin, La retorted that nothing would please her more than to revert to being a bachelor girl. Patrick added that the shouting match had been but the worst in a whole series of arguments, triggered by his having arranged to stay with Lois in a flat at Sandgate in Kent, and said he was seriously considering a permanent return to his first wife. The whole business had clearly plunged Patrick into profound gloom, but Bruce was at first unaware of the depths of his brother's depression. Paradoxically, the gravity of Patrick's condition only became clear to Bruce when he noticed that his brother was not drinking much but,

> ... seemed lost, and at moments almost incapable of speech. He was miserable and looked it. We went to cricket; Sussex were playing his favourites, Middlesex. But he could work up no interest, except for a little disappointment when Denis Compton was unluckily run out, and he could not settle down in his seat. For not more than half an hour at any one time did he sit quietly by me, for the rest he was walking, round and round the ground and round again. So it was on this day and the next, after which he wouldn't even enter the ground.

After three or four days of this dumb misery, Lois arrived and took charge of the situation in her usual capable way, moving Patrick out of his 'slit of a boarding-house room' into her hotel near the seafront and thence to more spacious accommodation in a house where they planned to stay a couple of days before driving to Sandgate. While they were there, Bruce read in his morning paper that Patrick's old friend and agent, Bill Linnit, had died:

> It was no good putting it off. I went into Patrick's room and told him. It was like hitting a man who was down.
> For the moment, he took it fairly well. But that afternoon he and Lois and I were in my room. We were both trying to distract him, one might almost say to wake him. Presently Lois and I were shocked to find Patrick in tears. He cried as he had as a child, not

noisily; I had never seen him cry as a man. He was thinking of his lost friend.

Patrick steeled himself to go to Linnit's memorial service in London and then departed with Lois for Sandgate. Left as usual to clear up the wreckage in his brother's wake, Bruce found himself drawn into tortuous negotiations with La, who had returned to London, about whether Patrick should go back to her or stay with Lois. Eventually Patrick did come back to London and La, where she did her best to shake him out of his apathy. It was now time for Bruce to return to Barbados, and he made his farewells to his brother in the Six Bells pub in the King's Road with a sore and heavy heart.

Once back on the island, Bruce did his best to put Patrick to the back of his mind while he set about what proved to be his own last novel. A series of cables from one or other of the wives told him that things were much the same, but then, in December, a wire from Lois announced a complete cure and added that Patrick was writing himself to fill in the gaps. Patrick's letter, written in December 1956, but posted at the end of January 1957, is not only – at fifty pages – the longest he ever wrote his brother, but also a moving and revealing description of depression. He began his 'De Profundis' with a perky prefatory note explaining that the letter was the first thing he had written since his recovery from,

> an illness compared to which my accident of 1932 was a more or less cheerful episode ... I became so pleased merely by the fact that I was using my pen again, and then so absorbed by the narration of the horrors I went through before my cure ... that I just went on and on completely disregarding my handwriting or method of expression ...
>
> What I should, though, have mentioned, was the *hopelessness* which went with it all. In almost any ordinary illness one hopes either to get *better* or to *die*. With this one had neither of these consolations, and that, really, was what made it so terrible ... What I was suffering at Hove, *ghastly* as it was, was nothing near the worst. At Hove I could still, occasionally, just *read*. But that went completely at last, and in the last phase I had moments of sheer *panic* at my misery.

You know how one reads in the papers about suicides who have been 'depressed for a long while'. I now wonder whether this famous 'depression' in any way resembles mine. I *contemplated* suicide *incessantly* ... but discovered how bloody difficult, and *doubtful* a business the attempt is. I stood at countless high windows but knew that, in spite of all my agony, I simply *physically funked it*! And then suppose one miraculously survived the jump! I similarly funked trains. I had what should be a safe Medinal dose (100 tablets) but I didn't have *any* confidence in its safety, and where and how did you take it? And if one did it ... with Lois, there was the horror involved for her – I mean discovering me in the morning, and having to *wait hours* before announcing, in case she should have me saved by doctors. (You will remember that poor Lalla went through this sort of horror.)

So one was reduced to the ridiculous hope that one might be run over accidentally in the street (but of course it was no use being purposely *careless*, because it might not be *fatal*, and simply being horrible *damaged* would, if such a thing were possible, only make matters worse!) ... Of course, nobody who has not been through this illness can possibly understand it fully. Nor can anybody who has been through it possibly explain it fully. To talk of 'depression' or '*hideous depression*' or '*unspeakable* depression' all sound so *tame*! People can only think of the most ghastly depression they themselves have ever been through, and imagine that this sort of thing is going on all the time in the case of a sufferer from this illness. But to think this is not really to touch even the fringe of the real horror which, although indescribable, I must nevertheless attempt, feebly, to describe to you. Imagine, then, that you have read in the papers about a small boy who has been made by his parents to 'stand in the corner' of a locked and empty room *all day and all night* for a *year* – the only relief he gets being in the few hours of sleep which he takes on his feet (still conscious, in the moments of his waking from this coma, of the torture which awaits him next day). You have, of course, to imagine that this is physically possible.

Now imagine that you are yourself this small boy. Go, if you like, into the corner of a deserted room *now*! And stand up in it for only twenty minutes! Or *two* minutes! Try it now! And, having endured the twenty minutes, think of the *next* twenty minutes after *that*, and then the *hour* after that, and then all the *hours* after *hours* after *that*, before you get your next coma! And then the *days* after that, and the *months*, and the *years*!

Think of the counting of every *minute*, and the watching of every *hour*, while waiting for the brief coma, which is *so* brief and useless!

Is not this a fair description of hell? – one might say *eternal* hell!

But this, really, is not all. If you or I were put in such a corner we *might* work out *some* scheme for coping with it – let's say writing a novel in one's mind and, as a daily task, memorising what one has written.

But such pleasures are denied one! – for one simply can't take the *faintest* interest in *anything* to *do* with the mind! ... Here I must concede that one was at least spared from *worry*! A million pounds (income tax free) given one – death of one's dearest (you, Lois, La) – a new world war – *complete* destitution – all bores, bores, *bores*!!!

The striking thing about this document, over and above the metaphor for catatonic depression, is the realisation that Patrick's lifelong sado-masochistic complexes, his obsession with pain and punishment, had finally arisen from the recesses of his unconscious to destroy him. He continued his account by describing how he had confessed to Dr Dent that his cure had failed, and how the doctor had replied that only drastic measures could now stave off disaster, telling Patrick that he looked like a case in need of ECT.

Electro Convulsive Treatment was, during the 1950s, a form of therapy much in vogue for treating severe and intractable cases of depression. Its dangers were then, of course, not fully realised. (Coincidently, Malcolm Lowry, also a depressive alcoholic, was undergoing similar shock therapy at a London hospital at the same time as Patrick. It failed to prevent his alcohol-induced death in 1957.) Dent got in touch with a colleague, Dr Hobson, who was pioneering ECT in Britain, and arranged an appointment for Patrick at the Woodside Hospital in Muswell Hill. Although Patrick was convinced that the treatment was worse than useless, he had committed himself to undergo at least six ECT sessions, spread over three weeks, and had promised Hobson, La and Lois to stick it out:

I am told (by Lois and La) that I was looking *awful* at this time, that my voice was fearfully weak, and that every now and again I was giving way to sheer terror ... I can remember the *unspeakably* optimistic Hobson coming to see me nearly every day, and I can remember clinging *desperately* to chess problems to pass the time with. But they bored me *stiff* ... and, sometimes, I couldn't understand the solution even *after* I had looked up the *key*! Hobson, who is a crack player, used to explain them to me.

Patrick was taken up by a sympathetic fellow patient, an elderly actor who had once played in a provincial production of *The Duke in Darkness*. This man diverted him with talk, mimicry of mutual friends like Val Gielgud, and even the occasional outing to a nearby pub for a beer. Although allowing that these activities faintly alleviated his agony, after undergoing his sixth and final ECT, Patrick felt there had been no fundamental change in his condition, which seemed as wretched as ever. Hobson remained relentlessly cheerful, assuring him that he was all but cured, and when he demurred, roared, 'And the patient's *always* the last to know ... Always the *last*'. Patrick was eager to leave hospital and return to Sandgate at once, but Lois was unable to put him up immediately and it was decided that he should remain at Woodside for another week and submit to a seventh ECT session, 'So', as the hearty Hobson put it, '... that you'll be done to a turn'.

Patrick had the final treatment on a Wednesday morning. He was visited by La in the afternoon who, despite his denials, said she found him to be improving. She left some library books by his bed, and after supper, Patrick started to casually flip through one of them, an account of a famous trial: slowly, as he listlessly leafed through the book, the occasional passage caught Patrick's attention, and when he put the book down and settled himself for sleep he admitted 'a tiny feeling of pleasure' that 'perhaps here I had a little *something* to cling to, to look *forward* to – that I *might*, as an *experiment*, see if I could go on reading it in the morning'.

Sure enough Patrick awoke with his enthusiasm for the book intact and when he had finished it, decided to take a bus into central London to get more books from Foyle's and the London Library. On the way he looked at the people and places around him with actual interest – a sensation he had not experienced for months – and felt 'almost cheerful'. At the end of the week he went back to Sandgate with Lois. But one disturbing aspect of the treatment was that Patrick seemed to have lost his main interests and hobbies:

> I need hardly tell you that I was not grudging in my gratitude to Dr Hobson. On the last day he played chess with me blindfold (he can do seven tables blindfold!) and still wiped the floor with me – hurtling through my defences in rather the same way as the Germans crashed through France. At Sandgate other faculties returned (including, believe it or not, the notion that I can write again!) ... The matter of my returning faculties is interesting for against certain things I have taken a violent dislike – a dislike which may, I feel, last all my life and these are exactly the things with which, during my depression, I sought to pass the time and alleviate my misery. They are: (1) *Cricket*! (I shall never forget a particular moment of misery, which I didn't tell you about ... at the County Ground you and I stopped at the nets and saw, among others, Langridge bowling at somebody, and me realising how utterly *utterly* uninterested I was in Langridge, and in the game we were going to watch). (2) *Chess problems* (and, indeed, chess altogether). Again I shall never forget a moment after tea at the C.G., when I had left you (I left you as much as possible, you will remember, for to inflict my own misery and restlessness on you considerably *added* to the agony of my mind) and sat on the south side of the ground ... and tried, tried, *tried* to interest myself in a chess problem, but at last gave in and walked round and round the ground with my mind set on my first whisky at the pub. Drinks, at this time, used to give me a faint, *faint* relief ... (3) *Golf*. When I got to Sandgate from Hove I thought I'd have a terrible spell of *physical* exercise as an attempt to cure myself, and started golf. I can't *describe* to you what suffering I went through for many mornings (I gave it up after about a week) on the very pleasant Folkestone course.
>
> And, finally, (but this is not really in the same category, for I had almost completely lost my taste for them while in the best of health), *anything to do with films or the theatre*. At Sandgate Lois

prevailed upon me to see a film (quite a good one) and I do not
know how I managed to keep in my seat for as long as I did in my
effort not to disappoint her too much. All these things not only
fail to interest me – they fill me with a sort of dread! . . . But these
small neuroses are not bothering *me*, believe me!

Although Patrick *was* in fact to renew his fondness for chess and
golf, this wholesale renunciation of the recreations which had
been his lifelong diversions and pleasures, was a sinister foreshadowing of the onset of what he called 'Oblomovism', a withdrawal from the world as though in preparation for a death he
knew was not far away.

La had found another house at Blakeney called Kettle Hill, to
which Patrick repaired after his stay with Lois at Sandgate. He
was delighted with the surroundings:

> . . . a lovelier place I have never been in . . . It is, as it were, like
> something situated in the remotest part of a long country walk.
> Or again, a sort of 'Sans Souci' or 'Mon Repos' (with every mod.
> con.) put down in a wilder than Wuthering Heights setting . . .

Although he attempted no new literary projects, Patrick occupied
his time and mind by starting to compile a dictionary of
synonyms. He also tried to teach himself French with a book
bought at Foyle's. When this failed he tackled Latin, but this
effort, too, was soon abandoned. These abortive mental exercises, coupled with an increasing tendency in his correspondence
to repeat things he had written before, and even to play back to
Bruce his own opinions and thoughts, alerted his brother to
Patrick's alarming mental deterioration. Not even the most
robust of brains can escape the effect of thirty years' marination
in alcohol, rounded off by, literally, being fried seven times.

Although unable to write creatively, his taste for reading, for
the moment, remained. But he turned on one of his youthful
literary heroes:

> I can never read about Keats nowadays without, in the midst of
> my unbounded admiration, enthusiasm, and pity, suddenly . . .
> crying out to myself 'Oh – what a *common* little man!' or 'Oh –

what a little bounder!' ... my lack of balance deriving from a
desire for *exhilaration* at any cost – the exhilaration either of
worshipping or tearing down. But I think I shall be able to think
of Keats more sensibly before long.

While the iconoclastic mood was on him, Patrick set about
another, more fundamental piece of demolition. Writing in the
wake of the Suez crisis and Prime Minister Eden's resignation,
he finally made an open avowal of a change in his political position that his brother had long suspected was under way,
claiming that without in any way abandoning his Marxist convictions, he intended to vote Tory at the next election:

> Listen. When you go into bat at Cricket your object is ... to defeat
> the bowlers and fieldsmen and make runs. But if the stumps are
> suddenly snatched away, the umpires and fieldsmen disappear,
> and you find that the game being played is no longer Cricket, but,
> say Lacrosse, you feel decidedly lost and foolish standing there in
> your beautiful white flannels, pads, gloves and bat. Well, that, I
> feel, is how a Marxist stands in this atomic, stratospheric, what-
> have-you era! The game has completely changed. It has not done
> this as suddenly as I've described it – for one's seen it coming for
> a long time – but I have come to a complete realisation of the
> complete change with almost the same sort of suddenness (a
> dialectical leap, if you like).
>
> But why on earth *Tory*, you may be asking in bewilderment,
> and my reasons are many and perhaps slightly complicated.
>
> (1) Now that the dream of Marxist Socialism, of the brother-
> hood of man, has not exactly faded, but become *meaningless*, I feel
> entirely justified in selfishly pursuing my own *material* and
> *cultural* interests. These, naturally, will be those of my own
> nation, and my own nation is, I think, likely to be best served by
> the Tory party.
>
> (2) You already know of my almost pathological hatred of the
> Labour Party – but now there has been something added to this –
> a genuine *contempt* for what largely supports it, the British
> Working Class, which has proved itself *despicably* incapable of
> what might have been its historic task, and instead of the Red
> Flag, has hoisted a stout and defiant Television Mast against the
> evils of capitalist exploitation. (If you want to feel truly ennobled,

stand on an eminence in any industrial town and see the densely serried ranks upon ranks upon ranks of these magnificent banners of emancipation stretching away on all sides to the distant horizon . . .).

(3) The Tory party is at least technically opposed to the Labour Party, and I think that events go more and more to justify my opinion of the latter.

Noting that the right-wing *Daily Express* was backing the anti-Eden/Suez line of Labour, Patrick added,

Now when the *Daily Express* supports anything you can be practically certain that it (the thing) is more or less putrid to the core, but in the case of the Labour Party one doesn't have to think twice about it.

What has happened, as I see it, is that the class which the *Daily Express* represents – a class which I shan't call the 'capitalist' class (though it is this) but just the scum of the earth – has now decided that it can rule better, or wholly, through what Lenin called its 'Labour Lieutenants', rather than through the Tory Party, which, with its *faint* remnants of honesty, conviction, and 'ideals' is likely to be unrealistic and obstructive. And this shows you what the Labour Party has come to. (Though why, remembering its grisly political lineage – the Thomases, Macdonalds, etc. – I say 'come to' I don't know.)

(4) In addition to their technical opposition to the Labour people, the Tories are, I feel, certainly going to serve this country (which means my own material and cultural interests) best both *as* a country and in the field of foreign affairs – Russia, America, etc. Their abhorrence of Russia is naive and genuine rather than diseased, complicated and ineradically venomous (as in the case of Labour – their leaders especially); and they retain a streak of 'patriotism' which has begun at last to show real signs of taking a stand against American domination. (I don't know which I hate most – Labour ascendancy within or American domination without.)

I must say I was at first a good deal disturbed on learning that Macmillan had become Prime Minister, but to tell you the truth I am now rather coming round to this man! I thought, in fact, that his first broadcast speech . . . was just about as good as it could be. In its *extremely* clear intimation that we were neither a second-rate power nor a satellite, it gave me a lift of the heart such as I had never hoped to experience again. So far as I know this declaration (that we are not the 49th State) has not once been *explicitly* made by any responsible public man for ten years at least – ever since the days, in fact, when my heart sank on seeing a newsreel of Attlee (on his trip to America, just after coming to power) *rushing* up some steps ... with a *ghastly* sychophantic grin on his face to *fawn* on President Truman, whose look of embarrassment I shall never forget.

Macmillan's entirely novel action of liberation may, of course, be a dream – but it is a noble dream, and I propose to succumb both to it and to these who propagate it.

Also I am with that section of the Tory Party which believes in taking the firmest possible hand (or stand!) with Egypt! I believe (as Marxists must) in the sacred right of *majorities*, and, now that there is absolutely no thought anywhere of international revolution and consequent world-union, I do not see why pipsqueak, corrupt little nationalist messes should be permitted to be in a position absolutely to *hamstring* (and this is really happening over the Suez business) *vast organisations and populations* such as those of Great Britain and France. (This, surely is the attitude Russia took when she had no nonsense with 'poor little Finland'.)

Patrick was of course right in recognising that the conditions of the 1950s were very different from those of the 1930s and 1940s when he had espoused Marxism. Capitalism had, partly thanks to the war, and partly thanks to the natural boom/slump cycle, succeeded in temporarily solving the conditions of worldwide depression and economic crisis which had prevailed when he had first embraced Communism.

Having seen the dreams of his youth and early middle age rejected by the class who were supposed to benefit most from socialism, Patrick, like a spurned adolescent lover, now reacted with rage and spite against the proletariat in a manner in which his father would have been proud. When he talked of his contempt for the despicable class which had perversely declined to take up its historic task (as defined by middle-class Marxists like himself), preferring the present joys of cars and television to a future Utopia, Patrick was revealing his own bourgeois prejudices and preconceptions. It might have been Bernard or Mummie inveighing against their Hove neighbours for being in trade. It is interesting that Patrick did not merely move to the political centre but that he specifically aligned himself with the most reactionary, imperialist sort of conservatism. He remained an extremist; simply leaping from one edge of the political spectrum to the other. He retained a few Communist attitudes – his affection for Russia and hostility to America – but these could be comfortably slotted into the world-view of the sort of Little Englander Toryism he now embraced. His closing remarks about patriotism and the need to teach upstart Third World countries a lesson virtually amounted to a reversion to the Edwardian racism and colonialism which dominated his youth and which he spent most of his life suppressing. Now he too could join his once-despised Kipling in deriding those 'lesser breeds without the law'.[2] Patrick remained a romantic idealist; but his essential political optimism and naivety was informed and fuelled by the middle-class prejudices of his youth; prejudices which he renewed in La's company at the end of his life.

Bruce made another flying visit to Britain in the summer of 1957, partly to cover the West Indian cricket tour for the *Barbados Advocate* newspaper. Because of this commitment, and because there was no room for him to stay with Patrick at Kettle Hill, Bruce met his brother only briefly on a few occasions in London. They went mainly to old haunts like the pubs of Earls Court and they also made some joint expeditions to the London Library, which Patrick treated as an alternative London club, borrowing books for years and refusing to return them despite repeated entreaties.

Bruce was disturbed by his brother's appearance and condition, his 'wrecked' and ravaged face betrayed the depredations of years of alcoholic abuse:

> He was not drinking prodigiously, but certainly more than he could happily absorb at this stage in his life. He was much in the Savile Club, and that of course was not helpful.[3]

Although taciturn and gloomy, Patrick was not deemed by

Bruce to be seriously depressed. After his eloquent letter earlier in the year, he made almost no references to his illness and 'cure' and the only time he talked of the ECT was when he blurted out to his brother:

> Do you know, there are some people who go back for ECT again and again, *begging* to be given fits. *Fits!*

If there were such people, Patrick was not destined to be one of them – he only returned to Woodside once more in his life, and never again fell into the paralysing despair that had prompted his first visit. Bruce did his best to keep Patrick out of bars (he found that he became fuddled and repetitious after only a couple of beers), but even when he inveigled him onto a Wimbledon-bound bus for a walk on the Common, Patrick insisted on making a 'literary' call at the Telegraph pub, where the Victorian poet Swinburne was allowed his daily ration of a pint of mild by his minder, Theodore Watts-Dunton.

Often alone, and once in Patrick's company, Bruce met Lois, who was still carrying a torch for her wayward ex-husband despite at least one offer of marriage from another man. As was his wont when not with La, Patrick was disparaging about his second wife. Patrick's domestic life had formed a fixed pattern that endured until his death: when in relatively good health and sobriety he lived with La in Norfolk; but when his edgy relationship with her grated too much, or he was drinking more than was tolerable, he would head like a homing pigeon towards Henley and the familiar, mothering care of Lois. Here he would recover and dry out and once sufficiently patched up, would be despatched back to La. It says much for the patience and devotion of both women that they were prepared to put up with this unorthodox *ménage à trois* for as long as they did, but it also says something for the charm that Patrick, even in his lamentable terminal condition, was still able to exert.

As had become their habit, just before Bruce's return to Barbados in September, the Hamilton brothers arranged to spend a week alone together. This time they went to Oxford but sadly what proved to be their last joint vacation was a disaster from beginning to end. From the start, the weather was against them: they had the ill luck to hit upon one of those English weeks when the rain, persistent and dispiriting, refused to let up. As a result, they were reduced to mooching through the town's traffic-punished streets from hotel to pub and back again. Once they had exhausted Blackwell's bookshop, the Bodleian Library and one or two of the colleges, they were, in Bruce's words 'almost literally driven to drink', for lack of a dry alternative.

The pattern of Patrick's drinking followed a rising curve as the days progressed: starting with beer in the morning, he would graduate to gin at lunchtime, and by the evening he would be hitting the whisky bottle. Bruce stuck to beer:

> I did this not from preference, but because in England . . . I could not afford to drink spirits on any scale which would cheer and enliven me.[4]

Although pressed by Patrick to accept drinks from him, Bruce steadfastly refused to sponge off his brother, and this disparity between their drinking habits steadily built a higher barrier between them as the wet week wore on:

> So we would sit in the saloon – he sometimes turning a glance of distaste upon my beer . . . Until the last day it provoked nothing like a quarrel, only a small discomfort. We talked, but . . . not quite so freely and happily as of old. And Patrick's repetitious-ness became depressing to me – not from boredom, but because the spectacle of such a wreckage of the mind of the person I had loved and revered above all others caused me distress.[5]

Patrick evidently noticed Bruce's dismay, and suggested that they might liven up their last evening in Oxford with a visit to the theatre. Bruce was doubtful, remembering Patrick's recently declared distaste for all things connected with the stage as well as his inability to sit still in one place for long, but his brother's mind was made up, and his stronger will prevailed. Patrick primed himself for the ordeal ahead by a more than usually heavy intake of scotch and as a result by the time they arrived at the theatre the show had begun, and Patrick was 'tight – tighter than usual'. In some confused corner of his mind there lingered a memory of his active days in the theatre; the existence of rover tickets which permitted the holder to walk about all over the house. This was obviously just the thing for the restless Patrick and he went to the box-office and asked for two of them. The girl had never heard of such things. Patrick was insistent and belligerently demanded to see the manager. A compromise was suggested and the brothers were given numbered tickets but told that the freedom of the house was theirs.

Embarrassing as this episode was, worse was to follow: Patrick had hardly been in his seat for five minutes when he arose and announced that he was going to the bar. Soon after, Bruce followed and discovered him in incoherent conversation with the barmaid. He heard Patrick slur, 'Of course, I know this theatre well. I've had several plays of my own on here.' A minute later, he repeated this information, and then said it a third time. Bruce was horrified:

> It was, to me, unspeakably dreadful. Not that he should have got high and be making a public fool of himself – though indeed, being usually an unobtrusive drinker in public, he seldom did this. It was the *sort* of fool he was making of himself. What filled me with an inexpressible sense of loss was the realisation that I might have been sitting with our father. 'I'm an author myself, so I don't want any trash.' What was the difference? Thus, after nearly 40 years, a full cycle had been completed. This was where we came in.[6]

Almost in tears, Bruce kept his silence; but his thoughts were all too obvious and, soon after, the brothers left the theatre for their hotel (stopping en route at a pub to have one for the road). They found a cold supper laid on in the empty hotel restaurant, where the wretched week came to its sad climax. Bruce took up the tale:

> My face must indeed have told much, and no doubt it must have suggested disapproval. And I can only think that it was this ... that suddenly brought him up from his chair in a swift blind rage ... What he shouted at me I have altogether forgotten, except that at the end, waving his fists and almost jumping up and down, he

cried 'Come on, fight me! You want to fight me, don't you? Come
on!' I answered, propitiatingly, 'But I *don't* want to fight you.' I
suppose what he might fairly have regarded as a bit of bloody
Tolstoy-cum-Jesus sanctimonious meekness could easily have
sent him further off the handle; but it didn't. He calmed down.[7]

They adjourned to Bruce's bedroom, where the quarrel was
made up; Patrick explaining that the cumulative depression of
the rain, plus the disaster at the theatre, had finally got him
down. He ended, 'For God's sake let's get to hell out of this
place.'

Next morning, arrangements were made to go and stay with
Lois at nearby Henley. As if to seal their peace, the rain stopped,
the sun came out, and they took their train in a cheerful mood.
Soon afterwards Bruce left for Barbados. Patrick returned to La
and after the tenancy of the Kettle Hill house expired they moved
briefly a few miles down the coast to a house at Cley-next-the-
Sea, 'Long Acre'. When this proved unmanageable, they took a
flat in a large house named 'Martincross' in the nearby resort of
Sheringham. This was to be Patrick Hamilton's last home.

29

The Silence of Snow

MARTINCROSS WAS A RAMBLING, TURN-OF-the-century building: appropriately for a life turning full circle it was architecturally very similar to Patrick's Sussex birthplace, Dale House. Between the wars it had been home to Ralph Vaughan Williams, but by the time Patrick arrived it had been divided into four flats; La and Patrick's was on the first floor.

Patrick's retirement to this quiet haven was almost immediately overshadowed by the deaths of a whole string of friends, which he reported to Bruce in a tone of semi-jocularity which masked the heartache he felt:

> ... all within about six weeks. (1) Vernon Sylvaine (the farce-writer and old drinking friend of mine). (2) Anthony Ireland, who first played Granillo in *Rope* (... Both of these, who died absurdly young – A.I. was only 55 – were nostalgically very important to me.) Then, of course, the *real* blow, Michael Sadleir. You can imagine how much this upset me – but perhaps not fully imagine – for I myself could not have imagined how much it would (and still does) distress me. It somehow gave me a delayed reaction to Bill Linnit's death (which, as you know, I never *properly* reacted to because of my depression when it happened). As well as being my oldest friends, they were both so closely bound up with my *writing* life – as well as my concrete, business, *everyday* life ... The two pillars have now collapsed – the two vitally important eggs have been destroyed with the basket. And then, just to

complete the business, Audrey Heath. I haven't seen her for
years, and so it should, really, have meant nothing. But it did, for
it was she who started me (and you) upon my/our writing life.

In a wry reference to the 1958 Munich air crash, which had
destroyed the brilliant young football team, 'the Busby Babes',
Patrick added, 'One feels like a surviving player for Manchester
United.' Despite this litany of gloom, Patrick was still able to take
a distant pleasure in world events, such as the launch of the first
Soviet sputnik satellite, which prompted once more his loyalty to
Russia. He also made his habitually optimistic report on his
health, which, he maintained, was 'excellent ... all things
considered, but then a lot of things have to be considered!'

Among those things was yet another lapse into wild whisky
drinking, which brought him back to the ever-patient Dr Hobson
in the spring of 1958.[1] Patrick reported that his boozing had
reached a bottle-a-day level on his trips to Henley and London.
He concluded that it was time for a spell inside what he called
the 'cooler'. This 'cure' consisted of alternating injections of
insulin and super vitamin B. At the end of it, Patrick proclaimed:

> I was looking ten and feeling about thirty years younger – as well,
> in fact, as I have ever been in my *life* – this includes both of the
> Norfolk periods – Overy and Highfield – and here I am in Norfolk
> again, maintaining the situation *superbly*! What I owe to this man
> Hobson is absolutely fantastic.

Towards the end of the year, in November, he burbled:

> I'm still *wonderfully* well, and have just finished a gloriously
> successful (from a drinking point of view) month in London – one
> in which I met *all* my old drinking-cum-business friends, and
> didn't overstep the mark *once*.

But all too soon, the tell-tale signs of trouble began: his letters
became less frequent, and their cheerful tone less pronounced,
with fewer self-congratulatory references to his battles with the
bottle. And, although he was not explicit, hints and evasions told
Bruce that his domestic life with La had again become problematic.

Patrick liked to maintain that he was driven to drink by rows with his wife, but this was surely the confirmed alcoholic's typical evasion of the truth. Neurotic and super-nervous La may have been, but she did, in her fashion, stand by her man; until he became too much for her jangled nerves when she would either decamp to her sister Audrey in Wales, or pack Patrick off to Lois at Henley for a curative holiday. She was undoubtedly deeply disturbed by his drinking.

In 1958 she published a novel, *The Elopement*, which portrayed her early days with Patrick in Hove in a heavily romanticised form. As an epigraph to the book, La quoted Patrick's bible, Dr Dent's work on anxiety and alcoholism, warning of the hereditary causes of the condition:

> Children after puberty should be told that there has been addiction in the parents or grandparents, just as they should know of any other hereditary weakness. They must be warned that they may be more liable to fall victims to drink than their fellows.

Patrick, of course, had his own thoughts about addiction. In a letter in August 1959, written towards the end of a radiant summer, he ramblingly expounded his views to Bruce on the addictions of work, drink, golf, chess and bridge; of these he thought the last the most dangerous.

In the same letter, Patrick commented on the social changes which were transforming Britain as the increasingly prosperous 1950s ended. In doing so, he adopted the persona of a curmudgeonly, conservative country gent; a sort of 'sickened of Sheringham', especially when speaking of his once-beloved London in complaining of inefficient buses, 'vilely expensive' tube trains and exhaust fumes. The letter also showed that he was completely out of touch with youth, particularly represented by the Teddy boys (whose penchant for coffee he thought unwise) and he railed against Italians and Germans for their various national failings.

This blimpish blather shows clearly one reason – apart from alcoholism – why Patrick was unable to write any fiction during the closing years of his life. He had, quite simply, cut himself off from his sources. The rural recluse of Sheringham was no longer the man who had walked twenty thousand London streets as, like blotting paper, he absorbed – along with his whisky – the talk and tone of the times. He had become alienated from his people and had failed to find another constituency. But even in this sad state there was still an occasionally perceptive remark that showed an all-too brief flash of the old Patrick: in the same letter, apropos of Shelley, he told Bruce:

> I have an idea that he was rather oddly sexed – in rather the same way that I am. Although, clearly, he slept with girls, I don't think that this was what he was *really* after. I think he liked *yearning* for them – *spooning*. What he *really* enjoyed was the emotion I had for Maruja. I don't agree that the 'Dejection' thing was in any way 'self-pitying'. A *huge* amount of the greatest poetry is *superb self-pity*. The best bits of Shakespeare are a sort of self-pity – 'Tomorrow and tomorrow and tomorrow' . . . 'the insubstantial pageant faded' thing – and many other examples.
>
> The great poets were, on the whole, *mortophiles* (is this the right word for those who woo death – extinction?) And the funny thing is that these people adored life and lived it to the full!

But Patrick himself, by now, was losing his zest for life. In the spring of 1960 he confessed, 'I am very well, but very lazy – almost a complete Oblomov.' What disturbed Bruce about this and many other references to the bed-bound hero of Goncharov's satiric novel – which Patrick had not actually read – was that his brother spoke of 'Oblomovism' as though it were a positive and considered philosophy: 'So perhaps it was to him; but one of despair.'

In the spring of 1960, Bruce paid his last visit to Britain in Patrick's lifetime. As soon as he arrived, he made arrangements to stay with his brother in Sheringham. Bruce shared Patrick's fondness for the Martincross flat:

> The living room was attractive and sunny, the bedrooms were also attractive but facing north and rather cold – though this was corrected by gas fires used without stint.[2]

As there were only two bedrooms, Bruce was installed for bed and breakfast in a nearby boarding-house until La went away for one of her frequent holidays, whereupon Patrick insisted on his brother moving in to his bedroom at Martincross, while he occupied La's. Once left alone, the brothers resumed their old, comfortable mode of life: Patrick would occupy his early morning with letter-writing or the latest move in his continual game of correspondence chess with Dr Hobson, although even at nine o'clock he had a glass of Guinness close at hand. For the first couple of hours of the day, Patrick would be quite clear-minded, though slow in his reactions. During this period he would get through the contents of three or four small Guinness bottles and about ten cigarettes. After eleven, the brothers would take a stroll through the quiet seaside town, usually stopping at a tobacconist, the post office and a chemist who sold Patrick a bottle of whisky. Back at the house Patrick would graduate from Guinness to gin, chain-smoking as he did so. Lunch, prepared by the middle-aged help, Mrs Cooper, was served at 1.30; but it took at least half an hour for Patrick to be coaxed to the table. Even when he was seated he would remain without eating for perhaps fifteen minutes; then, as if gritting his teeth for an ordeal, he would stub out his cigarette, swallow his drink, and bolt his food as quickly as possible.

As the day progressed and the level of the whisky bottle lowered, Patrick's reflexes slowed, his speech became laboured and slurred and he struggled in vain to take in what was being said, continually repeating himself when he tried to reply to a question. About nine o'clock, after an egg supper, it would be bed and barbiturates.

Conversation during this final fortnight of unbroken amity was relaxed and casual, partly because Bruce had resolved to go out of his way to avoid being 'censorious' or to express the disappointment and despair he felt about Patrick's condition, which had resulted in the savage quarrels of his last visits.

But he was not unaware of what I was seeking to conceal. One evening I had a partial failure. After he had twice repeated some not very inspired dictum I protested 'But you said that just now, dear boy! Twice!' He smiled wryly, and presently said 'It must be a bloody awful experience, coming back and finding a degenerate brother.' I answered 'But you're not degenerate! It's just that you're stupefying yourself.' He smiled again, but didn't answer.[3]

Patrick talked vaguely of starting a new novel, but he seemed more keen on a project he had first considered when young: a dictionary of rhyming slang, of which he had been collecting examples, on and off, all his life. But any sustained intellectual effort seemed beyond him. He read little, and what he did was hardly demanding: the Sherlock Holmes stories (for the umpteenth time) or trashy Westerns like Hopalong Cassidy. He did, however, recommend to Bruce the novels of George Gissing, the poet of the turn-of-the-century London nether-world of whom Patrick was in many ways a disciple and successor.

He also spoke – reluctantly but honestly – of his sexual life; telling Bruce for the first time the full, sad story of his hopeless pursuit of Paulette Goddard. Here Patrick also touched on his present domestic difficulties and admitted that alcoholism had periodically affected his potency, but he added that something of his original powerful physical passion for La still survived.

Unbeknownst to Bruce, his brother's fitful sexual desire for his wife – and her negative response – caused something of a scandal in sedate Sheringham. The couple had separate bedrooms, and to discourage Patrick's advances, La had a Yale lock fitted to the inside of her door. The neighbours in Martin-cross were occasionally disturbed, but no doubt entertained, to hear Patrick's cries and entreaties as he battered at his wife's bedroom, begging to be allowed to enjoy his conjugal rights.

Possibly for this reason, at the time of Bruce's visit, Patrick was in a state of sexual tension and also 'vehemently anti-La'. His alcoholism was removing some of the inhibitions that governed his repressed sexuality, and as Bruce blandly recorded:

It would be wrong to suggest that he was sexually dead or even indifferent. He took an innocent sensual pleasure in seeing little girls being trotted on shilling horseback rides round a large circle visible from his bedroom window; and there were other small indications.[4]

As to La:

> I am quite sure that throughout the remainder of his life his
> feelings towards her were ambivalent, and he alternated between
> almost hating the sight and sound of her and being utterly and
> affectionately dependent on her.[5]

After a fortnight's stay, Bruce bid farewell to his brother
without making a clear arrangement to meet again during his
time in England. Patrick seemed unwilling to leave Sheringham,
even for the briefest of visits to the now-detested London. In July
Bruce heard that there had been another domestic crisis with La,
with the usual pattern of a furious drinking bout, followed by a
sudden descent on Lois at Henley. Here Bruce saw Patrick for
one day. It proved to be their final meeting.

> There is so little to say about this, the last of so many happy days.
> But it *was* entirely happy. He seemed well and cheerful, and so
> did Lois ... The nine o'clock Guinness sequence was not being
> followed. We had coffee in the middle of the morning, and a
> couple of large gins apiece an hour before lunch. He was in excel-
> lent form, with his mind working clearly. After lunch, before
> going to rest, he pulled off a shelf a book of Max Beerbohm's
> stories, particularly urging me to read, before I nodded off on my
> sofa, 'Savonarola Brown'. I did this. We had tea, and talked, what
> about (except Max) I don't remember. I think I had some whisky
> and a bite of supper before leaving, some time near dusk ...
> Patrick did not come with me to Henley station. When I left he
> had not quite finished his evening's drinking, which had however
> neither stupefied him nor slowed him down. There were other
> troubles on my mind, but about him at least I felt comforted.[6]

In October, Bruce himself fell victim to a mildly depressive
condition, and feeling, like his brother, in need of some of Lois'
tender care, he made arrangements to visit her at Henley. He had
heard in the interim that Patrick, having recovered from the July
crisis and returned to La, had suffered yet another upheaval, his
worst yet, although there were few details. When Bruce met Lois,
she filled him in. Patrick's drinking had precipitated serious
physical illness at Sheringham and he had arrived at Henley in a

state of collapse; an appalling apparition witnessed by Lois' young friend, Timothy Boulton,[7] who was staying with her at the time. Patrick had made the long journey from Norfolk in a hired car, drinking all the way. He said he felt he was dying, and tried to crawl up the stairs, having to be undressed and put to bed by Lois. A doctor was summoned, who administered tranquillisers by injection. Once again the familiar pattern was repeated. Under Lois' tender ministrations, Patrick recovered himself enough to make the journey back to Sheringham. But this time Lois told Patrick firmly that she would not put him up again: she could take no more of the physical and emotional punishment he was putting her through and, to underline her resolve, she packed up and dispatched to Norfolk most of the possessions Patrick had left with her – a grim task in which Bruce assisted. Sadly, but without protest, Patrick acquiesced in the arrangement; he could see that he had driven even the patient Lois to the end of her tether.

What Bruce tragically called Patrick's 'death-in-life' continued for nearly two years after his brother flew back to Barbados in November 1960. Patrick wrote another dozen letters to him in his own hand during 1961, but after November of that year he could write no more, and La took up the sad job of telling Bruce of Patrick's last illness and death.

It was some while before Bruce realised from La's letters that this time his brother's case had become hopeless. Though Patrick's letters were shorter than usual, their tone remained resolutely cheery, albeit rather vague, with suggestions of a loss of grip, though there were 'remarkable flashes of memory and complete clarity of mind'. At first, Patrick continued to go out and about in Sheringham. He hardly ever visited London. His contact with Constable had virtually ceased upon Michael Sadleir's death, when it was realised that there would be no more work forthcoming from him. Sadleir's son Richard had taken over his father's editing at the firm, but he was not a drinking man and did not enjoy the duty that devolved upon him of escorting Patrick on a pub-crawl whenever this burned-out star of the company felt like dropping in at Constable's Orange Street office.

Patrick toyed with the idea of various new literary projects: he continued to dream of his rhyming slang dictionary, and actually began to jot down a dialogue about pubs, 'The Licensed Trade', in collaboration with William Jenner, a drinking acquaintance from Sheringham. He claimed to have given up chess completely, and his long involvement with the game of golf definitively ended after he staggered on to the Sheringham links one day, and to his horror hit three air shots in succession.

In the last year of his life, a kind of creative energy returned to him although, alas, not the ability to shape and control his material. He began two projects; a novel called *The Happy Hunting Grounds*[9] and a sort of autobiography of his early life that he thought of calling *The House of Hangover* before settling on the candid *Memoirs of a Heavy Drinking Man*.[10] The novel, which was to have told the story of yet another female victim, lured into a suicide pact for love of a stronger man, began well enough but speedily trailed off into a succession of repetitions, feeble plays on words ('Full marks to Karl Marx') and a maddening series of didactic dialogues between the know-all hero and his incredibly credulous (and cretinous) victim. Patrick announced its onset in a cable to Bruce in April 1961 – 'GLORIOUS HEALTH AND WRITING BOOK' – but had not made much progress with it when he was visited by Angus Hall that July. He told Hall that the book began with the hero asking his pick-up, 'Will you come with me, love?', to which she assented, not realising that the invitation was to join him in death. Patrick explained the title to Hall thus:

> It's a good title . . . London's a place where you're forever hunting for happiness – and even if you find it it's soon taken away from you. I can't explain why this idea of achievement and revocation appeals to me so much. There's no bile that I know of poisoning my system . . . but I feel that death is not far away from me.

Ironically, bile, from his damaged liver, was just what was poisoning his system. Patrick managed to scrawl six chapters of *The Happy Hunting Grounds* into one of his hard-covered, lined notebooks, bound in red watered silk – before abandoning it.

Reading the results, it is hard to dissent from Bruce's bleak verdict on the abortive book.

Memoirs of a Heavy Drinking Man is much more rewarding. Inspired by Patrick's final visit to Dr Hobson at Woodside in February 1961 – during which he ran away for a night's debauch at the Savile Club and was told that if he wanted to live any longer he should stop drinking completely – he had also been questioned by two medical students seeking to discover the roots of his alcoholism. This interrogation had got him thinking about his childhood, and he set down some of his memories and reflections. Most revolved around anecdotes of some of Bernard's more extravagant episodes, but there were also passages explaining his lifelong groping for the certainties that he felt had been promised him in childhood, before being cruelly and inexplicably snatched away. This essay in autobiography filled two notebooks before it was abruptly broken off, presumably by the onset of his final disease.

Thoughts of mortality, as Angus Hall learned, were much with Patrick, and in August 1961 he told Bruce, almost casually, and with his by now habitual mental confusion, that he had drawn up his will:

> I again *think* I've told you that I've made a will – very much *against* my will, as I hate what are called 'testamentary dispositions'. You are *mentioned*, but as far as I can make out you don't get any bees and honey [Rhyming slang for 'money'] unless you survive both Lois and La. Have you made a will? If you do make one, you might mention me. For instance you might say, 'As for that little sod, I leave *him* no pounds, no shillings and no pence.'

This will was to be the subject of much acrimony and controversy before and after Patrick's death. Bruce learned that all Patrick's royalties – by then his only means – had been left to La. He pleaded with his brother to change the document to include the loyal Lois, and prevailed insofar as she was eventually left one third of his royalties with the remaining amount going to La. Bruce was both affronted and suspicious, concluding that La took advantage of Patrick's hatred of business and state of disorder, to rush him into making a will which he did not fully understand. After La's death, it was found that she had left her two-thirds share of Patrick's royalties to her nephew Charles, Lord Ingestre (now the Earl of Shrewsbury) and her niece Charlotte. 'Thus,' wrote Bruce, '... contrary to Patrick's wishes, and at the expense of the devoted Lois, who had very little income beyond her one-third share of the royalties, most of the posthumous proceeds of Patrick's work have gone to enrich the not altogether impoverished Talbot family.'

Bruce's bitterness is partially explained by the fact that he received nothing from his brother's estate apart from Patrick's papers, family relics and a chest of drawers given him by Lois. He claimed that La had promised – and it was Patrick's intention – that her share of the royalties would go to Lois if La pre-deceased her. He was profoundly shocked when he discovered after her death that she had changed her will in favour of her niece and nephew. The sums involved were not inconsiderable; in the late 1980s, Lois' one-third share of the royalties, left by her to the Society of Authors, still amounted to some £10,000 a year.

Patrick's gloomy thoughts can only have been sharpened by the news that in June Bruce had suffered a coronary. Worried, he begged his brother to follow his example, stop working and 'do bugger all', and he recalled with graveyard humour, 'I remember how – when I was in dear old St Mary Abbots hospital I heard a man in the next bed reassuring his mother that he was *much* better. Within about six hours he was dead! Don't do this sort of thing on me, please.'

La's thirty long letters to Bruce portraying Patrick's decline in harrowing detail began in mid-February 1961, describing how she had got Patrick from Sheringham to Woodside for his last stay. From the outset, she refused to hide or disguise the gravity of her husband's condition from his brother:

He is *very* ill, his memory except for occasional lucid flashes *quite* gone, he can hardly walk, scalded his side with a hot water bottle about a month ago, it has healed but is still very painful. He has had a fall ... he was gentle and co-operative, it is desperately

upsetting to see ... what to do about the future I can't think, but
one must take one step at a time.

By the last months of 1961, the symptoms of liver cirrhosis
were clearly declaring themselves: La told Bruce that Patrick,
'had a continual feeling of nausea and giddiness, fell about very
easily, looked a ghastly colour and went into long, alarming kind
of sleeps, almost comas'. His GP, Dr Geldard, prescribed large
injections of vitamins to make up for the nutritional deficiencies
caused by his malfunctioning liver. Patrick at first refused the
treatment but, with La standing over him, at last surrendered.
Privately, La asked the doctor how long Patrick could live and
was told that if he continued to drink, two or three years at the
outside, but possibly only for months. This turned out to be an
accurate prediction.

By the following August, a month before the end, La was
telling Bruce:

> I am afraid he is going terribly down. I am glad you are not here
> to see it. He hardly gets out of bed at all, can only *just* walk. I
> dread the moment for him when he finds he is *utterly* bedridden,
> and I know that, although I have watched it happening day by
> day for so long, it will come as a great shock to me.

In his extremity Patrick had asked to see Lois, and La had overcome her reluctance and booked her in at a nearby guesthouse
for four days. Two other visitors also arrived during the final
weeks: John Davenport, who made the nine-hour round trip
from his home near Cambridge in order to take leave of his old
friend and La's nephew Charles, the future Lord Ingestre, who
had cheered Patrick earlier in his illness.

On 8 September, two weeks before the end, La wrote that
Patrick was 'much more ill'. She reported that his kidneys were
packing up under the impact of the vast amount of liquid he was
now consuming, including tea laced with whisky, as well as
straight scotch. His usual sleeping drugs were failing to work,
and he was being given nightly injections to help him sleep.
Another new complication was that Patrick was becoming

incontinent, and to add to his misery, he complained of ear and toothache.

In the final days, a nurse or the matron from the local nursing-home slept at Martincross within earshot of the dying man to give La some relief. By 15 September Patrick was totally bedridden; he fell if he tried to get out of bed, and he had virtually ceased eating. His bladder condition had worsened and Dr Geldard was forced to perform a painful catheterisation. Lois stayed for three days, and La claimed she had left her alone with Patrick much of the time, but had found her tidying his room and going through his papers which had irritated her. She reported that Patrick had said, 'She's all right really, but you must remember she is a fool.' La's next letter, written on 27 September, reported the circumstances of Patrick's death on Sunday, 23 September.

She began by detailing Patrick's last reference to his brother. He had, she told Bruce, suddenly said, 'You know, Bruce and I had a wonderful relationship, we were more than brothers', to which La had loyally replied that Bruce was still devoted to him. Patrick's final decline had begun on Friday, 21 September:

On Friday P. was very much more ill, on Saturday more so. Dr G. said his chest and heart were not at all good. Matron said the time was coming when they would have to take over altogether and be with him all the time, but as they were so short-handed over the weekend she and the little sister would come in and out whenever they could. He had a *very* bad day. Matron came to get him settled for the night and give him an injection – the paraldehyde which he had been having because it 'had no side effects' was no longer doing any good, he was feeling very restless and 'crotchety', they had decided on Saturday to give him sparine injections every four hours.

She was here most of Saturday afternoon. When she had settled him for the night the little sister took over for the night. He had a dreadful night and became *very* difficult, throwing off the bedclothes, knocking over the lamp, etc., calling for matron, calling for me. I got up and helped her several times and managed to quieten him. He was shouting for his Nembutal, we had to let him have it, he was becoming unmanageable.

I took over when she had to go back to the home at 7.30
(Sunday morning). I couldn't leave him at all until Matron came
back as soon as she could. He was obviously so *very* ill, I told the
night sister just to wash his face and not disturb him more than
she need.

They sent for Dr Geldard and one or other was with him till
11.30, then Dr Geldard came, stayed with him quite a long time,
talked to him, soothed him and made him feel better, told him he
must try to sleep off all the dope, the Nembutal was no longer
working, only making him more dopey and ill and I think he gave
him a sparine injection, drew the curtains and was very kind and
we made him as comfortable as we could and hoped he would
sleep.

I think he slept for about an hour, then became much more ill,
Matron came over at two and we were with him together, then
she made me go and rest and then came and told me that he *must*
have morphine, and she rang Dr Geldard and he said she was to
try paraldehyde once more. She gave him another injection, then
we both sat with him, we had to hold the cigarettes in his mouth,
then she *had* to go back to the home.

She told me I mustn't leave him at all except to ring her for
help until someone relieved me. I sat with him lighting and
holding cigarette after cigarette in his mouth and I realised we
were beginning to run out of cigarettes, and he was dropping
them, smoking faster and faster, very confused and wild, still
asking for Nembutal. I put the bell in his hand, put the cigarette
out and said he must just wait a *moment* while I got some more
matches and rang matron, she told me to ring Dr Geldard and
that she would send sister over until she could come herself.

Dr G. came at *once*. He said, 'You need *sleep*, my dear fellow,
you're tired out, you must sleep, I'm going to make you sleep.'
All the time I had been saying, 'You'll be better when you've had
a sleep, you'll hold the cigarettes yourself again when you have
been to sleep.' P. said to Dr G., 'You won't, you know,' and
laughed and Dr G. said, 'We'll see.' Then he gave him the injection and said, 'Now you'll sleep. Your wife is with you and you'll
sleep,' and he said he was coming back about 9.30. P. said,
'You're a good doctor and a good man.' Those were his last
words. I sat with him holding his hand until he fell asleep. Sister
then arrived and I said, 'Is it all right if I go out for some cigarettes, if he wants to smoke when he comes round and we run out

of cigarettes it will be terrible.' She said yes, he was all right, she would sit there and I had better get some air – I was totally exhausted. I went to the bar at the Grand for the cigarettes but it was shut, walked down to the sea, it was very still, the sun setting, went to the Burlington, got the cigarettes and came in.

P. was asleep, quite unconscious, breathing rather heavily. Sister said he was quite all right, she would go over to the home to see if matron wanted her and one of them would be back as soon as possible. We left his door open. I asked her if I should disturb him if I washed up the tea, and she said no, he was unconscious.

I got into a dressing gown, listened to P.'s breathing, then went into the kitchen, snatched a biscuit and cheese, washed up the tea, too tensed up to sit and do nothing, then went to listen to P. again – there was silence. I have never been in a house where there has been a death before – it seemed to be filling the whole house, engulfing it – the silence of snow. I couldn't go in.

I stood in the passage in the dark not knowing what to do. I went again and again to the doorway, listened, and the silence became more and more overwhelming. I stood in the passage again and then in the drawing room doorway till matron came. I said, 'The silence, this silence', and then I could see that she had heard it.

Epilogue

L A WAS CONSUMED WITH GUILT THAT Patrick might have woken and called her just before the end, but both the matron and Dr Geldard assured her that this was impossible, his heart had failed and he had died peacefully in his sleep with his eyes closed. La commented:

> How merciful, they say that had he lived any longer the complications would have been terrible ... I saw him the next day. He looked very peaceful, his beautiful mouth firmly shut, all the blemishes and the bloatedness of his illness gone. I thought it beautiful and terrifying, and the deathly silence seemed to bring with it a great peace.[1]

She busied herself with funeral arrangements and sending announcements of Patrick's death to *The Times*, the *Daily Telegraph* and the local paper in Norfolk. In its single-column obituary, *The Times* described Patrick as,

> ... a genuine minor poet (to use the term in its broad, modern sense) of the loneliness, purposelessness, and frustration of contemporary urban life.
> His novels communicate rather than merely record the featureless, unsatisfying anonymity to which the modern city condemns many of its inhabitants. His plays turn frequently to intelligently effective melodrama but in them too an implied vigorous morality operates powerfully ...

La had thought about Patrick's funeral even before he had died, writing to Bruce to recommend interment at Blakeney churchyard, within sight and sound of the sea's melancholy roar. In fact she eventually decided upon cremation, as it avoided 'that barbaric standing around the graveside'. So it was that the cremation ceremony was held at Blakeney at noon on Wednesday, 26 September. There was only a handful of mourners: La and Lois, glaring at each other over the coffin; Angus Hall, who had come up from London, and who escorted Lois back by train; and La's Blakeney friends, Christopher and Marnie Rhodes. That was all.

La ordered a wreath of red geraniums – 'Patrick's favourite flower' – and Mrs Cooper and the matron and nurse also sent flowers. La had a passage from Shelley's 'Lines written in Dejection at Naples' read at the secular service. Patrick's ashes were scattered along one of his favourite walks on Blakeney flats, within sight of the sea and La wrote wistfully to Bruce that she liked to think that some wild flowers would grow where the ashes fell. Her letter concluded:

> Just one more thing to say: however difficult my life with P. has been in the last few years, I don't regret it. I am glad I have had it, and of the experience; he has taught me so much and I am grateful to him for so many things.[2]

After a recuperative stay with friends in the New Forest, La lost little time in packing up and leaving Martincross with its sad memories. She continued to write effusively to Bruce – a little too effusively, he thought, when she took great pains to insist that Patrick had been totally *compos mentis* when composing his will. The warfare between La and Lois, so evident at the funeral, continued to be waged via La's Sheringham solicitor, the unfortunately named Mr Bent. There were squabbles over money, property and Patrick's estate, and Lois' suspicious suggestions that Patrick's death had been somehow avoidable ('I think she is a little mad,' La wrote).

When she was packing up Patrick's papers and few possessions, La offered Bruce a few sentimental relics: Patrick's ring, embossed with the Hamilton crest, which he had inherited from his father; Byron's swordstick; the family Bible; and an engraving of Newstead Abbey.[3] Not much for a life of fifty-eight years. She confided to Bruce:

> I have also felt that I want to write about him, but I shouldn't do it without consulting you and of course I could only do it in a very disguised way ... 'The Drinking Life of Roderick Anderson' ... would be a wonderful title. It *could* be used for a novel, but I should do nothing about it without a great deal of thought ... It is very sad here. Very empty. Very silent. I shall be glad to go.

She left Martincross for good on 10 December 1962.

Discussing her life with Patrick, La mused:

> I have often wondered, too, how things would have been if P. and I had met sooner, but I think I shouldn't have been right for him – *if I ever* was, and then illness would in time have run its course, possibly sooner if he had kept up with all his drinking friends and because of the inner misery which *no one* could help or reach – possibly later if he had gone on working. I think his work came out of a different *kind* of misery which he *didn't* feel with me and this is terrible and tragic, but if I was able to make him, even for a short time, a little happier it isn't all wasted, and we *were*, for a time, very happy and he was already finding it more and more difficult to work when he met me, and in any case he had already achieved his – I think one can say *great* reputation and, I think, reached his peak in *The Slaves of Solitude* and was perhaps coming to the end of that vein and I don't think he could ever have worked in any other. To me it always seemed that his *intense* brilliance *was* in the narrowness of his range – the pub life, the half-world.

As things turned out, La would never write at length about her husband. After leaving Norfolk she moved restlessly around – Hampshire, Wales, Sicily, the USA – where she had an encounter with Carlos Mackehenie which left her referring to him as 'that old Peruvian roué' – and a visit to Bruce and Aileen in Barbados. In the mid-1960s, she married for the fourth time – an old friend who owned an estate on Jersey. One evening in 1966 Lois was in London and saw a newspaper placard: EARL'S

SISTER DIES IN AIR CRASH. Something impelled her to buy the paper, and she found herself reading an account of her old rival's death: La and her husband had been in a small plane flying between Jersey and Alderney when it had lost power and come down in the sea, killing both them and the pilot. Lois herself survived for another decade, continuing to live in Henley surrounded by a small circle of friends until her death in 1975.

Of Patrick's other nearest and dearest, John Davenport soon followed him: depressed by marital strife, beset by drink and the deaths of two of his closest drinking friends, Patrick and Malcolm Lowry, Davenport took his own life.

Claud Cockburn survived into the 1980s. By then he was no longer an active Communist, though he remained an anti-Establishment gadfly who, in that peculiarly English metamorphosis, somehow became part of the Establishment himself. Carlos Mackehenie, too, survived into the early 1980s, eventually dying of a heart attack while visiting his sister Josefina in Spain. His other sister, Patrick's first love, Maruja, at the time of writing, lives on in Lima; and the other great extra-marital love, Geraldine Fitzgerald, still lives in New York. Both of these sprightly ladies recall Patrick, despite all the distress he caused them, with love and affection. Patrick's cousin, Frank Bridger, and his former brother-in-law and best man, Vane Sutton Vane, one a rich man, the other poor, kept in touch with Bruce and died in the 1970s.

Bruce himself, last and most stable of the Hamiltons, retired and left Barbados in the late 1960s, loaded with respect and honours from the community he had made his own. He and Aileen settled in Brighton, where he devoted himself to his brother's memory; setting about the writing of his memoir, *The Light Went Out* (a title suggested by Aileen), which Constable brought out in 1972, along with new editions of Patrick's two best novels, *Hangover Square* and *The Slaves of Solitude*. There was a brief flurry of revived interest in Patrick – all three books were respectfully and widely reviewed and Claud Cockburn was wheeled out to say that it was such a shame that Bruce had underestimated and played down the immense influence of Marxism on his brother.

The following year, 1973, Aileen was told that her husband had terminal cancer: Bruce had been in the habit of deceiving her by going out for walks and sitting in the park smoking, which he never did while at home. Lung cancer had spread to the brain, and in March 1974, he died peacefully at his home in Brighton. There is a tragic photograph taken a few days before his death showing Bruce surrounded, almost submerged, by editions of Patrick's books – a suitable symbol of their lifelong relationship – and yet there is something noble in Bruce's selfless devotion to his brother; without his love and effort, Patrick might be just one more forgotten literary sot.

The recovery of Patrick Hamilton's reputation was slow in coming. His isolation at Sheringham at the end of his life was mirrored by critical neglect. La, despite telling Bruce that one day someone would want to write Patrick's life, was notably discouraging when John Russell Taylor proposed to do just that. Rightly or wrongly, Russell Taylor was given the impression that La was quite happy to see Patrick's reputation decline into obscurity.[4]

Taylor abandoned the biography, but did write an article in 1966 describing Patrick's novels as 'hypnotically gripping' and adding:

> Patrick Hamilton is certainly not one of those writers who will suddenly turn out posthumously to have been, all unsuspected, a key figure in 20th-century literature. But as a giver of large and lasting pleasure ... it is difficult to believe we have heard the last of him.

Two years later the critic and biographer Michael Holroyd lamented in *The Times* the neglect of writers like Jean Rhys, William Gerhardie, Hugh Kingsmill and Patrick Hamilton. Soon afterwards, Constable agreed to take on Bruce's biography and to publish the reprints of the two novels.

The most discerning critics in the 1930s and 1940s always prized Patrick as a writer. They praised the contrived craftsmanship of the plays, but reserved their real accolades for the novels, which dig just that bit deeper into the rich social strata of the times. Patrick Hamilton was a divided self, who personified the strains and stresses of his age, his class and his country in his life and work. Born into England's governing class at the apparent acme of British imperialism, he saw, at an early age, the hollowness and the incipient decay behind the grandiose façade; saw that there were no safe havens to escape to, that each individual was alone. Running from this discovery into drink, into fanatical commitment to a political ideal, and into the hopeless pursuit of dream women, he fashioned from his torments some of the funniest, and yet most powerful and penetrating English prose of this century. That Patrick was tormented and disturbed from childhood we now know to be certain: such, sadly, is the fate of many children. But few are haunted and hunted down by the experience over a lifetime, and fewer still have the power to transmute it into art.

Doris Lessing described Patrick at the end of his life as 'a dry, funny, lonely drinking man who was sorrowful about lost or postponed dreams of socialism'.[5] It is tempting to see Patrick as a sad clown but there is much more to him than that. Lessing mentioned his 'harsh and cold childhood' with its preached certainties and practised insecurities. Cockburn instanced the contrast between the sedate seafront at Hove and the simultaneous thunder of the guns slaughtering millions on the Western Front. Priestley believed these dislocations permanently retarded Patrick emotionally – his immaturity as a novelist being at once his great strength and weakness. The critic Michael Holroyd saw these tensions sometimes breaking through the structure of his work to involve his readers in the emotional wreckage of his life.

Some commentators have taken Patrick's Marxism at face value, as a considered response to a crazed society which elevated Hitler to the status of a psychopathic deity and made mass unemployment the norm. Others saw his brand of Communism as a convenient pot into which he could pour his subjective longings for a coherent belief system. All these views have some validity.

Patrick turned to Marxism as an answer to both his own and society's problems; when it failed to satisfy him – and millions of others – his personality, already fractured by his childhood, soured in a parallel decline. The Hamiltons were a crippled family, sharing the sterility and loss of purpose that afflicted their whole class. But beyond that, Patrick's personal wounds glistened raw; no social creed could heal them, only alcohol could – fatally – assuage them. So, alone, he drank himself to death.

Patrick's books follow the curve of his life; from the ripe comedy of *Craven House*, through the love- and drink-sodden agonies of *Twenty Thousand Streets* and *Hangover Square* to the sad and solitary worlds of *Solitude* and Gorse.

Ultimately, he confronts us, as few other English writers have dared, with the loneliness and futility, the evil and emptiness, the fatuous absurdity, of the human condition. He saw, as early as Hove, that there was no gleam of light in the final darkness, and so quenched his own.

Shelley's lines that had been read aloud at Patrick's funeral were appropriate:

Yet now despair itself is mild,
Even as the winds and waters are;
I could lie down like a tired child,
And weep away this life of care
Which I have borne and yet must bear,
Till death like sleep might steal on me,
And I might feel in the warm air
My cheek grow cold, and hear the sea
Breathe o'er my dying brain its last monotony.

La might also have asked them to read Patrick Hamilton's own words:

God help us, God help all of us, every one, all of us.

Appendix

Works by Patrick Hamilton in chronological order of publication (all published by Constable):

Monday Morning, 1925 (novel)
Craven House, 1926 (novel); revised edition 1943
Twopence Coloured, 1928 (novel); revised edition 1943
Rope, 1929 (stage play)
Published as the London Trilogy, *Twenty Thousand Streets Under the Sky*, 1935: *The Midnight Bell* (novel)
                      The Siege of Pleasure (novel)
                      The Plains of Cement (novel)
Gaslight, 1938 (stage play)
Impromptu in Moribundia, 1939 (novel)
Money with Menaces, 1939 (radio play)
To the Public Danger, 1939 (radio play)
Hangover Square, 1941 (novel)
The Duke in Darkness, 1943 (stage play)
The Slaves of Solitude, 1947 (novel)
The West Pier, 1951 (novel)
The Man Upstairs, 1952 (stage play)
Mr Stimpson and Mr Gorse, 1953 (novel)
Unknown Assailant, 1955 (novel)

In addition, Hamilton wrote three full-length stage plays, *The*

Procurator of Judea (n.d.), *John Brown's Body* (1929), and *The Governess* (1944), and one radio play, *Caller Anonymous* (1952), which were not published. The latter two survive in manuscript form. His unfinished final novel, *The Happy Hunting Grounds* (1961), and his incomplete autobiography, *Memoirs of a Heavy Drinking Man* (n.d.), likewise survived in his notebooks. The typescript of his only known short story, 'The Quiet Room' (c. 1925), was found by the author among his papers and published for the first time in Issue 1 of the literary magazine *The Printer's Devil* (S.E. Arts, May 1990).

Notes

Unless otherwise stated, the source of all information in this biography is the large archive of Hamilton papers kept by Bruce Hamilton and quoted with kind permission of Aileen Hamilton.

Introduction

1. Doris Lessing, *The Times*, 26 June 1968.
2. J.B. Priestley, Introduction to new editions of *Hangover Square* and *Slaves of Solitude*, Constable, 1972.
3. *Ibid.*
4. *Ibid.*

PART I

1: Forebears and Family

1. This ring was in turn inherited by Bruce and is presumably buried with him in Brighton.
2. Bruce is less informative about his mother's middle-class ancestry than he is about his father's noble descent.
3. Now an old people's home, it still bears this name.
4. A bust of Hugo was a constant presence on Bernard's desk.

2: When I was a Child

1. The account of the unveiling of this plaque by the *Brighton Evening*

Argus perpetuates the commonly held myth that Patrick's childhood was one of 'genteel poverty'. Patrick's many problems never included a lack of ready cash.

2. This and other written examples of Nellie's rule were lovingly preserved among the Hamilton family papers.

3. Author's interview with Aileen Hamilton, 1990.

4. C. Musgrave, *Life in Brighton*, J. Hallewell Publications, 1980.

3: Mummie's Boy

1. George Orwell, 'Such, Such were the Joys', *Collected Essays, Journalism and Letters*, Volume 4, Penguin, 1970.

2. In *The West Pier* the school is called Rodney House.

3. He makes Esther Downes's grandfather such a runner in *The West Pier*.

4. Patrick Hamilton, *Memoirs of a Heavy Drinking Man*, unpublished.

5. *Ibid.*

6. *Ibid.*

7. J.B. Priestley, 'The Thirties'.

8. I. Mylander, 'The Children of Alcoholic Fathers', *Acta Paediatrica Scandinavica*, 1960, 49 Suplement 121.

9. *Memoirs of a Heavy Drinking Man.*

10. *Ibid.*

11. The Hamiltons, despite their differences, were united in a conspiracy of silence about the source of the family fortune. It was not until much later that the children learned that Bernard's lavish lifestyle was financed by money originally generated by the West Indian slave trade.

12. Bruce's discovery sheds light on one of the century's more unlikely minor literary controversies; a dispute between Charles Hamilton and George Orwell over the former's literary productivity. Charles Hamilton, who still holds pride of place in the *Guinness Book of Records* as the most prolific writer of all time, denied the charge in Orwell's essay 'Boy's Weeklies' (1940) that his work, appearing in the *Gem* and *Magnet* under the pen names 'Frank Richards' and 'Martin Clifford' over a thirty-year period, 'could hardly be the work of the same person every week'. Hamilton huffily replied, 'Mr Orwell finds it difficult to believe that a series running for thirty years can possibly have been written by one and the same person. In the presence of such authority, I speak with diffidence:

and can only say that, to the best of my knowledge and belief, I am only one person, and have never been two or three.' Faced with this statement, Orwell was forced to retract: 'These stories have been written throughout the whole period by "Frank Richards" and "Martin Clifford" who are one and the same person.' But Bruce's anecdote appears to give the lie to Hamilton's boast of sole authorship and provides a posthumous vindication of Orwell's original charge. (Orwell's essay and Charles Hamilton's reply can be found in Volume One of Orwell's *Collected Essays, Journalism and Letters*, Secker & Warburg, 1968.)

4: *Patrick the Poet*

1. *Memoirs of a Heavy Drinking Man.*
2. Rupert Brooke, 'Heaven', *The Poetical Works of Rupert Brooke*, edited by Sir Geoffrey Keynes, Faber & Faber, 1970 edition.
3. The two best modern books on Brooke are: John Lehmann, *Rupert Brooke: His Life and His Legend*, Quartet Books, 1981, and Paul Delaney, *Neo-pagans: Friendship and Love in the Rupert Brooke Circle*, Macmillan, 1987. Both books contain frank discussions of Brooke's ambiguous sexuality and politics.
4. See Part VI, Chapter 27.
5. I am heavily indebted for information on Westminster during the Great War to the school itself, and to Peter Parker's excellent study *The Old Lie: The Great War and the Public School Ethos*, Constable, 1987. For more on the neglected subject of homo-eroticism and the War see also Paul Fussell's brilliant *The Great War and Modern Memory*, OUP, 1982.
6. See Bernard R. Crick, *George Orwell: A Life*, Penguin, 1982.

5: *The Fractured Family*

1. J.B. Priestley, Introduction to new editions of *Hangover Square* and *The Slaves of Solitude*.
2. Michael Holroyd, Introduction to new edition of *Twenty Thousand Streets Under the Sky*, Hogarth Press, 1987.
3. See Richard Thurlow, *Fascism in Britain, A History 1918–1986*, Blackwell, 1987.
4. *Memoirs of a Heavy Drinking Man.*
5. Patrick Hamilton, *The Quiet Room*, discovered by the author in the

archives of Bruce Hamilton, and subsequently published in the literary magazine *The Printer's Devil*, S.E. Arts, May 1990.
6. *Memoirs of a Heavy Drinking Man.*
7. *Ibid.*
8. *Ibid.*
9. *Ibid.*
10. The hotel is still in existence.

PART II

6: *The Pursuit of Unhappiness*

1. Letters from Maruja Mackehenie to author, 1990.
2. *Ibid.*

7: *Stage-struck*

1. The amiable Vane was persuaded that this should include Patrick – despite the latter's complete lack of theatrical experience.
2. Angus Hall, 'After the Hangover', *Books and Bookmen*, July 1968.
3. Patrick was staying in Over Street when Bruce told him the story which formed the basis of *The Quiet Room*. The neighbouring Kemp Street was the scene of the Brighton Trunk Murder – one of the most notorious criminal cases of the inter-war years.
4. Patrick used the name Prest for one of his most sympathetic characters in his later novel *The Slaves of Solitude*.

8: *Monday Morning*

1. Michael Sadleir made a practice of changing the original working titles of Patrick's books; these and other changes were apparently accepted by the author with good grace until his relationship with Sadleir soured in the early 1950s.

9: *Craven House*

1. The inconsequential but amorous Lieutenant Pike in *The Slaves of Solitude* also hails from Wilkes-Barre.
2. Patrick used this scene to dramatic effect in his next novel *Craven House*.

3. 'After the Hangover'.

10: *Twopence Coloured*

1. *Memoirs of a Heavy Drinking Man.*

PART III

11: *Lily*

1. Patrick's fictional but archetypal London pub, The Midnight Bell, is an amalgam of several of his favourite watering holes. It probably owes most to the ambience of The Admiral Duncan, but from the evidence of the novels the physical model would appear to be a regular haunt of his in Warren Street, The Prince of Wales Feathers.

13: *Rope*

1. Bruce Hamilton, *The Light Went Out: A Biography of Patrick Hamilton*, Constable, 1972.
2. There are several factual accounts of this celebrated case, but the most interesting treatment – apart from *Rope* itself – is Meyer Levin's novel *Compulsion*, Muller, 1957. Levin was a Chicago reporter who covered the case.
3. Anti-semitism played no small part in the popular clamour for the execution of the two wealthy young murderers.
4. 'After the Hangover'.

14: *Lois*

1. Bernard's old friend and enemy, Arthur Conan Doyle, followed him one week later, perhaps to continue their disputes on the other side.
2. *The Light Went Out.*

15: *Accident*

1. 'Harbour View' and its adjacent cottages is now a single gentrified and comfortable residence, unrecognisable as the primitive dwelling found by the Hamiltons.

2. *The Light Went Out.*
3. The Ostrich still exists under that name, but is now a private house.
4. Patrick's accident jostled for space with other news stories of the day including a mutiny at Dartmoor prison; the arrest of Mahatma Gandhi by the British authorities in India; and the decision by the Home Secretary, the much-derided William Joynson-Hix, to reprieve a murderer named Donovan, sentenced to hang for his part in the killing of a Brighton chemist. Coincidentally, there was also an announcement of an article in the *Daily Mail* by Winston Churchill giving an account of his own experience of being knocked down and seriously hurt by a speeding car in New York.
5. J.B. Priestley, Introduction to *Twenty Thousand Streets Under the Sky*, Constable, 1935.
6. Claud Cockburn, Introduction to new edition of *The Slaves of Solitude*, OUP, 1982.
7. *The Light Went Out.*

PART IV

16: Marx Mad

1. Author's interview with Arthur Calder-Marshall, 1990.
2. Of the many accounts of Communist tactics in the Thirties I have found most useful David Caute, *Fellow Travellers: Intellectual Friends of Communism*, Weidenfeld, 1973, Andrew Boyle, *Climate of Treason*, Hodder & Stoughton, 1980, and Peter Stansky and William Abrahams, *Journey to the Frontier: Two Roads to the Spanish Civil War*, Constable, 1966.
3. *The Light Went Out.*
4. *Ibid.*
5. Author's interview with Sir Kenneth Robinson, 1990.
6. J.B. Priestley, Introduction to new editions of *Hangover Square* and *The Slaves of Solitude*.
7. See Peter Stansky and William Abrahams, *The Unknown Orwell*, Constable, 1972.
8. See *Christopher and His Kind*, Methuen, 1977, *All the Conspirators*, Cape, 1966, and other autobiographical writings by Christopher Isherwood.
9. Author's interview with Arthur Calder-Marshall.
10. See Douglas Day, *Malcolm Lowry: A Biography*, OUP, 1974.

18: The Age of Anxiety

1. This is the only volume from Patrick's vast Marxist library to survive in the archives of Bruce Hamilton.
2. Author's interview with Sir Kenneth Robinson.
3. Jason Gurney, *Crusade in Spain*, Faber & Faber, 1974.
4. Information from Lord Ted Willis to author, 1990.

19: The Road to War

1. Author's interview with Sir Kenneth Robinson.

20: Hangover Square

1. Davies was killed when a balcony at the Richmond Theatre gave way.
2. 'After the Hangover'.
3. The words in which Patrick describes Bone's tortured half-hearing of the 'murmuring' of the couple next door in the Brighton hotel room are almost the same as those he uses to describe himself overhearing his father 'mumbling' to Mummie during Bernard's feared visits to Hove.
4. Again a comparison with Pinter seems apposite. In *The Caretaker* Davies pursues a similarly single-minded fixation for Sidcup.
5. J.B. Priestley, Introduction to new editions of *Hangover Square* and *The Slaves of Solitude*.
6. Author's interview with Arnold Rattenbury, 1990.
7. *The Light Went Out*.

PART V

21: Darkness

1. The line is from the poem 'Spain', written during Auden's brief period as a Communist fellow-traveller. He later disowned the phrase and made every effort to suppress it.
2. Author's interview with Arnold Rattenbury. See also Rattenbury's 'Total Attainder and the Helots' in *The 1930s: A Challenge to Orthodoxy*, edited by John Lucas, Harvester Press, 1978.
3. Patrick never adopted the prevailing party line of 1940 and early

1941 i.e. that the war was an Imperialist battle and that true Communists should take no part in the struggle.

4. See Patricia Cockburn, *The Years of The Week,* Comedia, 1985.
5. See *I Claud,* Penguin, 1967, and Cockburn's other autobiographical books.
6. *Claud Cockburn Autobiography,* Hamlyn, 1965.
7. *Ibid.*
8. *Ibid.*
9. I am grateful to Douglas Hyde, then News Editor of *The Daily Worker,* for information on the Communist Party and its paper. See especially Mr Hyde's brilliant 'I Believed', probably the most honest ever *mea culpa* memoir of a former Communist.
10. *Claud Cockburn Autobiography.*
11. *Ibid.*
12. *Ibid.*
13. Geraldine Fitzgerald interview with author, 1990.

22: Victory – and Defeat

1. *The Light Went Out.*
2. *Ibid.*

23: The Slaves of Solitude

1. Claud Cockburn, Introduction to new edition of *The Slaves of Solitude.*
2. *Ibid.*
3. *Ibid.*
4. *The Light Went Out.*

24: Hollywood and Hitchcock

1. John Russell Taylor, *Hitch: The Life and Work of Alfred Hitchcock,* Faber & Faber, 1978.
2. *Ibid.*
3. *Ibid.*

PART VI

25: La

1. The Talbots' family seat, Alton Towers, is now a popular leisure and entertainments centre.

2. Introduction to Laura Talbot, *The Gentlewomen*, edited by Polly Devlin, Virago, 1985.
3. *Ibid.*

26: *Mr Heath and Mr Gorse*

1. See Patricia Cockburn, *Figure of Eight*, Brandon, 1989.
2. See Francis Selwyn, *Rotten to the Core: The Life and Death of Neville Heath*, Routledge, 1988.
3. See Walter Allen, *Tradition and Dream: The English and American Novel from the Twenties to Our Time*, Hogarth Press, 1986.
4. Patrick actually uses the phrase 'An evil dream' to describe his anti-hero's motivations in his next Gorse novel *Mr Stimpson and Mr Gorse*.
5. Author's interview with Aileen Hamilton.

27: *Swan-song*

1. *The Light Went Out.*
2. *Ibid.*
3. *Ibid.*
4. It is a peculiarity of the Gorse books, written in the early 1950s, that they are firmly set between the wars: Patrick seemed to wilfully shut himself off from the vastly different social reality of the post-war world, preferring to stay in the period of his own prime.
5. 'After the Hangover'.
6. Letter from Michael Sadleir to Patrick Hamilton, 1953, archives of Bruce Hamilton.
7. *Ibid.*
8. Claud Cockburn, Introduction to *The Slaves of Solitude*.
9. *The Light Went Out.*
10. *Ibid.*
11. *Ibid.*

28: *Crack-up and Cures*

1. *The Light Went Out.*
2. From Kipling's poem 'Recessional'. In fact it was a reference to the Germans.

3. *The Light Went Out.*
4. *Ibid.*
5. *Ibid.*
6. *Ibid.*
7. *Ibid.*

29: *The Silence of Snow*

1. Between cures, Patrick and Hobson stayed in touch with marathon games of correspondence chess.
2. *The Light Went Out.*
3. *Ibid.*
4. *Ibid.*
5. *Ibid.*
6. *Ibid.*
7. Author's interview with Timothy Boulton, 1990.
8. This abortive project survives in a notebook in the archives of Bruce Hamilton.
9. This, Patrick's final attempt at fiction, also survives in a notebook in the archives.
10. There are two draft versions of this fascinating, but tantalisingly incomplete attempt at an autobiography in the archives.

Epilogue

1. 'After the Hangover'.
2. Angus Hall interview with author.
3. These remain in the possession of Aileen Hamilton.
4. Author's interview with John Russell Taylor, 1990.
5. Doris Lessing, 'A Blank Look?' *Listener*, September 1987.

Select Bibliography

Allen, Walter. Discussion of Patrick Hamilton's novels in *Tradition and Dream: The English and American Novel from the Twenties to Our Time*, Hogarth Press, 1986

Cockburn, Claud. Introduction to paperback edition of *The Slaves of Solitude*, OUP, 1982

Croft, Andy. *Red Letter Days: British Fiction in the 1930s*, Lawrence and Wishart, 1990

Hamilton, Bruce. *The Light Went Out: A Biography of Patrick Hamilton*, Constable, 1972

Holroyd, Michael. *Unreceived Opinions*, Heinemann, 1976

Priestley, J.B. Introduction to new editions of *Hangover Square* and *The Slaves of Solitude*, Constable, 1972

Rattenbury, Arnold. 'Total Attainder and the Helots' in *The 1930s: A Challenge to Orthodoxy* edited by John Lucas, Harvester/Barnes & Noble, 1978

Widdowson, Peter J. 'The Saloon Bar Society: Patrick Hamilton's fiction in the 1930s' in *The 1930s: A Challenge to Orthodoxy* edited by John Lucas, Harvester/Barnes & Noble, 1978

Index